VICES PRESS PRESENTS

FORGOTTEN HOME™

VOLUME 1: FAMILY MATTERS

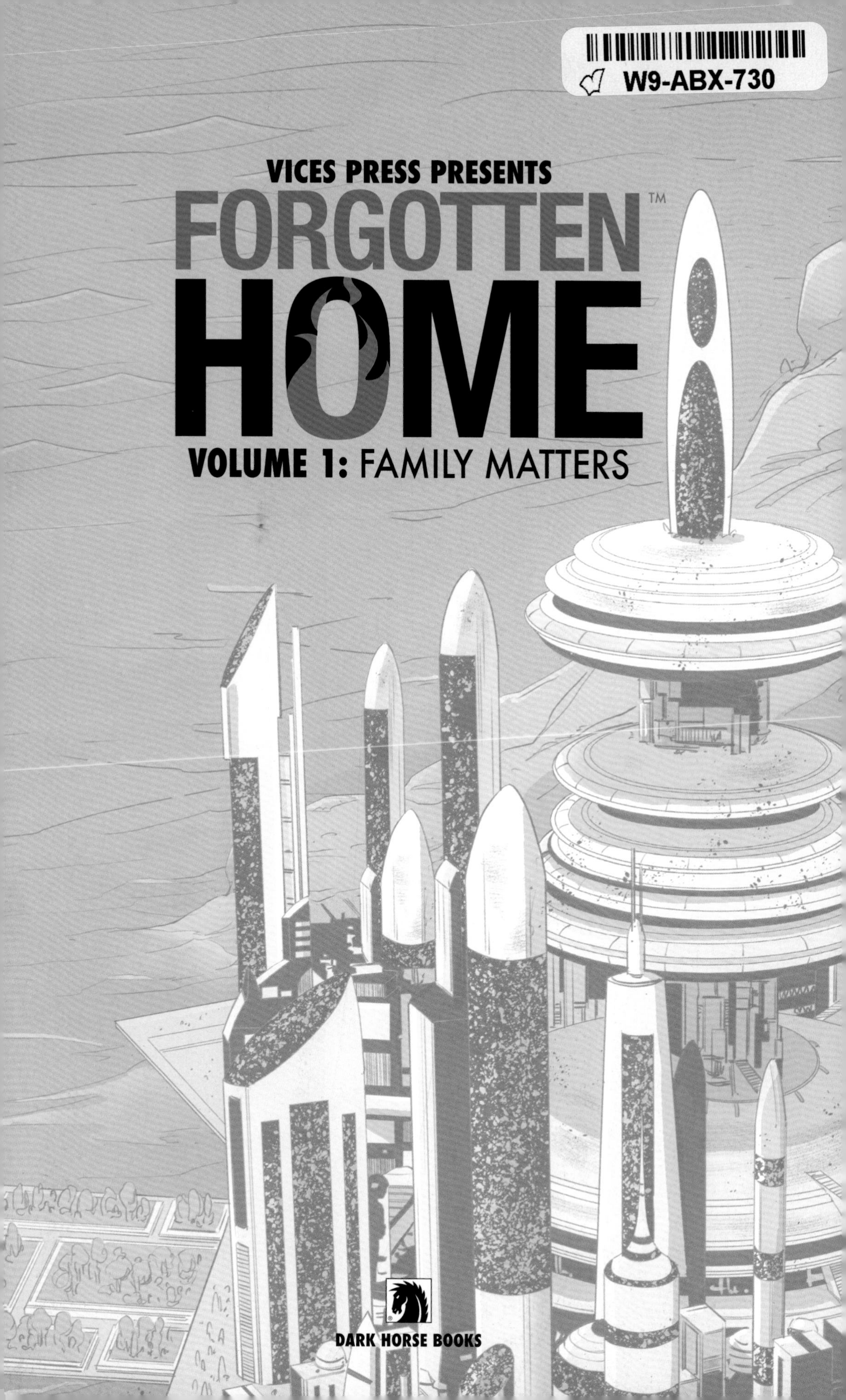

DARK HORSE BOOKS

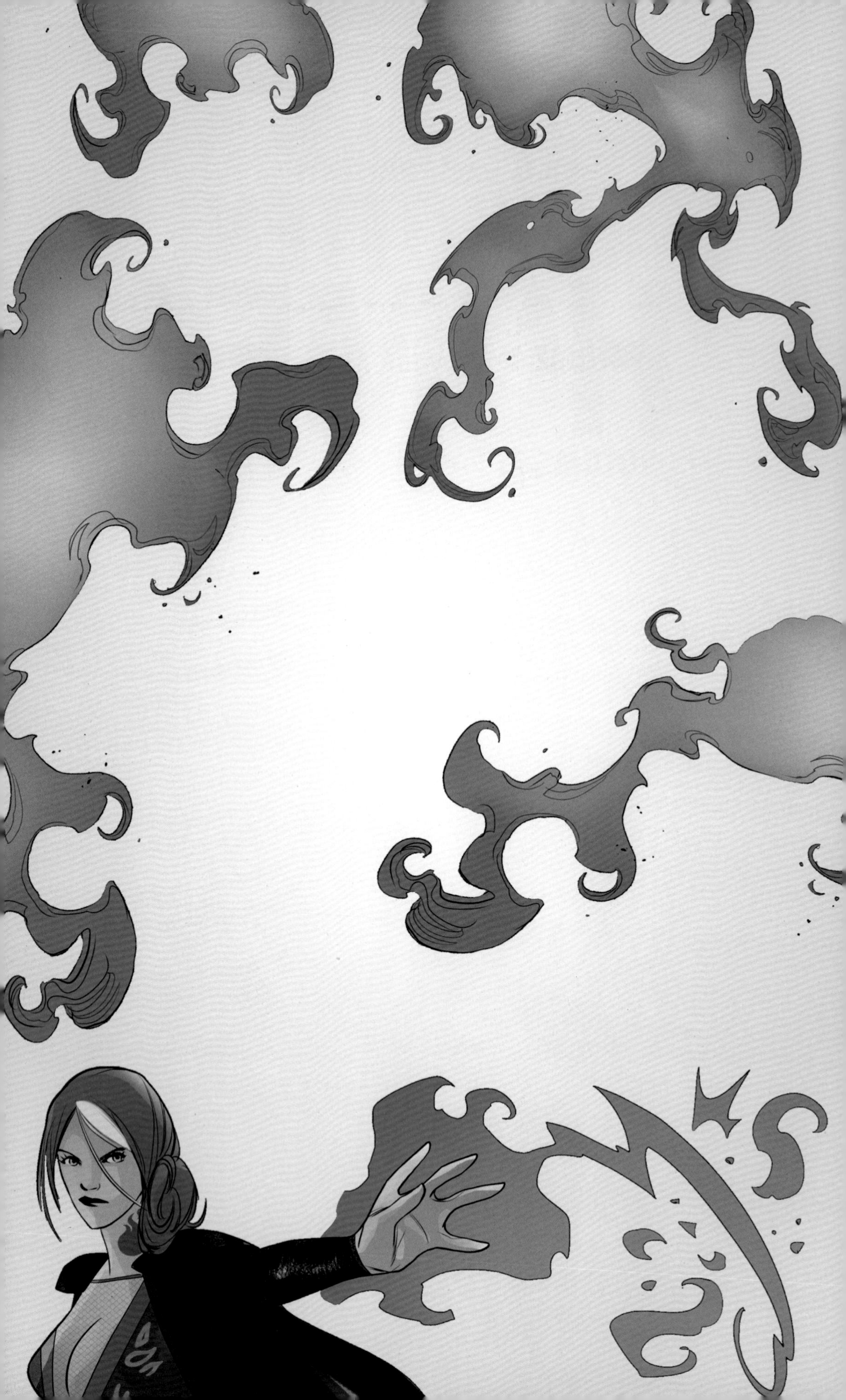

VICES PRESS PRESENTS
FORGOTTEN™
HOME

VOLUME 1: FAMILY MATTERS

WRITTEN BY
ERICA SCHULTZ

ART BY
MARIKA CRESTA

COLORS BY
MATT EMMONS

FOREWORD BY
SAM MAGGS

COLOR ASSISTS BY
CASSIE ANDERSON,
SAM BENNETT &
JACKIE VON SPANKS

LETTERING BY
CARDINAL RAE

CHAPTER TITLE COVERS BY
NATASHA ALTERICI

COVER BY
BILL SIENKIEWICZ

FORGOTTEN HOME LOGO
DESIGNED BY
KEVIN MAHER

ADDITIONAL EDITS BY
CHIP MOSHER
& A. J. SCHULTZ

FORGOTTEN HOME CREATED BY ERICA SCHULTZ

DARK HORSE TEAM

PRESIDENT AND PUBLISHER
MIKE RICHARDSON

EDITOR
DANIEL CHABON

ASSISTANT EDITORS
CHUCK HOWITT & KONNER KNUDSEN

DESIGNER
MAY HIJIKURO

DIGITAL ART TECHNICIAN
JASON RICKERD

SPECIAL THANKS DAVID STEINBERGER ♨ CHIP MOSHER ♨ BRYCE GOLD

Neil Hankerson Executive Vice President **Tom Weddle** Chief Financial Officer **Dale LaFountain** Chief Information Officer **Tim Wiesch** Vice President of Licensing **Matt Parkinson** Vice President of Marketing **Vanessa Todd-Holmes** Vice President of Production and Scheduling **Mark Bernardi** Vice President of Book Trade and Digital Sales **Randy Lahrman** Vice President of Product Development **Ken Lizzi** General Counsel **Dave Marshall** Editor in Chief **Davey Estrada** Editorial Director **Chris Warner** Senior Books Editor **Cary Grazzini** Director of Specialty Projects **Lia Ribacchi** Art Director **Matt Dryer** Director of Digital Art and Prepress **Michael Gombos** Senior Director of Licensed Publications **Kari Yadro** Director of Custom Programs **Kari Torson** Director of International Licensing

Published by Dark Horse Books
A division of Dark Horse Comics LLC
10956 SE Main Street, Milwaukie, OR 97222

First edition: April 2022
Trade paperback ISBN: 978-1-50672-454-6

1 3 5 7 9 10 8 6 4 2
Printed in China

Comic Shop Locator Service: comicshoplocator.com

FORGOTTEN HOME™ VOL. 1: FAMILY MATTERS

Collects *Forgotten Home* #1–#8, first published by Vices Press.

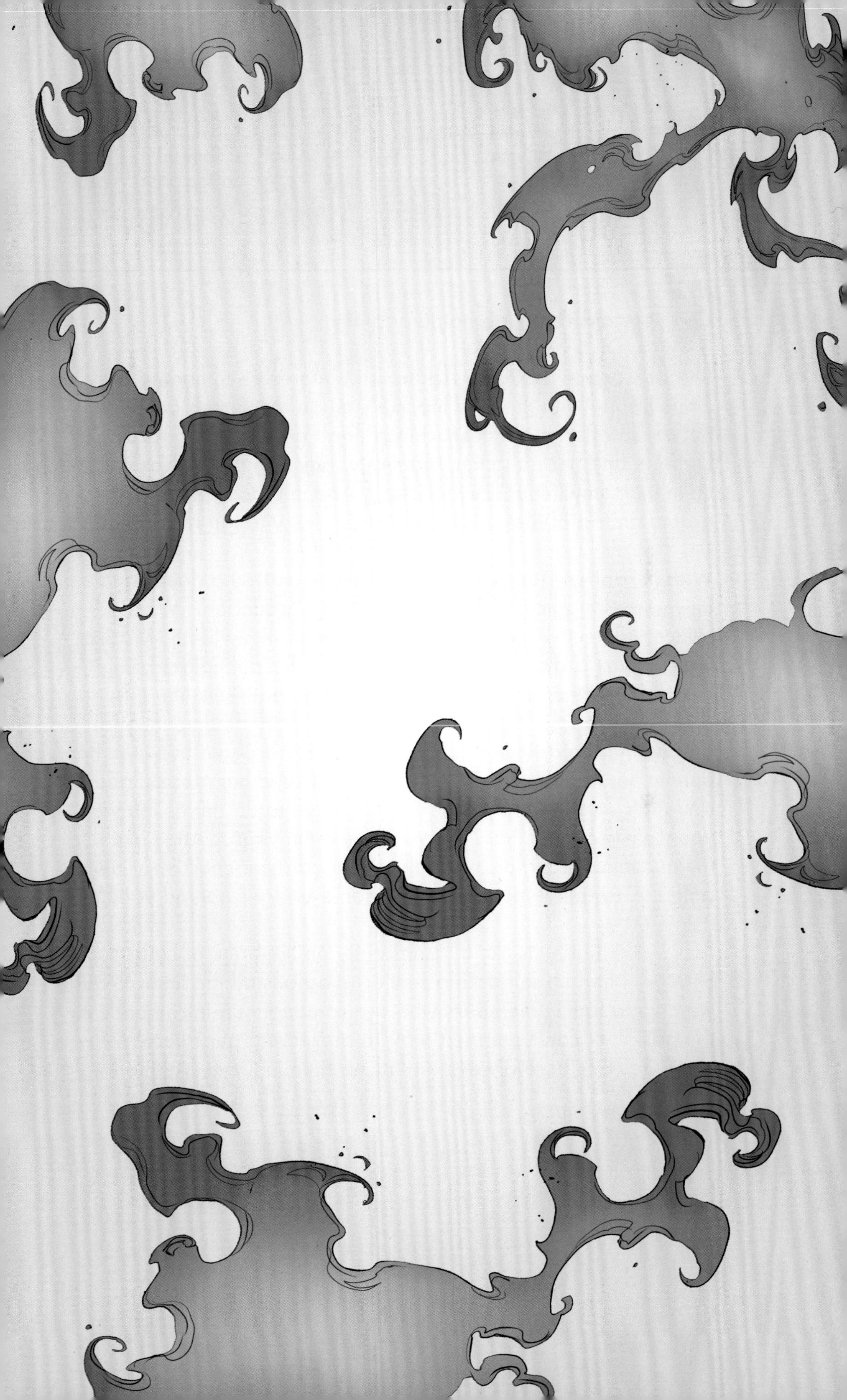

FOREWORD BY
SAM MAGGS

Can you ever really go home again?

Sheriff's deputy Lorraine Adalet isn't interested in finding out.
She's happy with the new life she's made for herself on Earth.
But, as so often is the case, things don't go according to plan.
Lorraine and her daughter Joanna quickly find themselves caught
up in their tumultuous family history. Add in a dash of magical royal
drama on top of that, and you get one very tough road home.

With *Forgotten Home*, Erica Schultz has crafted a deep, rich
universe as magical as its characters are grounded. (Witchy
princess detective? Where have you been all my life?!) Marika
Cresta's art is dynamic. Matt Emmons's vibrant colors bring
Lorraine and her powers to life in a way that feels like they
could jump off the page and into reality at any moment. And,
despite the fantasticality of it all, Lorraine's struggle between her
duty to her family and her duty to herself—and her morals, and her
daughter—feels entirely real. Do you have to do things the way
your family always has? Do you owe them your loyalty, even if it
means betraying your own values? Or can you chart your own
path . . . even if it means burning some bridges behind you?

In a world that feels like it's constantly on the brink of catastrophic
change, I find myself asking similar questions all the time. What do
we owe to family members who are so caught up in romanticizing
the past they can't see their way to preserving our future? Why is
there always an "us vs. them"? Does tradition hold
value, or is it simply made to uphold an unjust

establishment? These are all things we must consider when deciding what we owe to ourselves. Most importantly, we have to figure out how to be *kind* to ourselves when choosing what family and which traditions are meaningful. Not to other people. To *you.*

Lorraine's journey is a beautiful reflection of what it means to grow into the person you're meant to be. Really, home is the people you love and the values closest to your heart. And that is what *Forgotten Home* reminds us.

Be good to yourself,

Sam Maggs
February 2020

Sam Maggs is a best-selling author of books, comics, and video games. She's been a senior games writer, including work on *Marvel's Spider-Man*; the author of many YA and middle-grade books, like *The Unstoppable Wasp, Con Quest!, Tell No Tales,* and *The Fangirl's Guide to the Galaxy*; and a comics writer for beloved titles like *Marvel Action: Captain Marvel, My Little Pony,* and *Transformers.* She is also an on-air host for networks like Nerdist. A Canadian in Los Angeles, she misses Coffee Crisp and bagged milk.

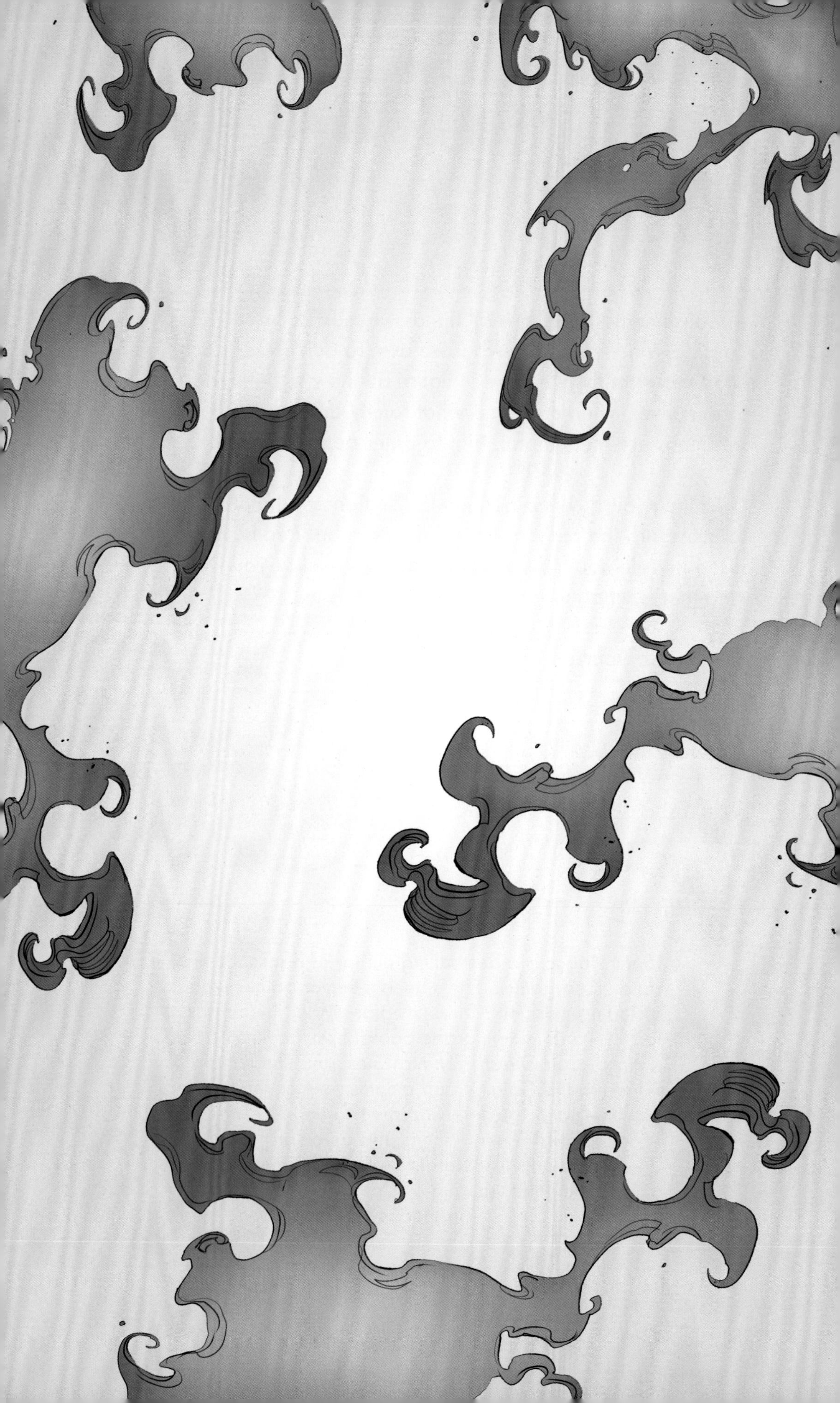

ONE

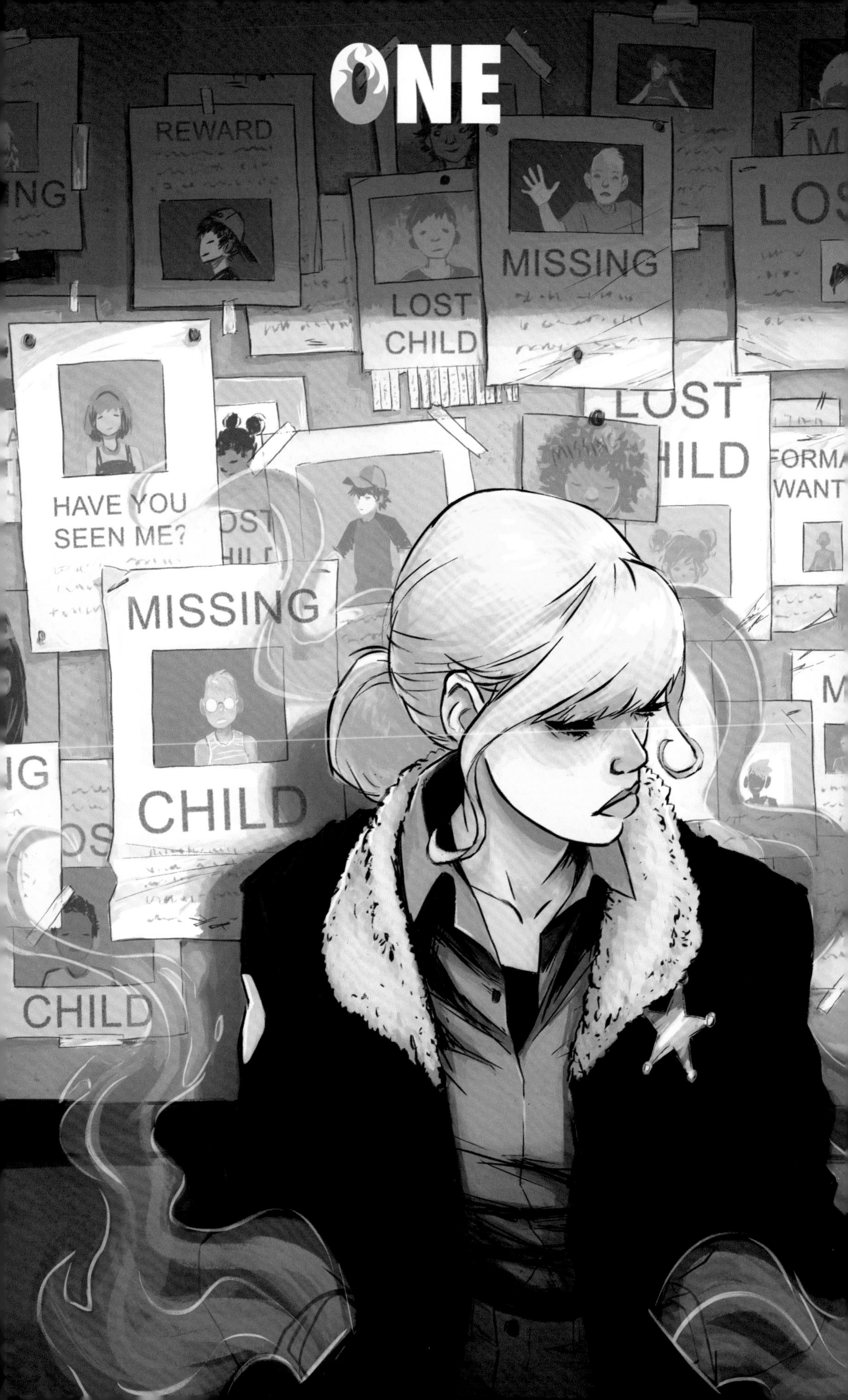
REWARD
LOST CHILD
MISSING
HAVE YOU SEEN ME?
MISSING CHILD
CHILD

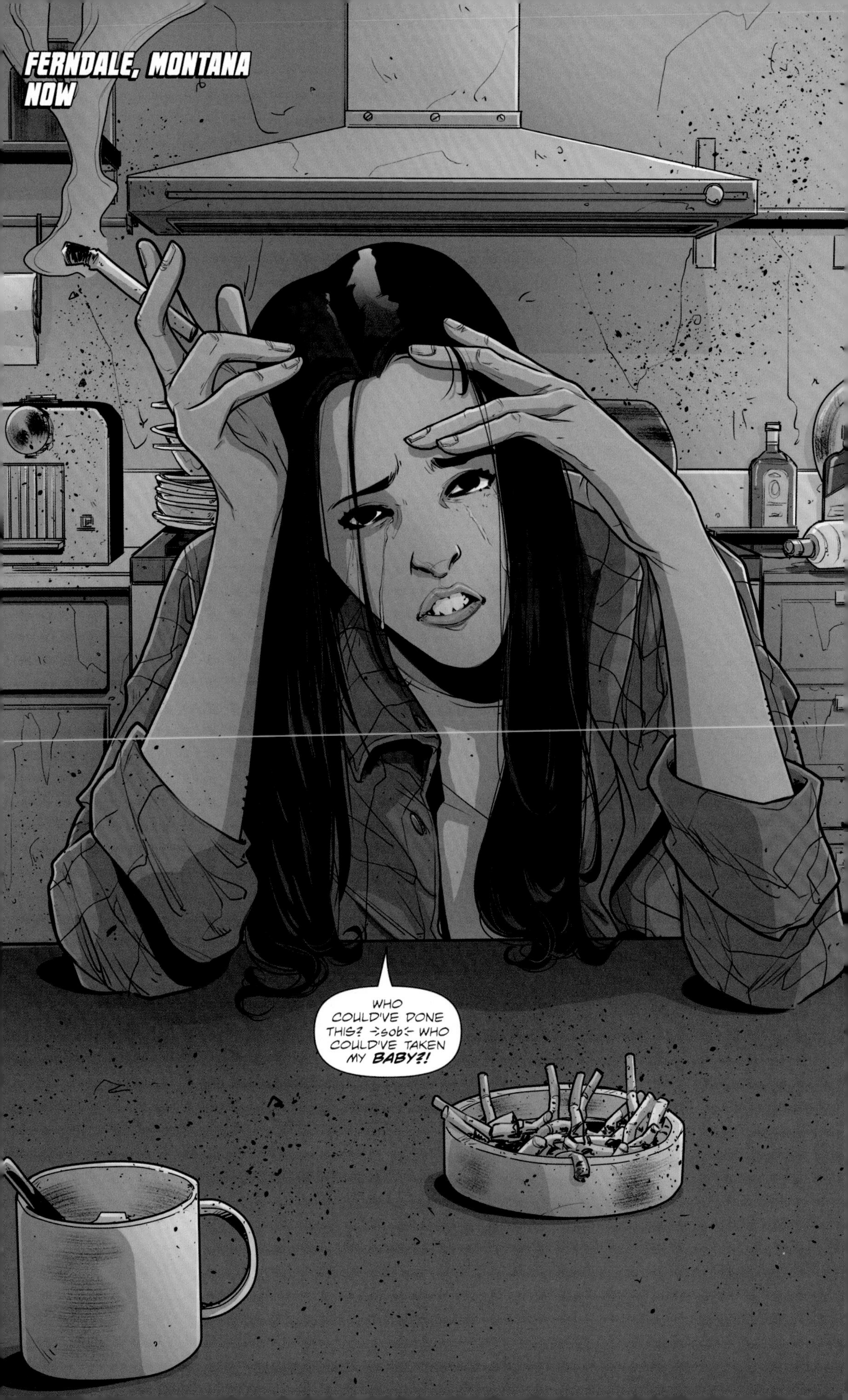
FERNDALE, MONTANA
NOW
WHO COULD'VE DONE THIS? -sob- WHO COULD'VE TAKEN MY BABY?!

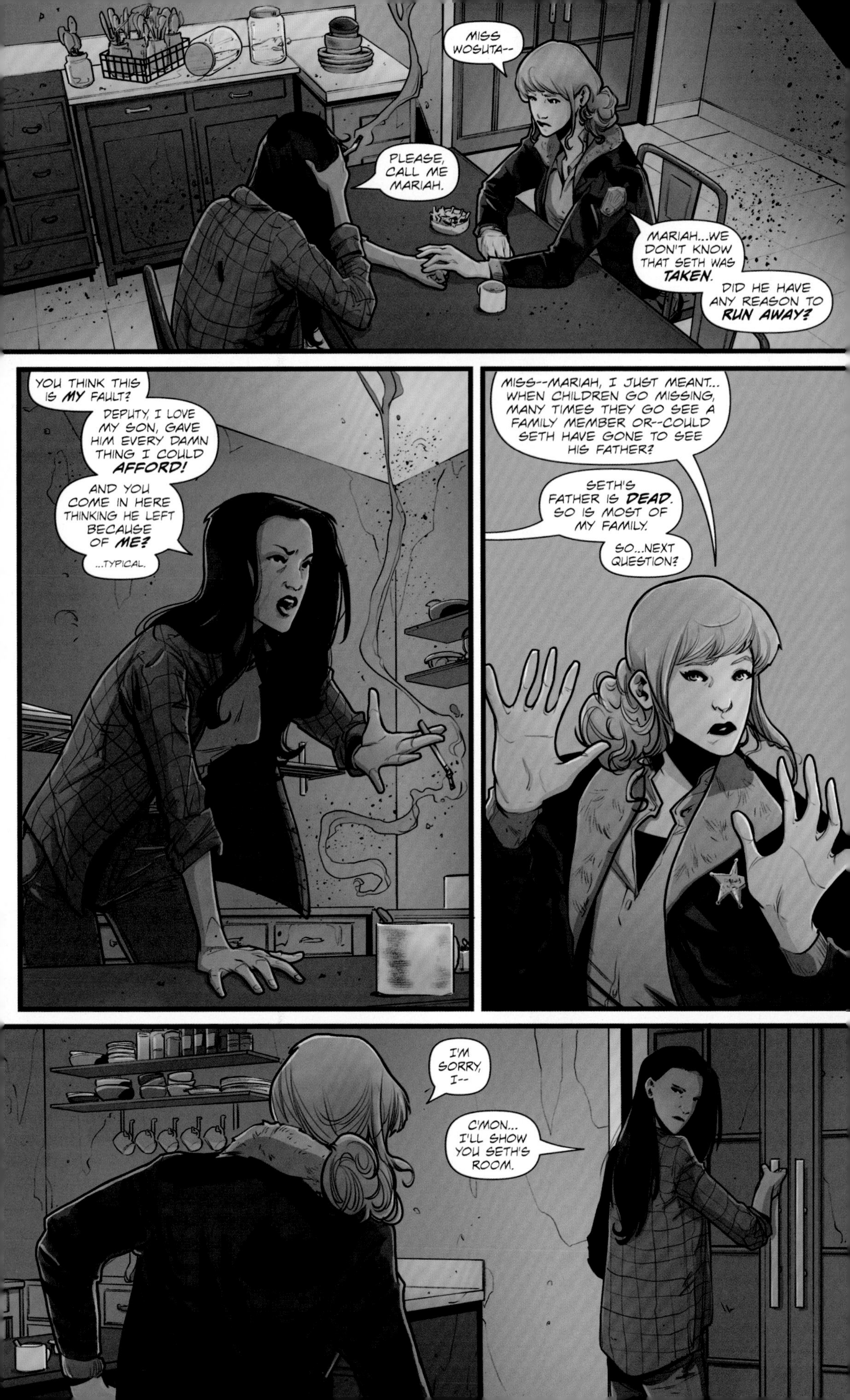
MISS WOSUTA--
PLEASE, CALL ME MARIAH.
MARIAH...WE DON'T KNOW THAT SETH WAS TAKEN.
DID HE HAVE ANY REASON TO RUN AWAY?
YOU THINK THIS IS MY FAULT?
DEPUTY, I LOVE MY SON, GAVE HIM EVERY DAMN THING I COULD AFFORD!
AND YOU COME IN HERE THINKING HE LEFT BECAUSE OF ME?
...TYPICAL.
MISS--MARIAH, I JUST MEANT... WHEN CHILDREN GO MISSING, MANY TIMES THEY GO SEE A FAMILY MEMBER OR--COULD SETH HAVE GONE TO SEE HIS FATHER?
SETH'S FATHER IS DEAD. SO IS MOST OF MY FAMILY.
SO...NEXT QUESTION?
I'M SORRY, I--
C'MON... I'LL SHOW YOU SETH'S ROOM.

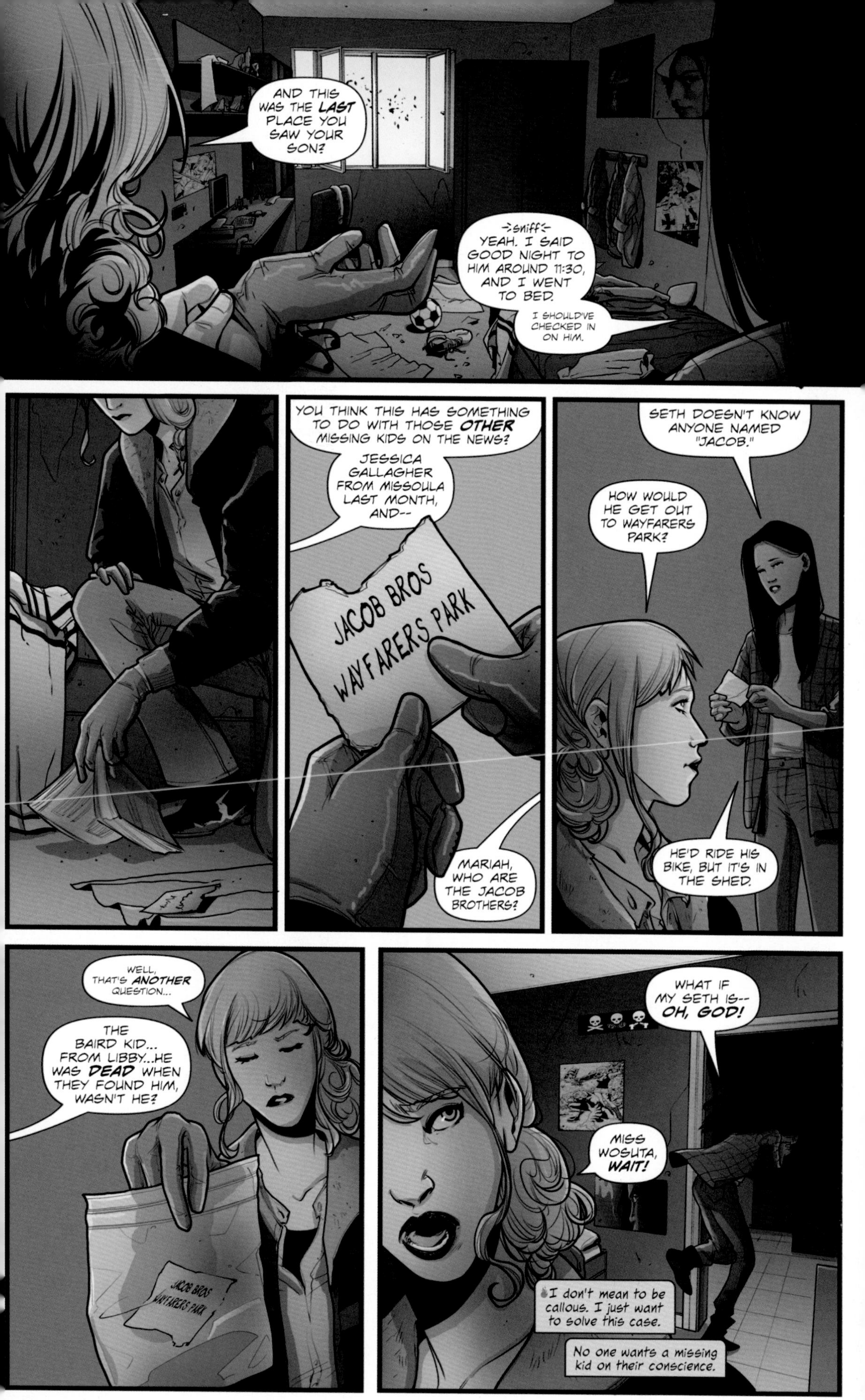
AND THIS WAS THE LAST PLACE YOU SAW YOUR SON?
-sniff- YEAH. I SAID GOOD NIGHT TO HIM AROUND 11:30, AND I WENT TO BED.
I SHOULD'VE CHECKED IN ON HIM.
YOU THINK THIS HAS SOMETHING TO DO WITH THOSE OTHER MISSING KIDS ON THE NEWS?
JESSICA GALLAGHER FROM MISSOULA LAST MONTH, AND--
JACOB BROS
WAYFARERS PARK
MARIAH, WHO ARE THE JACOB BROTHERS?
SETH DOESN'T KNOW ANYONE NAMED "JACOB."
HOW WOULD HE GET OUT TO WAYFARERS PARK?
HE'D RIDE HIS BIKE, BUT IT'S IN THE SHED.
WELL, THAT'S ANOTHER QUESTION...
THE BAIRD KID... FROM LIBBY...HE WAS DEAD WHEN THEY FOUND HIM, WASN'T HE?
JACOB BROS
WAYFARERS PARK
WHAT IF MY SETH IS-- OH, GOD!
MISS WOSUTA, WAIT!
I don't mean to be callous. I just want to solve this case.
No one wants a missing kid on their conscience.

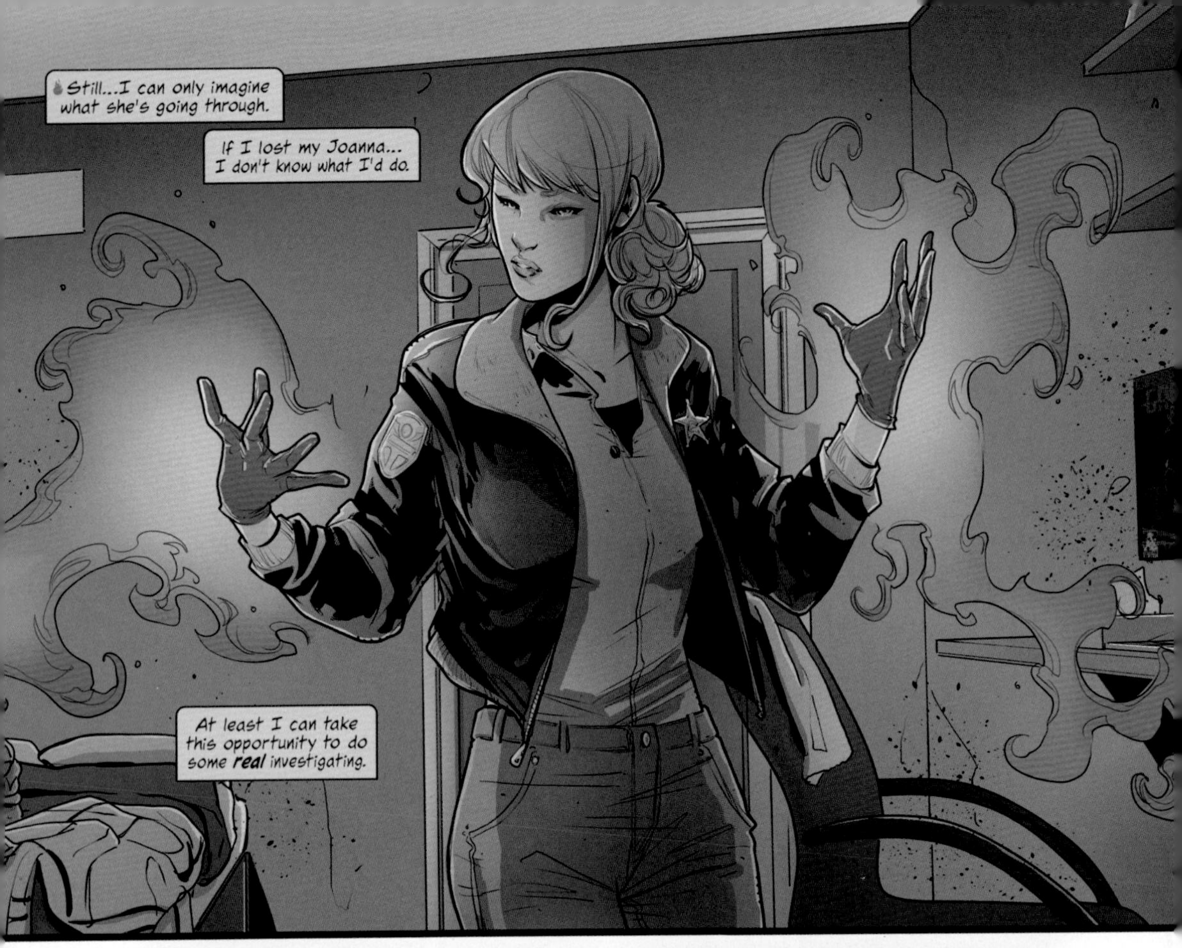
Still...I can only imagine what she's going through.
If I lost my Joanna... I don't know what I'd do.
At least I can take this opportunity to do some *real* investigating.

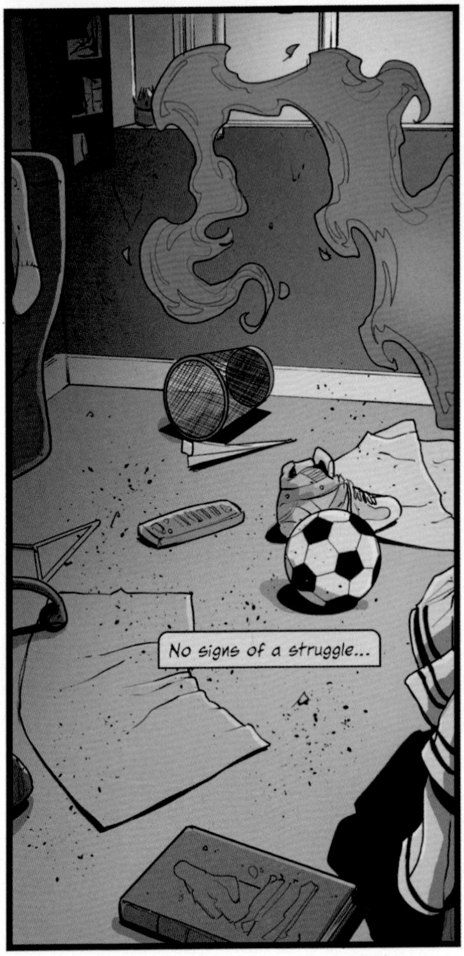
No signs of a struggle...

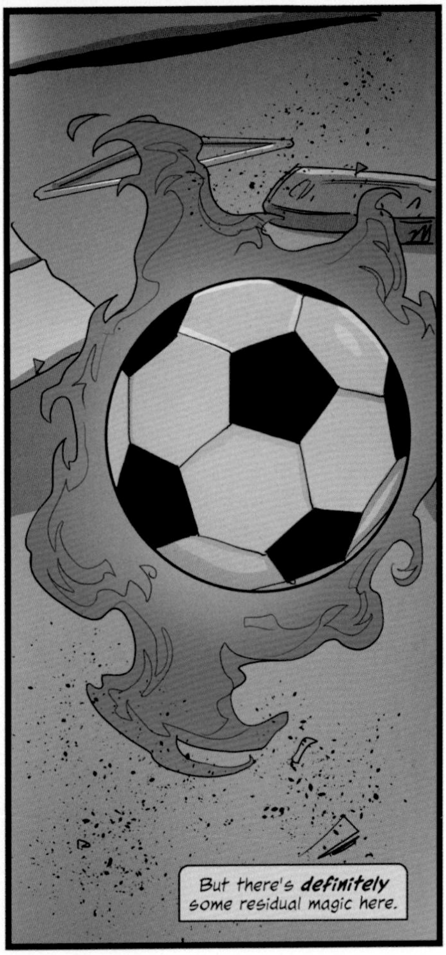
But there's ***definitely*** some residual magic here.

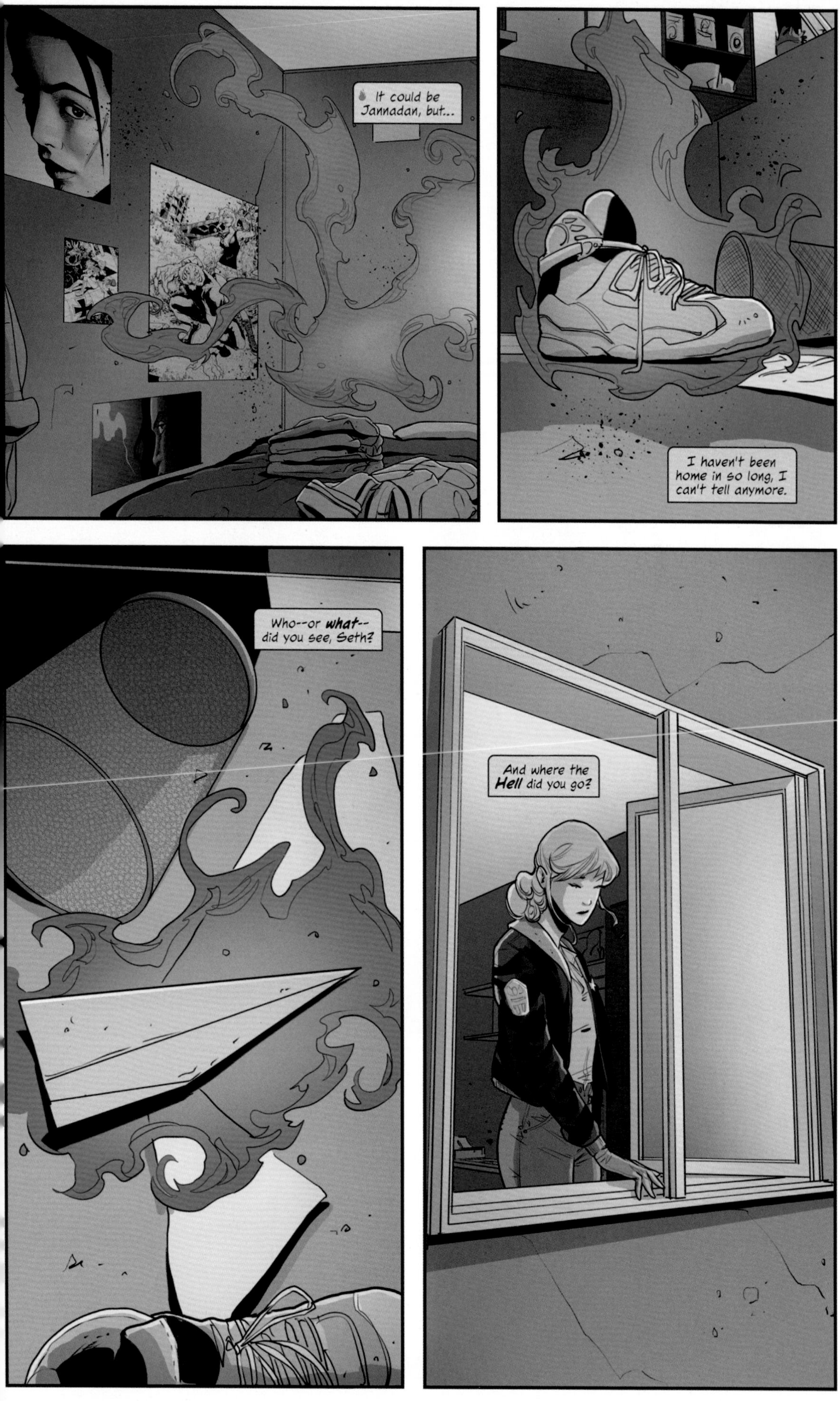

It could be Jannadan, but...
I haven't been home in so long, I can't tell anymore.
Who--or **what**--did you see, Seth?
And where the **Hell** did you go?

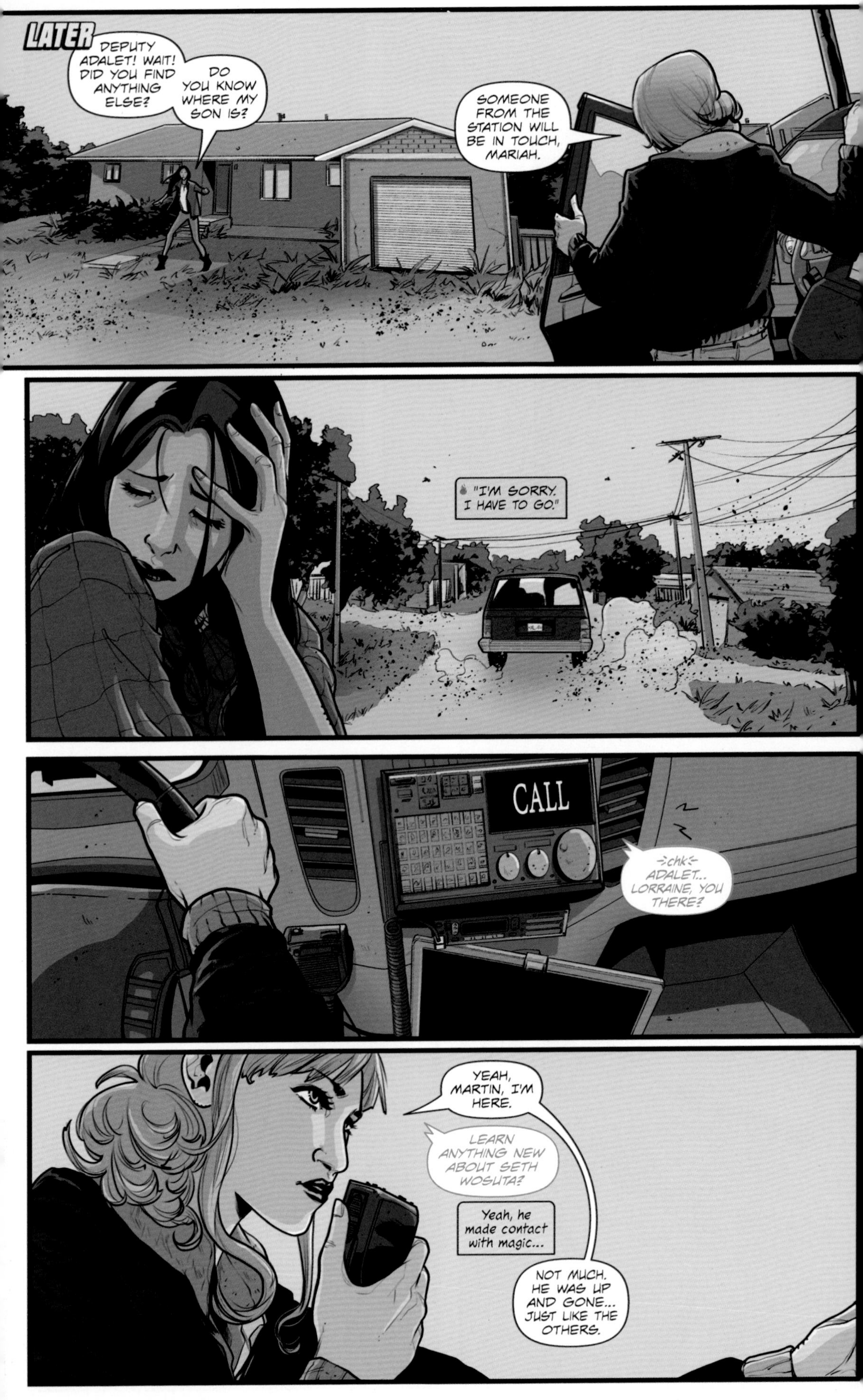
LATER
DEPUTY ADALET! WAIT! DID YOU FIND ANYTHING ELSE?
DO YOU KNOW WHERE MY SON IS?
SOMEONE FROM THE STATION WILL BE IN TOUCH, MARIAH.
"I'M SORRY. I HAVE TO GO."
CALL
chk ADALET... LORRAINE, YOU THERE?
YEAH, MARTIN, I'M HERE.
LEARN ANYTHING NEW ABOUT SETH WOSUTA?
Yeah, he made contact with magic...
NOT MUCH. HE WAS UP AND GONE... JUST LIKE THE OTHERS.

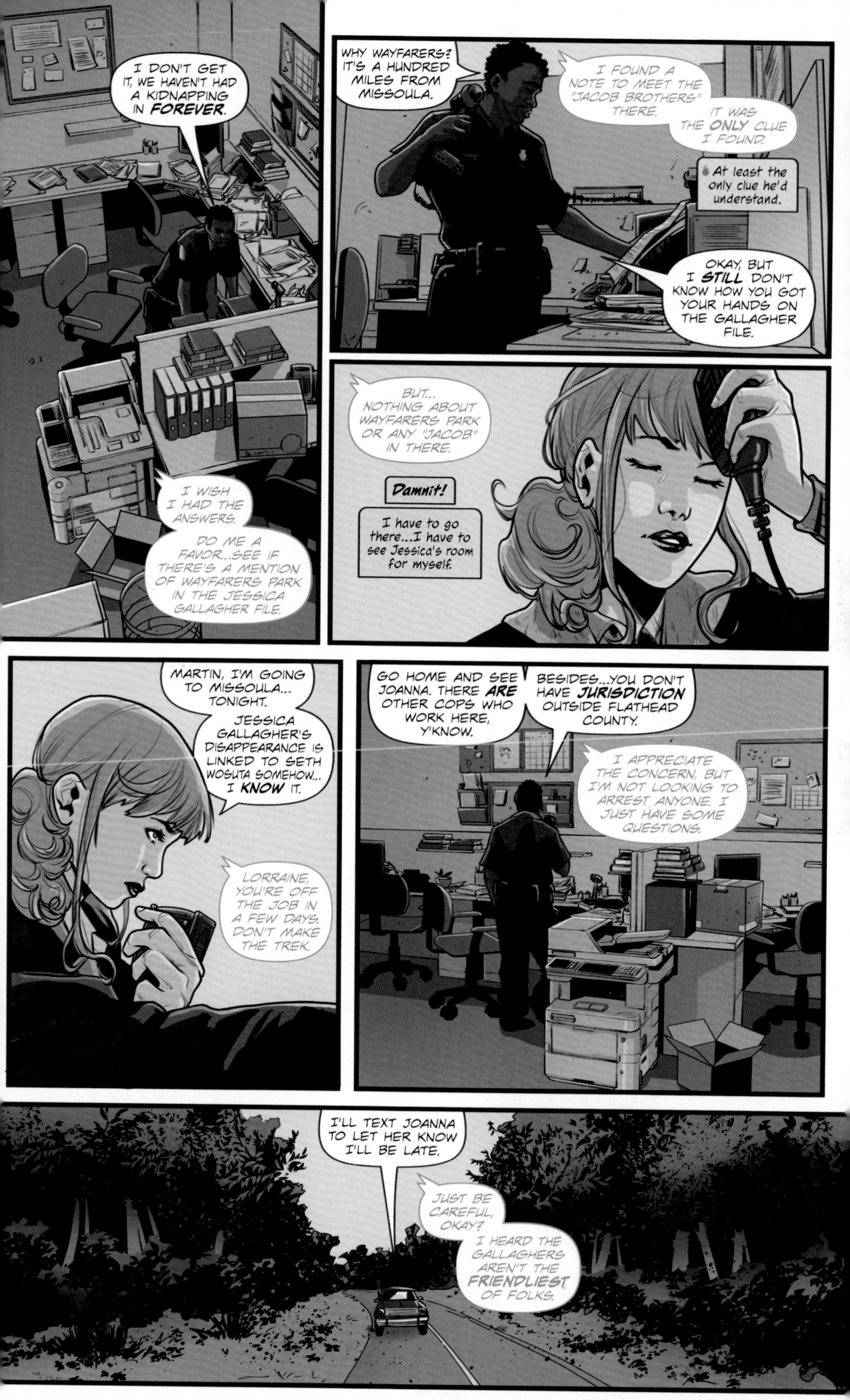
I DON'T GET IT, WE HAVEN'T HAD A KIDNAPPING IN FOREVER.
WHY WAYFARERS? IT'S A HUNDRED MILES FROM MISSOULA.
I FOUND A NOTE TO MEET THE "JACOB BROTHERS" THERE.
IT WAS THE ONLY CLUE I FOUND.
At least the only clue he'd understand.
OKAY, BUT I STILL DON'T KNOW HOW YOU GOT YOUR HANDS ON THE GALLAGHER FILE.
I WISH I HAD THE ANSWERS.
DO ME A FAVOR...SEE IF THERE'S A MENTION OF WAYFARERS PARK IN THE JESSICA GALLAGHER FILE.
BUT... NOTHING ABOUT WAYFARERS PARK OR ANY "JACOB" IN THERE.
Damnit!
I have to go there...I have to see Jessica's room for myself.
MARTIN, I'M GOING TO MISSOULA... TONIGHT.
JESSICA GALLAGHER'S DISAPPEARANCE IS LINKED TO SETH WOSUTA SOMEHOW... I KNOW IT.
LORRAINE, YOU'RE OFF THE JOB IN A FEW DAYS. DON'T MAKE THE TREK.
GO HOME AND SEE JOANNA. THERE ARE OTHER COPS WHO WORK HERE, Y'KNOW.
BESIDES...YOU DON'T HAVE JURISDICTION OUTSIDE FLATHEAD COUNTY.
I APPRECIATE THE CONCERN, BUT I'M NOT LOOKING TO ARREST ANYONE. I JUST HAVE SOME QUESTIONS.
I'LL TEXT JOANNA TO LET HER KNOW I'LL BE LATE.
JUST BE CAREFUL, OKAY?
I HEARD THE GALLAGHERS AREN'T THE FRIENDLIEST OF FOLKS.

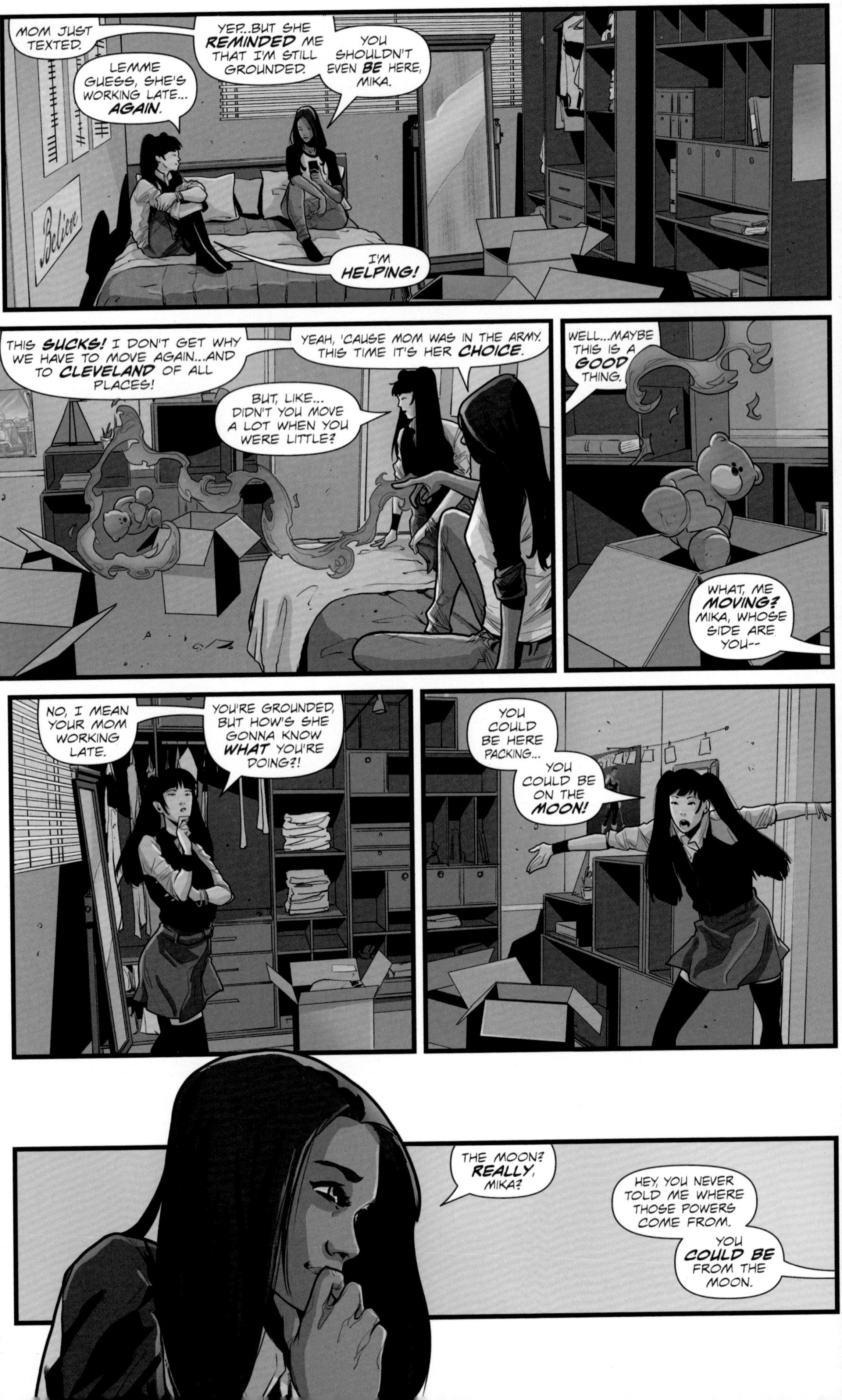
MOM JUST TEXTED.
LEMME GUESS, SHE'S WORKING LATE... AGAIN.
YEP...BUT SHE REMINDED ME THAT I'M STILL GROUNDED.
YOU SHOULDN'T EVEN BE HERE, MIKA.
I'M HELPING!
THIS SUCKS! I DON'T GET WHY WE HAVE TO MOVE AGAIN...AND TO CLEVELAND OF ALL PLACES!
BUT, LIKE... DIDN'T YOU MOVE A LOT WHEN YOU WERE LITTLE?
YEAH, 'CAUSE MOM WAS IN THE ARMY. THIS TIME IT'S HER CHOICE.
WELL...MAYBE THIS IS A GOOD THING.
WHAT, ME MOVING? MIKA, WHOSE SIDE ARE YOU--
NO, I MEAN YOUR MOM WORKING LATE.
YOU'RE GROUNDED, BUT HOW'S SHE GONNA KNOW WHAT YOU'RE DOING?!
YOU COULD BE HERE PACKING...
YOU COULD BE ON THE MOON!
THE MOON? REALLY, MIKA?
HEY, YOU NEVER TOLD ME WHERE THOSE POWERS COME FROM.
YOU COULD BE FROM THE MOON.

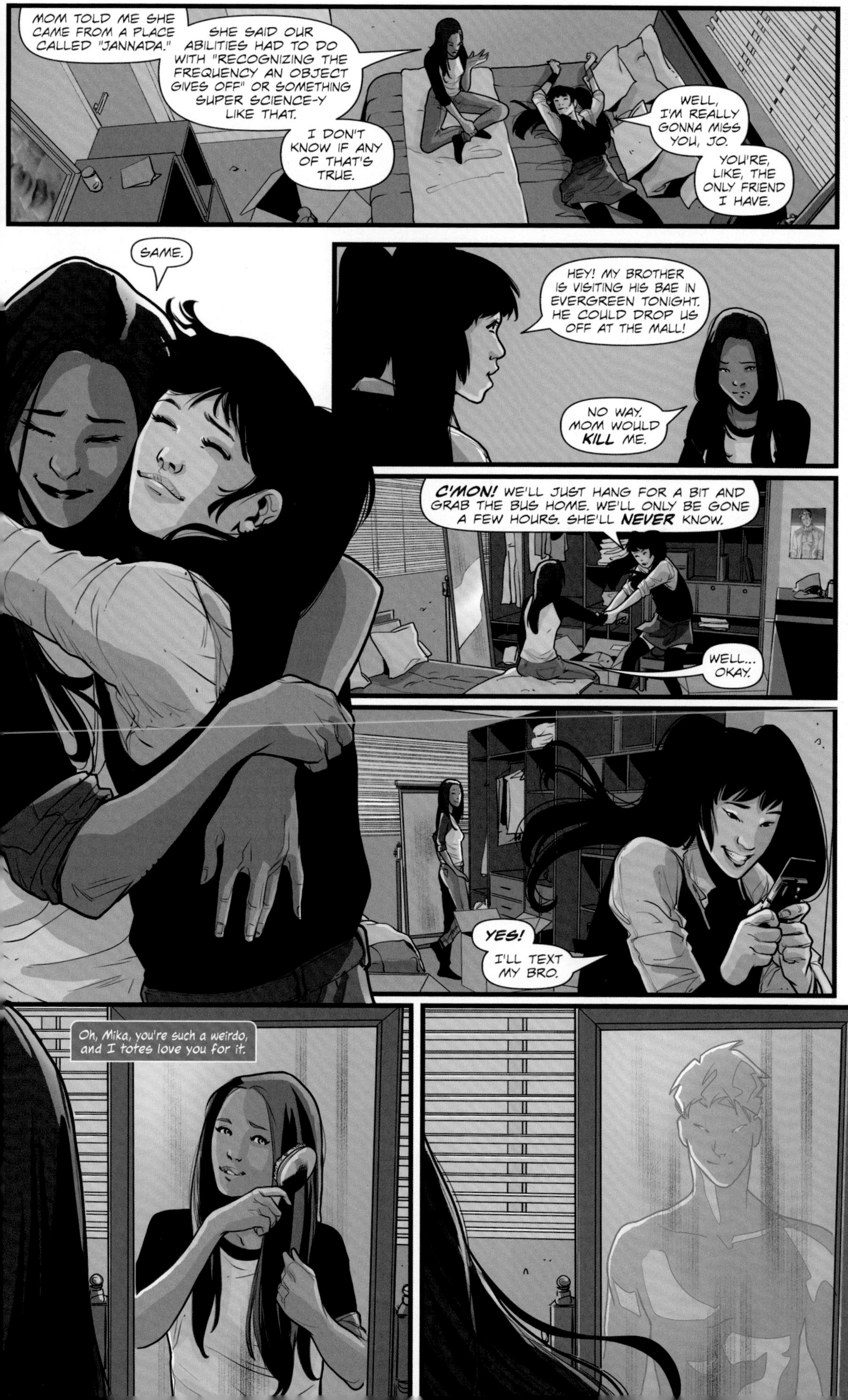
MOM TOLD ME SHE CAME FROM A PLACE CALLED "JANNADA."
SHE SAID OUR ABILITIES HAD TO DO WITH "RECOGNIZING THE FREQUENCY AN OBJECT GIVES OFF" OR SOMETHING SUPER SCIENCE-Y LIKE THAT.
I DON'T KNOW IF ANY OF THAT'S TRUE.
WELL, I'M REALLY GONNA MISS YOU, JO.
YOU'RE, LIKE, THE ONLY FRIEND I HAVE.
SAME.
HEY! MY BROTHER IS VISITING HIS BAE IN EVERGREEN TONIGHT. HE COULD DROP US OFF AT THE MALL!
NO WAY. MOM WOULD KILL ME.
C'MON! WE'LL JUST HANG FOR A BIT AND GRAB THE BUS HOME. WE'LL ONLY BE GONE A FEW HOURS. SHE'LL NEVER KNOW.
WELL... OKAY.
YES!
I'LL TEXT MY BRO.
Oh, Mika, you're such a weirdo, and I totes love you for it.

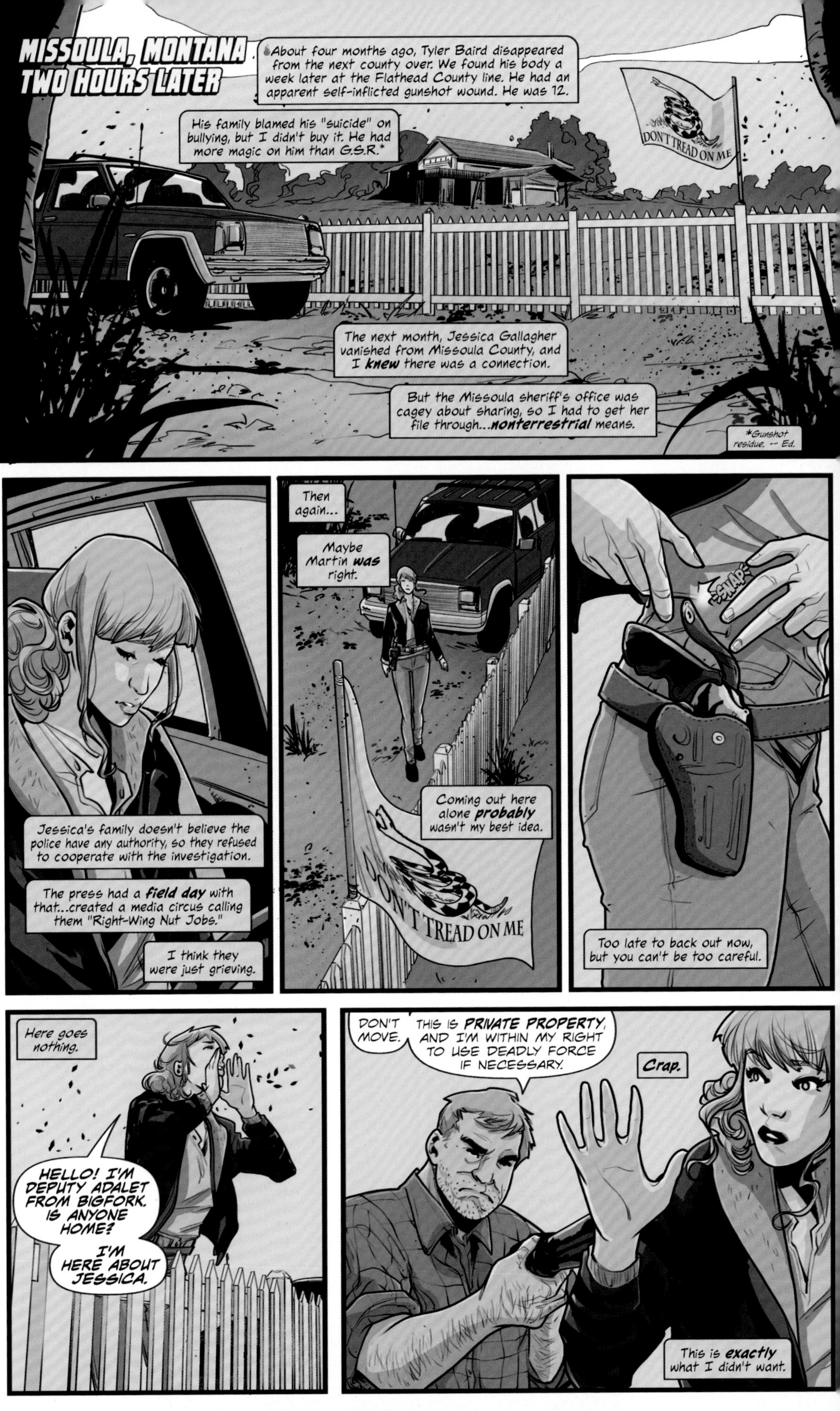
MISSOULA, MONTANA
TWO HOURS LATER
About four months ago, Tyler Baird disappeared from the next county over. We found his body a week later at the Flathead County line. He had an apparent self-inflicted gunshot wound. He was 12.
His family blamed his "suicide" on bullying, but I didn't buy it. He had more magic on him than G.S.R.*
DON'T TREAD ON ME
The next month, Jessica Gallagher vanished from Missoula County, and I *knew* there was a connection.
But the Missoula sheriff's office was cagey about sharing, so I had to get her file through...*nonterrestrial* means.
*Gunshot residue. -- Ed.
Jessica's family doesn't believe the police have any authority, so they refused to cooperate with the investigation.
The press had a *field day* with that...created a media circus calling them "Right-Wing Nut Jobs."
I think they were just grieving.
Then again...
Maybe Martin *was* right.
Coming out here alone *probably* wasn't my best idea.
DON'T TREAD ON ME
SNAP
Too late to back out now, but you can't be too careful.
Here goes nothing.
HELLO! I'M DEPUTY ADALET FROM BIGFORK. IS ANYONE HOME?
I'M HERE ABOUT JESSICA.
DON'T MOVE.
THIS IS *PRIVATE PROPERTY*, AND I'M WITHIN MY RIGHT TO USE DEADLY FORCE IF NECESSARY.
Crap.
This is *exactly* what I didn't want.

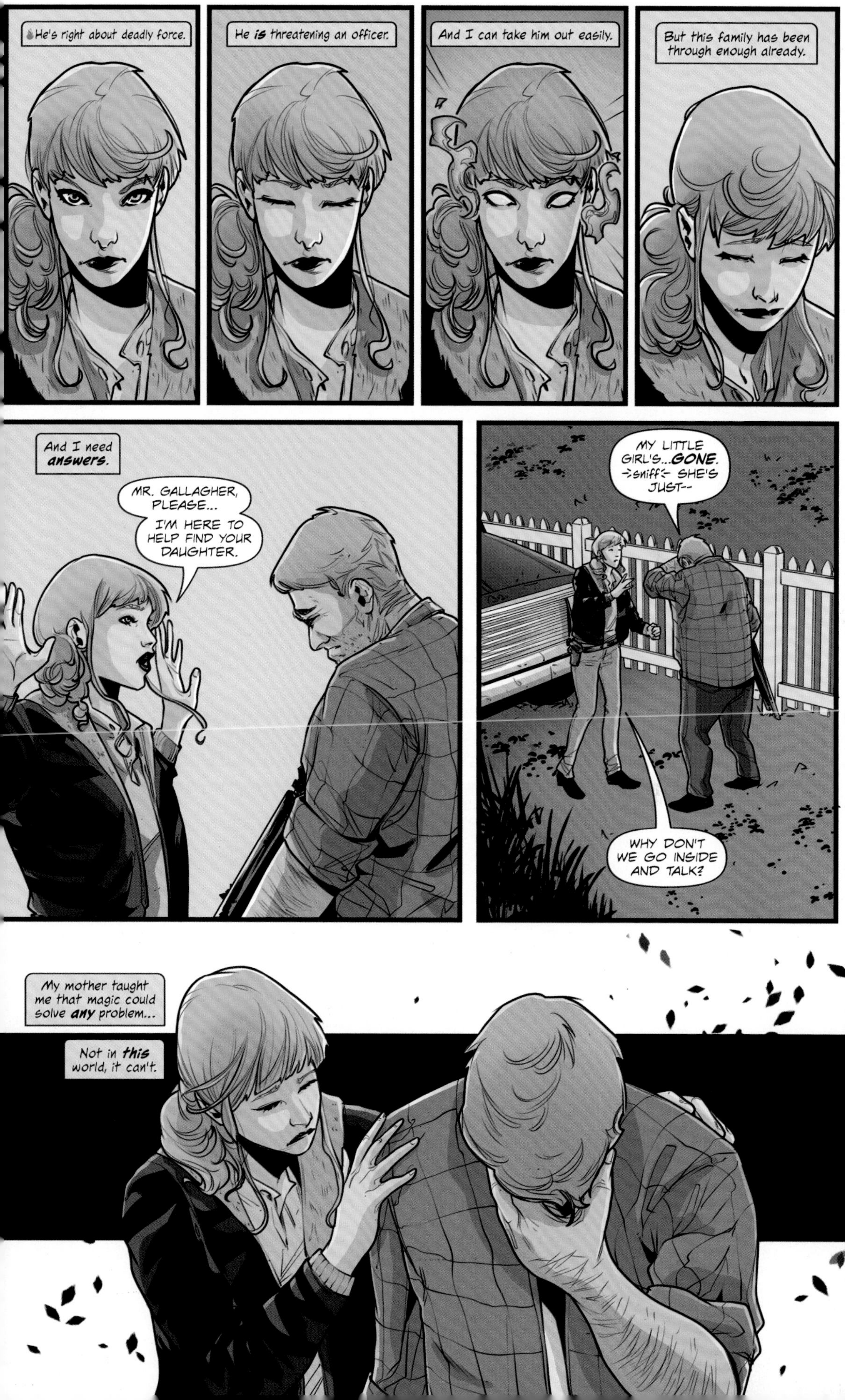
He's right about deadly force.
He *is* threatening an officer.
And I can take him out easily.
But this family has been through enough already.
And I need **answers.**
MR. GALLAGHER, PLEASE... I'M HERE TO HELP FIND YOUR DAUGHTER.
MY LITTLE GIRL'S...**GONE**. ~sniff~ SHE'S JUST--
WHY DON'T WE GO INSIDE AND TALK?
My mother taught me that magic could solve **any** problem...
Not in **this** world, it can't.

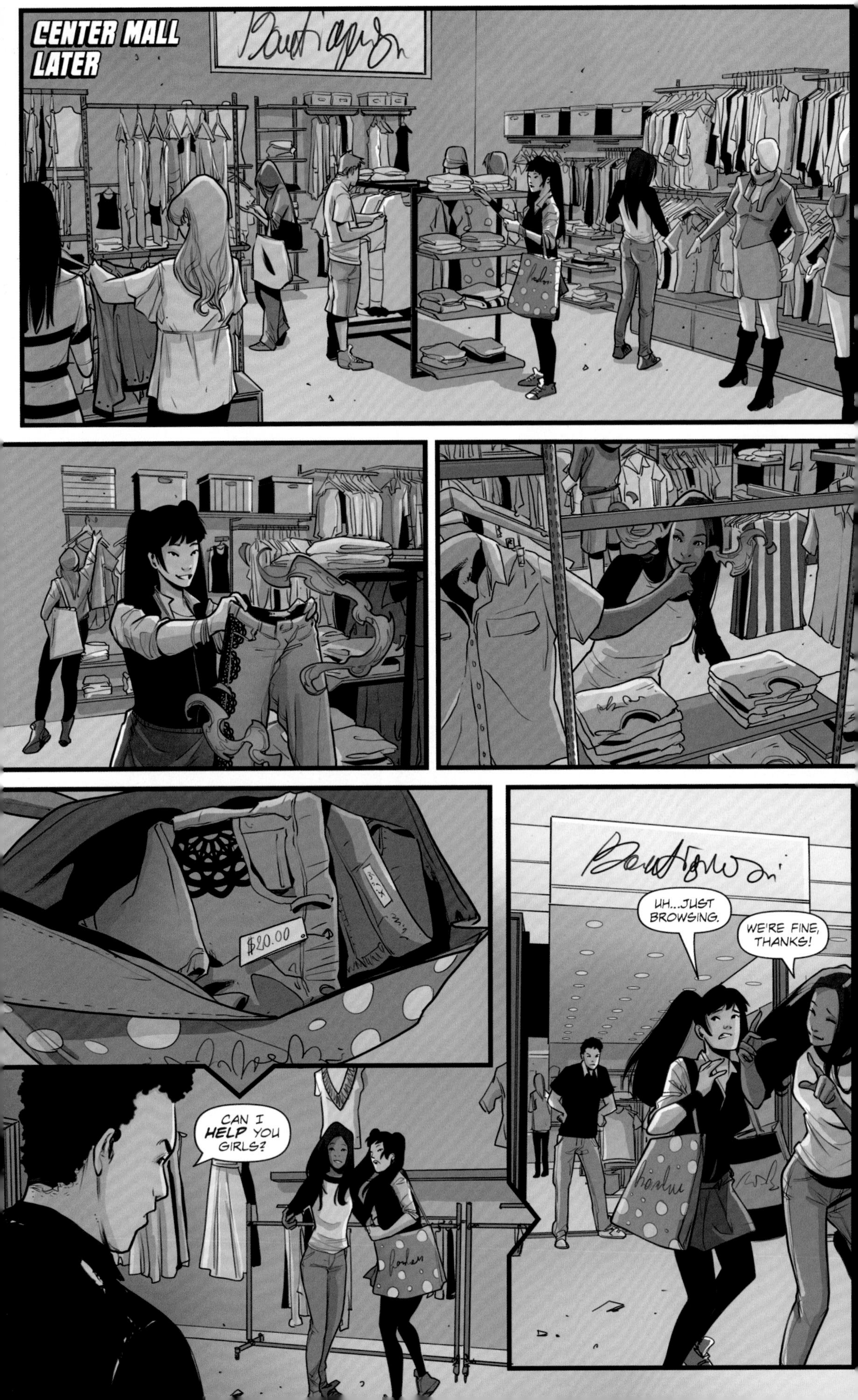
CENTER MALL
LATER
$20.00
CAN I HELP YOU GIRLS?
UH...JUST BROWSING.
WE'RE FINE, THANKS!

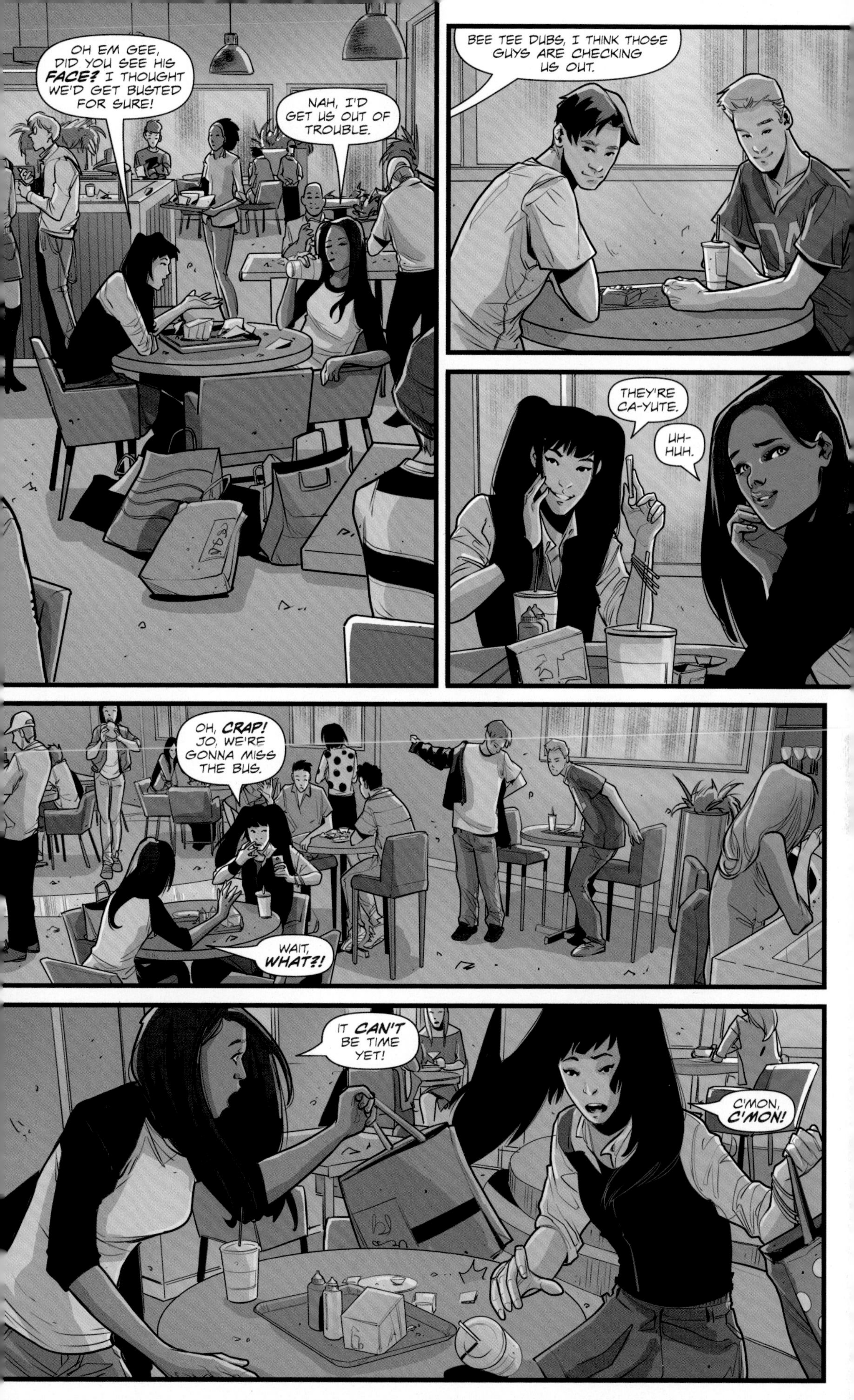
OH EM GEE, DID YOU SEE HIS FACE? I THOUGHT WE'D GET BUSTED FOR SURE!
NAH, I'D GET US OUT OF TROUBLE.
BEE TEE DUBS, I THINK THOSE GUYS ARE CHECKING US OUT.
THEY'RE CA-YUTE.
UH-HUH.
OH, CRAP! JO, WE'RE GONNA MISS THE BUS.
WAIT, WHAT?!
IT CAN'T BE TIME YET!
C'MON, C'MON!

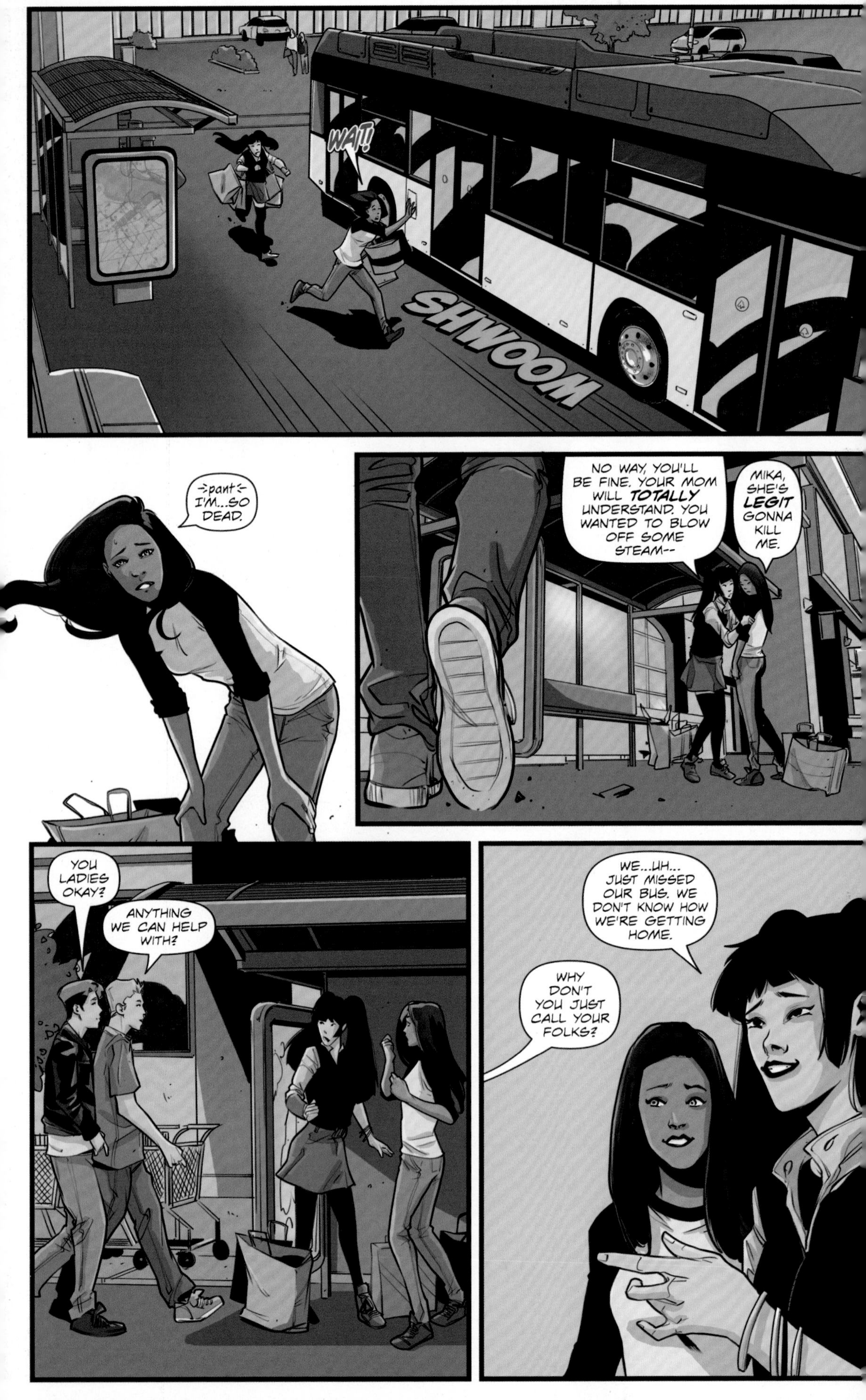
WAIT!
SHWOOM
-pant- I'M...SO DEAD.
NO WAY, YOU'LL BE FINE. YOUR MOM WILL TOTALLY UNDERSTAND. YOU WANTED TO BLOW OFF SOME STEAM--
MIKA, SHE'S LEGIT GONNA KILL ME.
YOU LADIES OKAY?
ANYTHING WE CAN HELP WITH?
WE...UH... JUST MISSED OUR BUS. WE DON'T KNOW HOW WE'RE GETTING HOME.
WHY DON'T YOU JUST CALL YOUR FOLKS?

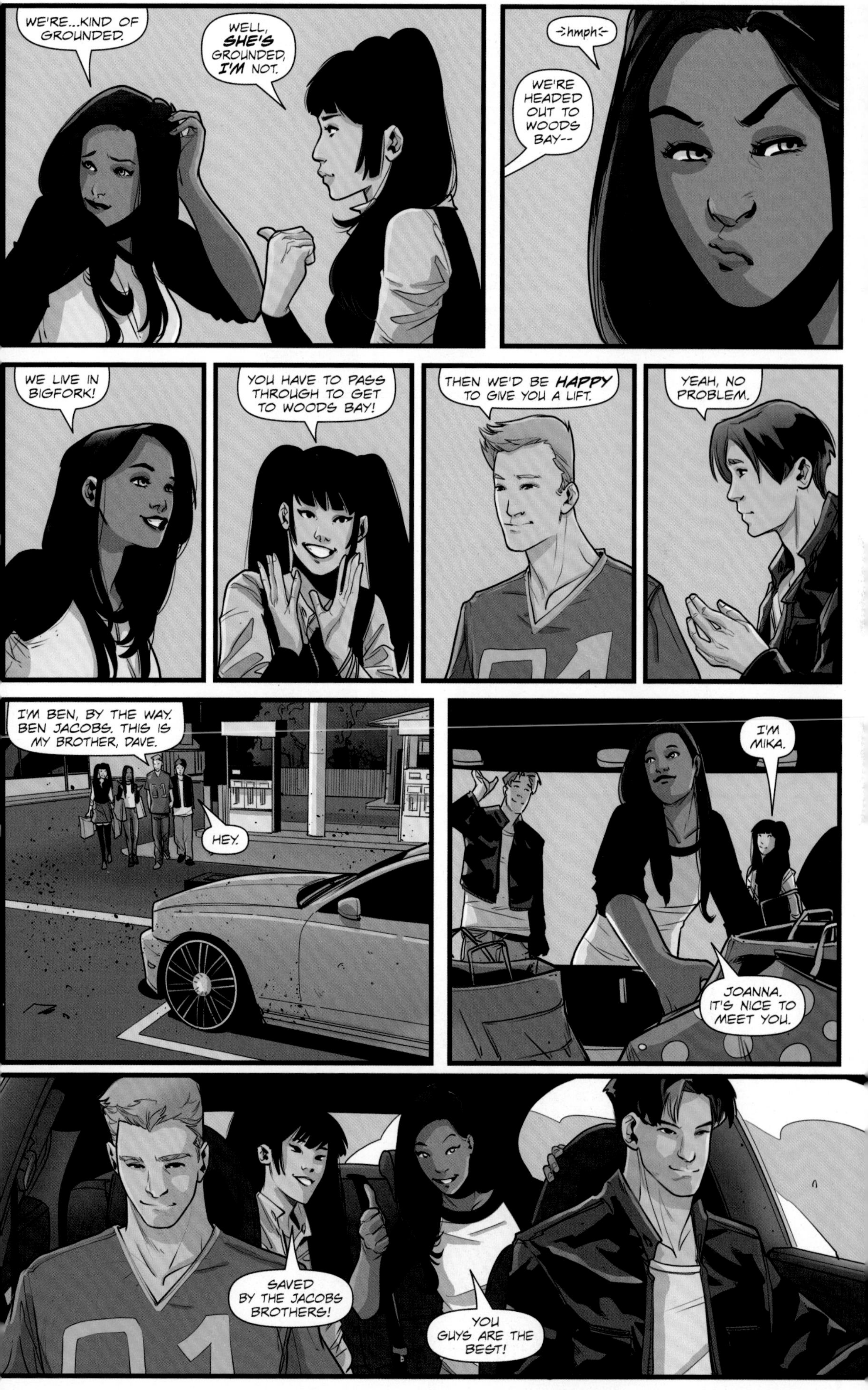
WE'RE...KIND OF GROUNDED.
WELL, SHE'S GROUNDED, I'M NOT.
-hmph-
WE'RE HEADED OUT TO WOODS BAY--
WE LIVE IN BIGFORK!
YOU HAVE TO PASS THROUGH TO GET TO WOODS BAY!
THEN WE'D BE HAPPY TO GIVE YOU A LIFT.
YEAH, NO PROBLEM.
I'M BEN, BY THE WAY. BEN JACOBS. THIS IS MY BROTHER, DAVE.
HEY.
I'M MIKA.
JOANNA. IT'S NICE TO MEET YOU.
SAVED BY THE JACOBS BROTHERS!
YOU GUYS ARE THE BEST!

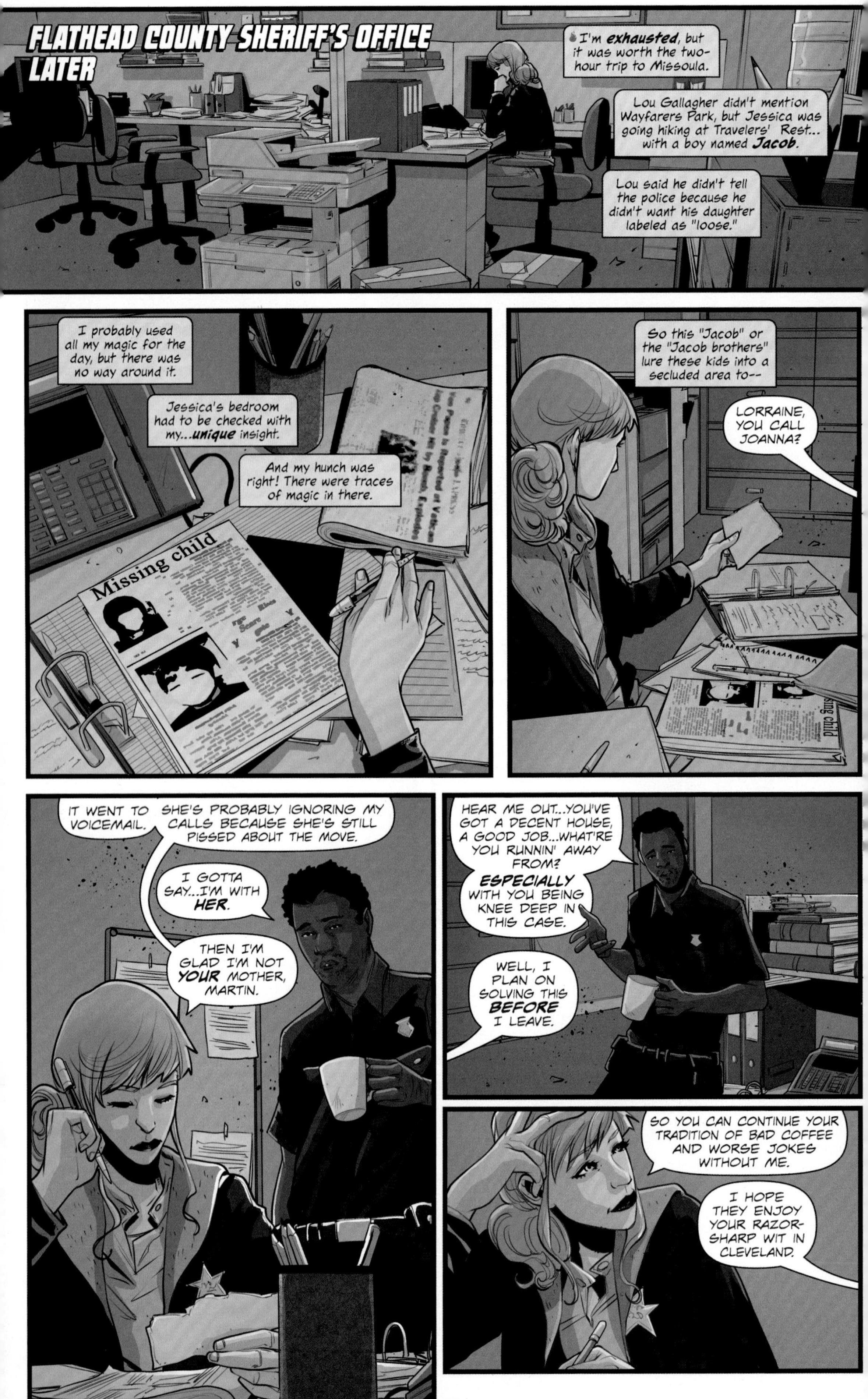
FLATHEAD COUNTY SHERIFF'S OFFICE
LATER
I'm exhausted, but it was worth the two-hour trip to Missoula.
Lou Gallagher didn't mention Wayfarers Park, but Jessica was going hiking at Travelers' Rest... with a boy named Jacob.
Lou said he didn't tell the police because he didn't want his daughter labeled as "loose."
I probably used all my magic for the day, but there was no way around it.
Jessica's bedroom had to be checked with my...unique insight.
And my hunch was right! There were traces of magic in there.
Missing child
So this "Jacob" or the "Jacob brothers" lure these kids into a secluded area to--
LORRAINE, YOU CALL JOANNA?
IT WENT TO VOICEMAIL.
SHE'S PROBABLY IGNORING MY CALLS BECAUSE SHE'S STILL PISSED ABOUT THE MOVE.
I GOTTA SAY...I'M WITH HER.
THEN I'M GLAD I'M NOT YOUR MOTHER, MARTIN.
HEAR ME OUT...YOU'VE GOT A DECENT HOUSE, A GOOD JOB...WHAT'RE YOU RUNNIN' AWAY FROM?
ESPECIALLY WITH YOU BEING KNEE DEEP IN THIS CASE.
WELL, I PLAN ON SOLVING THIS BEFORE I LEAVE.
SO YOU CAN CONTINUE YOUR TRADITION OF BAD COFFEE AND WORSE JOKES WITHOUT ME.
I HOPE THEY ENJOY YOUR RAZOR-SHARP WIT IN CLEVELAND.

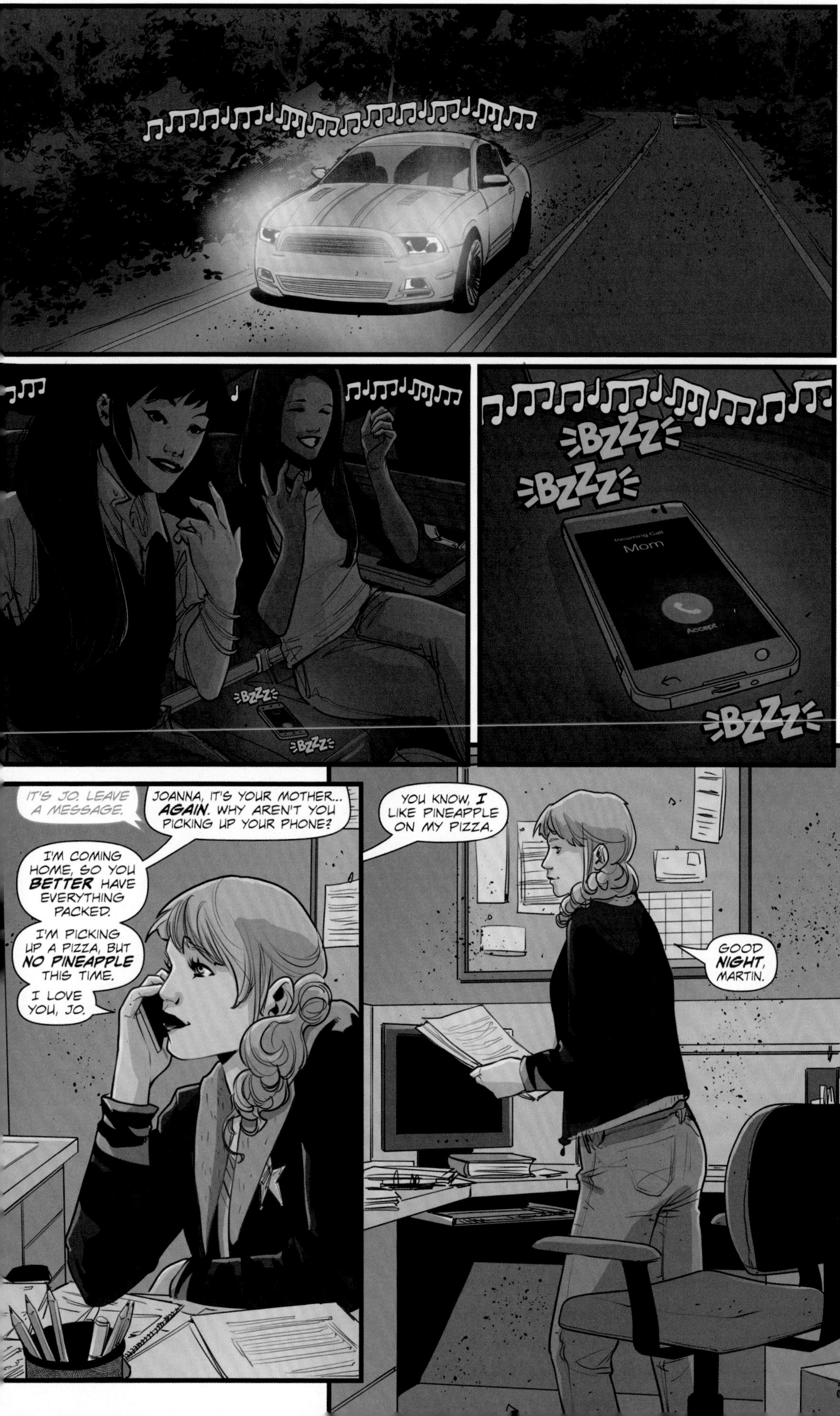
BZZZ
BZZZ
Incoming Call
Mom
Accept
BZZZ
BZZZ
BZZZ
IT'S JO. LEAVE A MESSAGE.
JOANNA, IT'S YOUR MOTHER... AGAIN. WHY AREN'T YOU PICKING UP YOUR PHONE?
I'M COMING HOME, SO YOU BETTER HAVE EVERYTHING PACKED.
I'M PICKING UP A PIZZA, BUT NO PINEAPPLE THIS TIME.
I LOVE YOU, JO.
YOU KNOW, I LIKE PINEAPPLE ON MY PIZZA.
GOOD NIGHT, MARTIN.

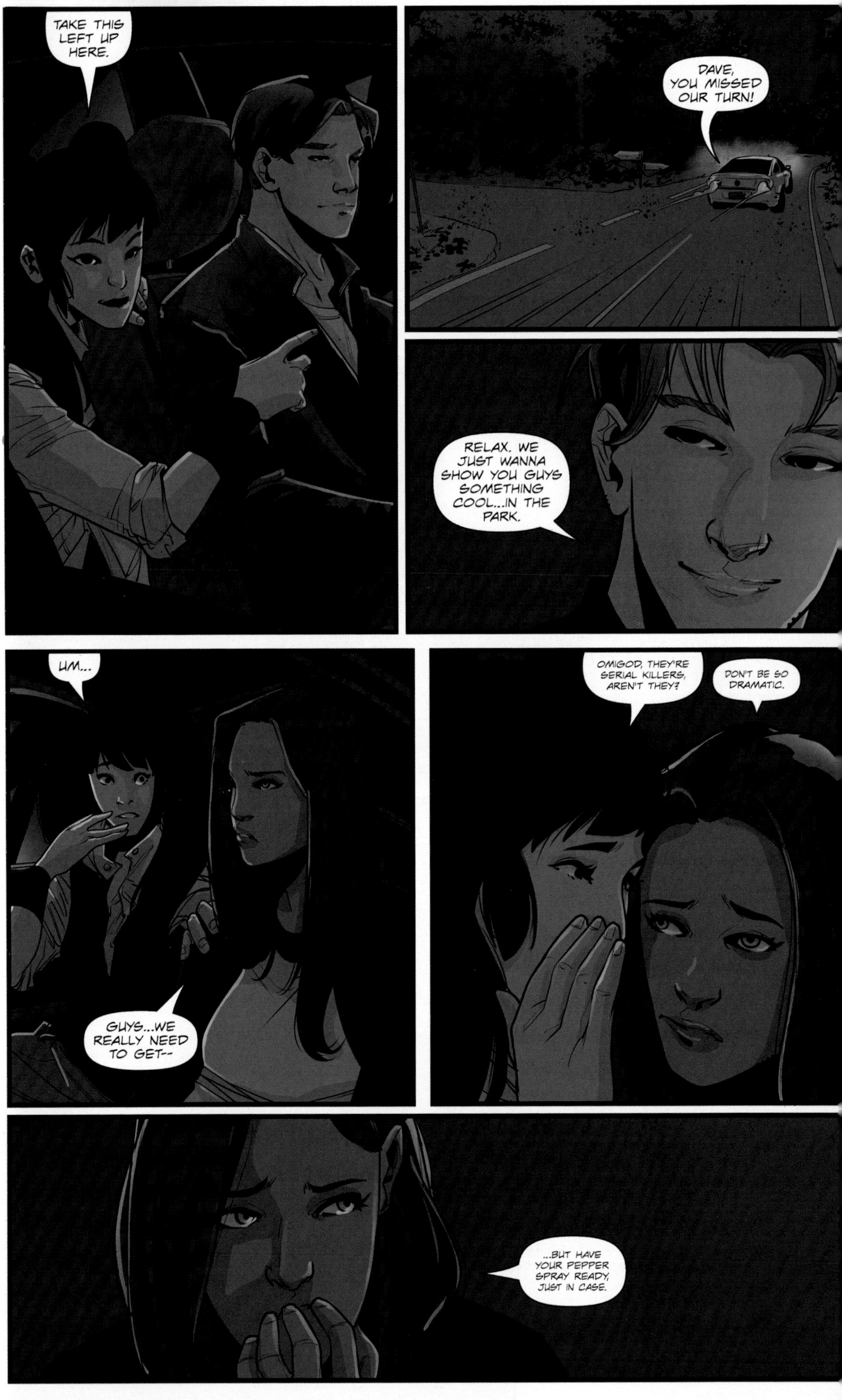
TAKE THIS LEFT UP HERE.
DAVE, YOU MISSED OUR TURN!
RELAX. WE JUST WANNA SHOW YOU GUYS SOMETHING COOL...IN THE PARK.
UM...
GUYS...WE REALLY NEED TO GET--
OMIGOD, THEY'RE SERIAL KILLERS, AREN'T THEY?
DON'T BE SO DRAMATIC.
...BUT HAVE YOUR PEPPER SPRAY READY, JUST IN CASE.

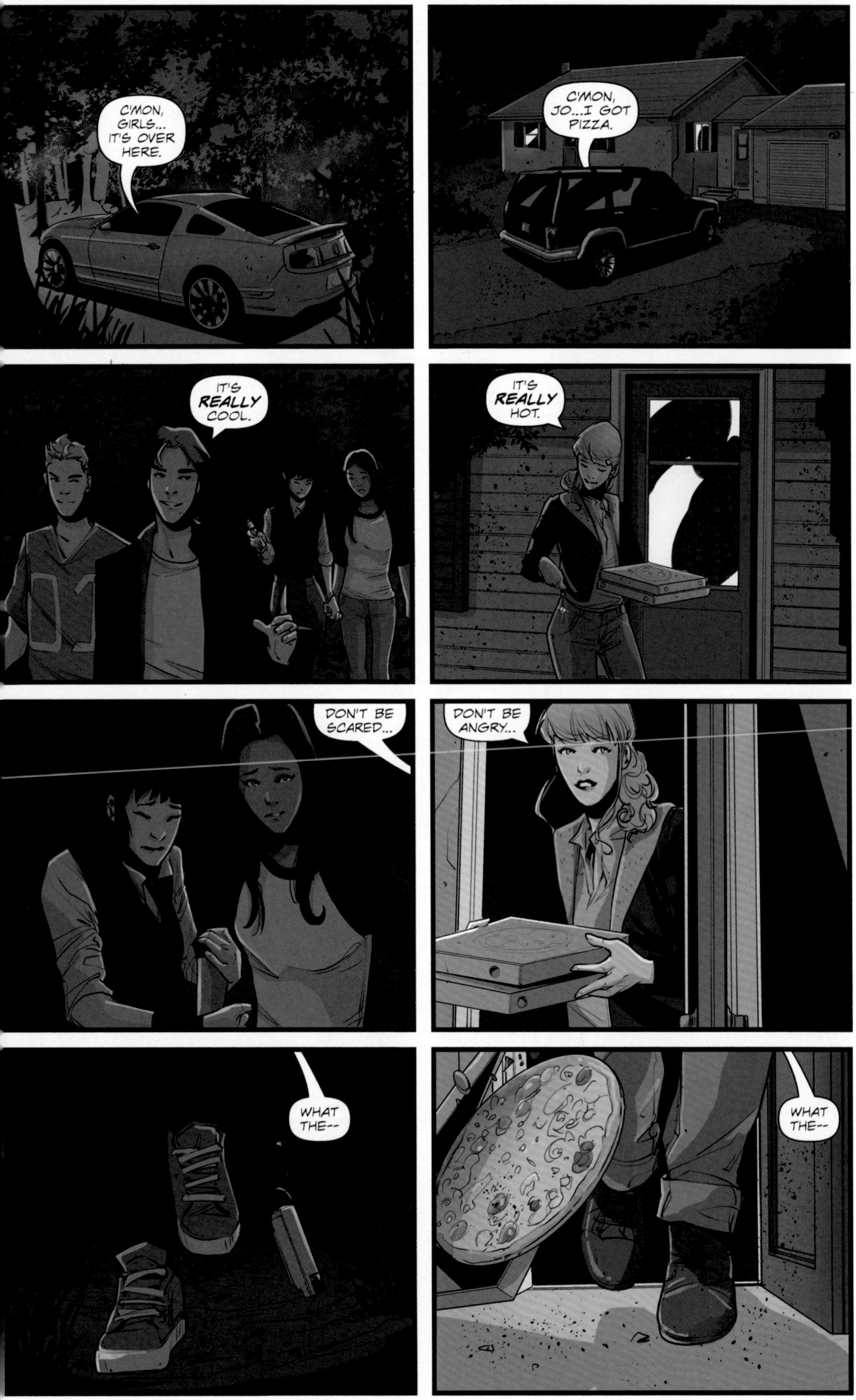
C'MON, GIRLS... IT'S OVER HERE.
C'MON, JO...I GOT PIZZA.
IT'S REALLY COOL.
IT'S REALLY HOT.
DON'T BE SCARED...
DON'T BE ANGRY...
WHAT THE--
WHAT THE--

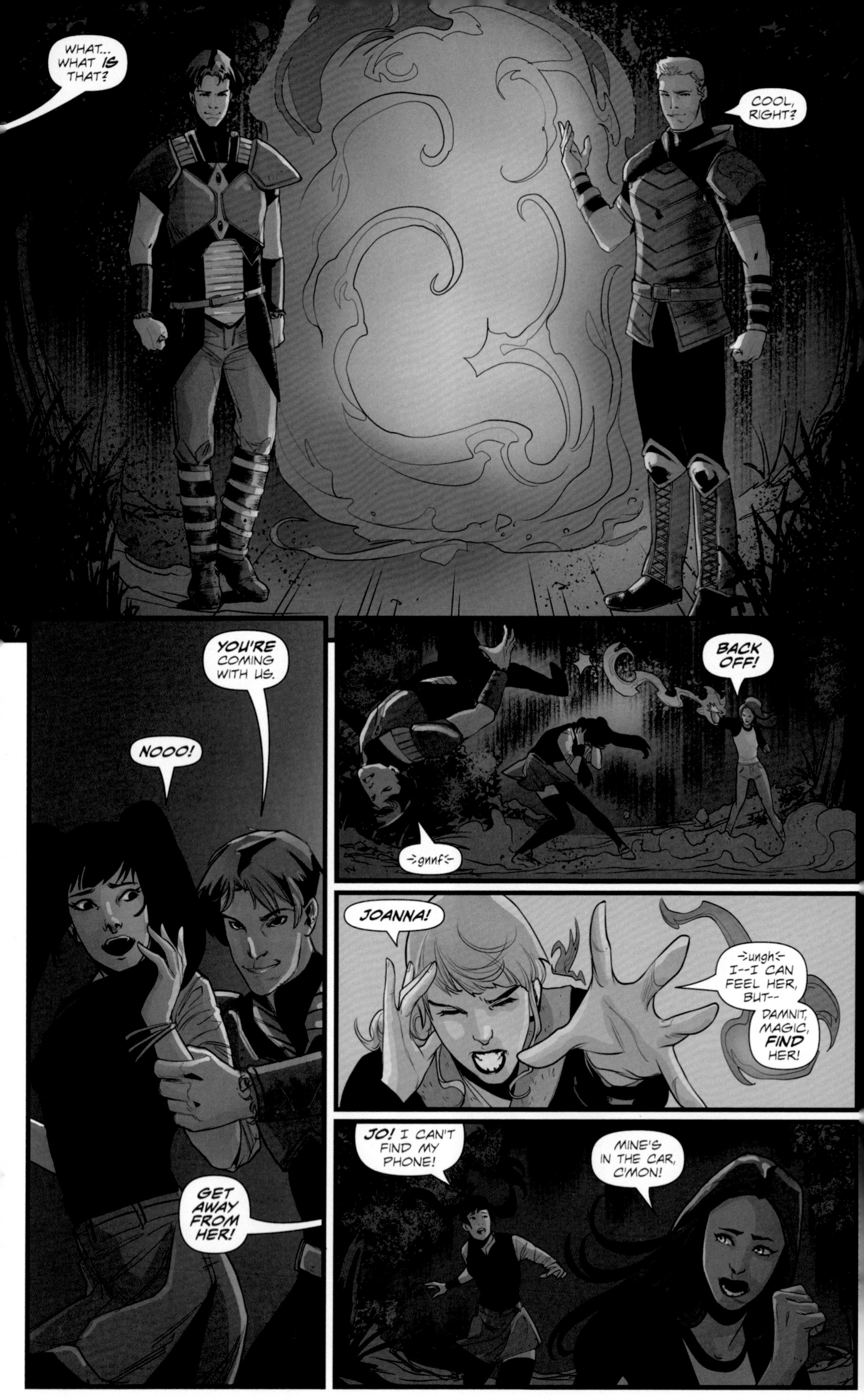
WHAT... WHAT IS THAT?
COOL, RIGHT?
YOU'RE COMING WITH US.
NOOO!
GET AWAY FROM HER!
BACK OFF!
gnnf
JOANNA!
ungh
I--I CAN FEEL HER, BUT--
DAMNIT, MAGIC, FIND HER!
JO! I CAN'T FIND MY PHONE!
MINE'S IN THE CAR, C'MON!

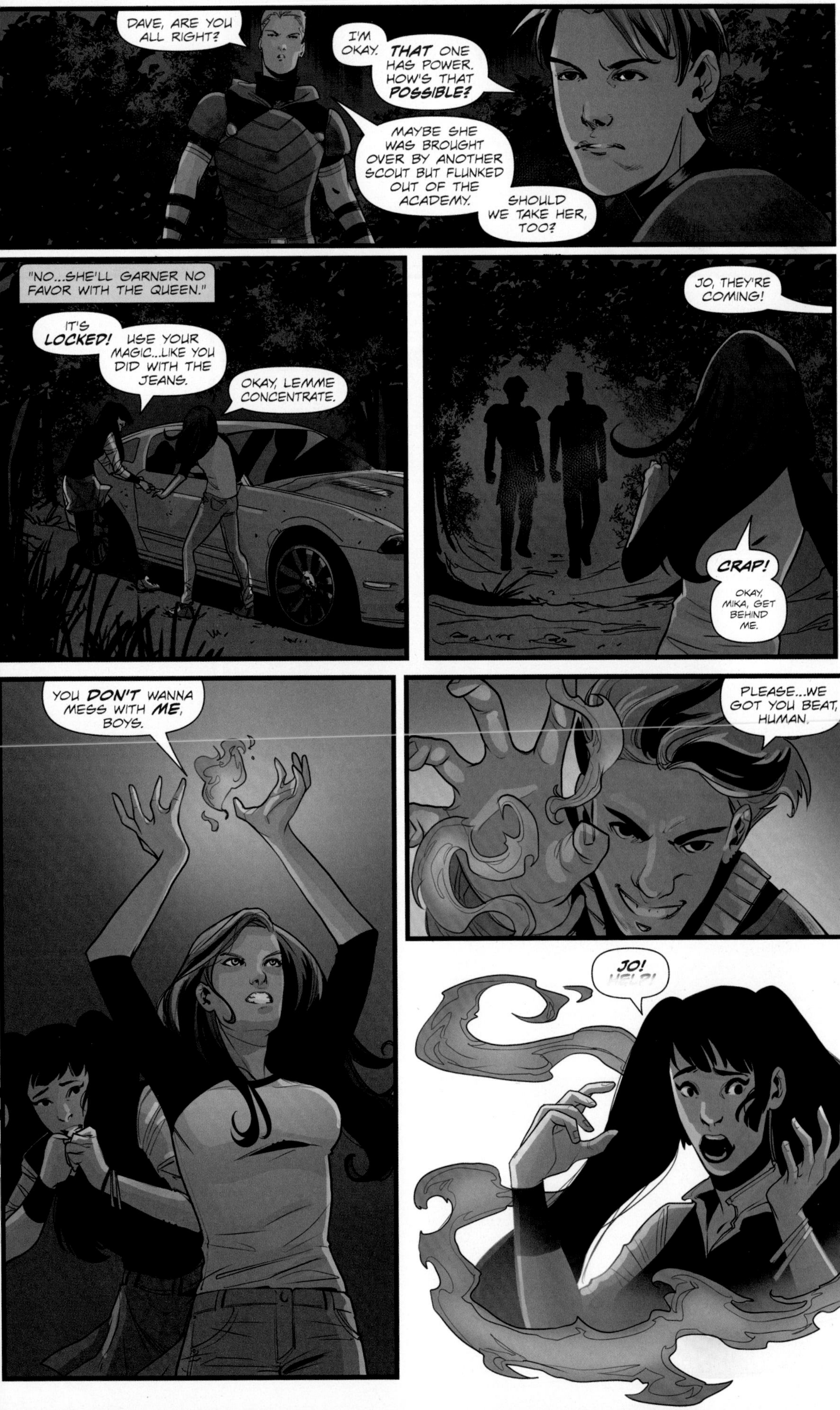
DAVE, ARE YOU ALL RIGHT?
I'M OKAY. THAT ONE HAS POWER. HOW'S THAT POSSIBLE?
MAYBE SHE WAS BROUGHT OVER BY ANOTHER SCOUT BUT FLUNKED OUT OF THE ACADEMY.
SHOULD WE TAKE HER, TOO?
"NO...SHE'LL GARNER NO FAVOR WITH THE QUEEN."
IT'S LOCKED! USE YOUR MAGIC...LIKE YOU DID WITH THE JEANS.
OKAY, LEMME CONCENTRATE.
JO, THEY'RE COMING!
CRAP!
OKAY, MIKA, GET BEHIND ME.
YOU DON'T WANNA MESS WITH ME, BOYS.
PLEASE...WE GOT YOU BEAT, HUMAN.
JO! HELP!

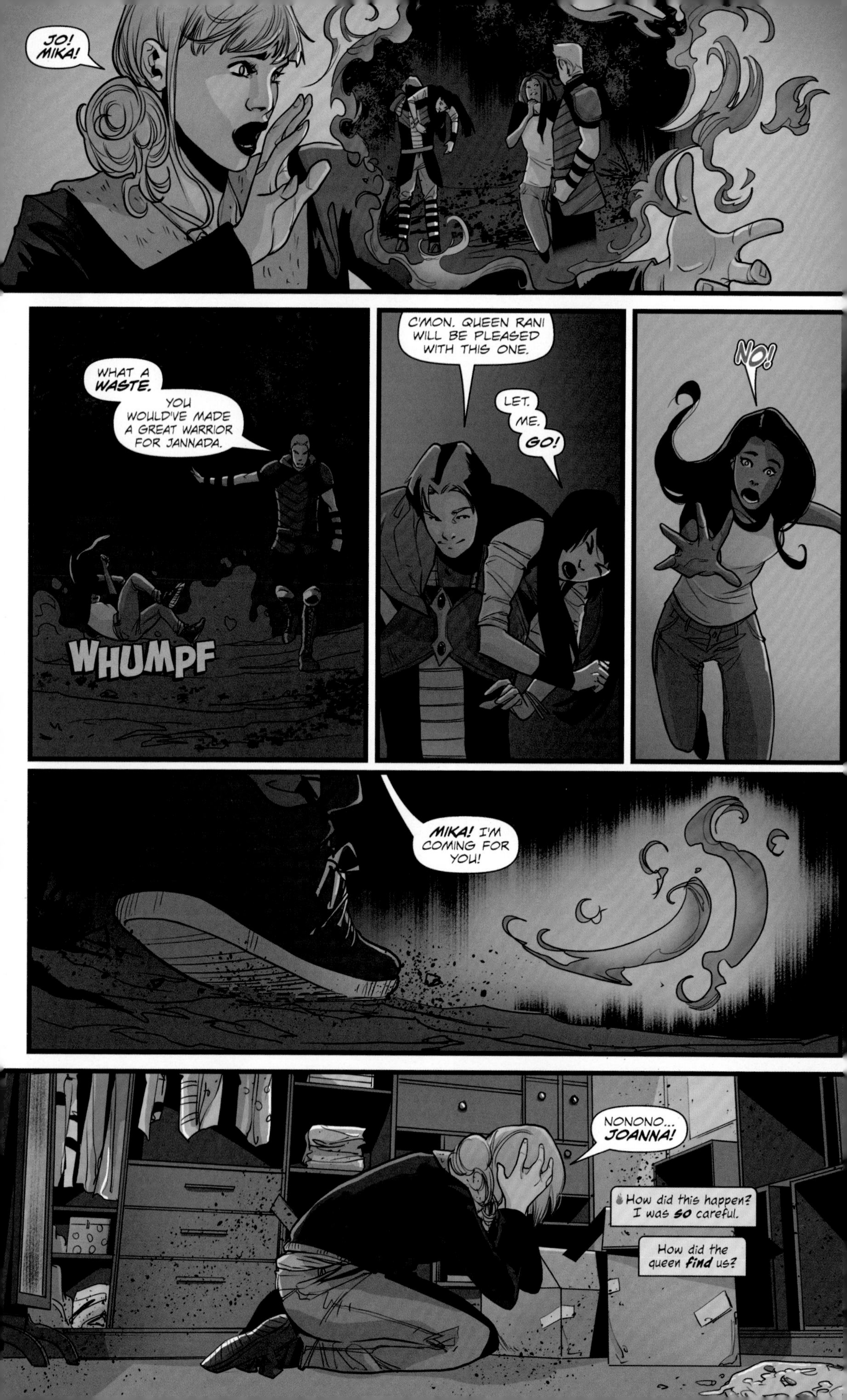
JO! MIKA!
WHAT A WASTE.
YOU WOULD'VE MADE A GREAT WARRIOR FOR JANNADA.
WHUMPF
C'MON. QUEEN RANI WILL BE PLEASED WITH THIS ONE.
LET. ME. GO!
NO!
MIKA! I'M COMING FOR YOU!
NONONO... JOANNA!
How did this happen? I was SO careful.
How did the queen find us?

TWO

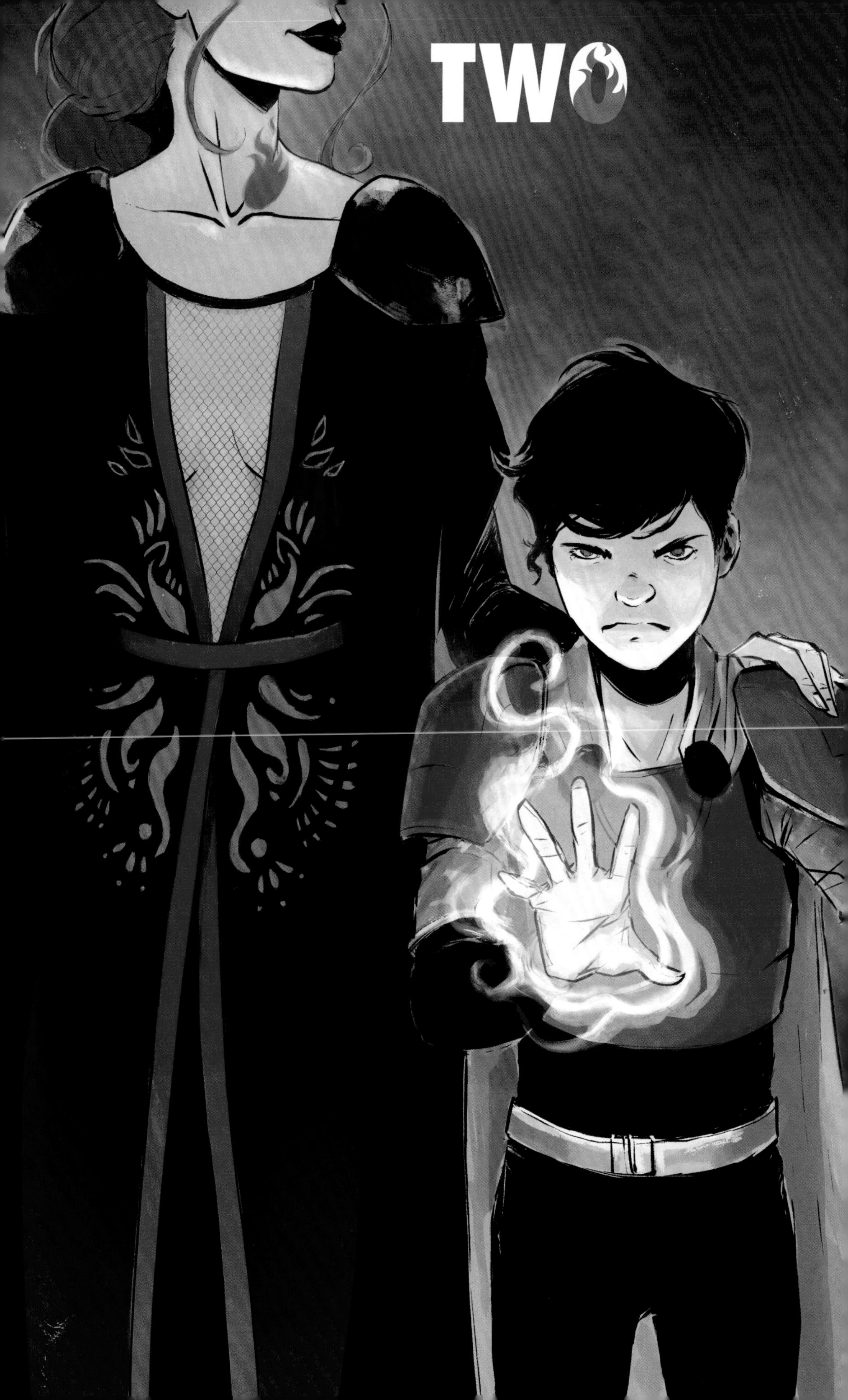

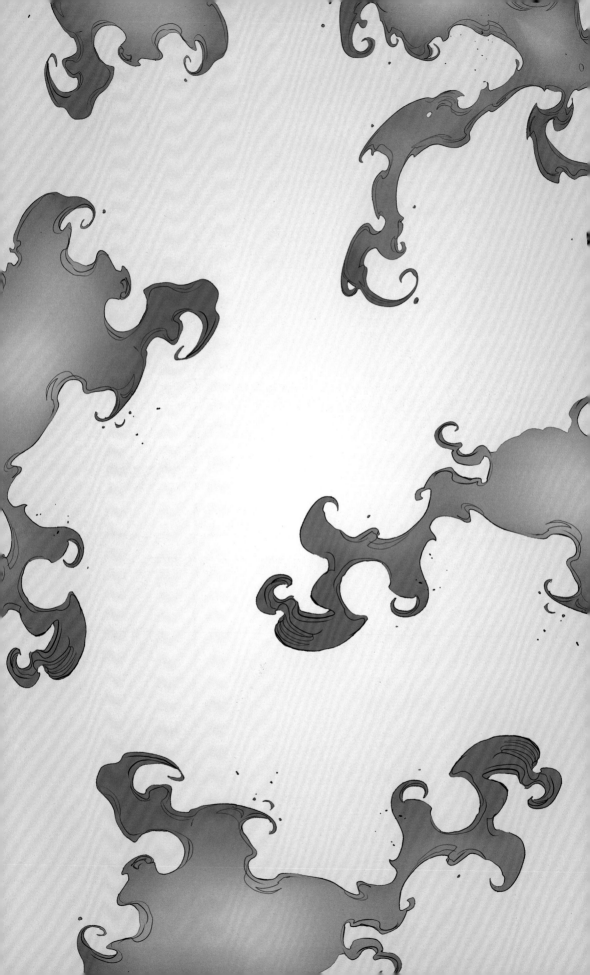

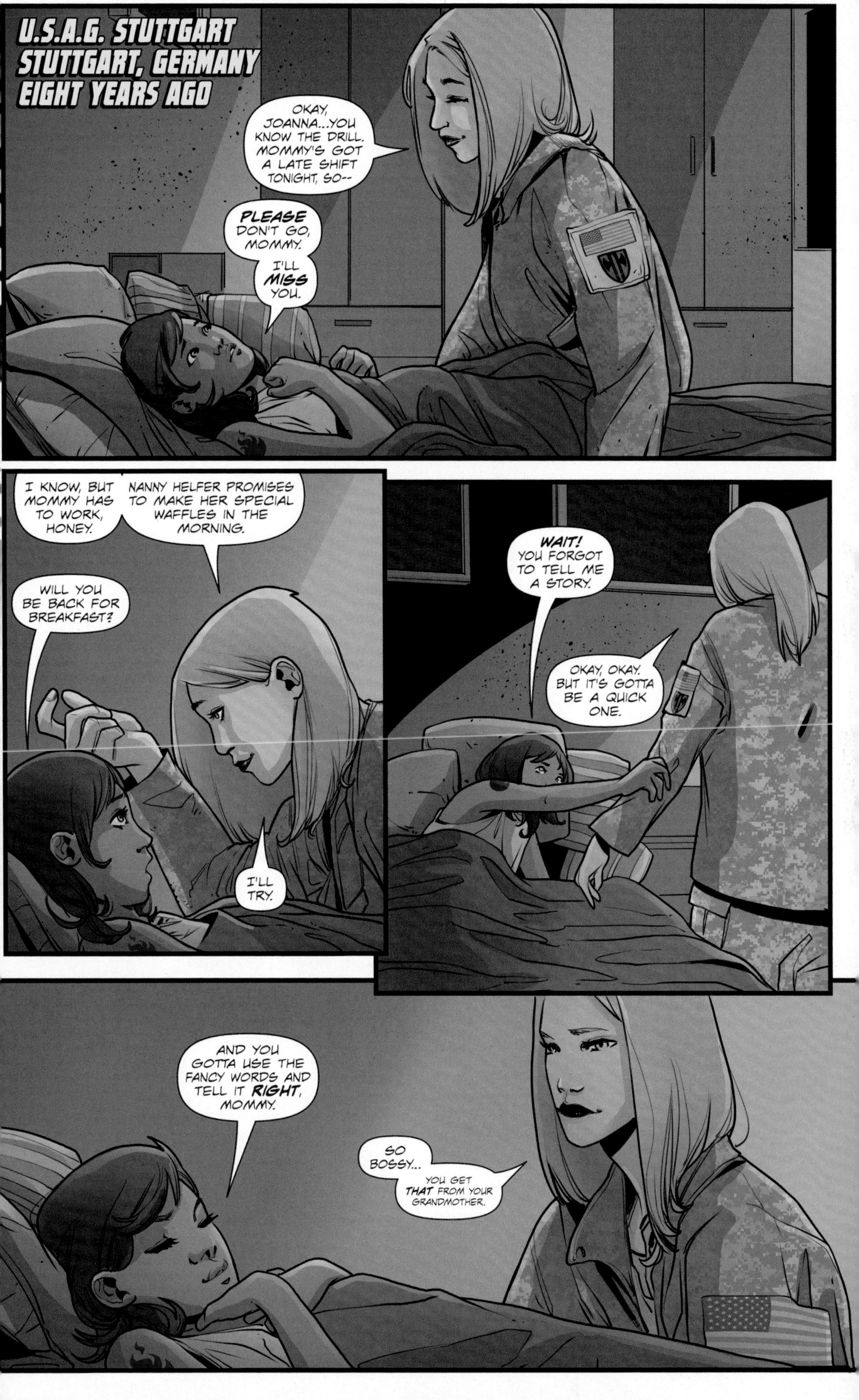
U.S.A.G. STUTTGART
STUTTGART, GERMANY
EIGHT YEARS AGO
OKAY, JOANNA...YOU KNOW THE DRILL. MOMMY'S GOT A LATE SHIFT TONIGHT, SO--
PLEASE DON'T GO, MOMMY.
I'LL MISS YOU.
I KNOW, BUT MOMMY HAS TO WORK, HONEY.
NANNY HELFER PROMISES TO MAKE HER SPECIAL WAFFLES IN THE MORNING.
WILL YOU BE BACK FOR BREAKFAST?
I'LL TRY.
WAIT! YOU FORGOT TO TELL ME A STORY.
OKAY, OKAY. BUT IT'S GOTTA BE A QUICK ONE.
AND YOU GOTTA USE THE FANCY WORDS AND TELL IT RIGHT, MOMMY.
SO BOSSY...
YOU GET THAT FROM YOUR GRANDMOTHER.

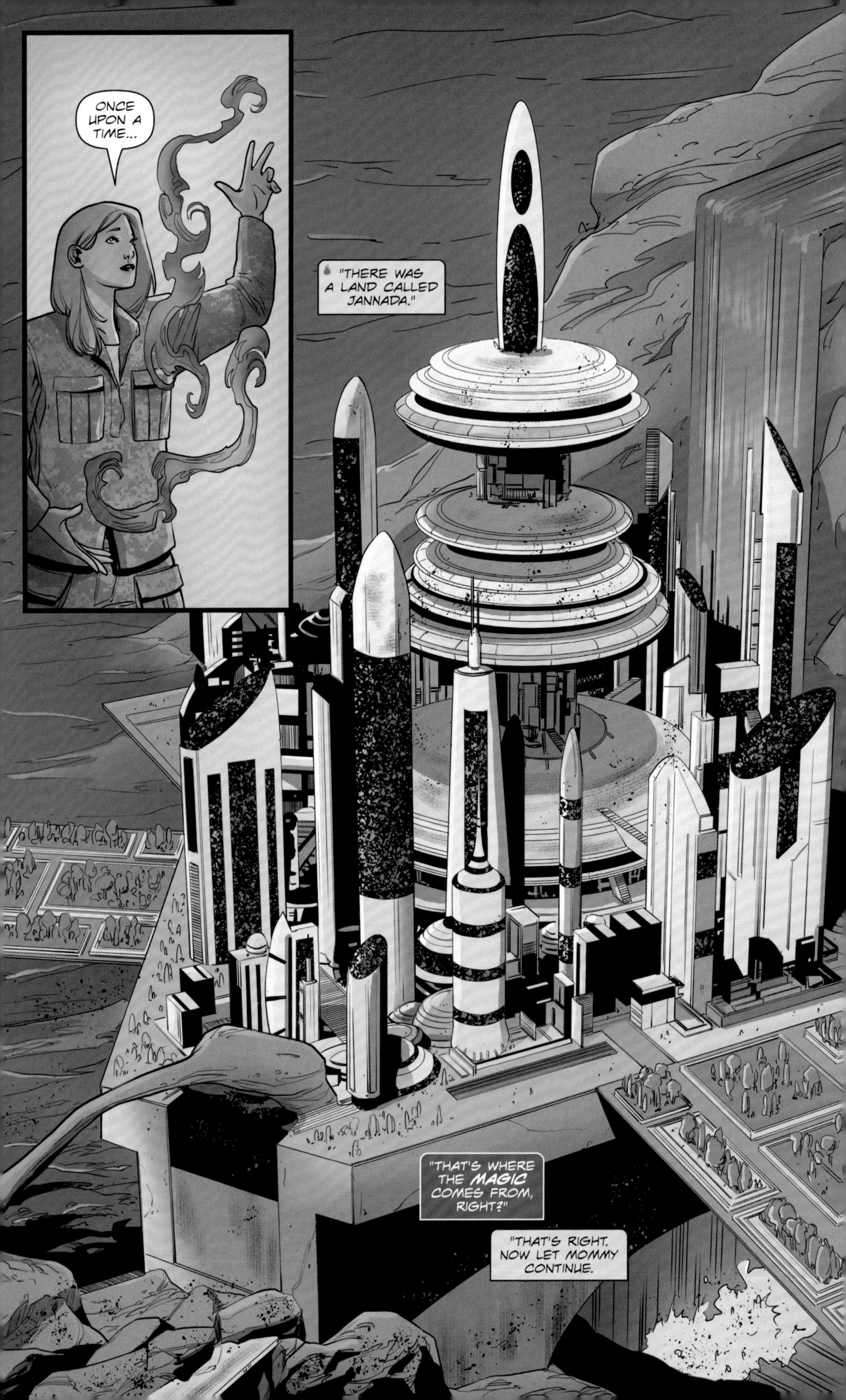

ONCE UPON A TIME...
"THERE WAS A LAND CALLED JANNADA."
"THAT'S WHERE THE MAGIC COMES FROM, RIGHT?"
"THAT'S RIGHT. NOW LET MOMMY CONTINUE.

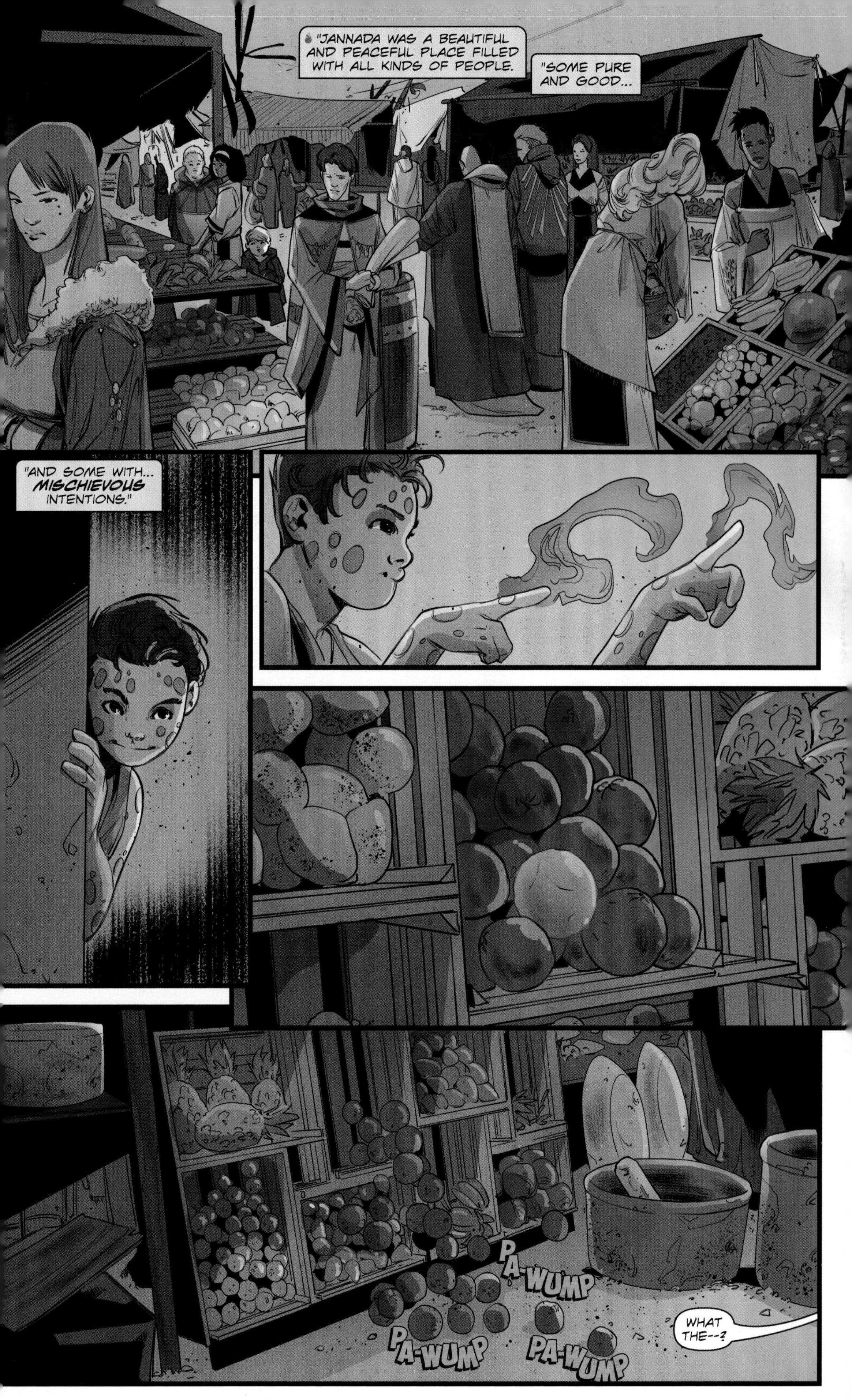
"JANNADA WAS A BEAUTIFUL AND PEACEFUL PLACE FILLED WITH ALL KINDS OF PEOPLE.
"SOME PURE AND GOOD...
"AND SOME WITH... MISCHIEVOUS INTENTIONS."
PA-WUMP
PA-WUMP
PA-WUMP
WHAT THE--?

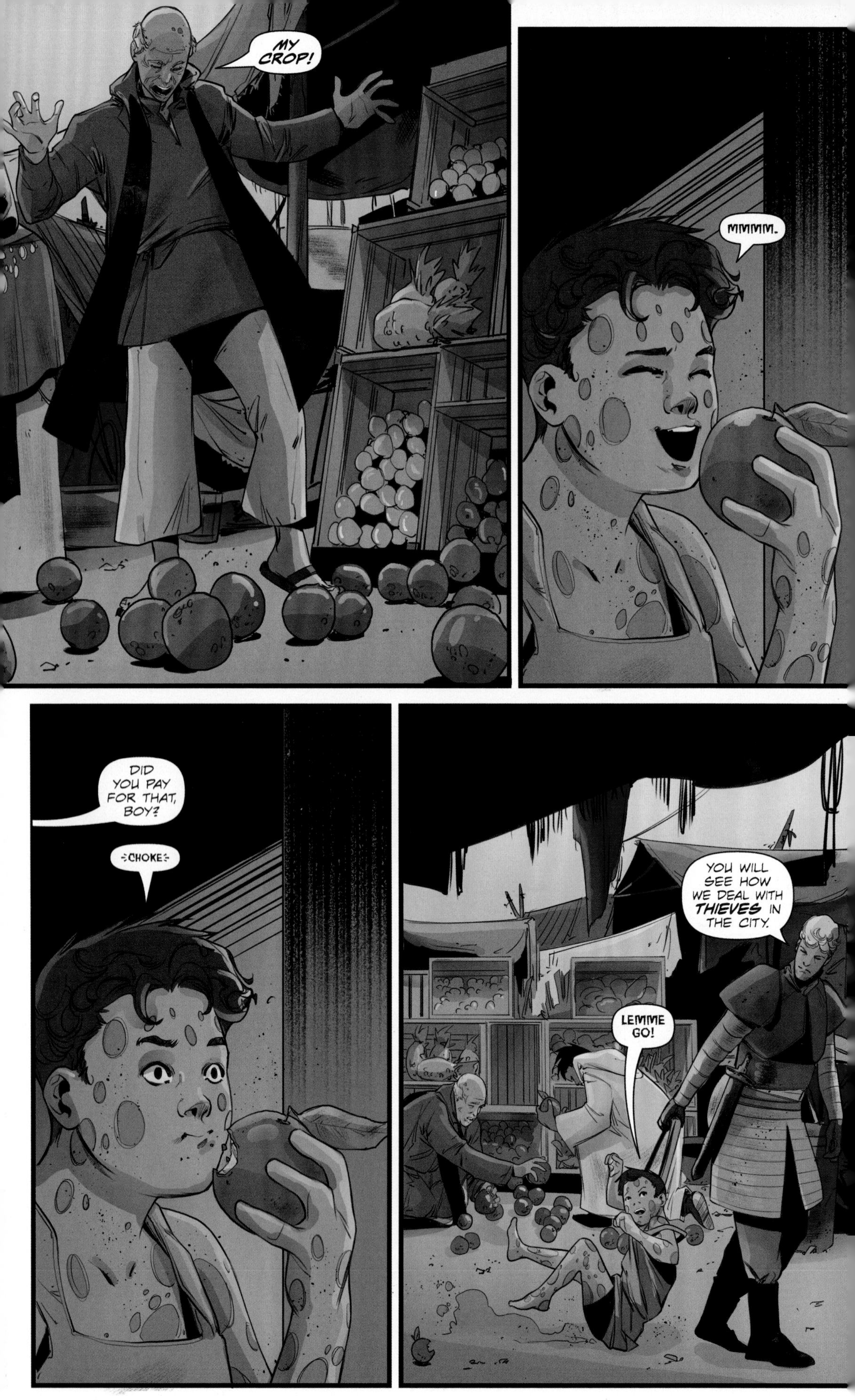
MY CROP!
MMMM.
DID YOU PAY FOR THAT, BOY?
CHOKE
YOU WILL SEE HOW WE DEAL WITH THIEVES IN THE CITY.
LEMME GO!

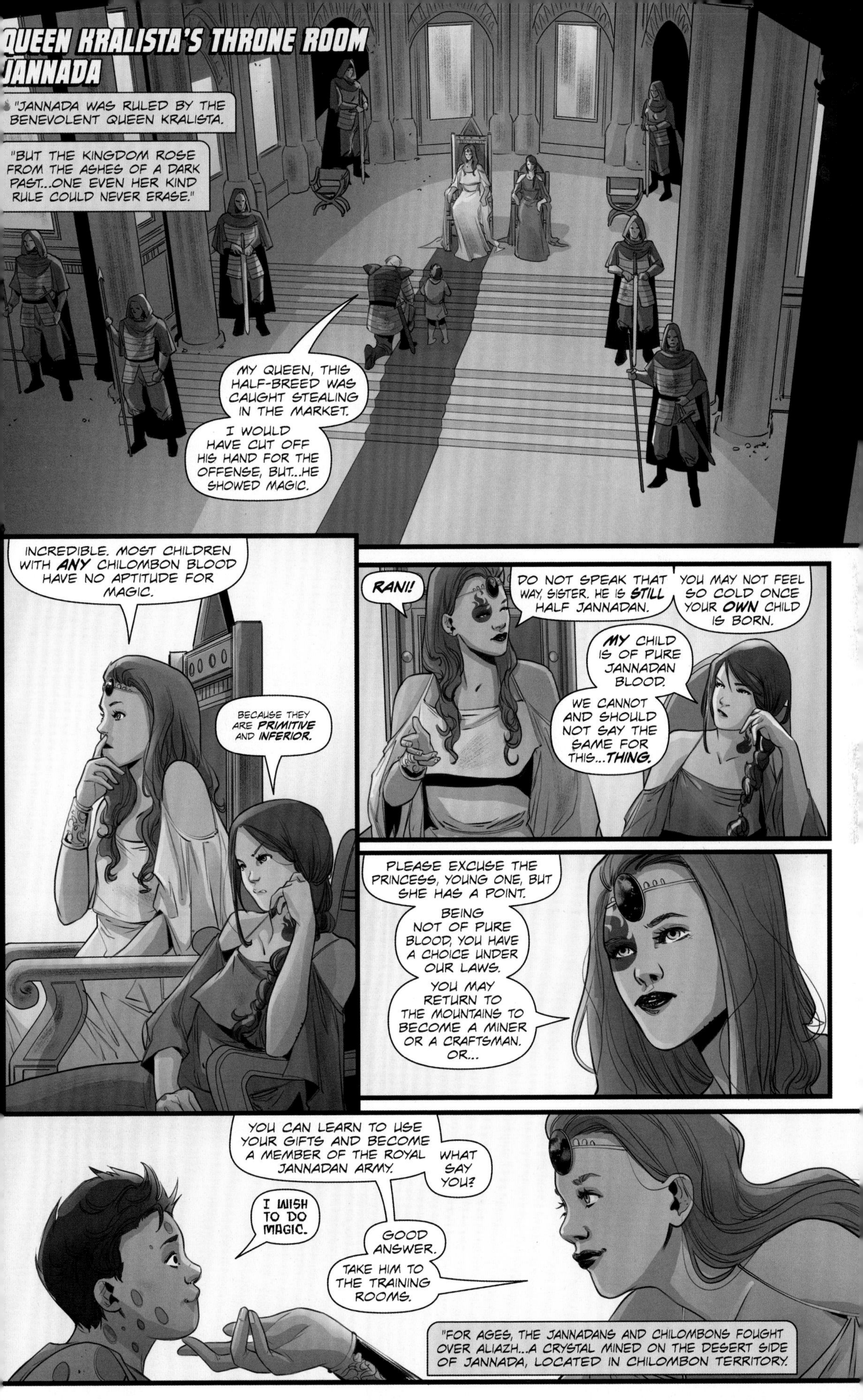

QUEEN KRALISTA'S THRONE ROOM
JANNADA
"JANNADA WAS RULED BY THE BENEVOLENT QUEEN KRALISTA.
"BUT THE KINGDOM ROSE FROM THE ASHES OF A DARK PAST...ONE EVEN HER KIND RULE COULD NEVER ERASE."
MY QUEEN, THIS HALF-BREED WAS CAUGHT STEALING IN THE MARKET.
I WOULD HAVE CUT OFF HIS HAND FOR THE OFFENSE, BUT...HE SHOWED MAGIC.
INCREDIBLE. MOST CHILDREN WITH ANY CHILOMBON BLOOD HAVE NO APTITUDE FOR MAGIC.
BECAUSE THEY ARE PRIMITIVE AND INFERIOR.
RANI!
DO NOT SPEAK THAT WAY, SISTER. HE IS STILL HALF JANNADAN.
YOU MAY NOT FEEL SO COLD ONCE YOUR OWN CHILD IS BORN.
MY CHILD IS OF PURE JANNADAN BLOOD.
WE CANNOT AND SHOULD NOT SAY THE SAME FOR THIS...THING.
PLEASE EXCUSE THE PRINCESS, YOUNG ONE, BUT SHE HAS A POINT.
BEING NOT OF PURE BLOOD, YOU HAVE A CHOICE UNDER OUR LAWS.
YOU MAY RETURN TO THE MOUNTAINS TO BECOME A MINER OR A CRAFTSMAN. OR...
YOU CAN LEARN TO USE YOUR GIFTS AND BECOME A MEMBER OF THE ROYAL JANNADAN ARMY.
WHAT SAY YOU?
I WISH TO DO MAGIC.
GOOD ANSWER.
TAKE HIM TO THE TRAINING ROOMS.
"FOR AGES, THE JANNADANS AND CHILOMBONS FOUGHT OVER ALIAZH...A CRYSTAL MINED ON THE DESERT SIDE OF JANNADA, LOCATED IN CHILOMBON TERRITORY.

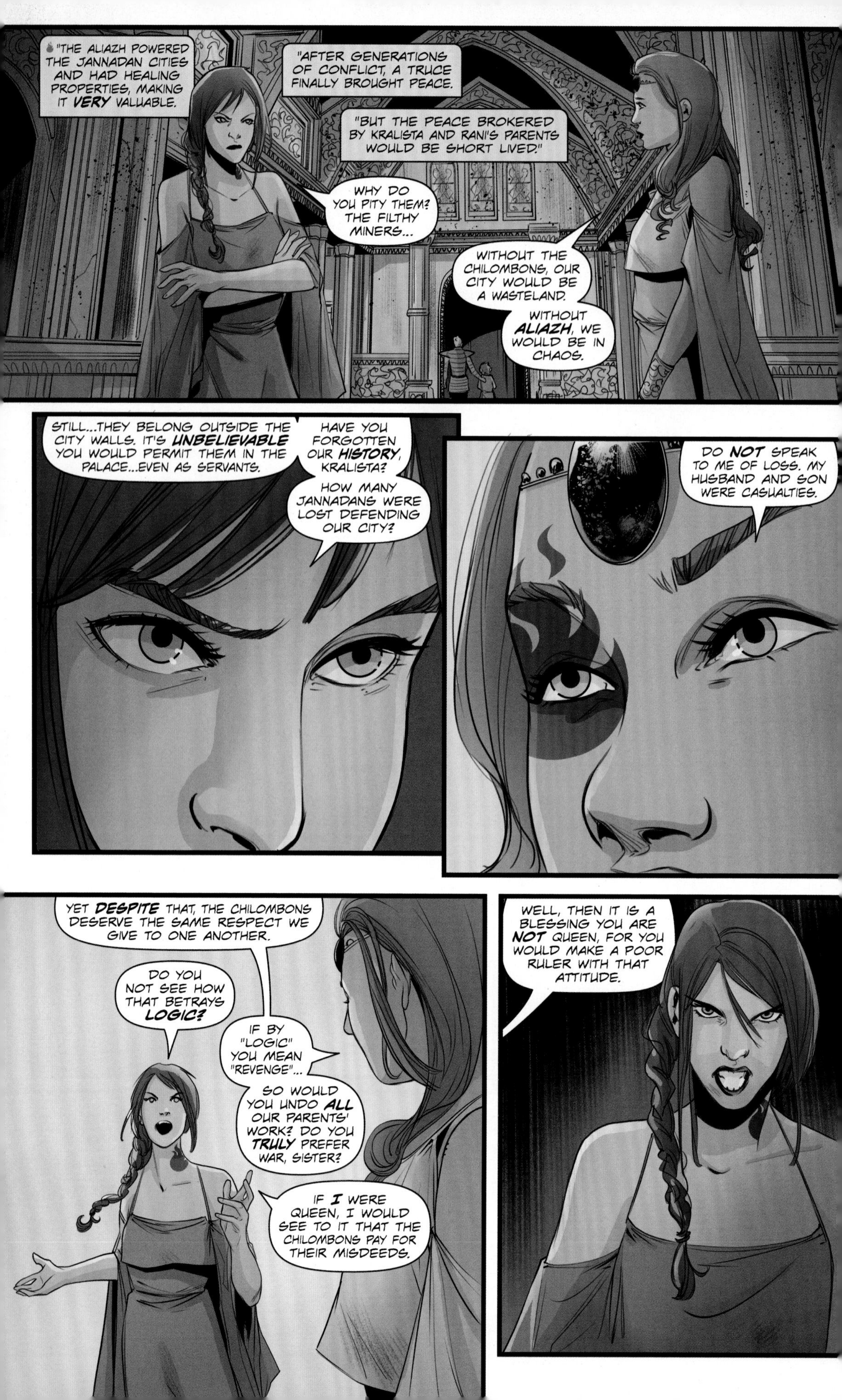
"THE ALIAZH POWERED THE JANNADAN CITIES AND HAD HEALING PROPERTIES, MAKING IT VERY VALUABLE.
"AFTER GENERATIONS OF CONFLICT, A TRUCE FINALLY BROUGHT PEACE.
"BUT THE PEACE BROKERED BY KRALISTA AND RANI'S PARENTS WOULD BE SHORT LIVED."
WHY DO YOU PITY THEM? THE FILTHY MINERS...
WITHOUT THE CHILOMBONS, OUR CITY WOULD BE A WASTELAND.
WITHOUT ALIAZH, WE WOULD BE IN CHAOS.
STILL...THEY BELONG OUTSIDE THE CITY WALLS. IT'S UNBELIEVABLE YOU WOULD PERMIT THEM IN THE PALACE...EVEN AS SERVANTS.
HAVE YOU FORGOTTEN OUR HISTORY, KRALISTA?
HOW MANY JANNADANS WERE LOST DEFENDING OUR CITY?
DO NOT SPEAK TO ME OF LOSS. MY HUSBAND AND SON WERE CASUALTIES.
YET DESPITE THAT, THE CHILOMBONS DESERVE THE SAME RESPECT WE GIVE TO ONE ANOTHER.
DO YOU NOT SEE HOW THAT BETRAYS LOGIC?
IF BY "LOGIC" YOU MEAN "REVENGE"...
SO WOULD YOU UNDO ALL OUR PARENTS' WORK? DO YOU TRULY PREFER WAR, SISTER?
IF I WERE QUEEN, I WOULD SEE TO IT THAT THE CHILOMBONS PAY FOR THEIR MISDEEDS.
WELL, THEN IT IS A BLESSING YOU ARE NOT QUEEN, FOR YOU WOULD MAKE A POOR RULER WITH THAT ATTITUDE.

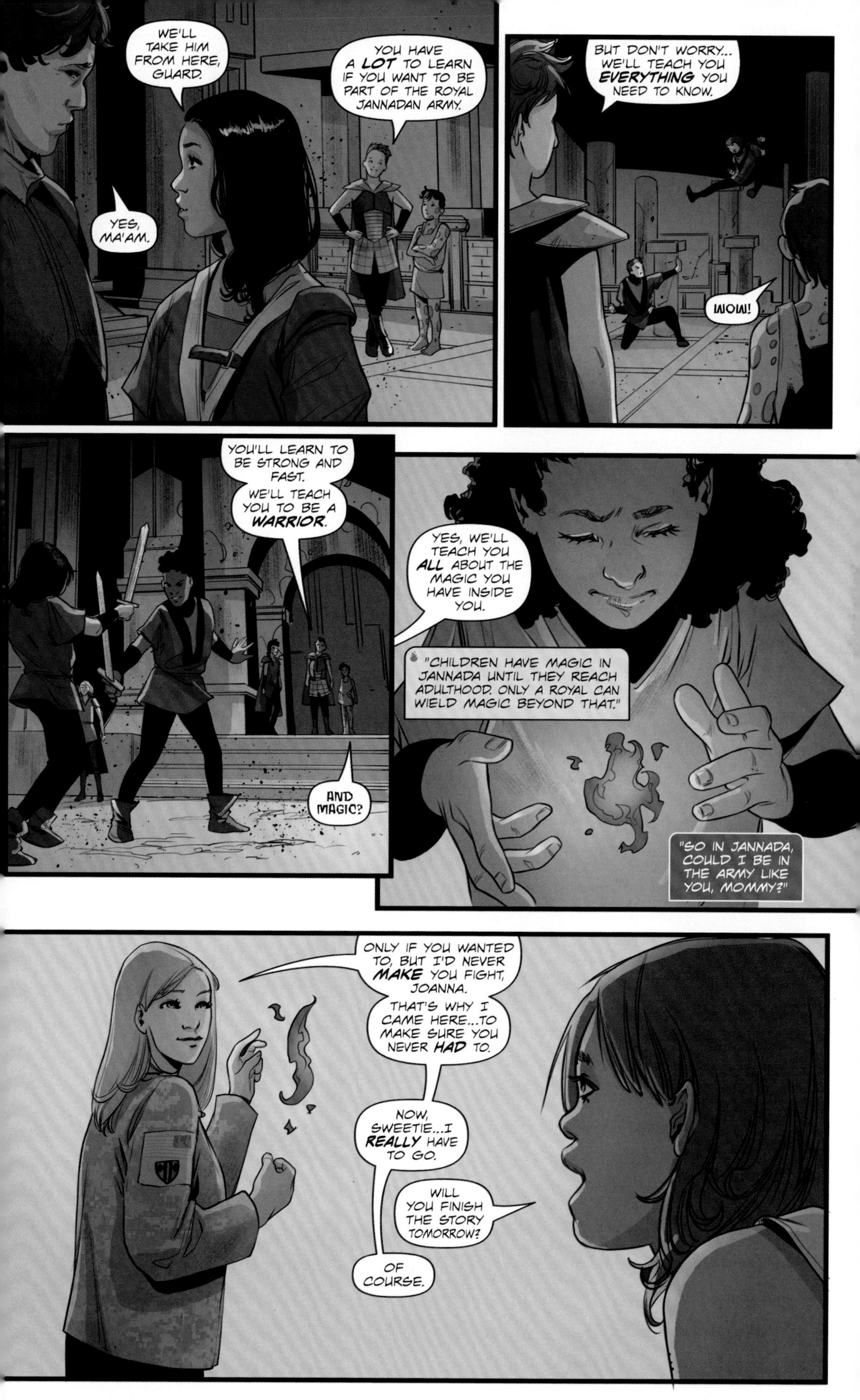

WE'LL TAKE HIM FROM HERE, GUARD.
YES, MA'AM.
YOU HAVE A LOT TO LEARN IF YOU WANT TO BE PART OF THE ROYAL JANNADAN ARMY.
BUT DON'T WORRY... WE'LL TEACH YOU EVERYTHING YOU NEED TO KNOW.
WOW!
YOU'LL LEARN TO BE STRONG AND FAST.
WE'LL TEACH YOU TO BE A WARRIOR.
AND MAGIC?
YES, WE'LL TEACH YOU ALL ABOUT THE MAGIC YOU HAVE INSIDE YOU.
"CHILDREN HAVE MAGIC IN JANNADA UNTIL THEY REACH ADULTHOOD. ONLY A ROYAL CAN WIELD MAGIC BEYOND THAT."
"SO IN JANNADA, COULD I BE IN THE ARMY LIKE YOU, MOMMY?"
ONLY IF YOU WANTED TO, BUT I'D NEVER MAKE YOU FIGHT, JOANNA.
THAT'S WHY I CAME HERE...TO MAKE SURE YOU NEVER HAD TO.
NOW, SWEETIE...I REALLY HAVE TO GO.
WILL YOU FINISH THE STORY TOMORROW?
OF COURSE.

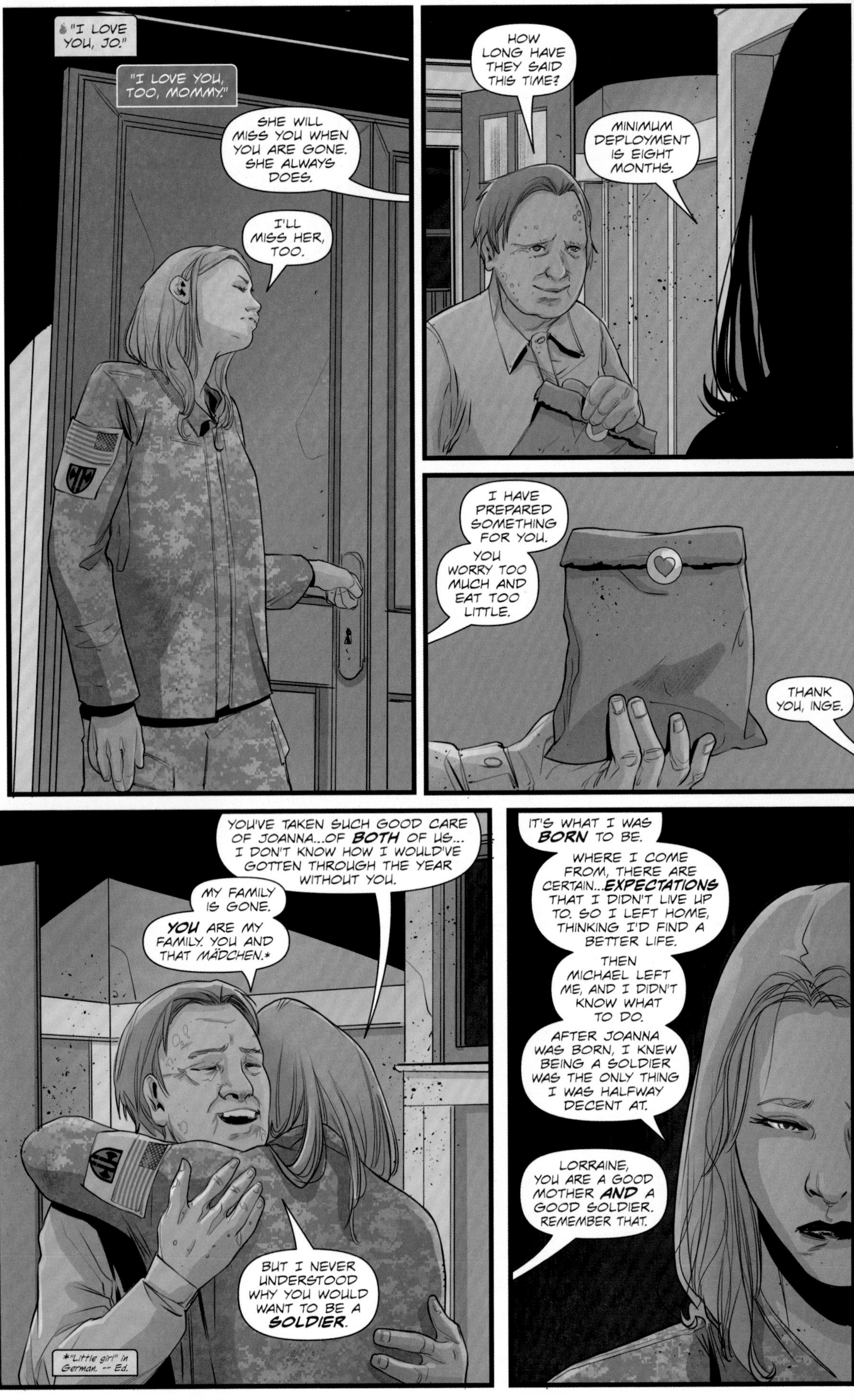
"I LOVE YOU, JO."
"I LOVE YOU, TOO, MOMMY."
SHE WILL MISS YOU WHEN YOU ARE GONE. SHE ALWAYS DOES.
I'LL MISS HER, TOO.
HOW LONG HAVE THEY SAID THIS TIME?
MINIMUM DEPLOYMENT IS EIGHT MONTHS.
I HAVE PREPARED SOMETHING FOR YOU.
YOU WORRY TOO MUCH AND EAT TOO LITTLE.
THANK YOU, INGE.
YOU'VE TAKEN SUCH GOOD CARE OF JOANNA...OF BOTH OF US... I DON'T KNOW HOW I WOULD'VE GOTTEN THROUGH THE YEAR WITHOUT YOU.
MY FAMILY IS GONE.
YOU ARE MY FAMILY. YOU AND THAT MÄDCHEN.*
BUT I NEVER UNDERSTOOD WHY YOU WOULD WANT TO BE A SOLDIER.
*"Little girl" in German. -- Ed.
IT'S WHAT I WAS BORN TO BE.
WHERE I COME FROM, THERE ARE CERTAIN...EXPECTATIONS THAT I DIDN'T LIVE UP TO. SO I LEFT HOME, THINKING I'D FIND A BETTER LIFE.
THEN MICHAEL LEFT ME, AND I DIDN'T KNOW WHAT TO DO.
AFTER JOANNA WAS BORN, I KNEW BEING A SOLDIER WAS THE ONLY THING I WAS HALFWAY DECENT AT.
LORRAINE, YOU ARE A GOOD MOTHER AND A GOOD SOLDIER. REMEMBER THAT.

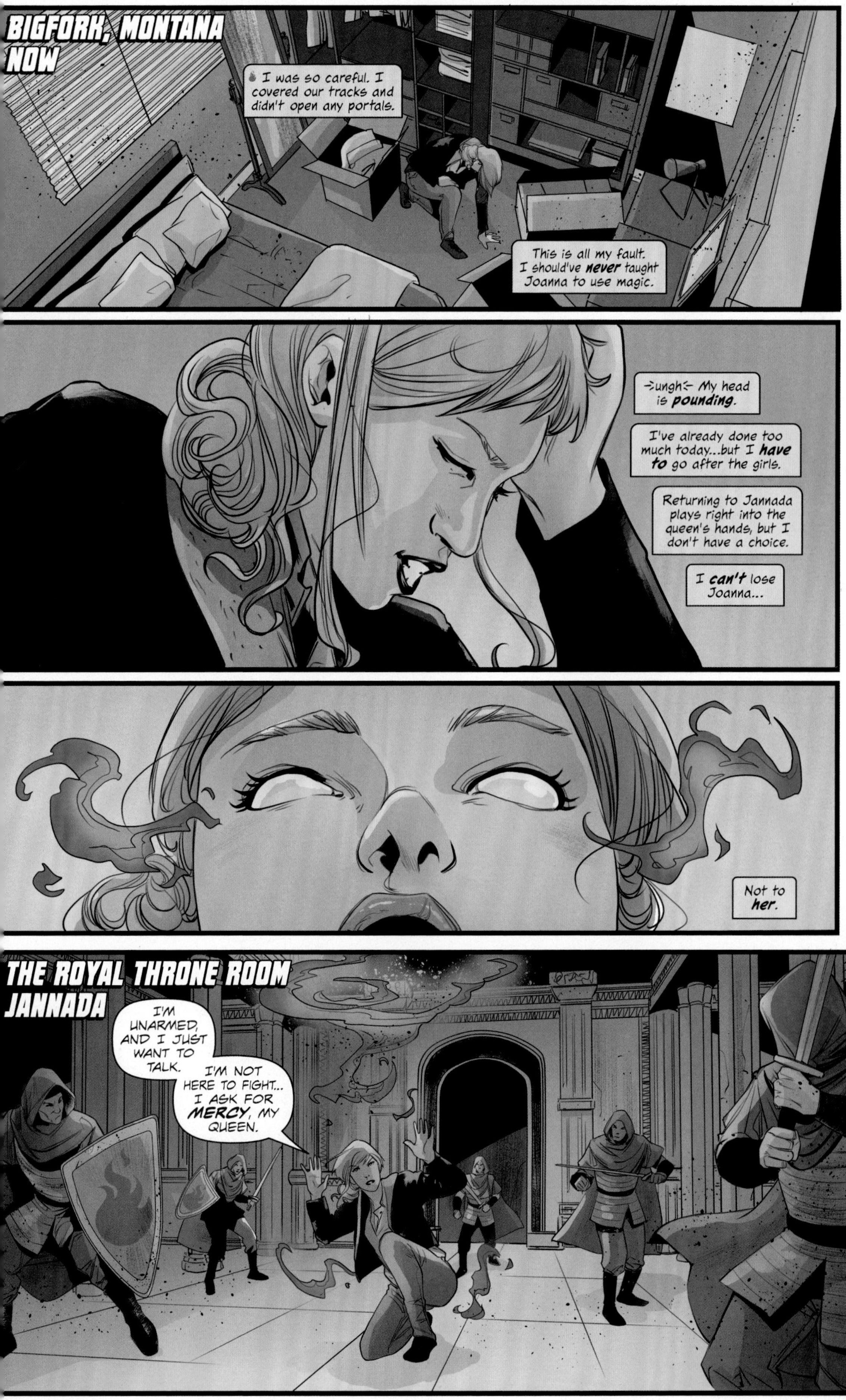
BIGFORK, MONTANA
NOW
I was so careful. I covered our tracks and didn't open any portals.
This is all my fault. I should've **never** taught Joanna to use magic.
–ungh– My head is **pounding**.
I've already done too much today...but I **have to** go after the girls.
Returning to Jannada plays right into the queen's hands, but I don't have a choice.
I **can't** lose Joanna...
Not to **her**.
THE ROYAL THRONE ROOM
JANNADA
I'M UNARMED, AND I JUST WANT TO TALK.
I'M NOT HERE TO FIGHT... I ASK FOR **MERCY**, MY QUEEN.

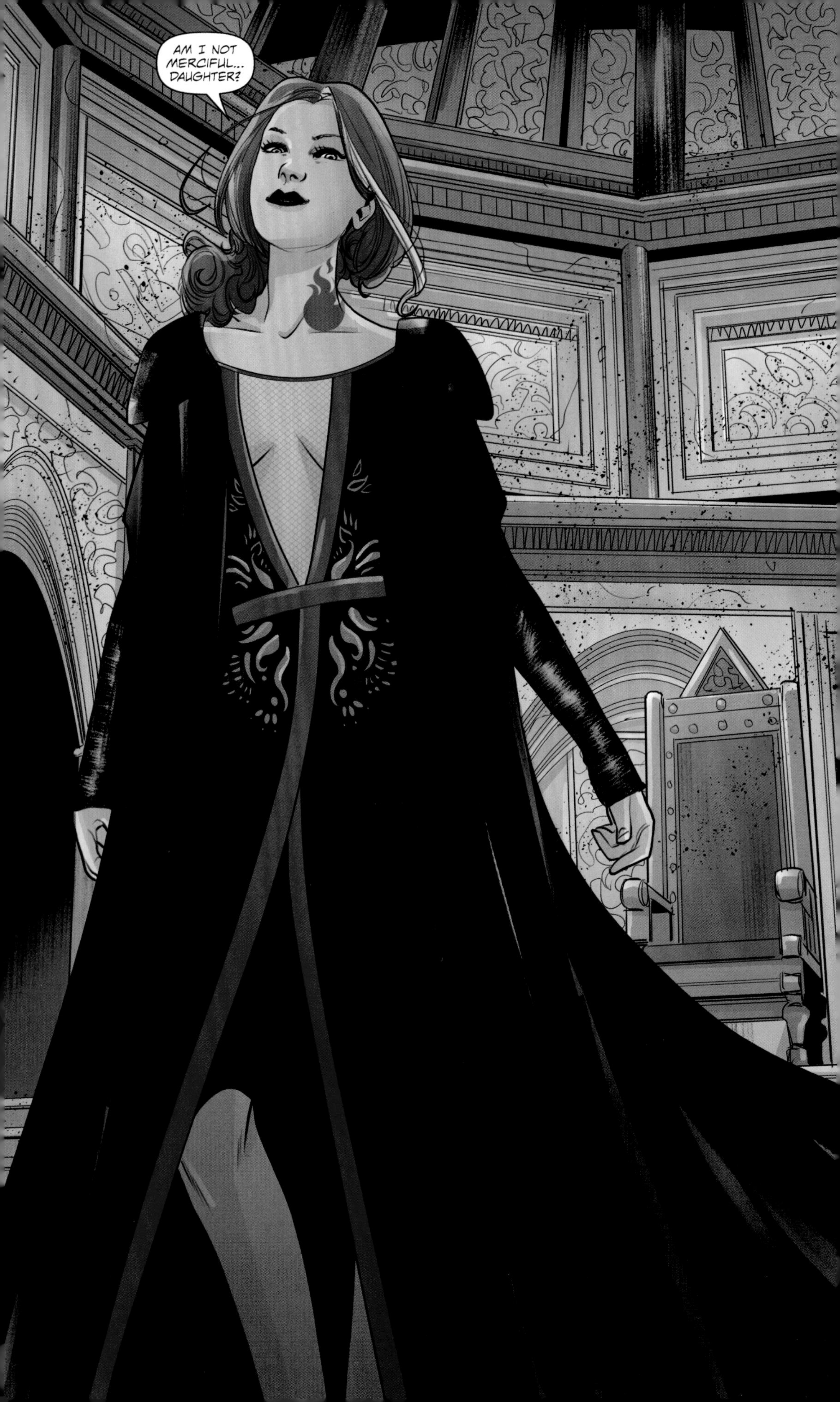
AM I NOT MERCIFUL... DAUGHTER?

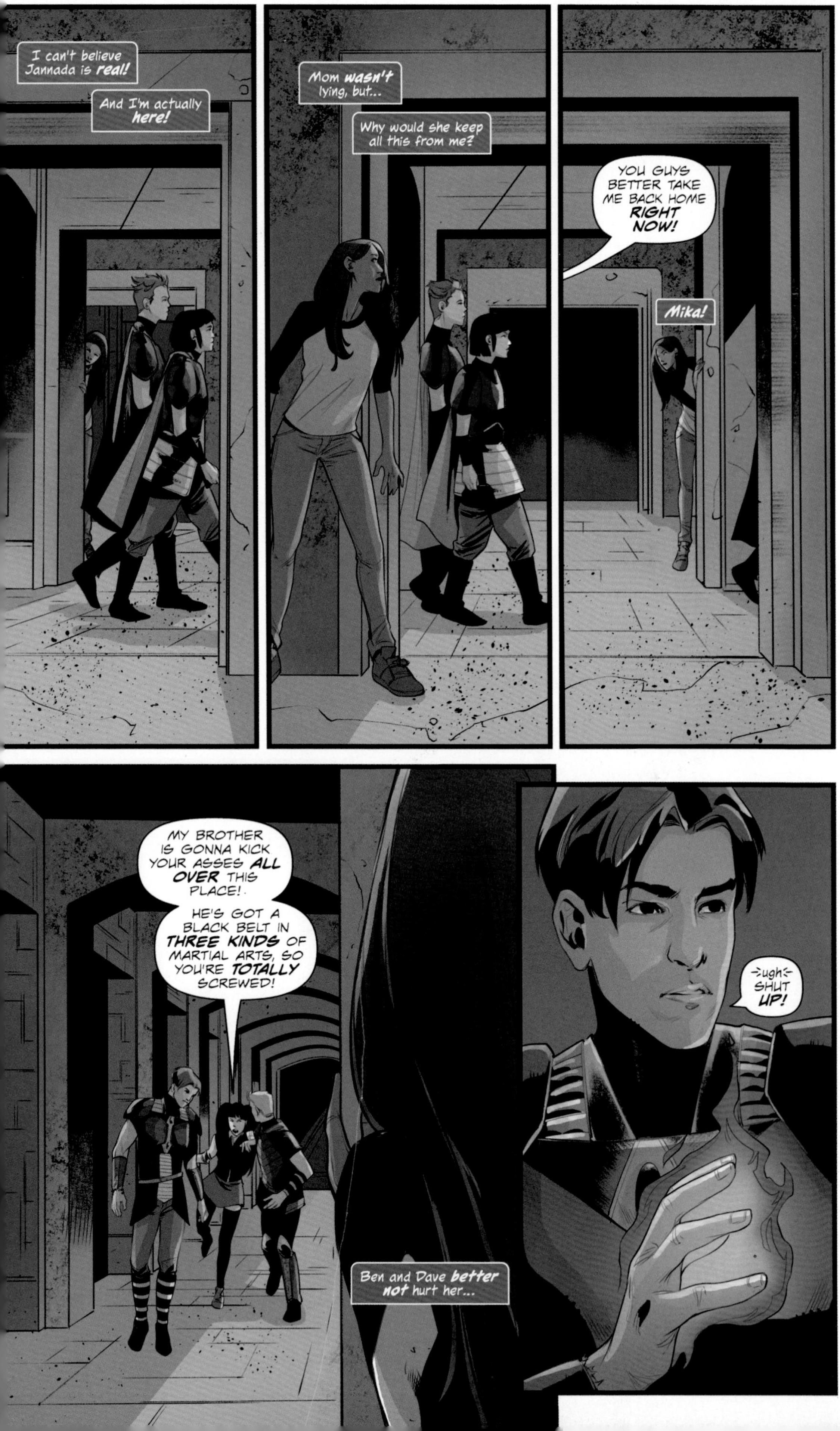
I can't believe Jannada is real!
And I'm actually here!
Mom wasn't lying, but...
Why would she keep all this from me?
YOU GUYS BETTER TAKE ME BACK HOME RIGHT NOW!
Mika!
MY BROTHER IS GONNA KICK YOUR ASSES ALL OVER THIS PLACE!
HE'S GOT A BLACK BELT IN THREE KINDS OF MARTIAL ARTS, SO YOU'RE TOTALLY SCREWED!
Ben and Dave better not hurt her...
ugh SHUT UP!

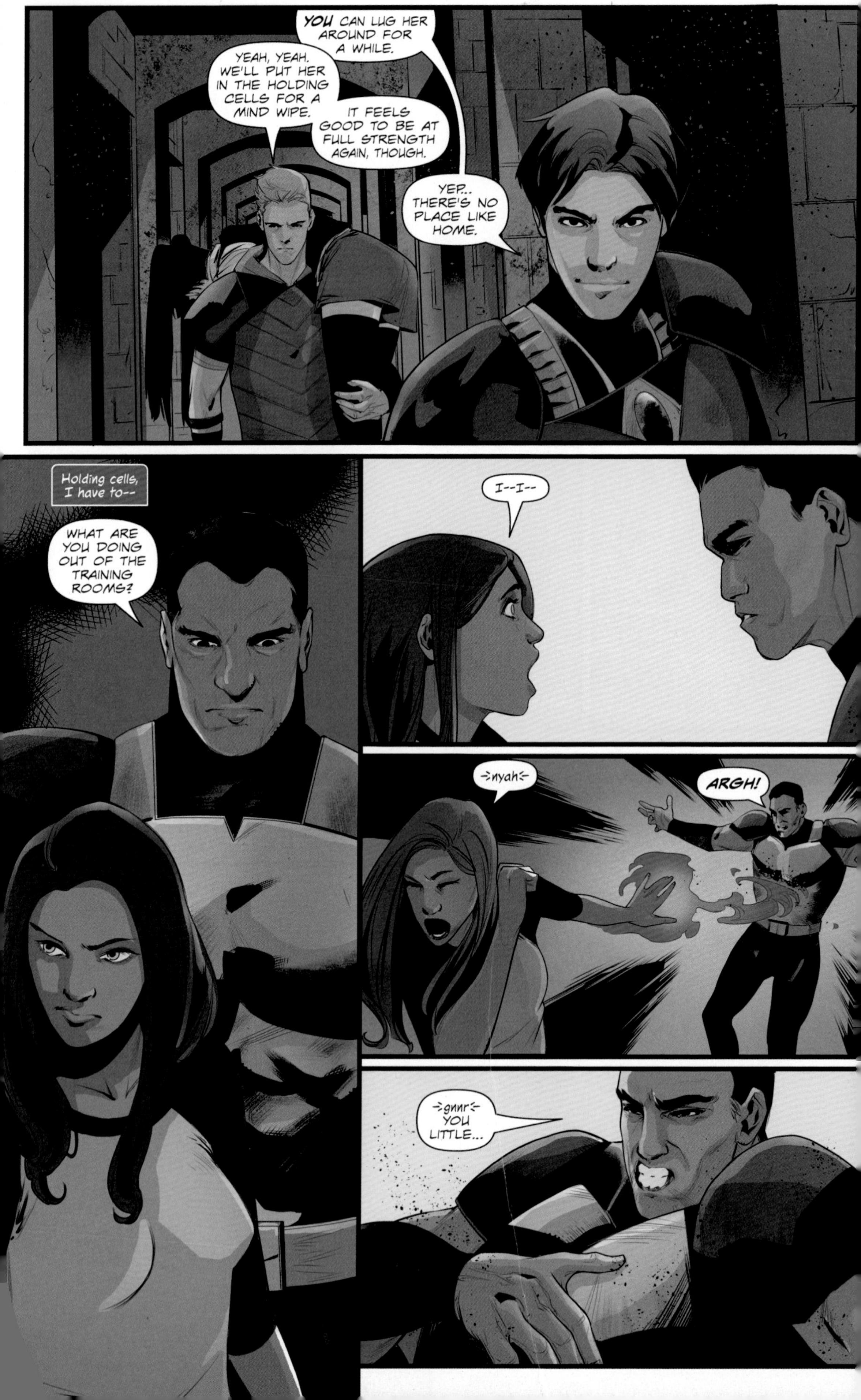
YEAH, YEAH. WE'LL PUT HER IN THE HOLDING CELLS FOR A MIND WIPE.
YOU CAN LUG HER AROUND FOR A WHILE.
IT FEELS GOOD TO BE AT FULL STRENGTH AGAIN, THOUGH.
YEP.. THERE'S NO PLACE LIKE HOME.
Holding cells, I have to--
WHAT ARE YOU DOING OUT OF THE TRAINING ROOMS?
I--I--
-nyah-
ARGH!
-gnnr- YOU LITTLE...

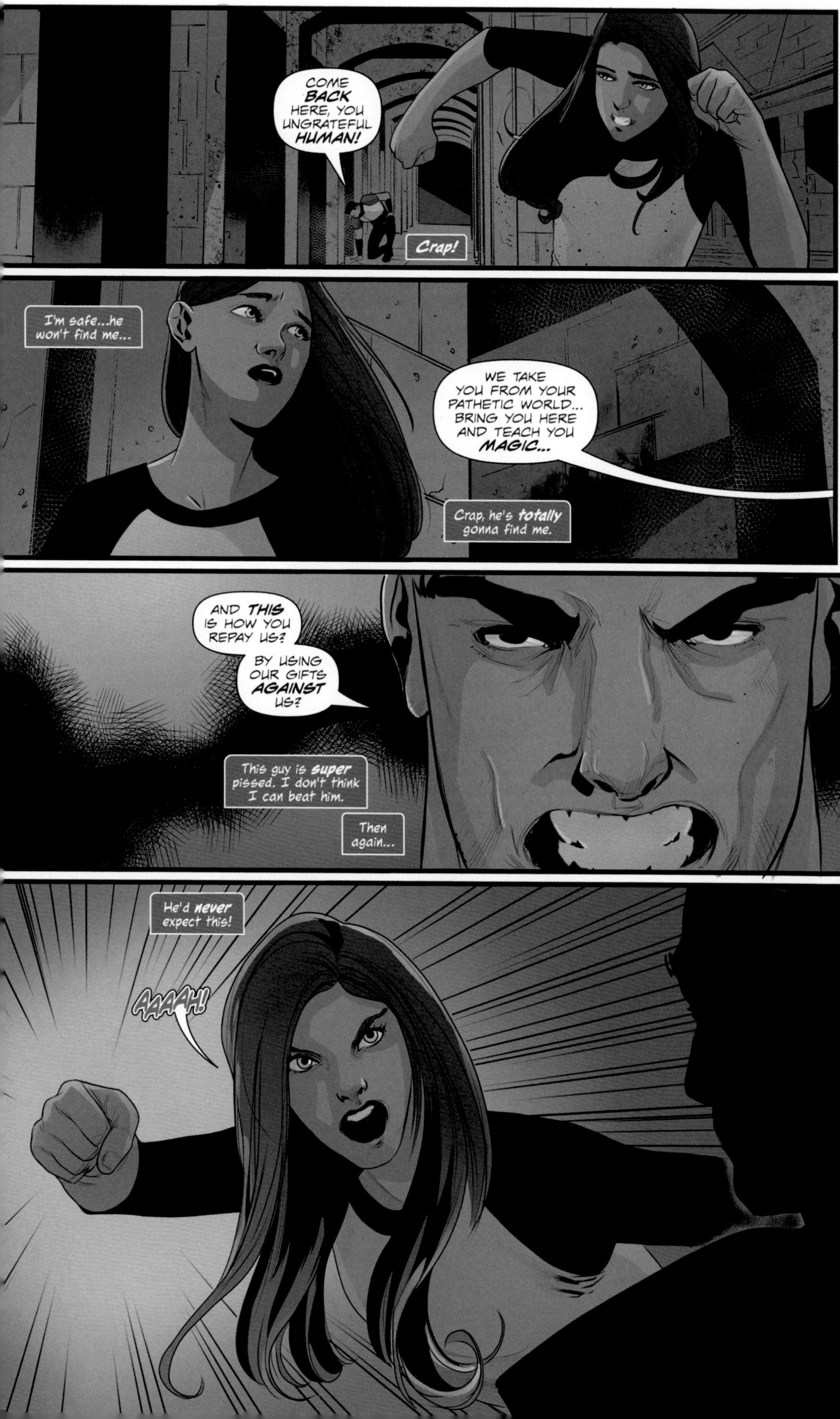
COME BACK HERE, YOU UNGRATEFUL HUMAN!
Crap!
I'm safe...he won't find me...
WE TAKE YOU FROM YOUR PATHETIC WORLD... BRING YOU HERE AND TEACH YOU MAGIC...
Crap, he's totally gonna find me.
AND THIS IS HOW YOU REPAY US?
BY USING OUR GIFTS AGAINST US?
This guy is super pissed. I don't think I can beat him.
Then again...
He'd never expect this!
AAAAH!

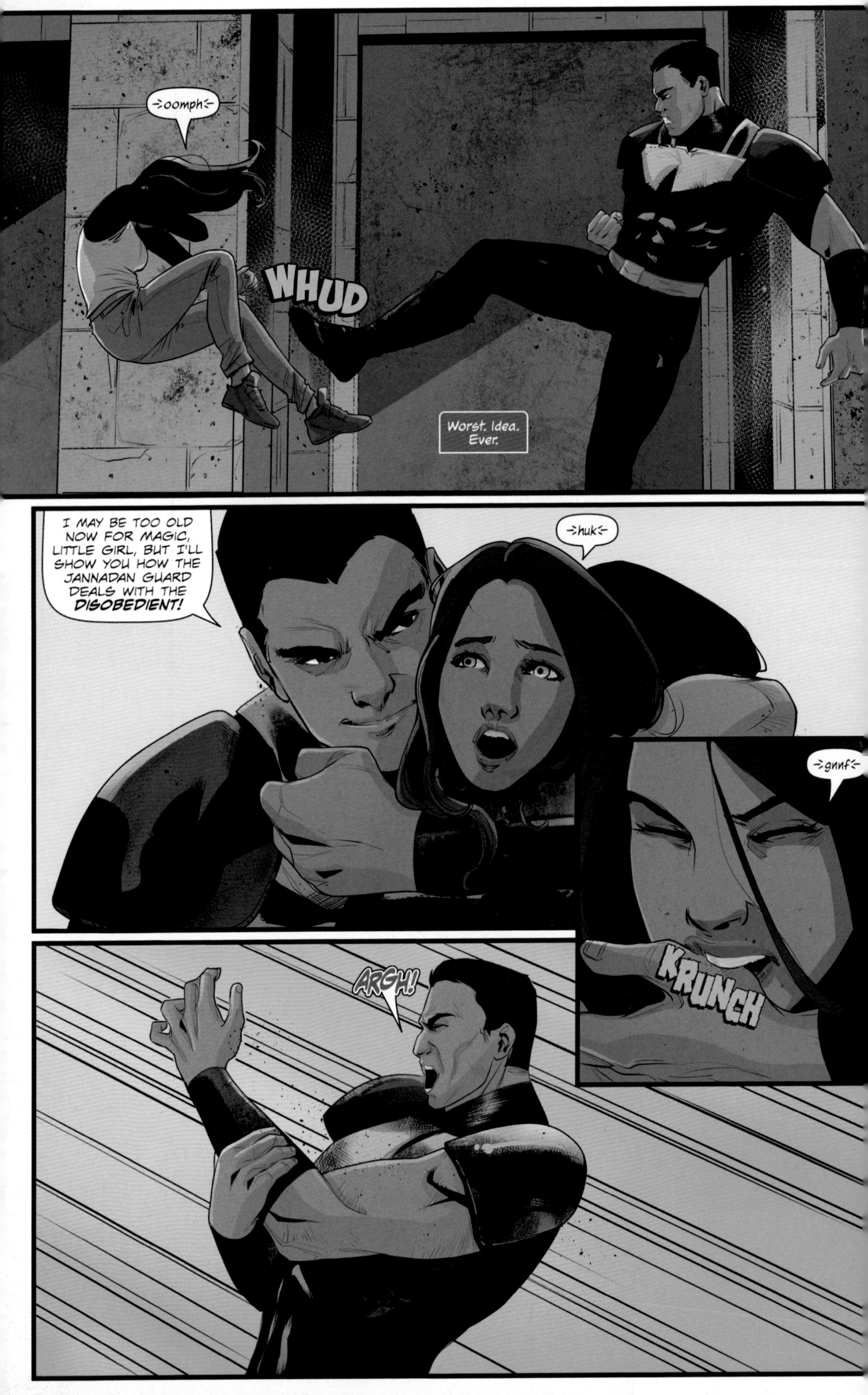
-oomph-
WHUD
Worst. Idea. Ever.
I MAY BE TOO OLD NOW FOR MAGIC, LITTLE GIRL, BUT I'LL SHOW YOU HOW THE JANNADAN GUARD DEALS WITH THE DISOBEDIENT!
-huk-
-gnnf-
KRUNCH
ARGH!

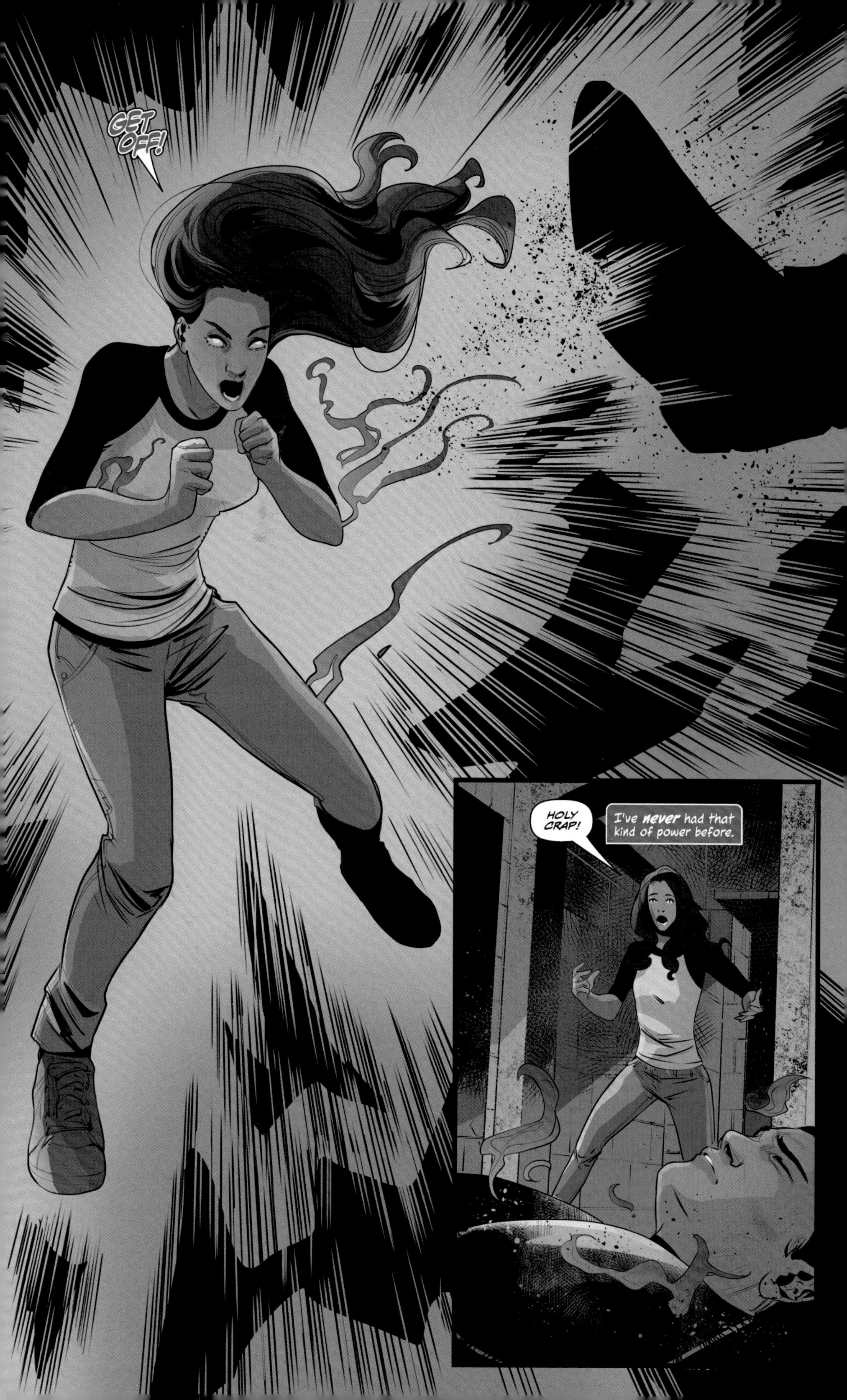
GET OFF!
HOLY CRAP!
I've never had that kind of power before.

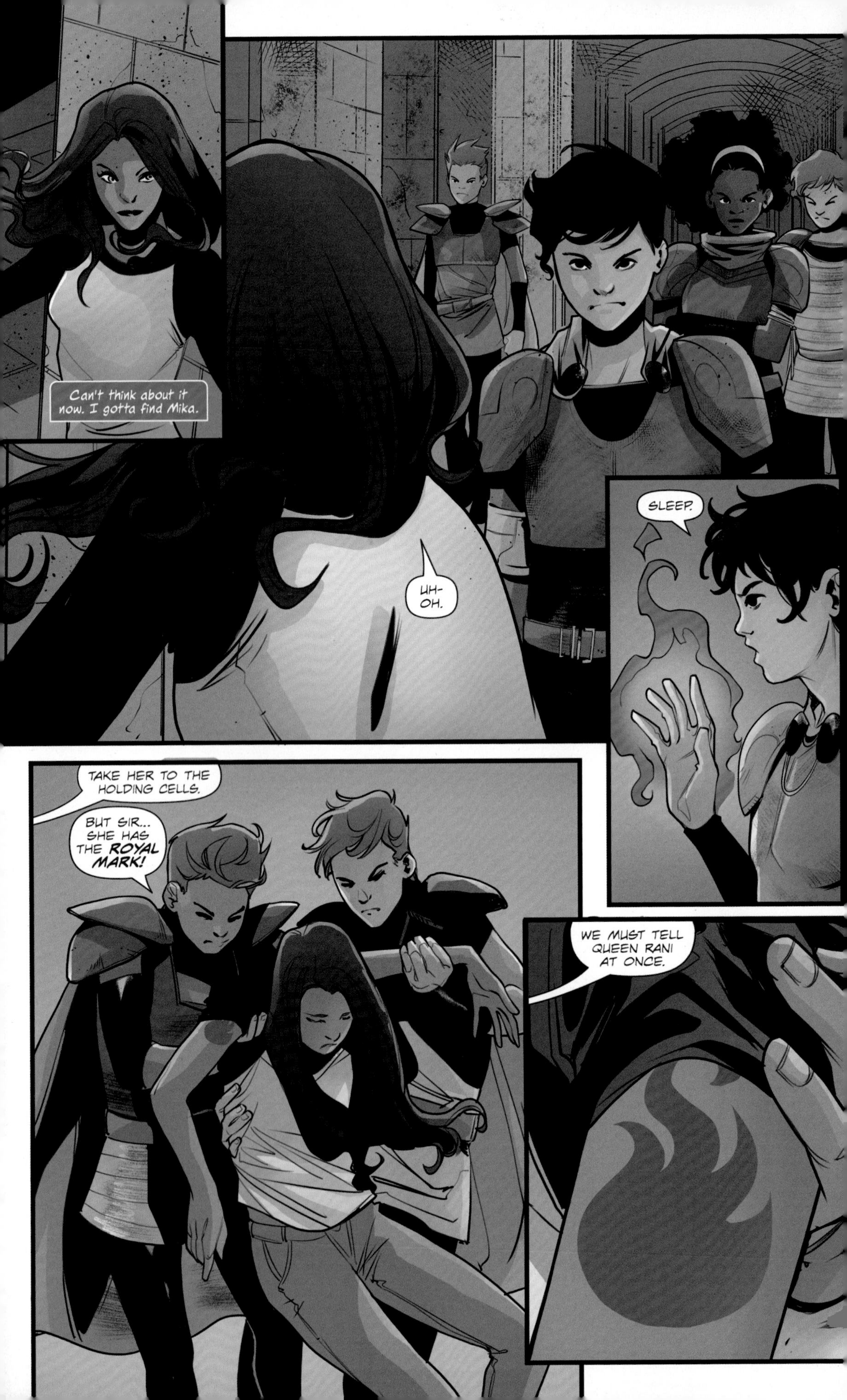

Can't think about it now. I gotta find Mika.
UH-OH.
SLEEP.
TAKE HER TO THE HOLDING CELLS.
BUT SIR... SHE HAS THE ROYAL MARK!
WE MUST TELL QUEEN RANI AT ONCE.

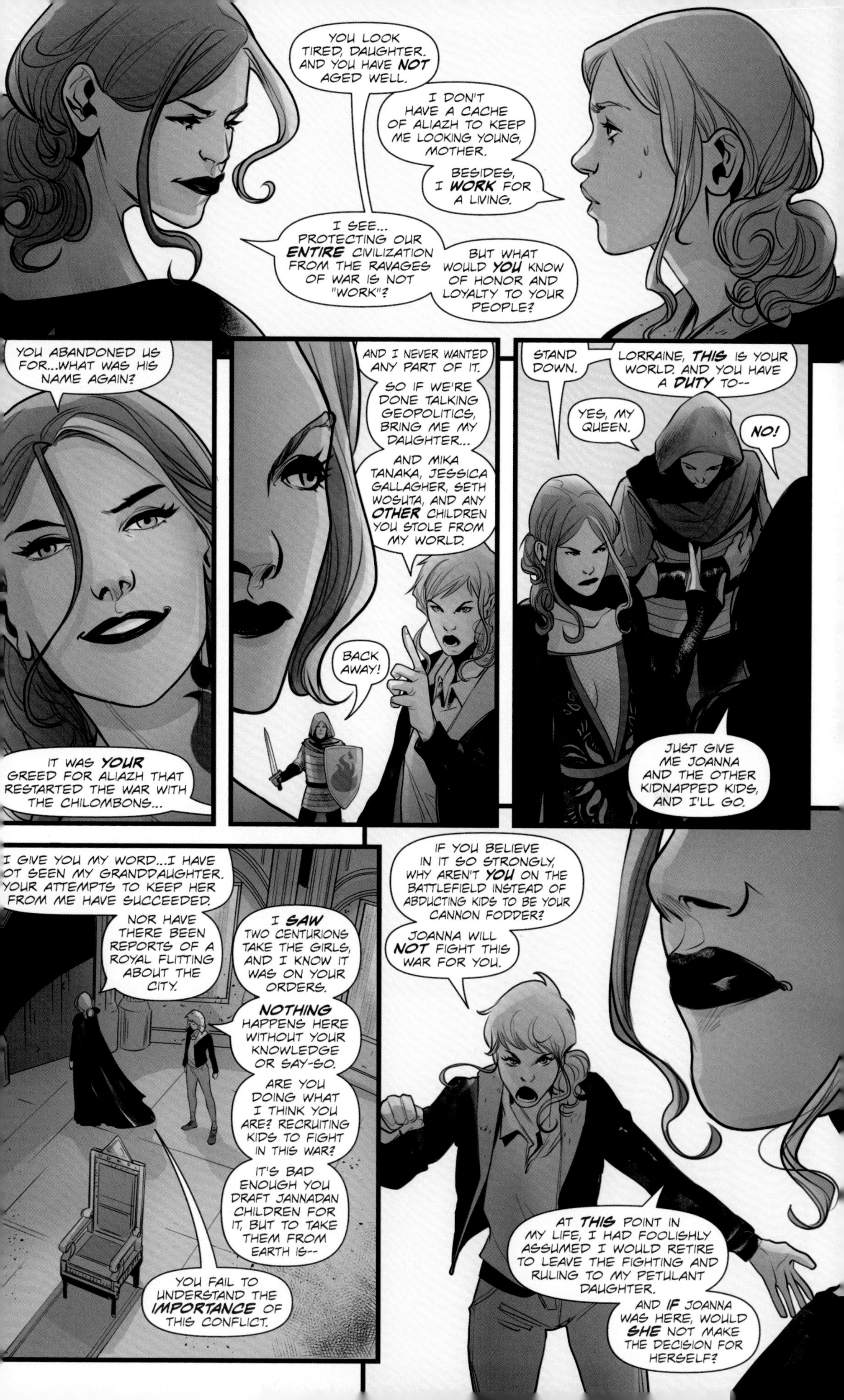

YOU LOOK TIRED, DAUGHTER. AND YOU HAVE NOT AGED WELL.
I DON'T HAVE A CACHE OF ALIAZH TO KEEP ME LOOKING YOUNG, MOTHER.
BESIDES, I WORK FOR A LIVING.
I SEE... PROTECTING OUR ENTIRE CIVILIZATION FROM THE RAVAGES OF WAR IS NOT "WORK"?
BUT WHAT WOULD YOU KNOW OF HONOR AND LOYALTY TO YOUR PEOPLE?
YOU ABANDONED US FOR...WHAT WAS HIS NAME AGAIN?
IT WAS YOUR GREED FOR ALIAZH THAT RESTARTED THE WAR WITH THE CHILOMBONS...
AND I NEVER WANTED ANY PART OF IT.
SO IF WE'RE DONE TALKING GEOPOLITICS, BRING ME MY DAUGHTER...
AND MIKA TANAKA, JESSICA GALLAGHER, SETH WOSUTA, AND ANY OTHER CHILDREN YOU STOLE FROM MY WORLD.
BACK AWAY!
STAND DOWN.
LORRAINE, THIS IS YOUR WORLD. AND YOU HAVE A DUTY TO--
YES, MY QUEEN.
NO!
JUST GIVE ME JOANNA AND THE OTHER KIDNAPPED KIDS, AND I'LL GO.
I GIVE YOU MY WORD...I HAVE OT SEEN MY GRANDDAUGHTER. YOUR ATTEMPTS TO KEEP HER FROM ME HAVE SUCCEEDED.
NOR HAVE THERE BEEN REPORTS OF A ROYAL FLITTING ABOUT THE CITY.
I SAW TWO CENTURIONS TAKE THE GIRLS, AND I KNOW IT WAS ON YOUR ORDERS.
NOTHING HAPPENS HERE WITHOUT YOUR KNOWLEDGE OR SAY-SO.
ARE YOU DOING WHAT I THINK YOU ARE? RECRUITING KIDS TO FIGHT IN THIS WAR?
IT'S BAD ENOUGH YOU DRAFT JANNADAN CHILDREN FOR IT, BUT TO TAKE THEM FROM EARTH IS--
YOU FAIL TO UNDERSTAND THE IMPORTANCE OF THIS CONFLICT.
IF YOU BELIEVE IN IT SO STRONGLY, WHY AREN'T YOU ON THE BATTLEFIELD INSTEAD OF ABDUCTING KIDS TO BE YOUR CANNON FODDER?
JOANNA WILL NOT FIGHT THIS WAR FOR YOU.
AT THIS POINT IN MY LIFE, I HAD FOOLISHLY ASSUMED I WOULD RETIRE TO LEAVE THE FIGHTING AND RULING TO MY PETULANT DAUGHTER.
AND IF JOANNA WAS HERE, WOULD SHE NOT MAKE THE DECISION FOR HERSELF?

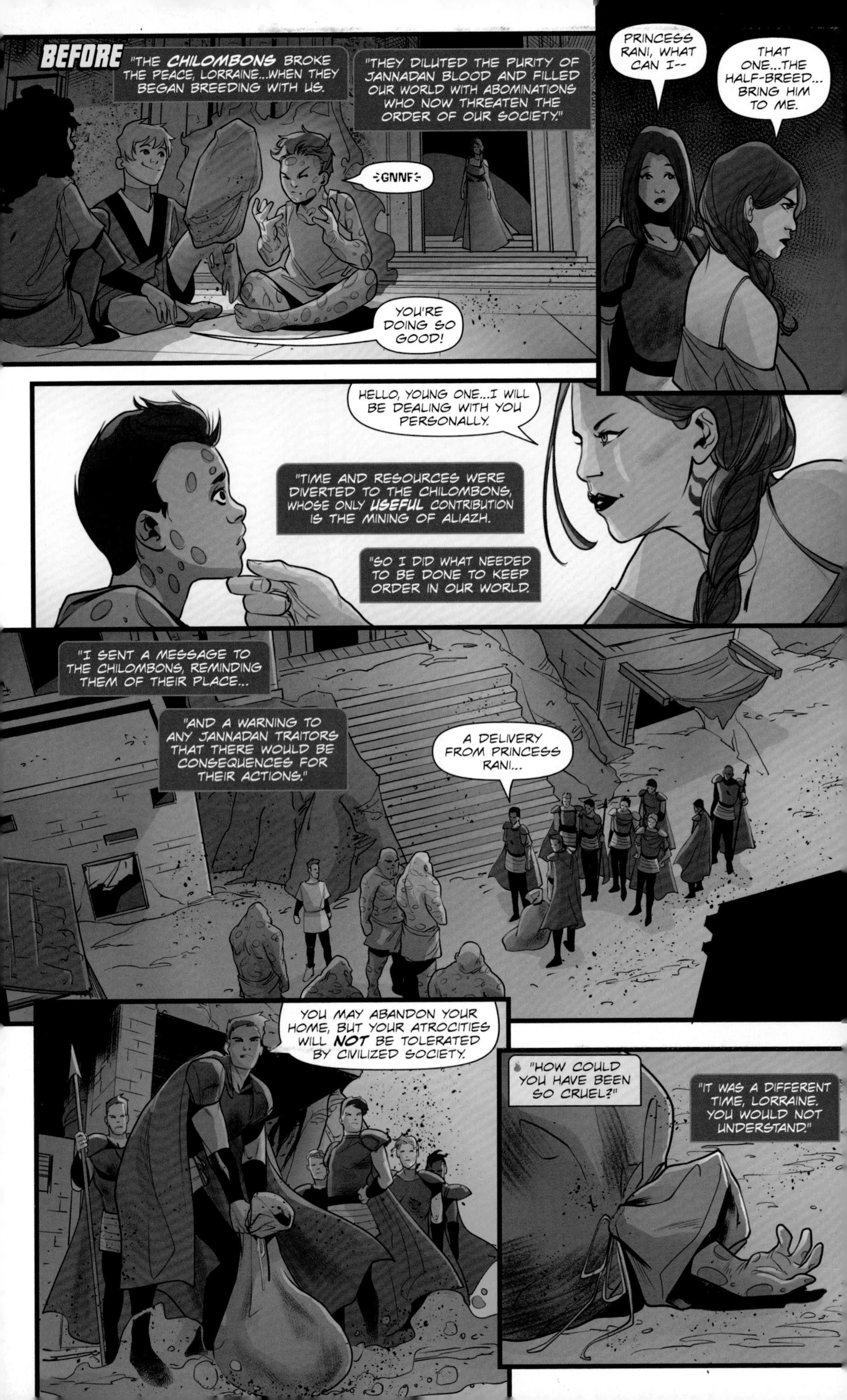
BEFORE
"THE CHILOMBONS BROKE THE PEACE, LORRAINE...WHEN THEY BEGAN BREEDING WITH US.
"THEY DILUTED THE PURITY OF JANNADAN BLOOD AND FILLED OUR WORLD WITH ABOMINATIONS WHO NOW THREATEN THE ORDER OF OUR SOCIETY."
GNNF
YOU'RE DOING SO GOOD!
PRINCESS RANI, WHAT CAN I--
THAT ONE...THE HALF-BREED... BRING HIM TO ME.
HELLO, YOUNG ONE...I WILL BE DEALING WITH YOU PERSONALLY.
"TIME AND RESOURCES WERE DIVERTED TO THE CHILOMBONS, WHOSE ONLY USEFUL CONTRIBUTION IS THE MINING OF ALIAZH.
"SO I DID WHAT NEEDED TO BE DONE TO KEEP ORDER IN OUR WORLD.
"I SENT A MESSAGE TO THE CHILOMBONS, REMINDING THEM OF THEIR PLACE...
"AND A WARNING TO ANY JANNADAN TRAITORS THAT THERE WOULD BE CONSEQUENCES FOR THEIR ACTIONS."
A DELIVERY FROM PRINCESS RANI...
YOU MAY ABANDON YOUR HOME, BUT YOUR ATROCITIES WILL NOT BE TOLERATED BY CIVILIZED SOCIETY.
"HOW COULD YOU HAVE BEEN SO CRUEL?"
"IT WAS A DIFFERENT TIME, LORRAINE. YOU WOULD NOT UNDERSTAND."

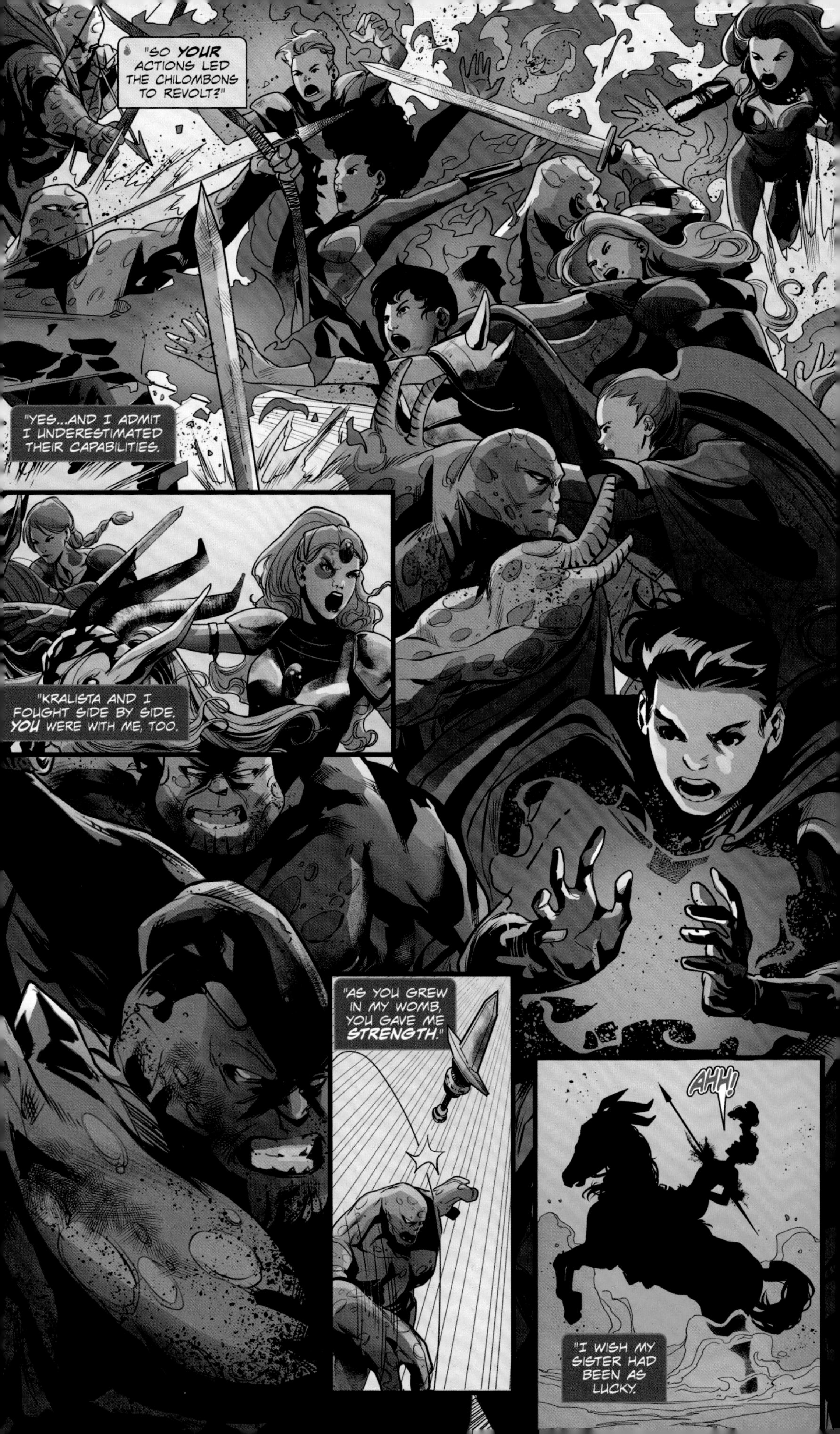
"SO YOUR ACTIONS LED THE CHILOMBONS TO REVOLT?"
"YES...AND I ADMIT I UNDERESTIMATED THEIR CAPABILITIES.
"KRALISTA AND I FOUGHT SIDE BY SIDE. YOU WERE WITH ME, TOO.
"AS YOU GREW IN MY WOMB, YOU GAVE ME STRENGTH."
AHH!
"I WISH MY SISTER HAD BEEN AS LUCKY.

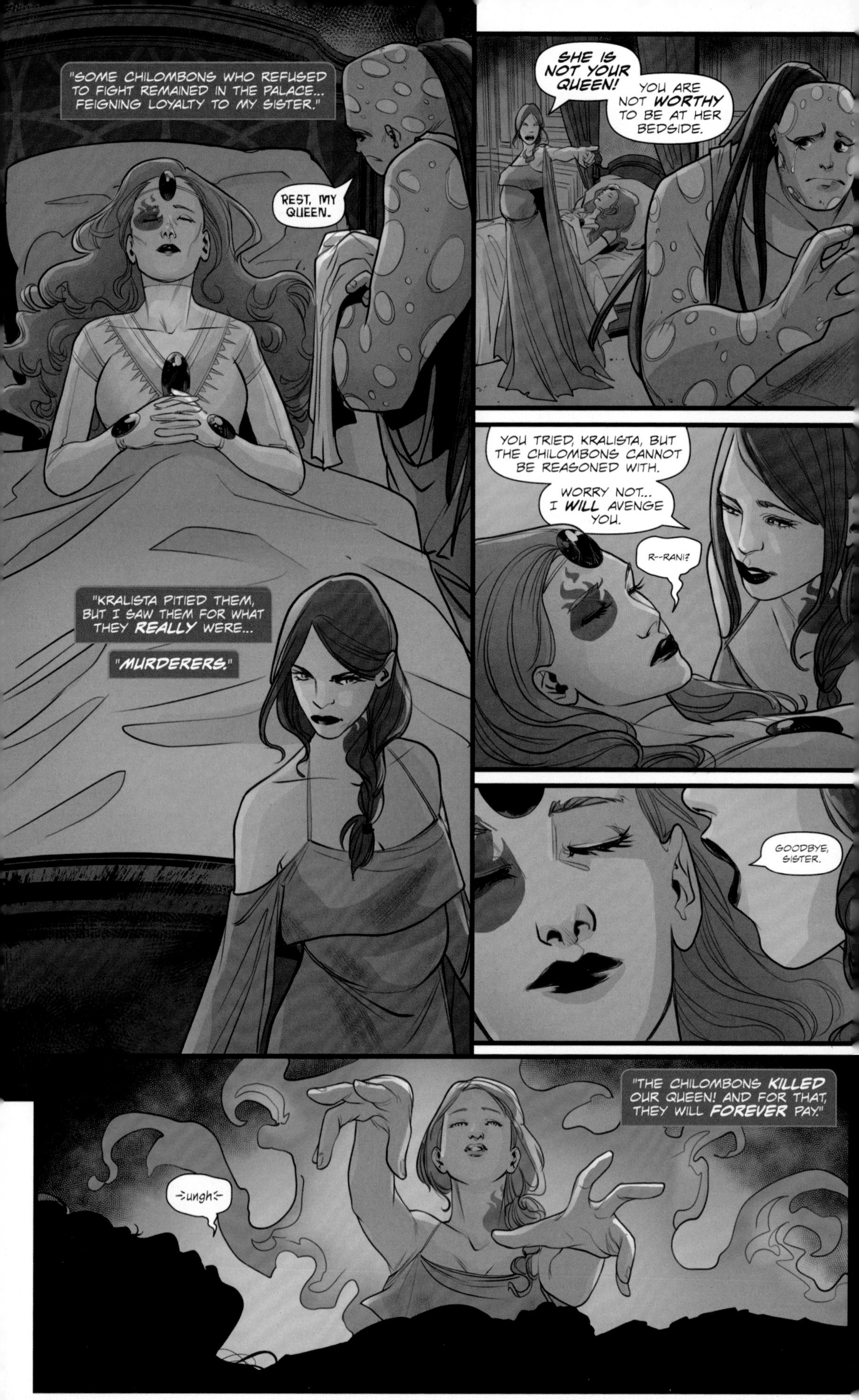
"SOME CHILOMBONS WHO REFUSED TO FIGHT REMAINED IN THE PALACE... FEIGNING LOYALTY TO MY SISTER."
REST, MY QUEEN.
"KRALISTA PITIED THEM, BUT I SAW THEM FOR WHAT THEY REALLY WERE...
"MURDERERS."
SHE IS NOT YOUR QUEEN!
YOU ARE NOT WORTHY TO BE AT HER BEDSIDE.
YOU TRIED, KRALISTA, BUT THE CHILOMBONS CANNOT BE REASONED WITH.
WORRY NOT... I WILL AVENGE YOU.
R--RANI?
GOODBYE, SISTER.
"THE CHILOMBONS KILLED OUR QUEEN! AND FOR THAT, THEY WILL FOREVER PAY."
ungh

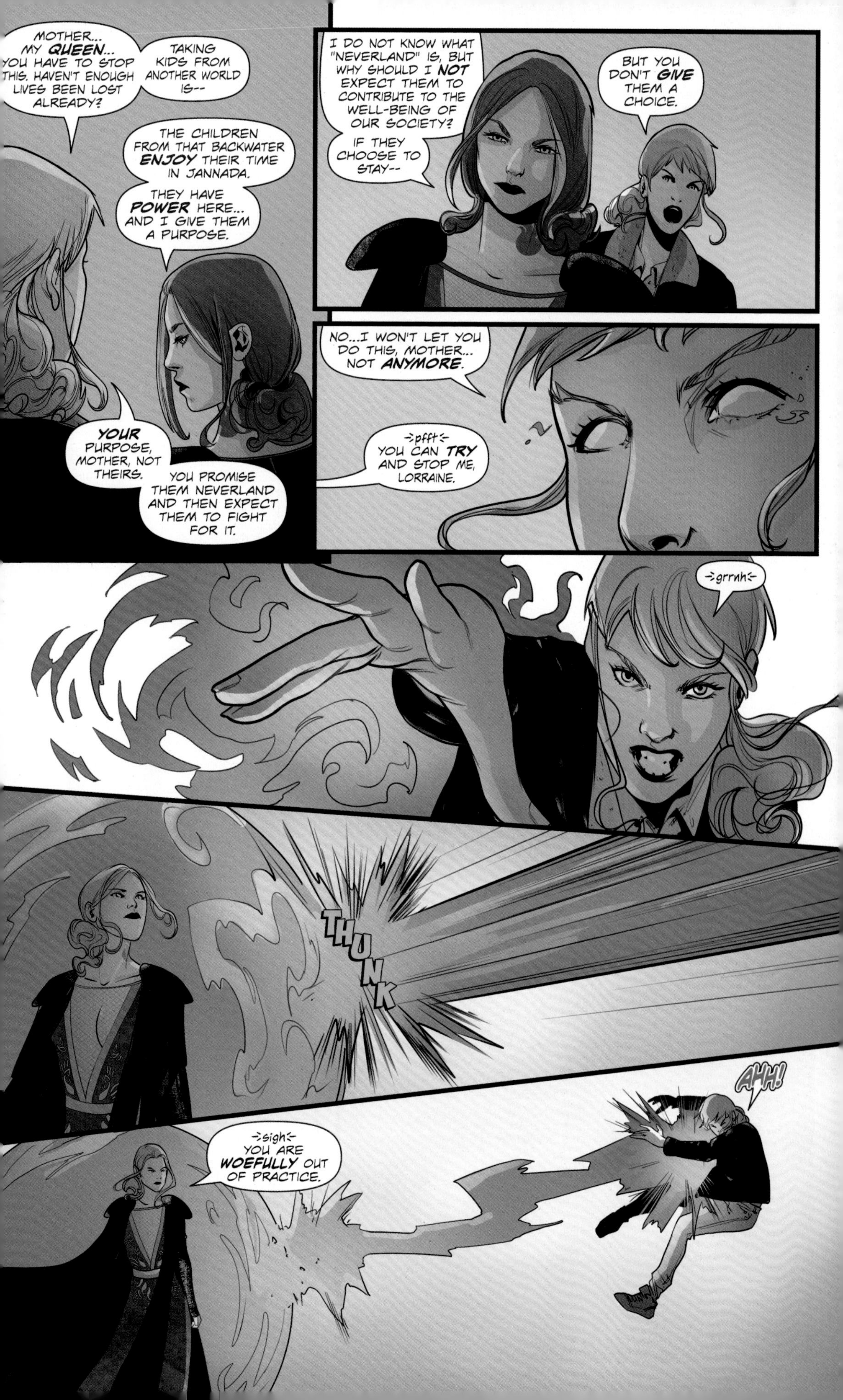
MOTHER... MY **QUEEN**... YOU HAVE TO STOP THIS. HAVEN'T ENOUGH LIVES BEEN LOST ALREADY?
TAKING KIDS FROM ANOTHER WORLD IS--
THE CHILDREN FROM THAT BACKWATER **ENJOY** THEIR TIME IN JANNADA.
THEY HAVE **POWER** HERE... AND I GIVE THEM A PURPOSE.
YOUR PURPOSE, MOTHER, NOT THEIRS.
YOU PROMISE THEM NEVERLAND AND THEN EXPECT THEM TO FIGHT FOR IT.
I DO NOT KNOW WHAT "NEVERLAND" IS, BUT WHY SHOULD I **NOT** EXPECT THEM TO CONTRIBUTE TO THE WELL-BEING OF OUR SOCIETY?
IF THEY CHOOSE TO STAY--
BUT YOU DON'T **GIVE** THEM A CHOICE.
NO...I WON'T LET YOU DO THIS, MOTHER... NOT **ANYMORE**.
pfft YOU CAN **TRY** AND STOP ME, LORRAINE.
grrnh
THUNK
AHH!
sigh YOU ARE **WOEFULLY** OUT OF PRACTICE.

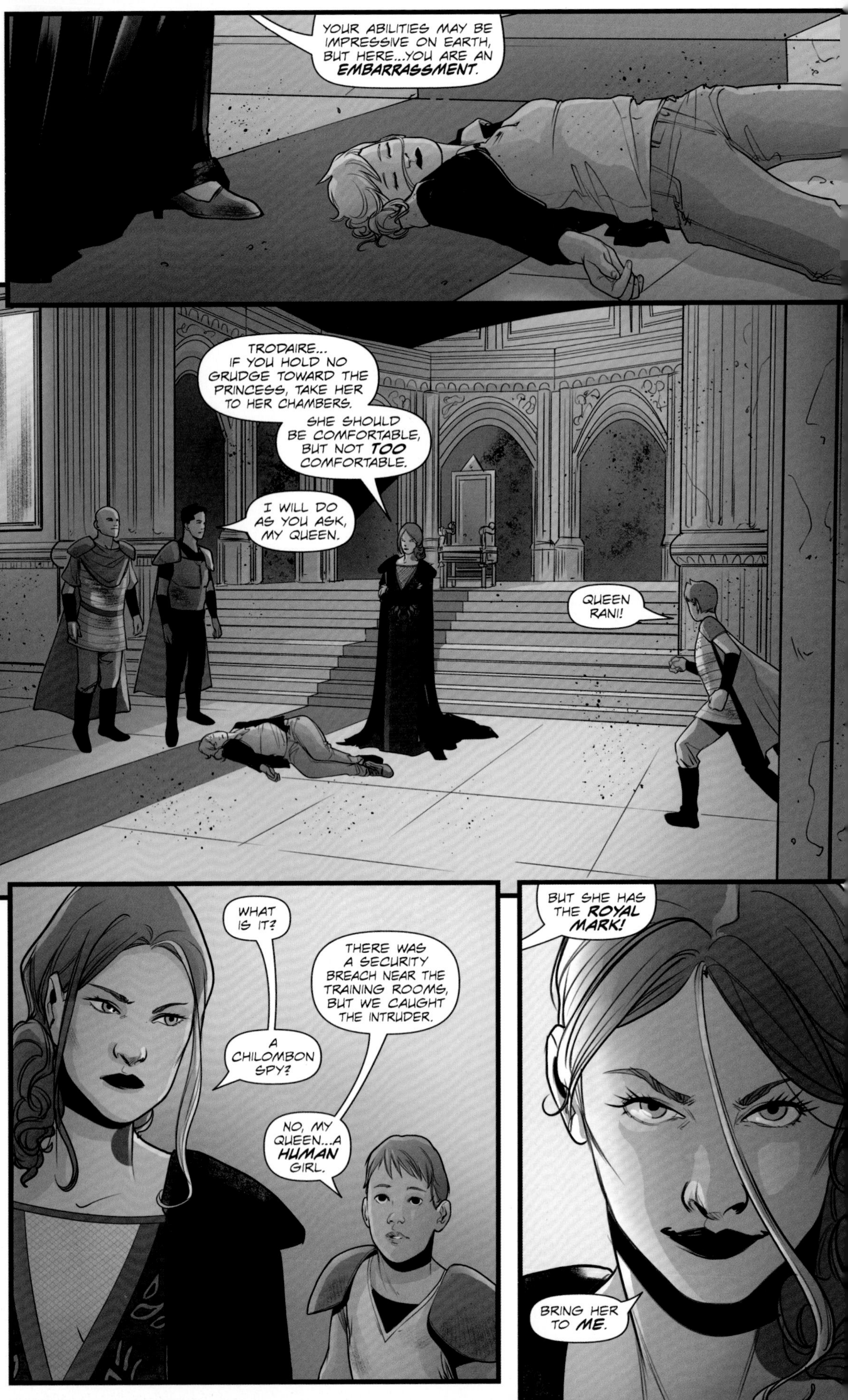
YOUR ABILITIES MAY BE IMPRESSIVE ON EARTH, BUT HERE...YOU ARE AN EMBARRASSMENT.
TRODAIRE... IF YOU HOLD NO GRUDGE TOWARD THE PRINCESS, TAKE HER TO HER CHAMBERS.
SHE SHOULD BE COMFORTABLE, BUT NOT TOO COMFORTABLE.
I WILL DO AS YOU ASK, MY QUEEN.
QUEEN RANI!
WHAT IS IT?
THERE WAS A SECURITY BREACH NEAR THE TRAINING ROOMS, BUT WE CAUGHT THE INTRUDER.
A CHILOMBON SPY?
NO, MY QUEEN...A HUMAN GIRL.
BUT SHE HAS THE ROYAL MARK!
BRING HER TO ME.

THREE

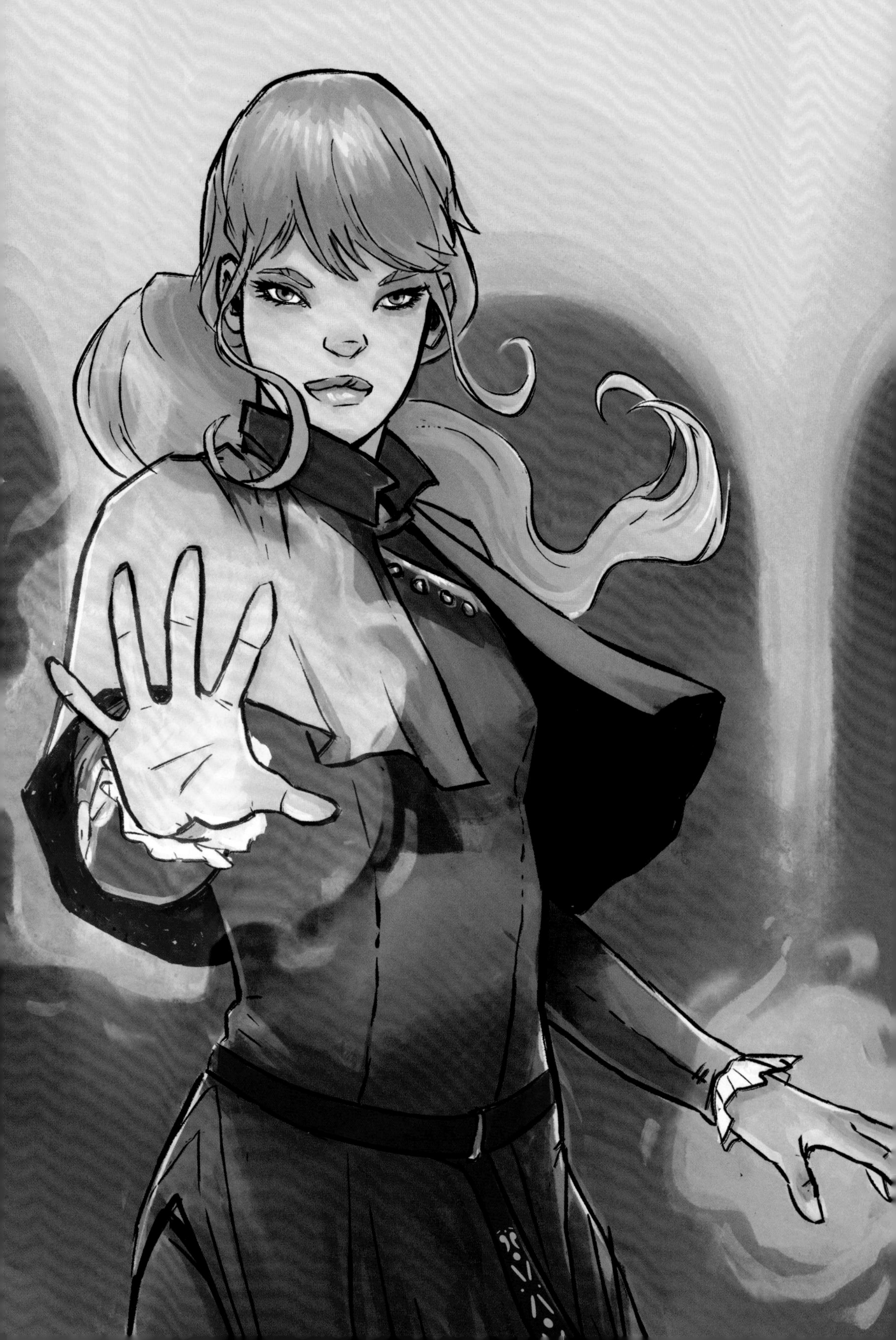

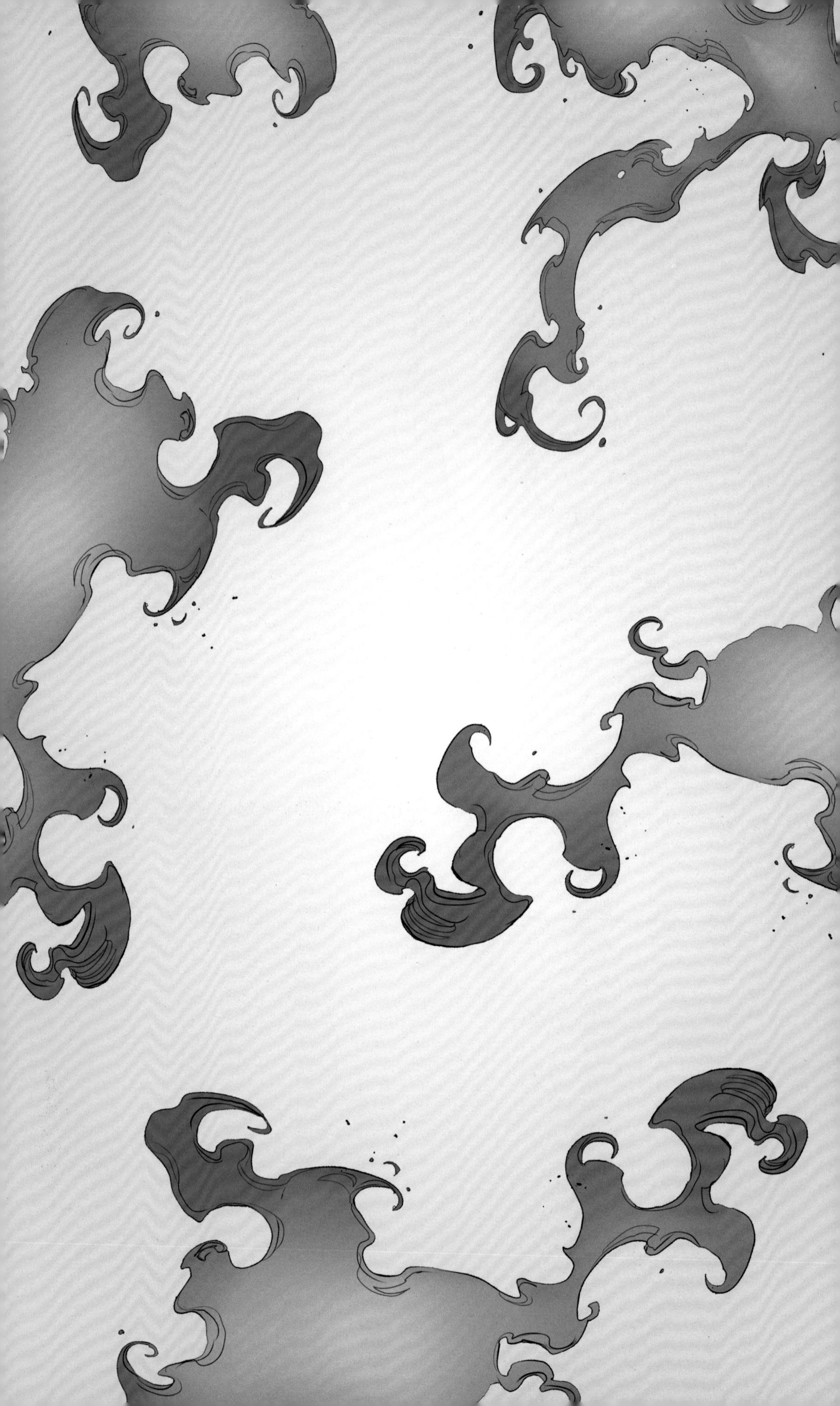

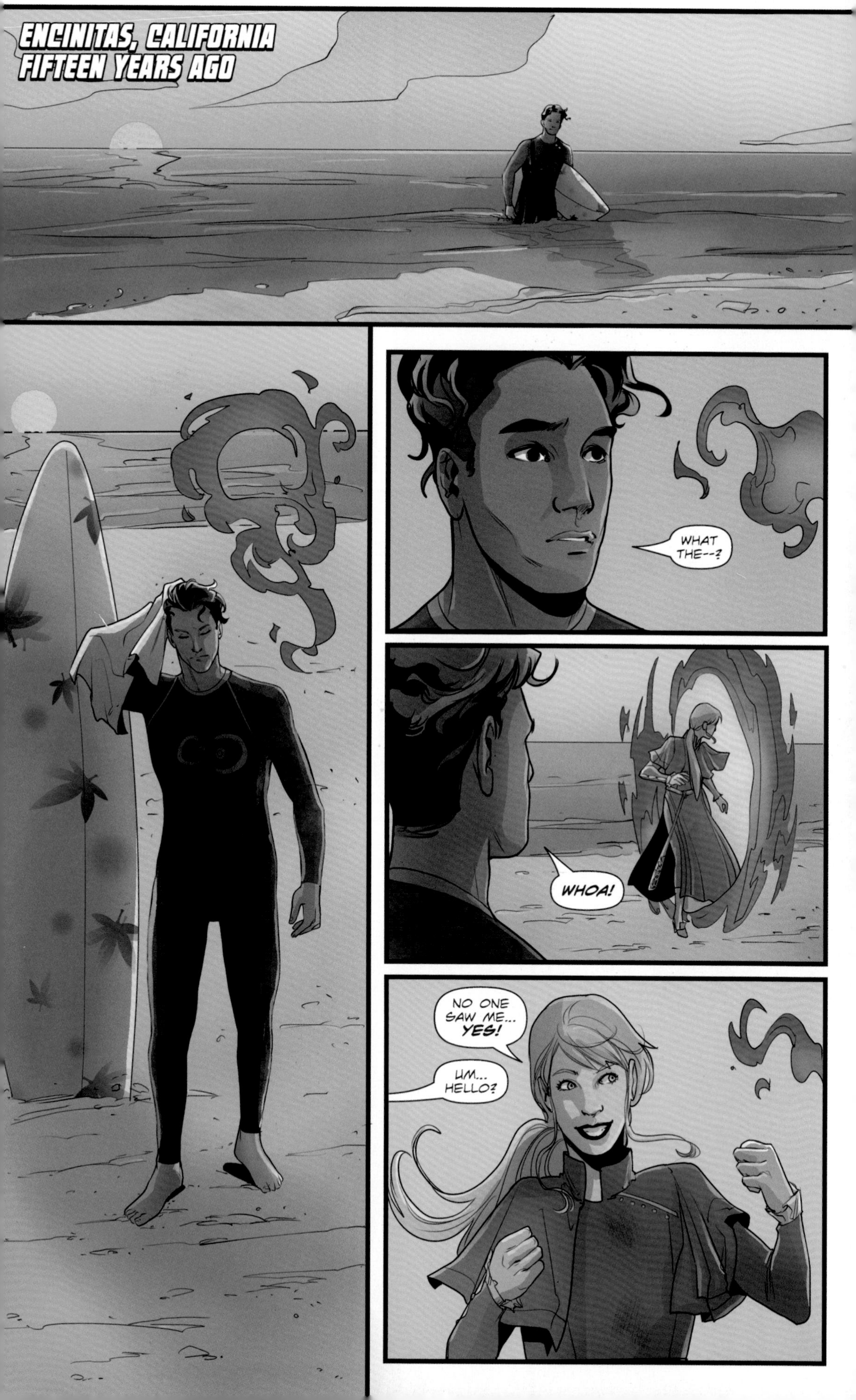
ENCINITAS, CALIFORNIA
FIFTEEN YEARS AGO
WHAT THE--?
WHOA!
NO ONE SAW ME... YES!
UM... HELLO?

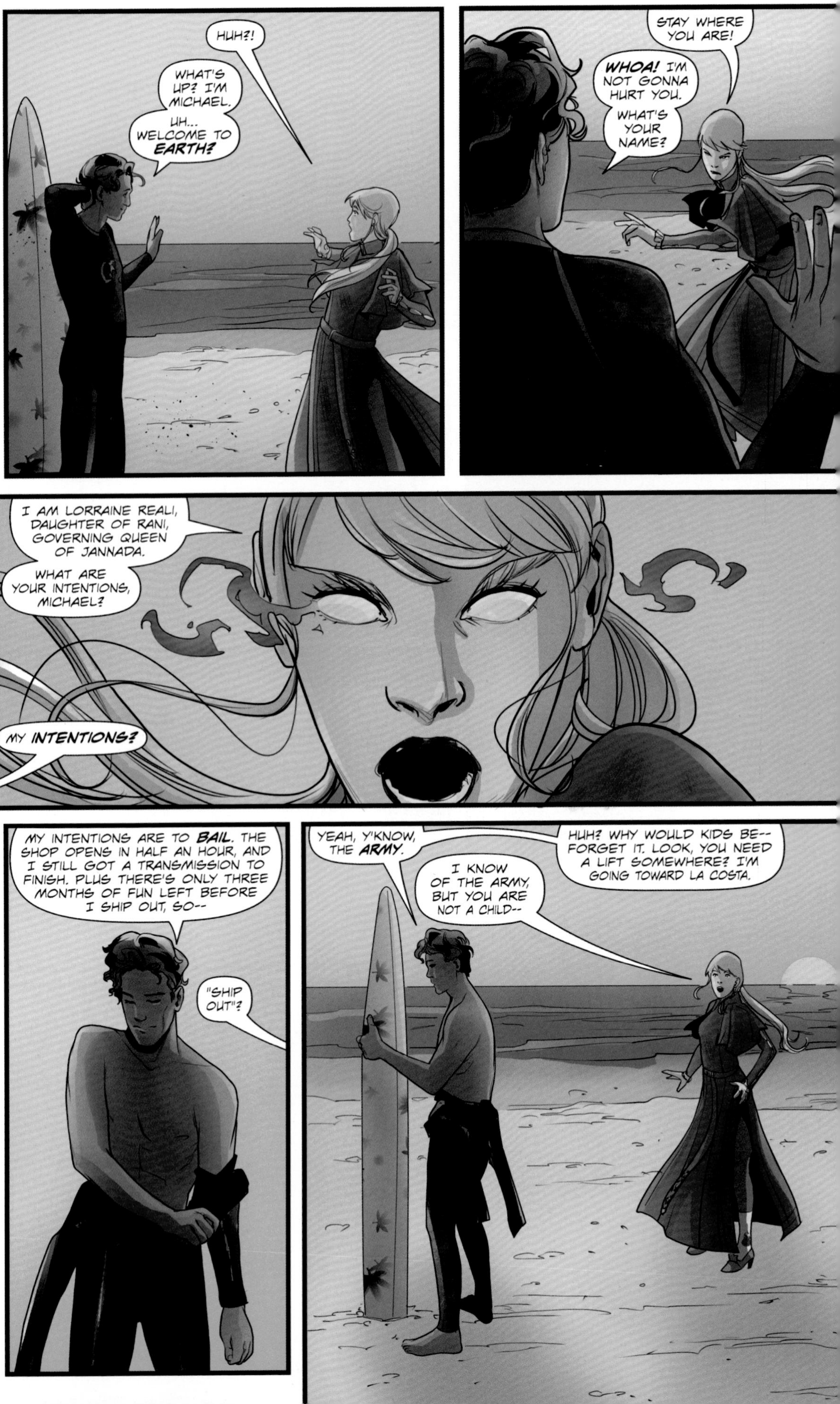
HUH?!
WHAT'S UP? I'M MICHAEL.
UH... WELCOME TO **EARTH?**
STAY WHERE YOU ARE!
WHOA! I'M NOT GONNA HURT YOU.
WHAT'S YOUR NAME?
I AM LORRAINE REALI, DAUGHTER OF RANI, GOVERNING QUEEN OF JANNADA.
WHAT ARE YOUR INTENTIONS, MICHAEL?
MY **INTENTIONS?**
MY INTENTIONS ARE TO **BAIL.** THE SHOP OPENS IN HALF AN HOUR, AND I STILL GOT A TRANSMISSION TO FINISH. PLUS THERE'S ONLY THREE MONTHS OF FUN LEFT BEFORE I SHIP OUT, SO--
"SHIP OUT"?
YEAH, Y'KNOW, THE **ARMY.**
I KNOW OF THE ARMY, BUT YOU ARE NOT A CHILD--
HUH? WHY WOULD KIDS BE-- FORGET IT. LOOK, YOU NEED A LIFT SOMEWHERE? I'M GOING TOWARD LA COSTA.

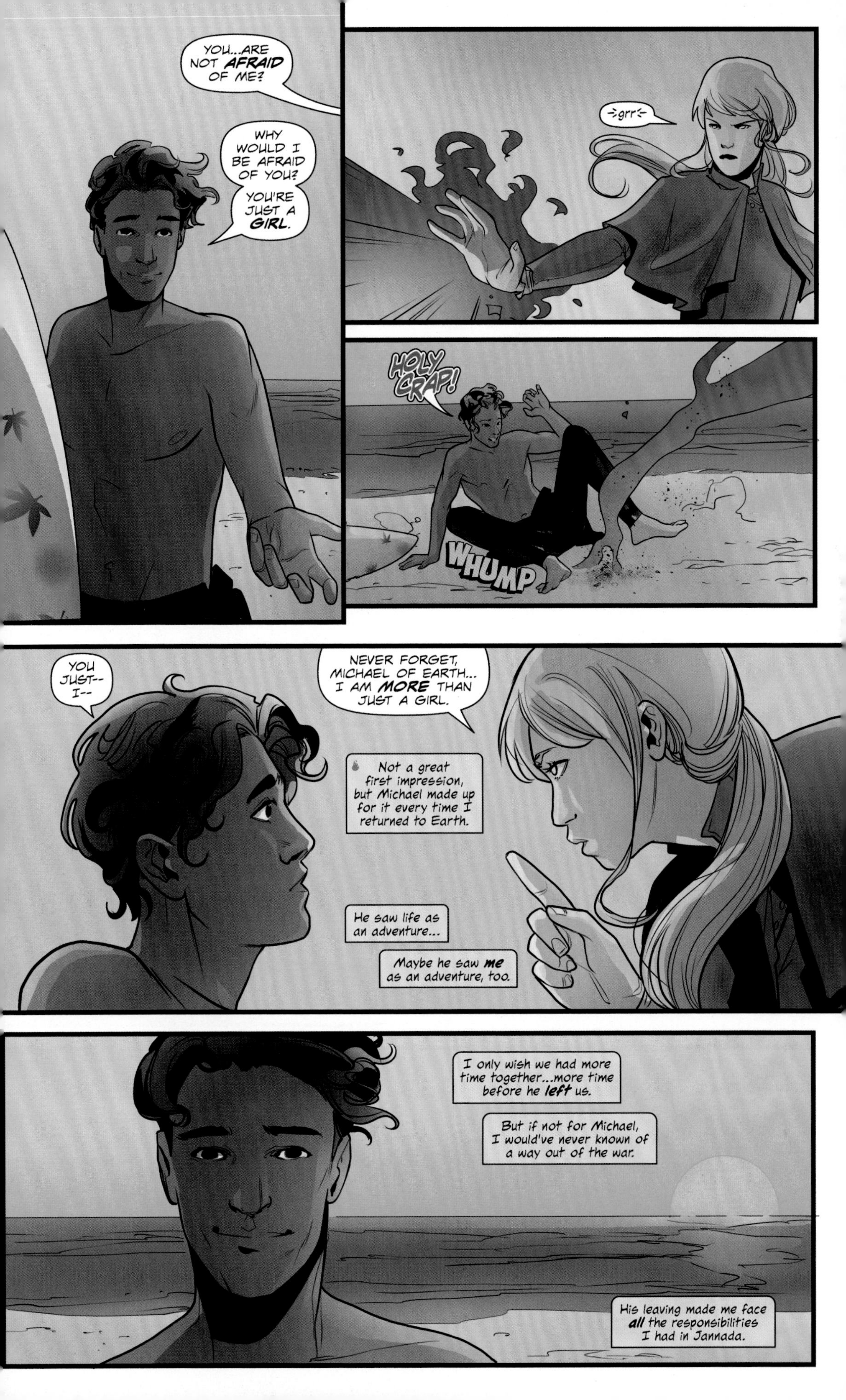

YOU...ARE NOT AFRAID OF ME?
WHY WOULD I BE AFRAID OF YOU?
YOU'RE JUST A GIRL.
-grr-
HOLY CRAP!
WHUMP
YOU JUST-- I--
NEVER FORGET, MICHAEL OF EARTH... I AM MORE THAN JUST A GIRL.
Not a great first impression, but Michael made up for it every time I returned to Earth.
He saw life as an adventure...
Maybe he saw me as an adventure, too.
I only wish we had more time together...more time before he left us.
But if not for Michael, I would've never known of a way out of the war.
His leaving made me face all the responsibilities I had in Jannada.

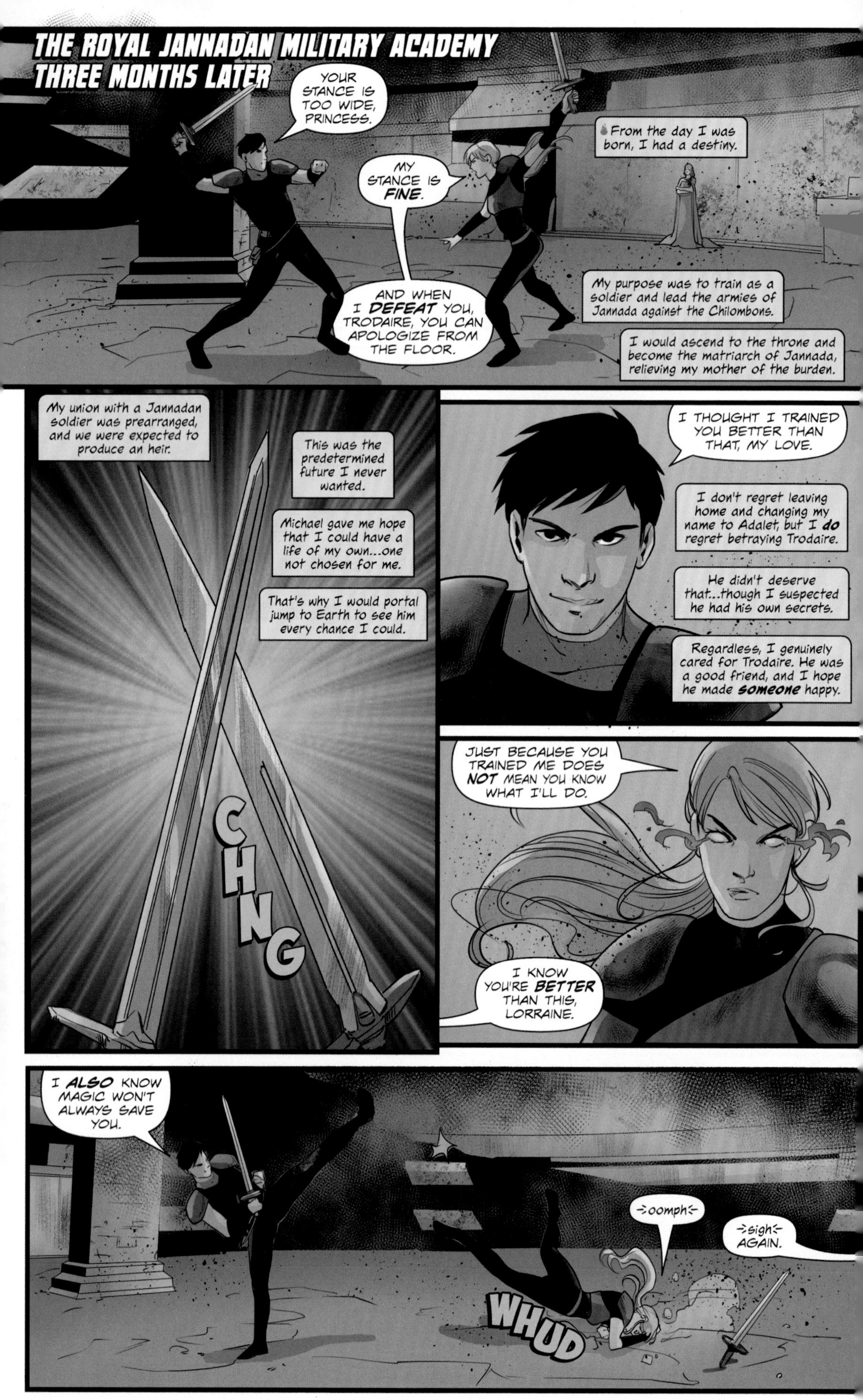

THE ROYAL JANNADAN MILITARY ACADEMY
THREE MONTHS LATER
YOUR STANCE IS TOO WIDE, PRINCESS.
MY STANCE IS FINE.
AND WHEN I DEFEAT YOU, TRODAIRE, YOU CAN APOLOGIZE FROM THE FLOOR.
From the day I was born, I had a destiny.
My purpose was to train as a soldier and lead the armies of Jannada against the Chilombons.
I would ascend to the throne and become the matriarch of Jannada, relieving my mother of the burden.
My union with a Jannadan soldier was prearranged, and we were expected to produce an heir.
This was the predetermined future I never wanted.
Michael gave me hope that I could have a life of my own...one not chosen for me.
That's why I would portal jump to Earth to see him every chance I could.
CHNG
I THOUGHT I TRAINED YOU BETTER THAN THAT, MY LOVE.
I don't regret leaving home and changing my name to Adalet, but I do regret betraying Trodaire.
He didn't deserve that...though I suspected he had his own secrets.
Regardless, I genuinely cared for Trodaire. He was a good friend, and I hope he made someone happy.
JUST BECAUSE YOU TRAINED ME DOES NOT MEAN YOU KNOW WHAT I'LL DO.
I KNOW YOU'RE BETTER THAN THIS, LORRAINE.
I ALSO KNOW MAGIC WON'T ALWAYS SAVE YOU.
oomph
sigh AGAIN.
WHUD

AND MUST I REMIND YOU, TRODAIRE, THAT MY DAUGHTER'S MAGIC **IS** HER GREATEST STRENGTH?

BEING A **KHAMIL**,* I DO NOT EXPECT YOU TO UNDERSTAND.

*A Jannadan who never had magic, even as a child. -- Ed.

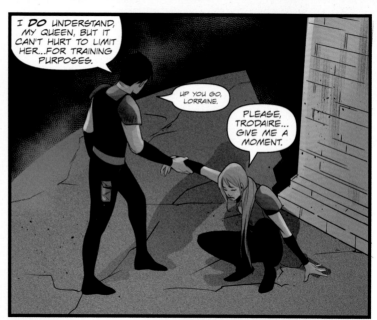

I **DO** UNDERSTAND, MY QUEEN, BUT IT CAN'T HURT TO LIMIT HER...FOR TRAINING PURPOSES.

UP YOU GO, LORRAINE.

PLEASE, TRODAIRE... GIVE ME A MOMENT.

PERHAPS MY BRIDE COULD HAVE TIME TO REST, YOUR HIGHNESS?

DO YOU THINK THE **ENEMY** WILL BE SO KIND?

BESIDES, IT IS THE **PRINCESS** WHO SHOULD BE TRAINING **YOU**, NOT THE OTHER WAY AROUND.

BUT PERHAPS TRODAIRE IS CORRECT, DAUGHTER...YOU **HAVE** RELIED TOO HEAVILY ON YOUR ABILITIES AND NOT ENOUGH ON **INSTINCT**.

MOTHER, PLEASE...

IF YOU CANNOT RECOVER QUICKLY ON THE BATTLEFIELD, YOU WILL BE **SLAUGHTERED**.

MY QUEEN--

THIS IS A LESSON YOU **MUST** LEARN, LORRAINE.

NO!

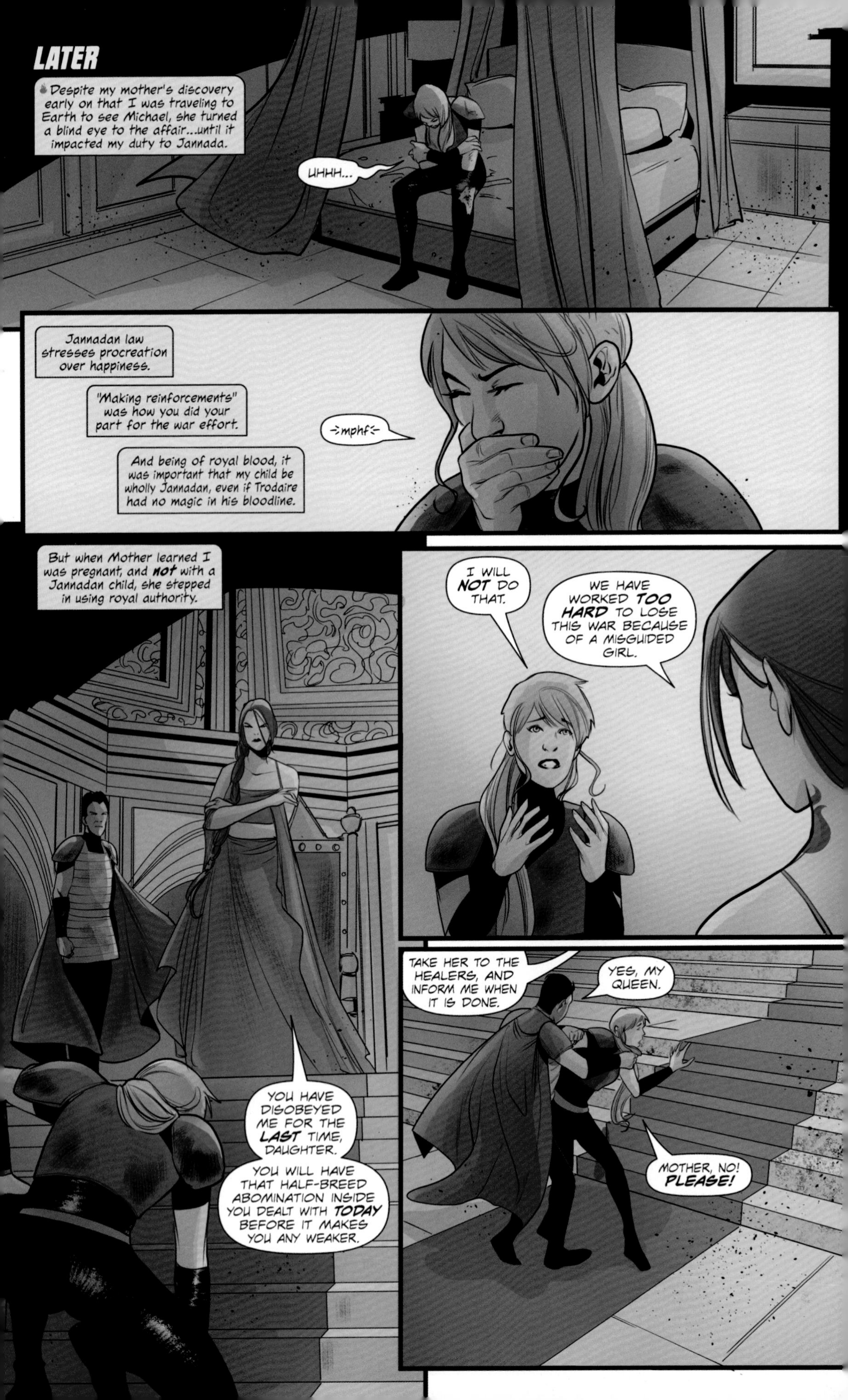
LATER
Despite my mother's discovery early on that I was traveling to Earth to see Michael, she turned a blind eye to the affair...until it impacted my duty to Jannada.
UHHH...
Jannadan law stresses procreation over happiness.
"Making reinforcements" was how you did your part for the war effort.
And being of royal blood, it was important that my child be wholly Jannadan, even if Trodaire had no magic in his bloodline.
mphf
But when Mother learned I was pregnant, and not with a Jannadan child, she stepped in using royal authority.
YOU HAVE DISOBEYED ME FOR THE LAST TIME, DAUGHTER.
YOU WILL HAVE THAT HALF-BREED ABOMINATION INSIDE YOU DEALT WITH TODAY BEFORE IT MAKES YOU ANY WEAKER.
I WILL NOT DO THAT.
WE HAVE WORKED TOO HARD TO LOSE THIS WAR BECAUSE OF A MISGUIDED GIRL.
TAKE HER TO THE HEALERS, AND INFORM ME WHEN IT IS DONE.
YES, MY QUEEN.
MOTHER, NO! PLEASE!

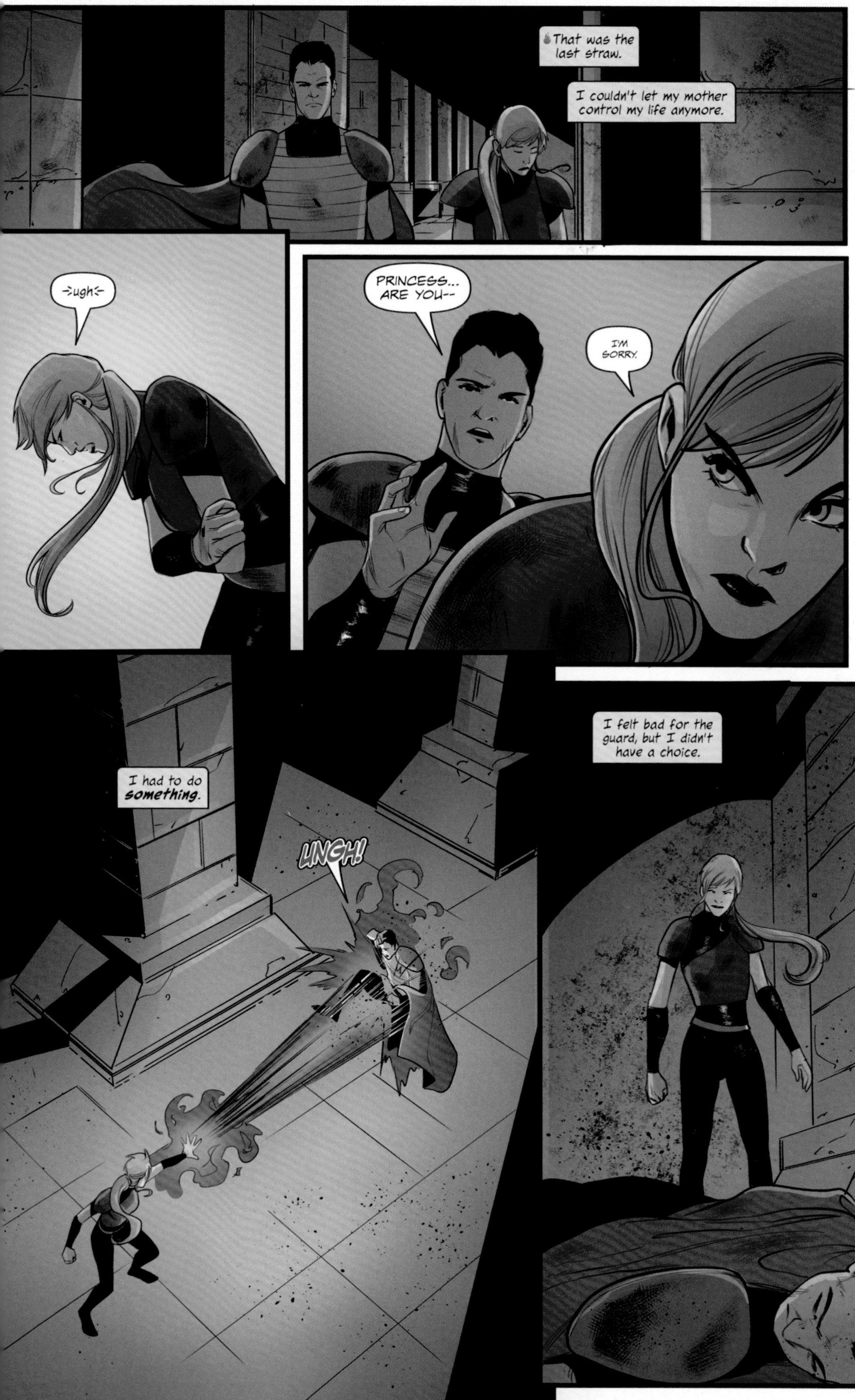
That was the last straw.
I couldn't let my mother control my life anymore.
ugh
PRINCESS... ARE YOU--
I'M SORRY.
I had to do something.
UNGH!
I felt bad for the guard, but I didn't have a choice.

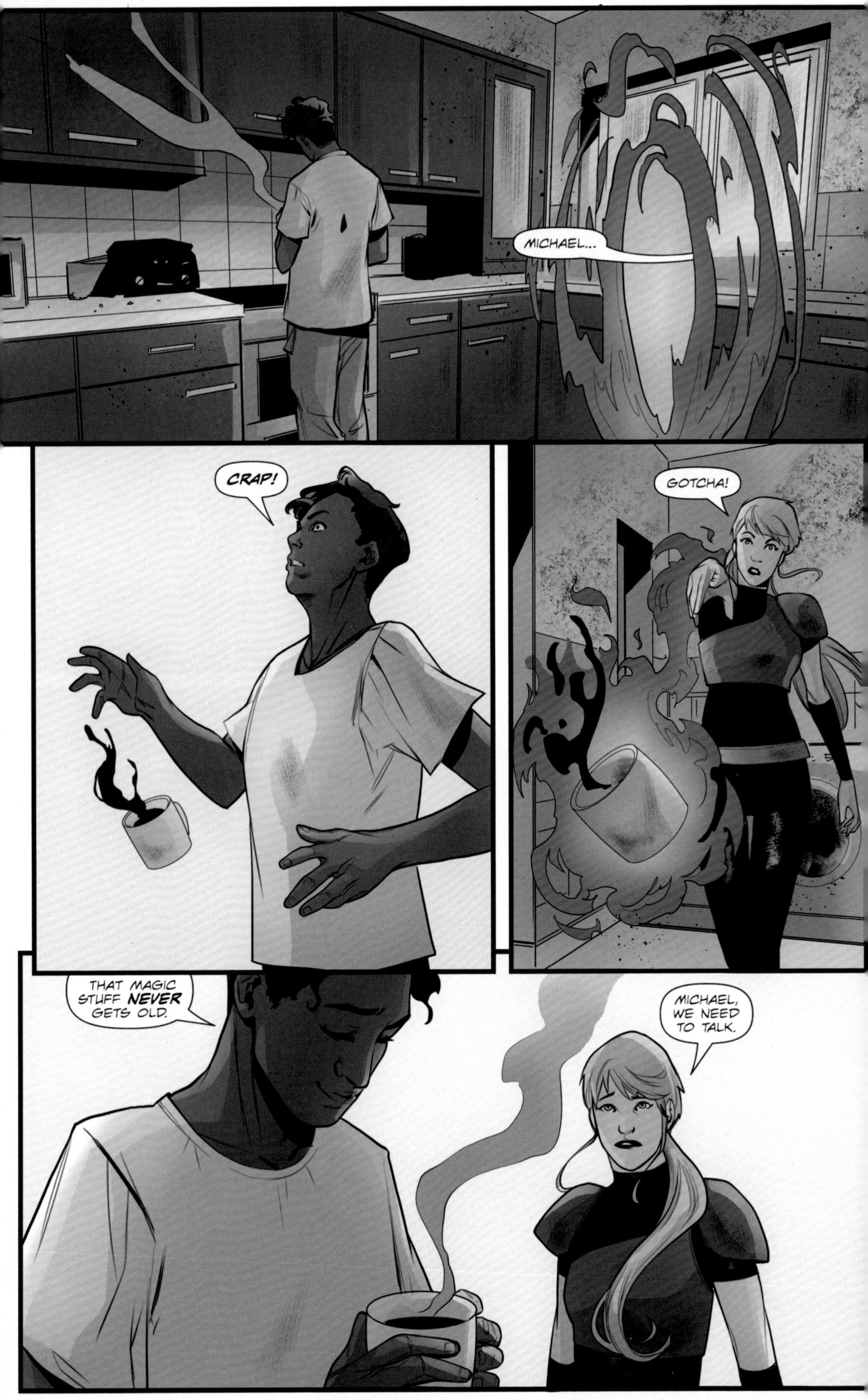
MICHAEL...
CRAP!
GOTCHA!
THAT MAGIC STUFF **NEVER** GETS OLD.
MICHAEL, WE NEED TO TALK.

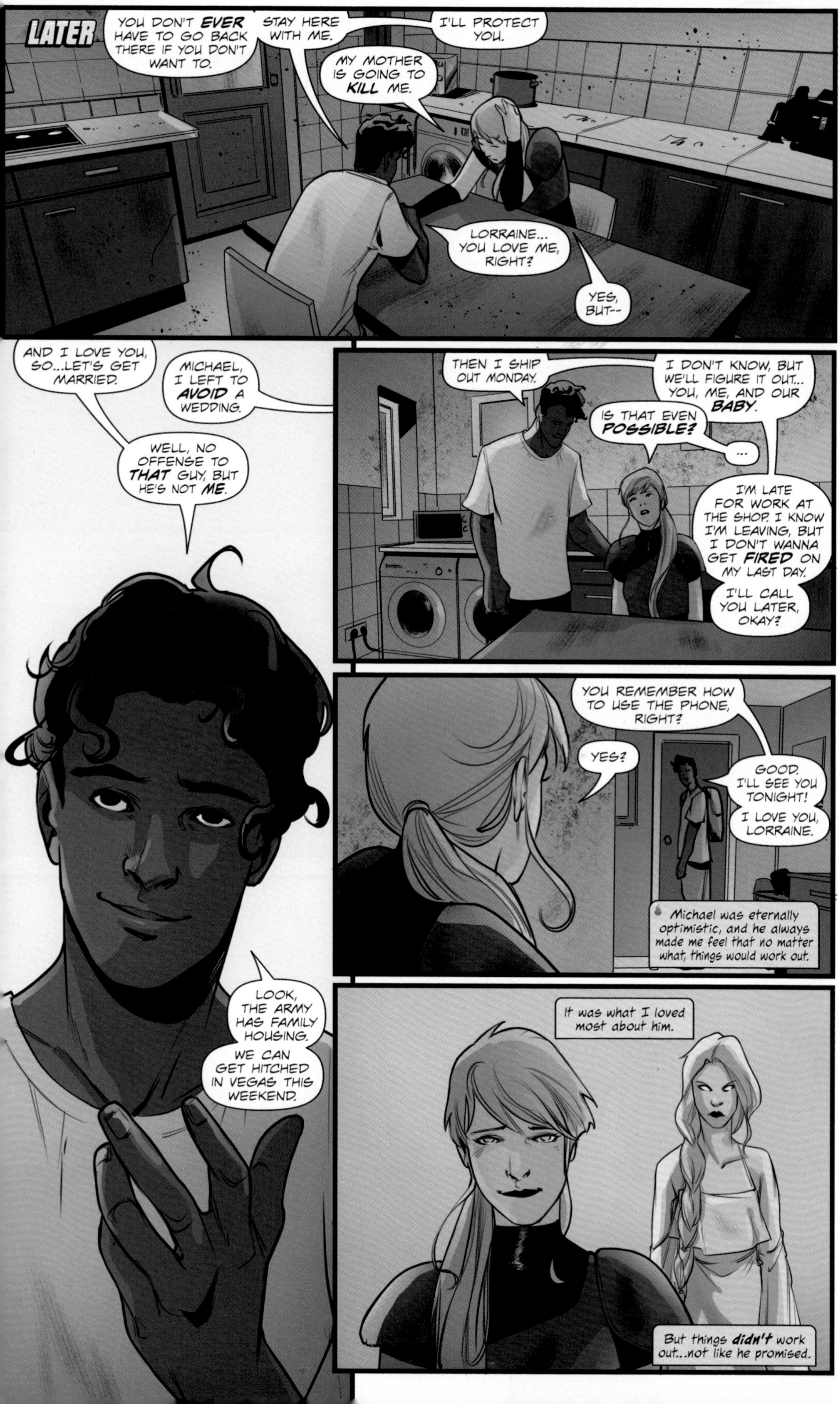
LATER
YOU DON'T EVER HAVE TO GO BACK THERE IF YOU DON'T WANT TO.
STAY HERE WITH ME.
I'LL PROTECT YOU.
MY MOTHER IS GOING TO KILL ME.
LORRAINE... YOU LOVE ME, RIGHT?
YES, BUT--
AND I LOVE YOU, SO...LET'S GET MARRIED.
MICHAEL, I LEFT TO AVOID A WEDDING.
WELL, NO OFFENSE TO THAT GUY, BUT HE'S NOT ME.
LOOK, THE ARMY HAS FAMILY HOUSING.
WE CAN GET HITCHED IN VEGAS THIS WEEKEND.
THEN I SHIP OUT MONDAY.
I DON'T KNOW, BUT WE'LL FIGURE IT OUT... YOU, ME, AND OUR BABY.
IS THAT EVEN POSSIBLE?
...
I'M LATE FOR WORK AT THE SHOP. I KNOW I'M LEAVING, BUT I DON'T WANNA GET FIRED ON MY LAST DAY.
I'LL CALL YOU LATER, OKAY?
YOU REMEMBER HOW TO USE THE PHONE, RIGHT?
YES?
GOOD. I'LL SEE YOU TONIGHT!
I LOVE YOU, LORRAINE.
Michael was eternally optimistic, and he always made me feel that no matter what, things would work out.
It was what I loved most about him.
But things didn't work out...not like he promised.

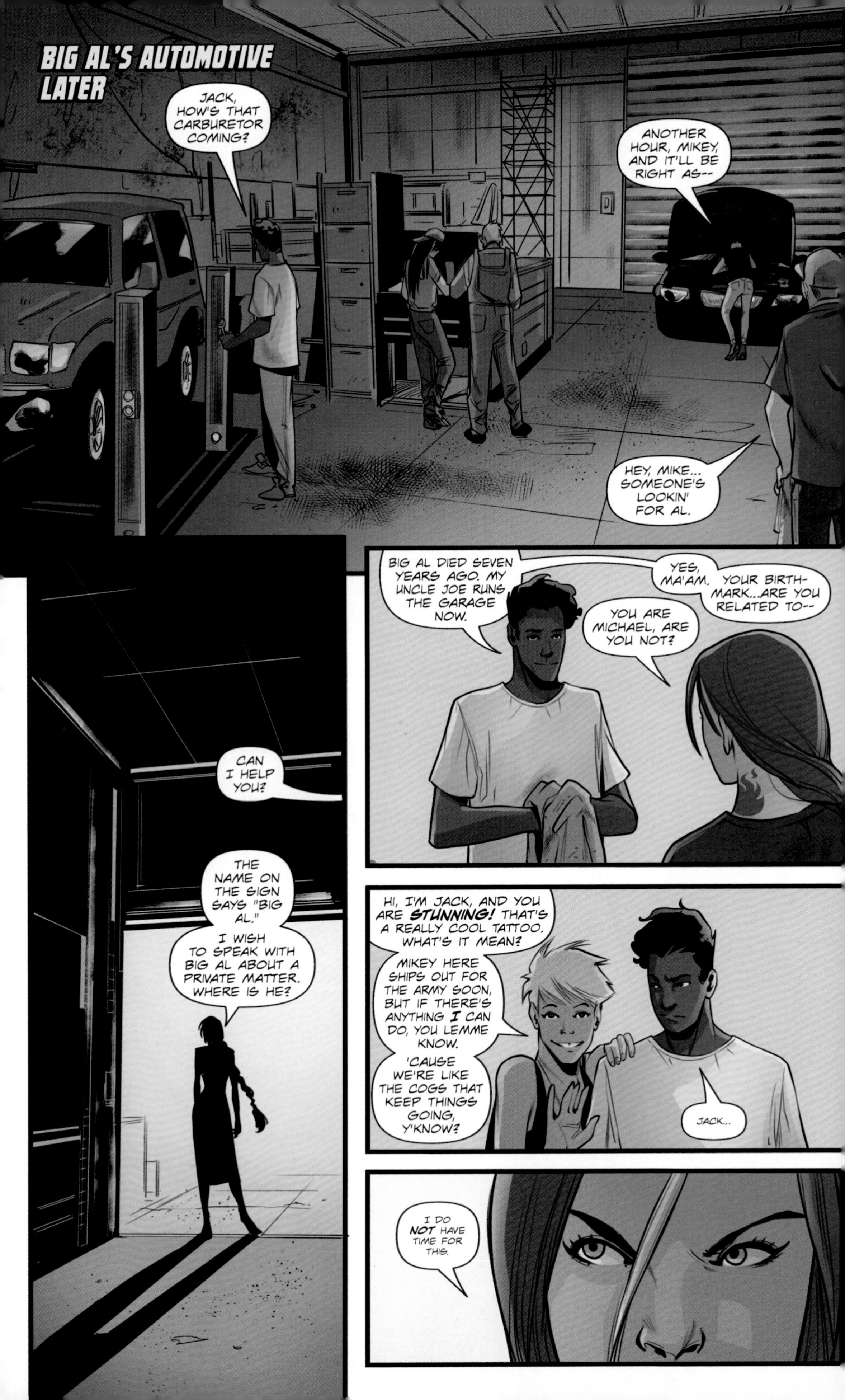
BIG AL'S AUTOMOTIVE
LATER
JACK, HOW'S THAT CARBURETOR COMING?
ANOTHER HOUR, MIKEY, AND IT'LL BE RIGHT AS--
HEY, MIKE... SOMEONE'S LOOKIN' FOR AL.
CAN I HELP YOU?
THE NAME ON THE SIGN SAYS "BIG AL."
I WISH TO SPEAK WITH BIG AL ABOUT A PRIVATE MATTER. WHERE IS HE?
BIG AL DIED SEVEN YEARS AGO. MY UNCLE JOE RUNS THE GARAGE NOW.
YOU ARE MICHAEL, ARE YOU NOT?
YES, MA'AM.
YOUR BIRTH-MARK...ARE YOU RELATED TO--
HI, I'M JACK, AND YOU ARE STUNNING! THAT'S A REALLY COOL TATTOO. WHAT'S IT MEAN?
MIKEY HERE SHIPS OUT FOR THE ARMY SOON, BUT IF THERE'S ANYTHING I CAN DO, YOU LEMME KNOW.
'CAUSE WE'RE LIKE THE COGS THAT KEEP THINGS GOING, Y'KNOW?
JACK...
I DO NOT HAVE TIME FOR THIS.

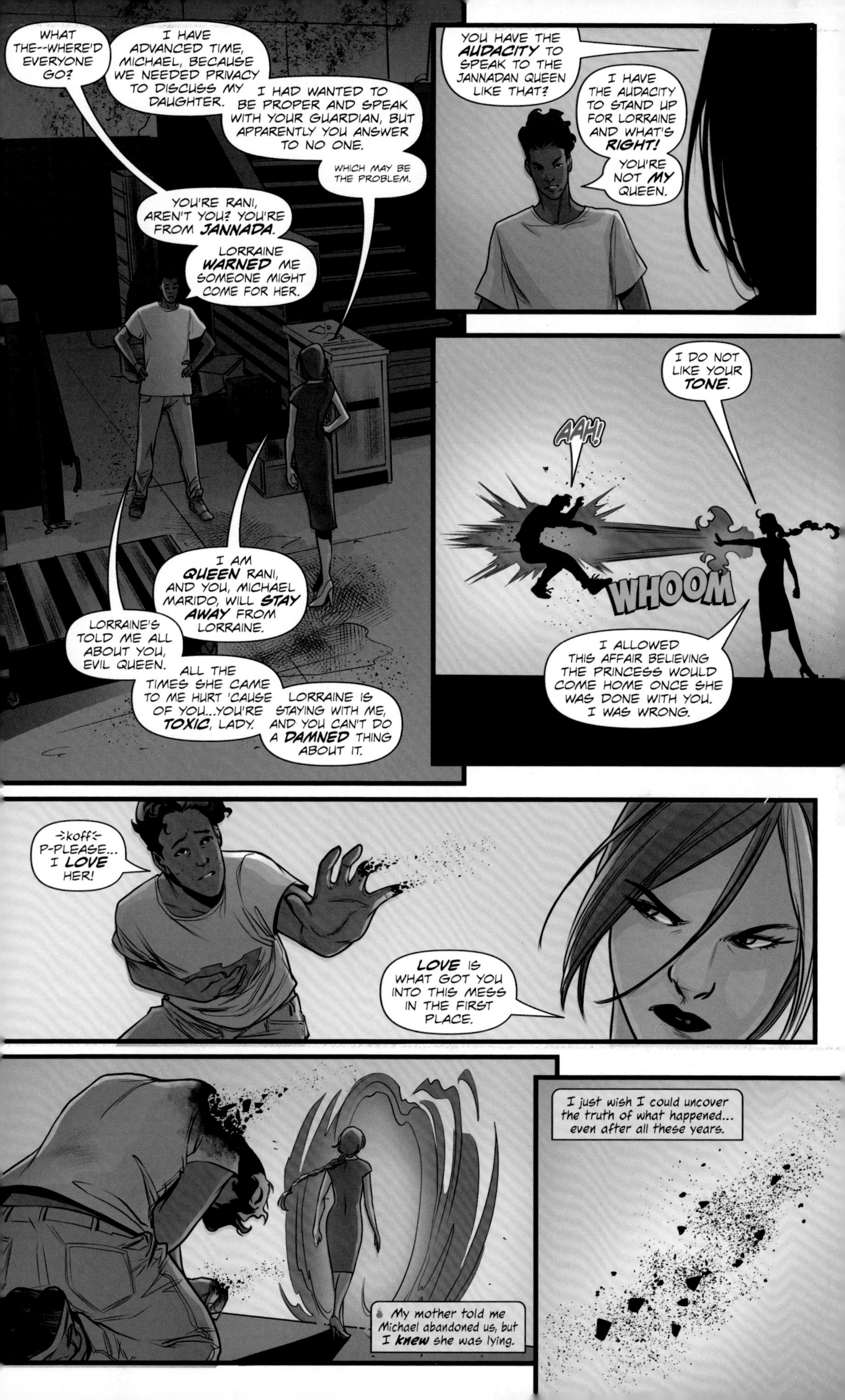
WHAT THE--WHERE'D EVERYONE GO?
I HAVE ADVANCED TIME, MICHAEL, BECAUSE WE NEEDED PRIVACY TO DISCUSS MY DAUGHTER.
I HAD WANTED TO BE PROPER AND SPEAK WITH YOUR GUARDIAN, BUT APPARENTLY YOU ANSWER TO NO ONE.
WHICH MAY BE THE PROBLEM.
YOU'RE RANI, AREN'T YOU? YOU'RE FROM JANNADA.
LORRAINE WARNED ME SOMEONE MIGHT COME FOR HER.
I AM QUEEN RANI, AND YOU, MICHAEL MARIDO, WILL STAY AWAY FROM LORRAINE.
LORRAINE'S TOLD ME ALL ABOUT YOU, EVIL QUEEN.
ALL THE TIMES SHE CAME TO ME HURT 'CAUSE OF YOU...YOU'RE TOXIC, LADY.
LORRAINE IS STAYING WITH ME, AND YOU CAN'T DO A DAMNED THING ABOUT IT.
YOU HAVE THE AUDACITY TO SPEAK TO THE JANNADAN QUEEN LIKE THAT?
I HAVE THE AUDACITY TO STAND UP FOR LORRAINE AND WHAT'S RIGHT!
YOU'RE NOT MY QUEEN.
I DO NOT LIKE YOUR TONE.
AAH!
WHOOM
I ALLOWED THIS AFFAIR BELIEVING THE PRINCESS WOULD COME HOME ONCE SHE WAS DONE WITH YOU. I WAS WRONG.
koff P-PLEASE... I LOVE HER!
LOVE IS WHAT GOT YOU INTO THIS MESS IN THE FIRST PLACE.
My mother told me Michael abandoned us, but I knew she was lying.
I just wish I could uncover the truth of what happened... even after all these years.

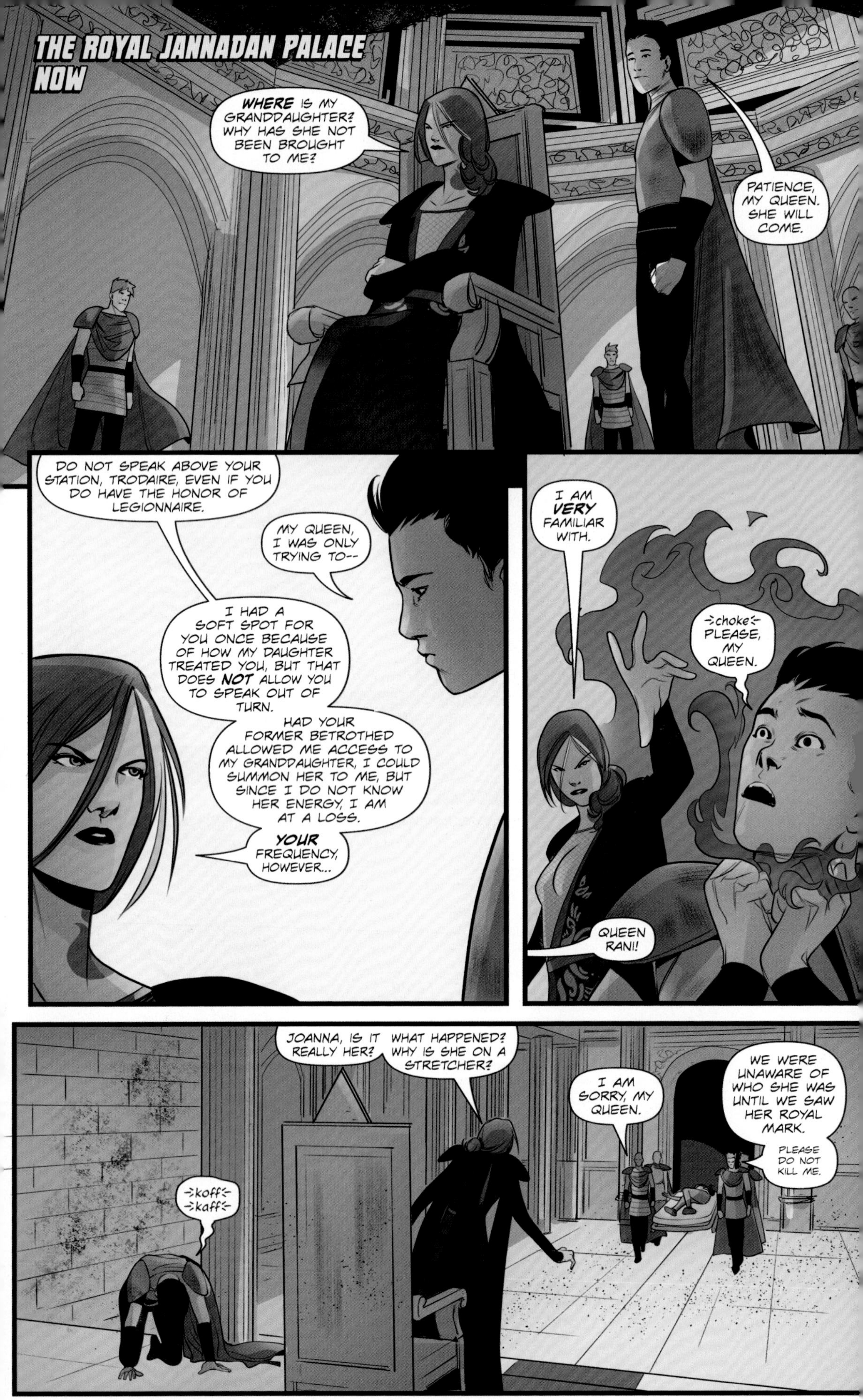
THE ROYAL JANNADAN PALACE
NOW
WHERE IS MY GRANDDAUGHTER? WHY HAS SHE NOT BEEN BROUGHT TO ME?
PATIENCE, MY QUEEN. SHE WILL COME.
DO NOT SPEAK ABOVE YOUR STATION, TRODAIRE, EVEN IF YOU DO HAVE THE HONOR OF LEGIONNAIRE.
MY QUEEN, I WAS ONLY TRYING TO--
I HAD A SOFT SPOT FOR YOU ONCE BECAUSE OF HOW MY DAUGHTER TREATED YOU, BUT THAT DOES NOT ALLOW YOU TO SPEAK OUT OF TURN.
HAD YOUR FORMER BETROTHED ALLOWED ME ACCESS TO MY GRANDDAUGHTER, I COULD SUMMON HER TO ME, BUT SINCE I DO NOT KNOW HER ENERGY, I AM AT A LOSS.
YOUR FREQUENCY, HOWEVER...
I AM VERY FAMILIAR WITH.
choke PLEASE, MY QUEEN.
QUEEN RANI!
JOANNA, IS IT REALLY HER?
WHAT HAPPENED? WHY IS SHE ON A STRETCHER?
koff kaff
I AM SORRY, MY QUEEN.
WE WERE UNAWARE OF WHO SHE WAS UNTIL WE SAW HER ROYAL MARK.
PLEASE DO NOT KILL ME.

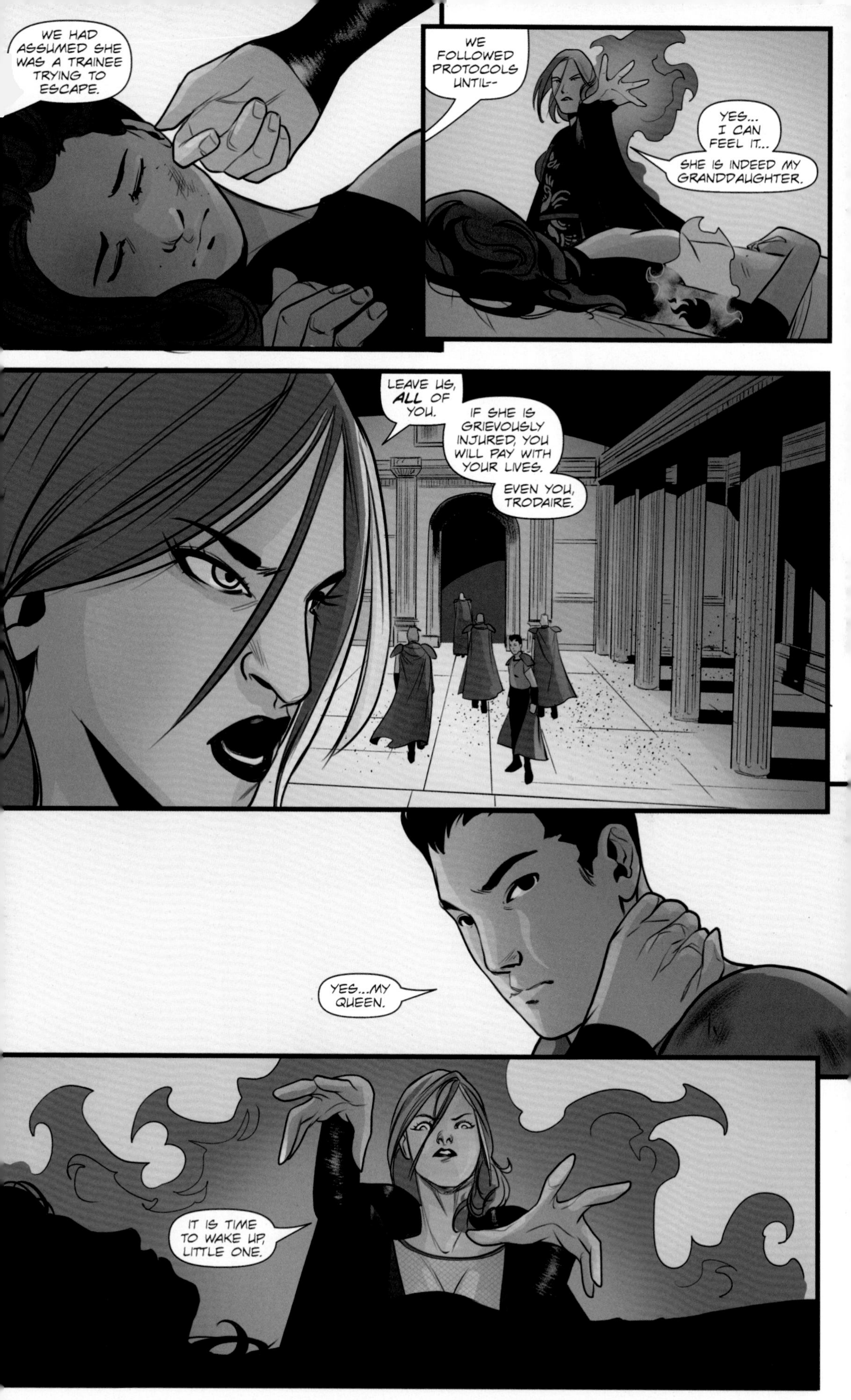
WE HAD ASSUMED SHE WAS A TRAINEE TRYING TO ESCAPE.
WE FOLLOWED PROTOCOLS UNTIL-
YES... I CAN FEEL IT...
SHE IS INDEED MY GRANDDAUGHTER.
LEAVE US, ALL OF YOU.
IF SHE IS GRIEVOUSLY INJURED, YOU WILL PAY WITH YOUR LIVES.
EVEN YOU, TRODAIRE.
YES...MY QUEEN.
IT IS TIME TO WAKE UP, LITTLE ONE.

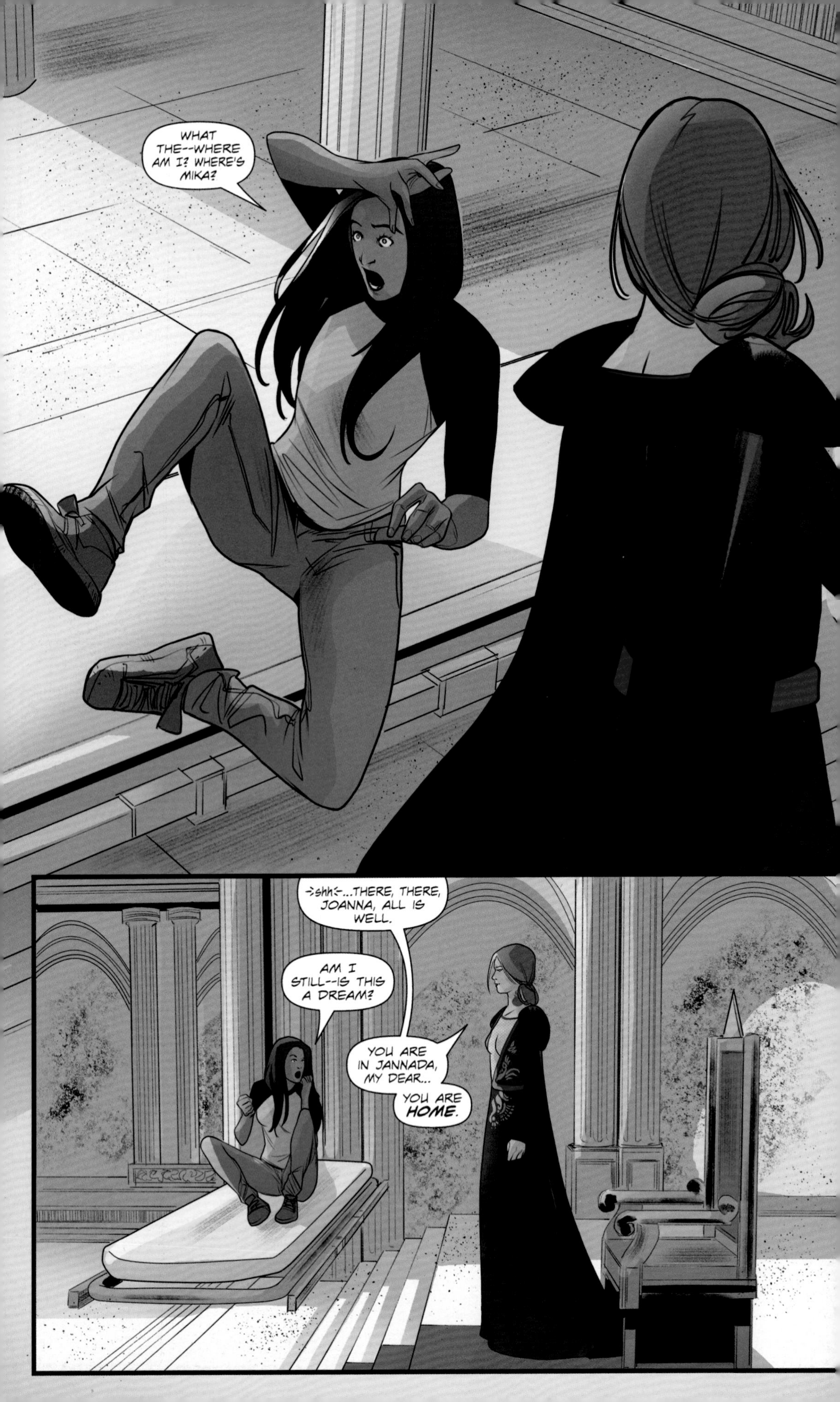
WHAT THE--WHERE AM I? WHERE'S MIKA?
-shh-...THERE, THERE, JOANNA, ALL IS WELL.
AM I STILL--IS THIS A DREAM?
YOU ARE IN JANNADA, MY DEAR...
YOU ARE *HOME*.

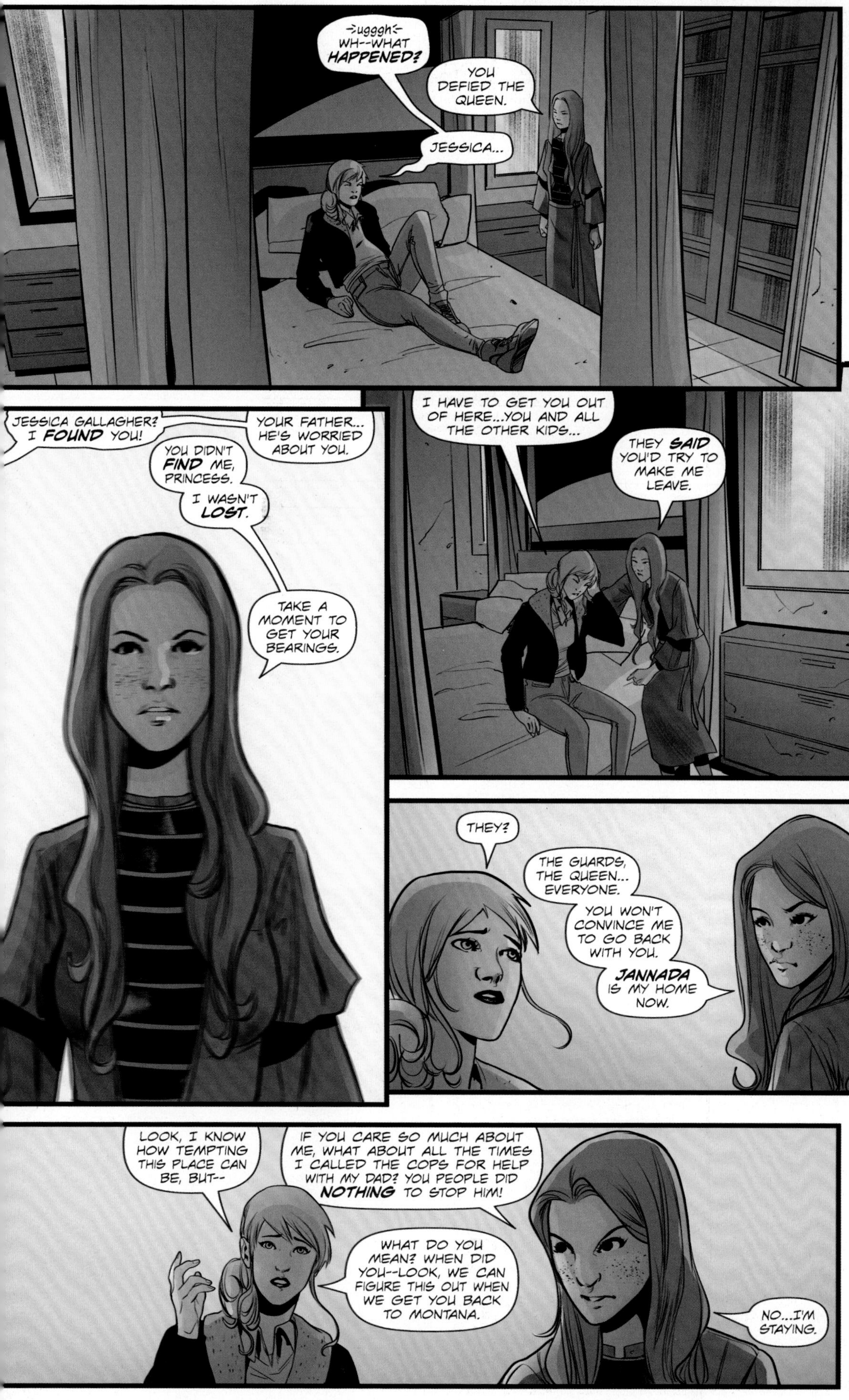

-uggggh-
WH--WHAT HAPPENED?
YOU DEFIED THE QUEEN.
JESSICA...
JESSICA GALLAGHER? I FOUND YOU!
YOUR FATHER... HE'S WORRIED ABOUT YOU.
YOU DIDN'T FIND ME, PRINCESS.
I WASN'T LOST.
TAKE A MOMENT TO GET YOUR BEARINGS.
I HAVE TO GET YOU OUT OF HERE...YOU AND ALL THE OTHER KIDS...
THEY SAID YOU'D TRY TO MAKE ME LEAVE.
THEY?
THE GUARDS, THE QUEEN... EVERYONE.
YOU WON'T CONVINCE ME TO GO BACK WITH YOU.
JANNADA IS MY HOME NOW.
LOOK, I KNOW HOW TEMPTING THIS PLACE CAN BE, BUT--
IF YOU CARE SO MUCH ABOUT ME, WHAT ABOUT ALL THE TIMES I CALLED THE COPS FOR HELP WITH MY DAD? YOU PEOPLE DID NOTHING TO STOP HIM!
WHAT DO YOU MEAN? WHEN DID YOU--LOOK, WE CAN FIGURE THIS OUT WHEN WE GET YOU BACK TO MONTANA.
NO...I'M STAYING.

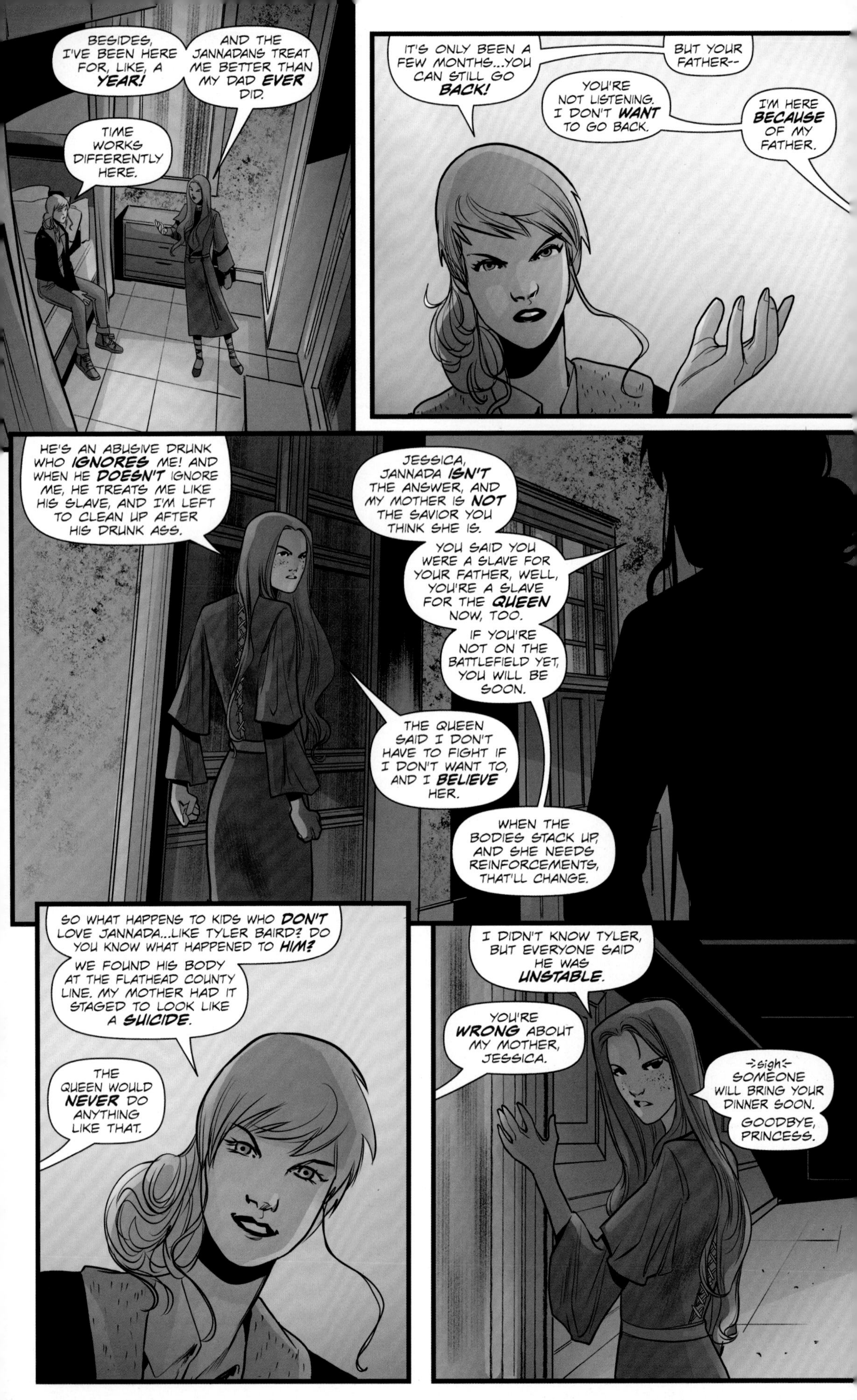
BESIDES, I'VE BEEN HERE FOR, LIKE, A YEAR!
AND THE JANNADANS TREAT ME BETTER THAN MY DAD EVER DID.
TIME WORKS DIFFERENTLY HERE.
IT'S ONLY BEEN A FEW MONTHS...YOU CAN STILL GO BACK!
BUT YOUR FATHER--
YOU'RE NOT LISTENING. I DON'T WANT TO GO BACK.
I'M HERE BECAUSE OF MY FATHER.
HE'S AN ABUSIVE DRUNK WHO IGNORES ME! AND WHEN HE DOESN'T IGNORE ME, HE TREATS ME LIKE HIS SLAVE, AND I'M LEFT TO CLEAN UP AFTER HIS DRUNK ASS.
JESSICA, JANNADA ISN'T THE ANSWER, AND MY MOTHER IS NOT THE SAVIOR YOU THINK SHE IS.
YOU SAID YOU WERE A SLAVE FOR YOUR FATHER, WELL, YOU'RE A SLAVE FOR THE QUEEN NOW, TOO.
IF YOU'RE NOT ON THE BATTLEFIELD YET, YOU WILL BE SOON.
THE QUEEN SAID I DON'T HAVE TO FIGHT IF I DON'T WANT TO, AND I BELIEVE HER.
WHEN THE BODIES STACK UP, AND SHE NEEDS REINFORCEMENTS, THAT'LL CHANGE.
SO WHAT HAPPENS TO KIDS WHO DON'T LOVE JANNADA...LIKE TYLER BAIRD? DO YOU KNOW WHAT HAPPENED TO HIM?
WE FOUND HIS BODY AT THE FLATHEAD COUNTY LINE. MY MOTHER HAD IT STAGED TO LOOK LIKE A SUICIDE.
THE QUEEN WOULD NEVER DO ANYTHING LIKE THAT.
I DIDN'T KNOW TYLER, BUT EVERYONE SAID HE WAS UNSTABLE.
YOU'RE WRONG ABOUT MY MOTHER, JESSICA.
sigh
SOMEONE WILL BRING YOUR DINNER SOON.
GOODBYE, PRINCESS.

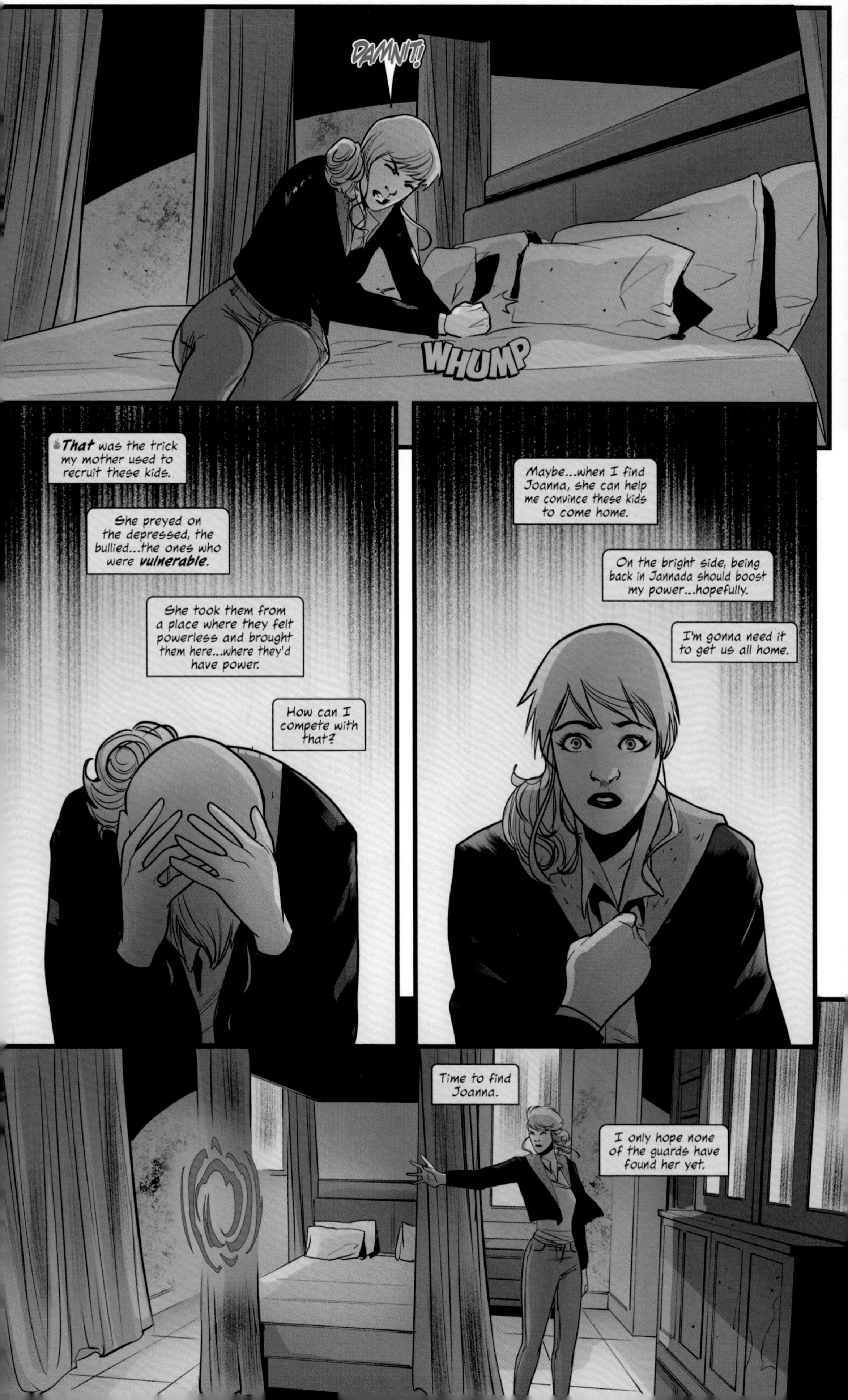
DAMNIT!
WHUMP
That was the trick my mother used to recruit these kids.
She preyed on the depressed, the bullied...the ones who were vulnerable.
She took them from a place where they felt powerless and brought them here...where they'd have power.
How can I compete with that?
Maybe...when I find Joanna, she can help me convince these kids to come home.
On the bright side, being back in Jannada should boost my power...hopefully.
I'm gonna need it to get us all home.
Time to find Joanna.
I only hope none of the guards have found her yet.

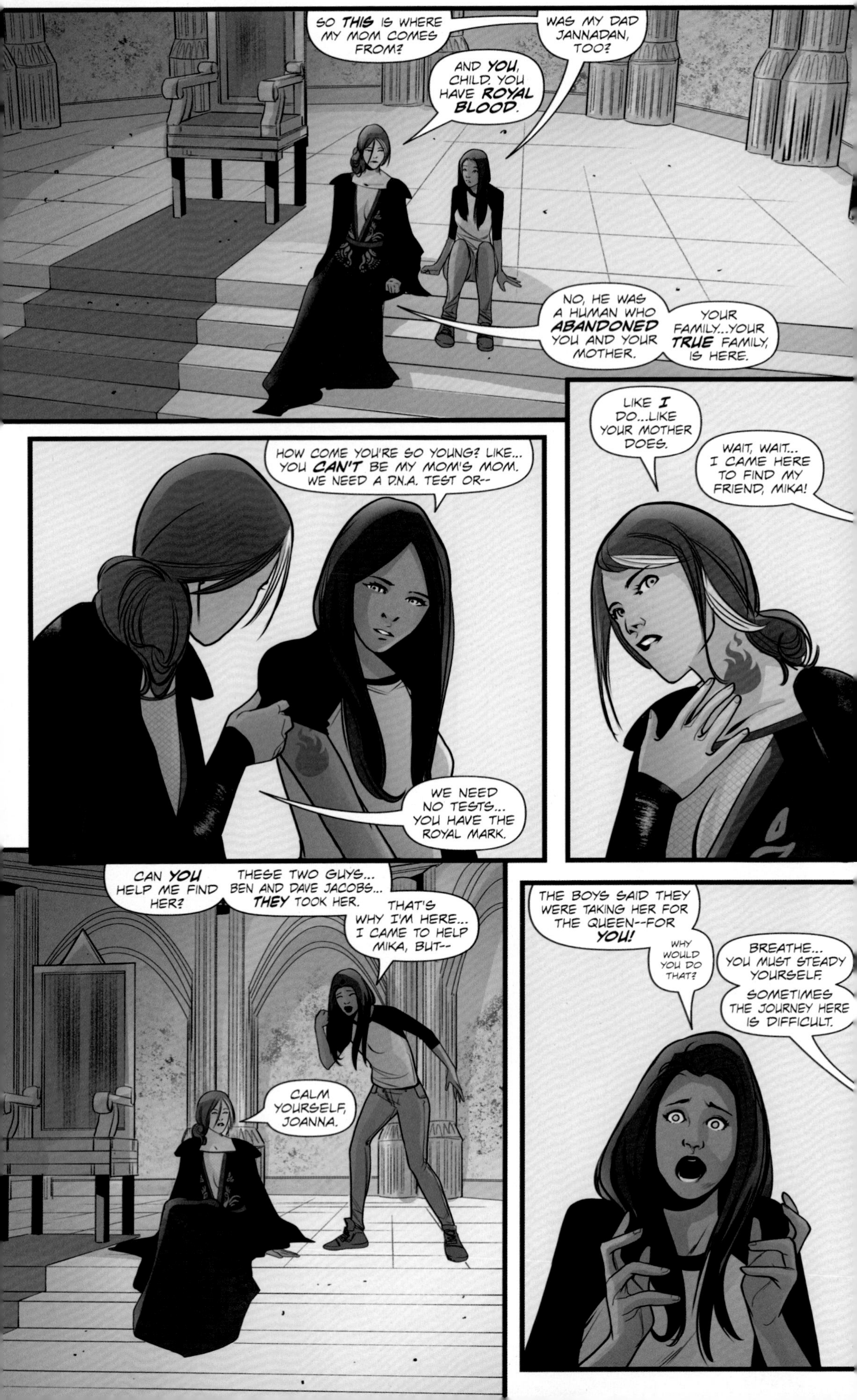
SO **THIS** IS WHERE MY MOM COMES FROM?
WAS MY DAD JANNADAN, TOO?
AND **YOU**, CHILD. YOU HAVE **ROYAL BLOOD**.
NO, HE WAS A HUMAN WHO **ABANDONED** YOU AND YOUR MOTHER.
YOUR FAMILY...YOUR **TRUE** FAMILY, IS HERE.
HOW COME YOU'RE SO YOUNG? LIKE... YOU **CAN'T** BE MY MOM'S MOM. WE NEED A D.N.A. TEST OR--
WE NEED NO TESTS... YOU HAVE THE ROYAL MARK.
LIKE **I** DO...LIKE YOUR MOTHER DOES.
WAIT, WAIT... I CAME HERE TO FIND MY FRIEND, MIKA!
CAN **YOU** HELP ME FIND HER?
THESE TWO GUYS... BEN AND DAVE JACOBS... **THEY** TOOK HER.
THAT'S WHY I'M HERE... I CAME TO HELP MIKA, BUT--
CALM YOURSELF, JOANNA.
THE BOYS SAID THEY WERE TAKING HER FOR THE QUEEN--FOR **YOU!**
WHY WOULD YOU DO THAT?
BREATHE... YOU MUST STEADY YOURSELF.
SOMETIMES THE JOURNEY HERE IS DIFFICULT.

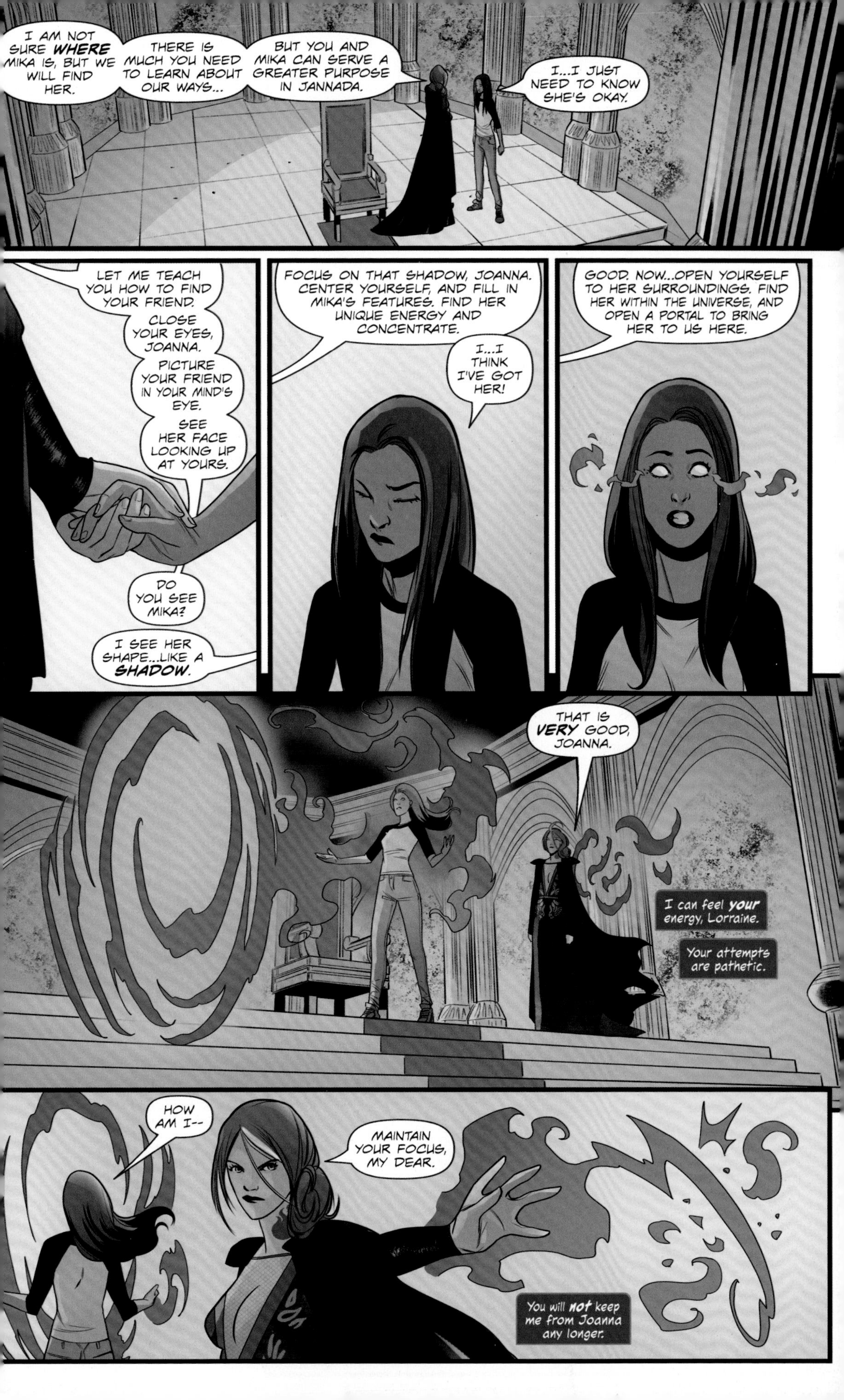

I AM NOT SURE WHERE MIKA IS, BUT WE WILL FIND HER.
THERE IS MUCH YOU NEED TO LEARN ABOUT OUR WAYS...
BUT YOU AND MIKA CAN SERVE A GREATER PURPOSE IN JANNADA.
I...I JUST NEED TO KNOW SHE'S OKAY.
LET ME TEACH YOU HOW TO FIND YOUR FRIEND.
CLOSE YOUR EYES, JOANNA.
PICTURE YOUR FRIEND IN YOUR MIND'S EYE.
SEE HER FACE LOOKING UP AT YOURS.
DO YOU SEE MIKA?
I SEE HER SHAPE...LIKE A SHADOW.
FOCUS ON THAT SHADOW, JOANNA. CENTER YOURSELF, AND FILL IN MIKA'S FEATURES. FIND HER UNIQUE ENERGY AND CONCENTRATE.
I...I THINK I'VE GOT HER!
GOOD. NOW...OPEN YOURSELF TO HER SURROUNDINGS. FIND HER WITHIN THE UNIVERSE, AND OPEN A PORTAL TO BRING HER TO US HERE.
THAT IS VERY GOOD, JOANNA.
I can feel your energy, Lorraine.
Your attempts are pathetic.
HOW AM I--
MAINTAIN YOUR FOCUS, MY DEAR.
You will not keep me from Joanna any longer.

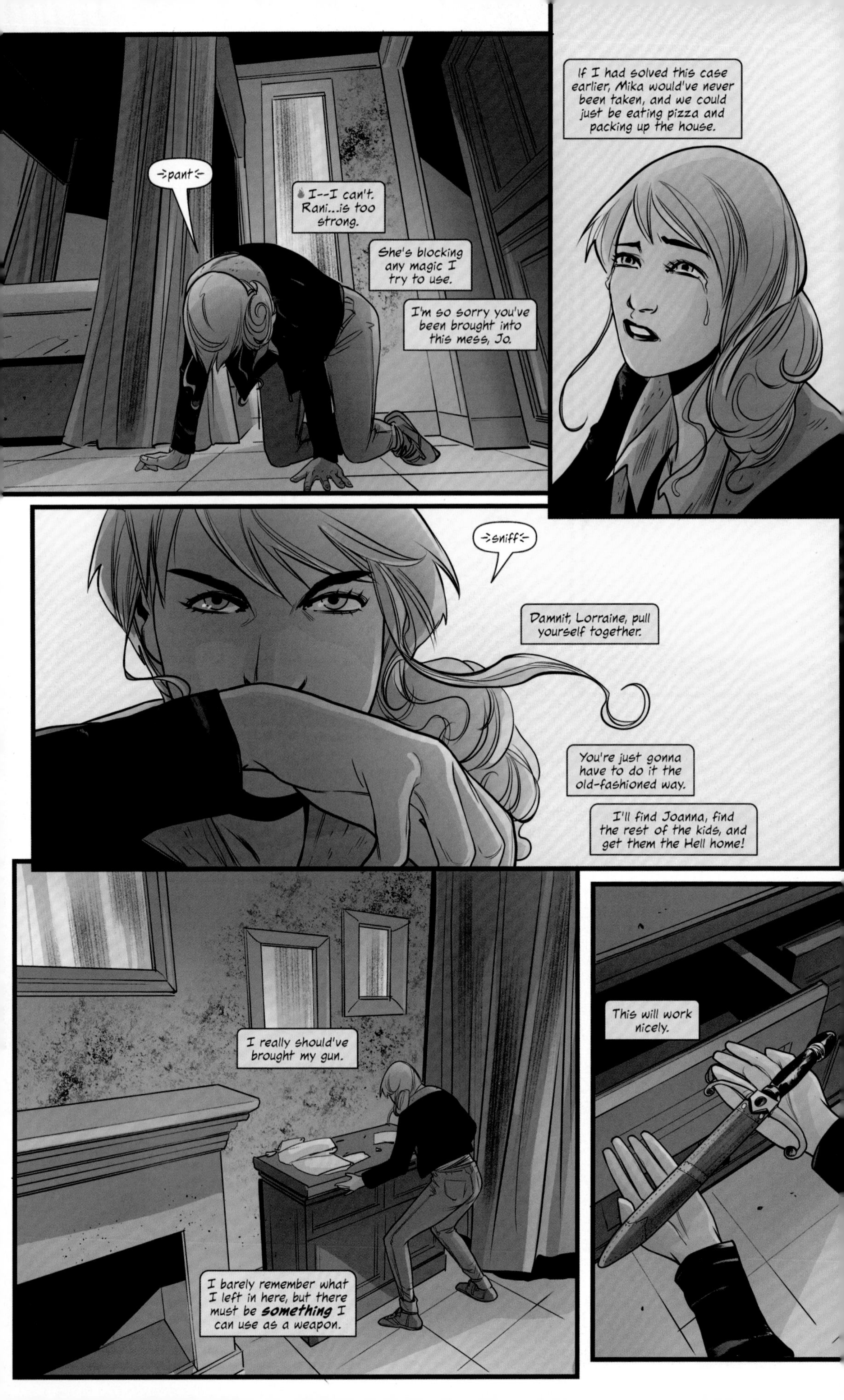

pant
I--I can't. Rani...is too strong.
She's blocking any magic I try to use.
I'm so sorry you've been brought into this mess, Jo.
If I had solved this case earlier, Mika would've never been taken, and we could just be eating pizza and packing up the house.
sniff
Damnit, Lorraine, pull yourself together.
You're just gonna have to do it the old-fashioned way.
I'll find Joanna, find the rest of the kids, and get them the Hell home!
I really should've brought my gun.
I barely remember what I left in here, but there must be **something** I can use as a weapon.
This will work nicely.

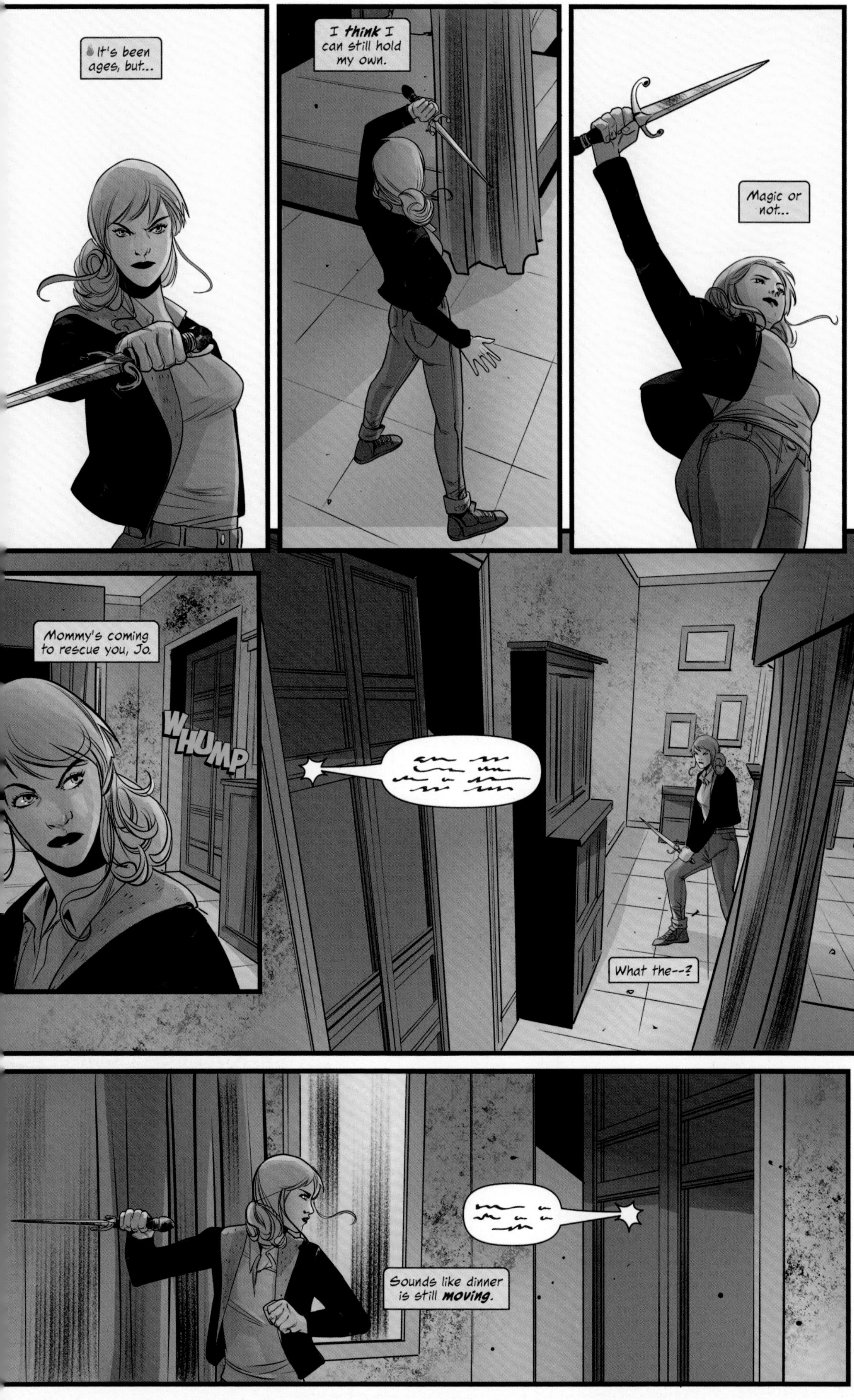
It's been ages, but...
I *think* I can still hold my own.
Magic or not...
Mommy's coming to rescue you, Jo.
WHUMP
What the--?
Sounds like dinner is still *moving*.

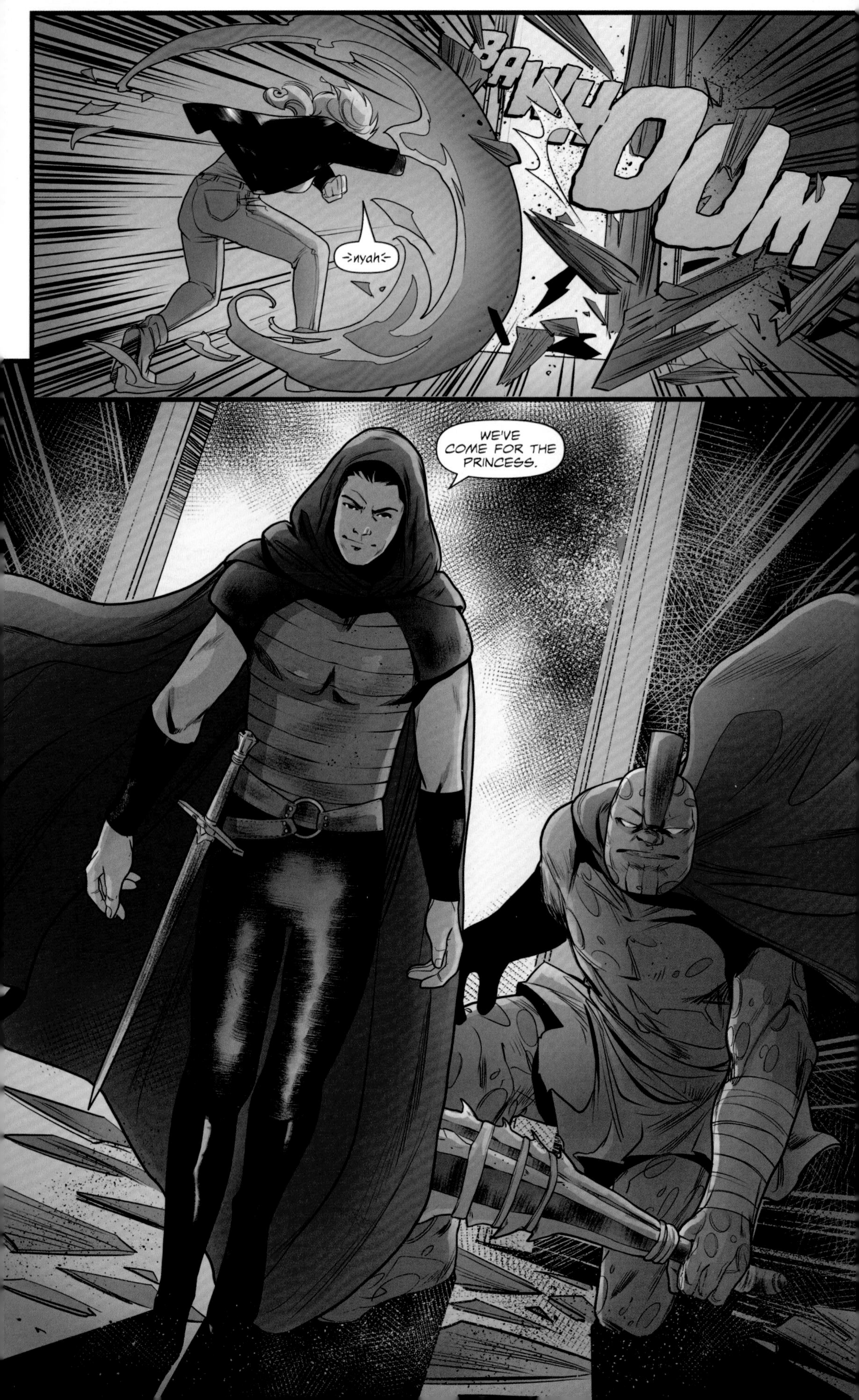
BAWHOOM
-nyah-
WE'VE COME FOR THE PRINCESS.

FOUR

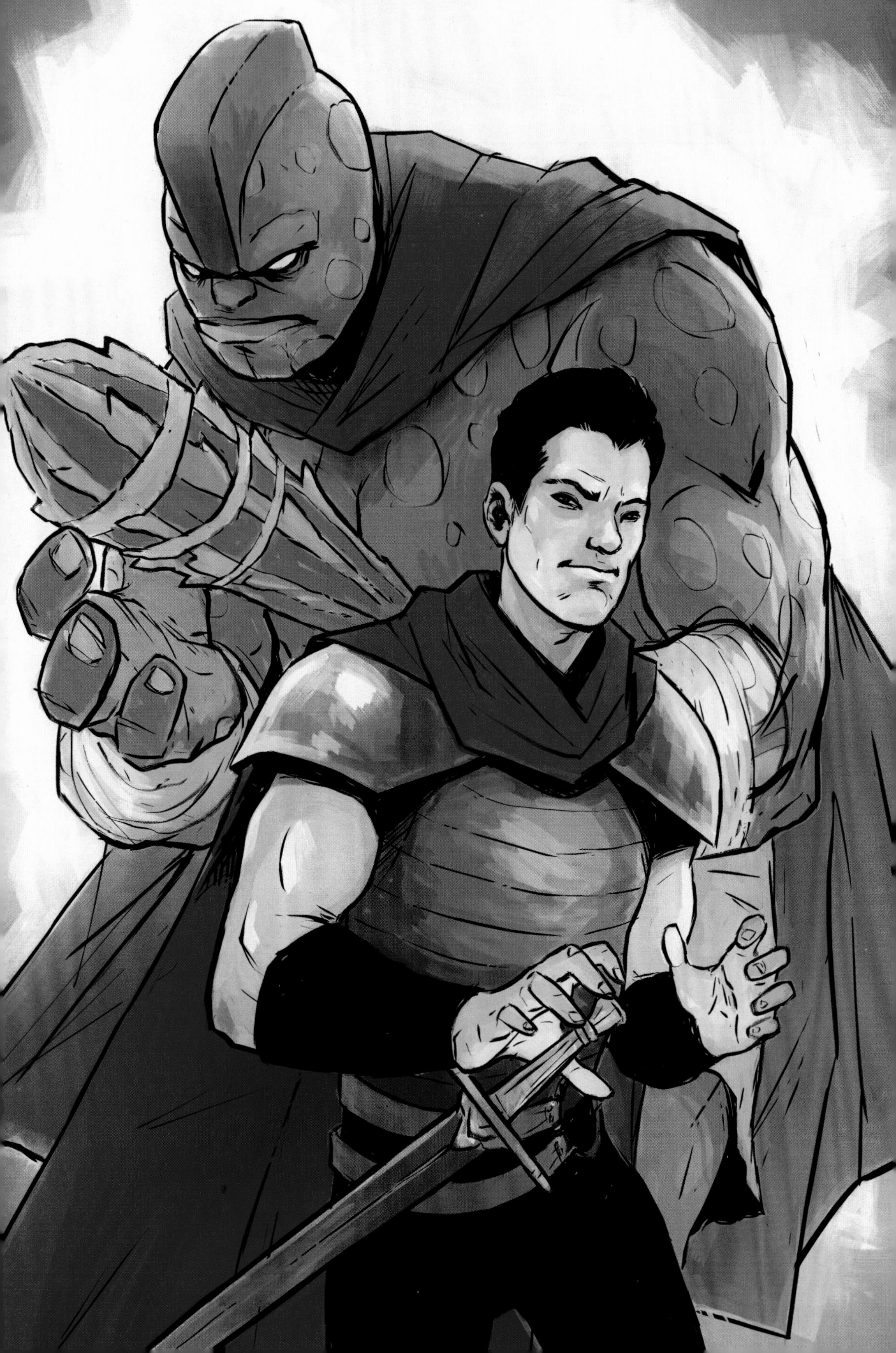

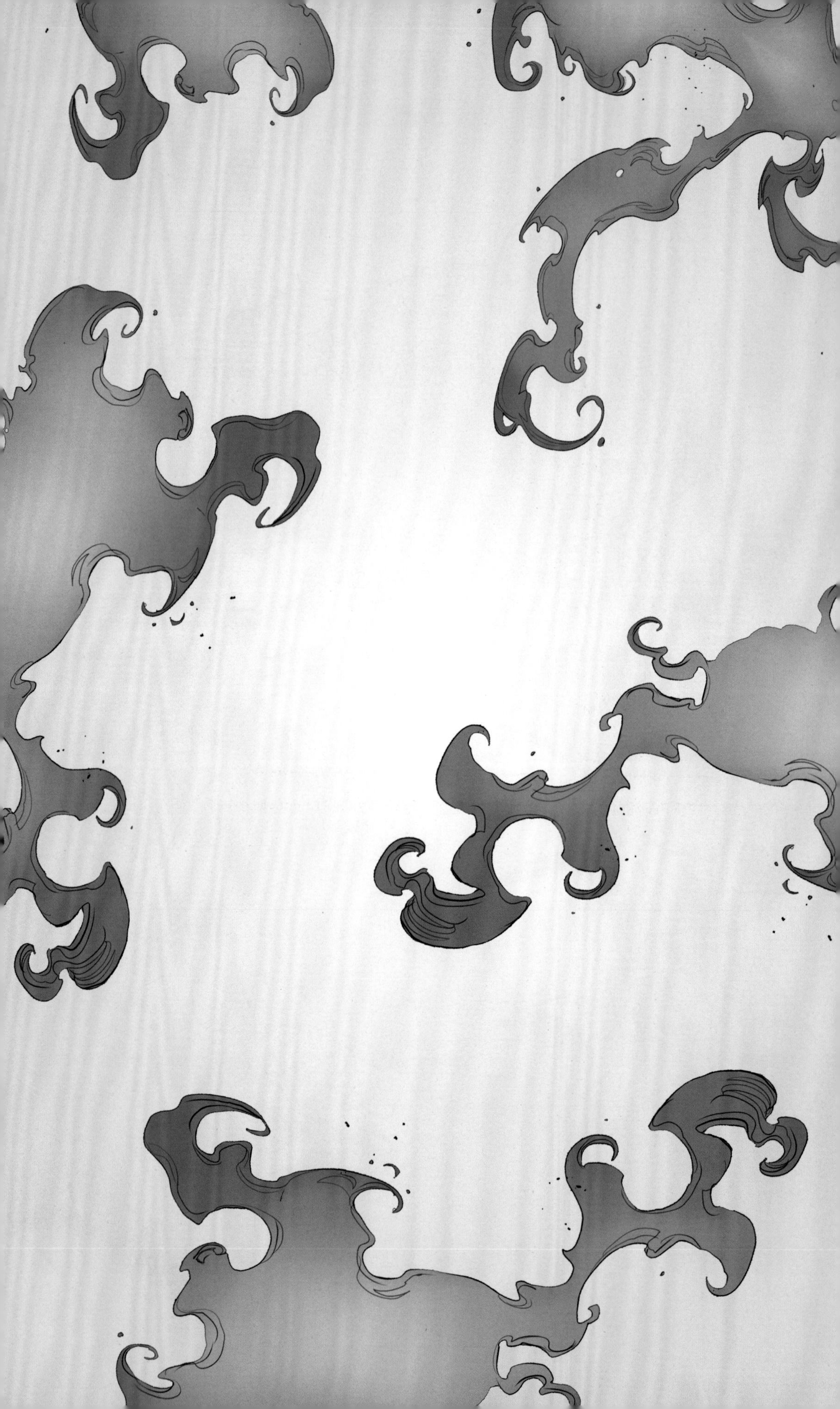

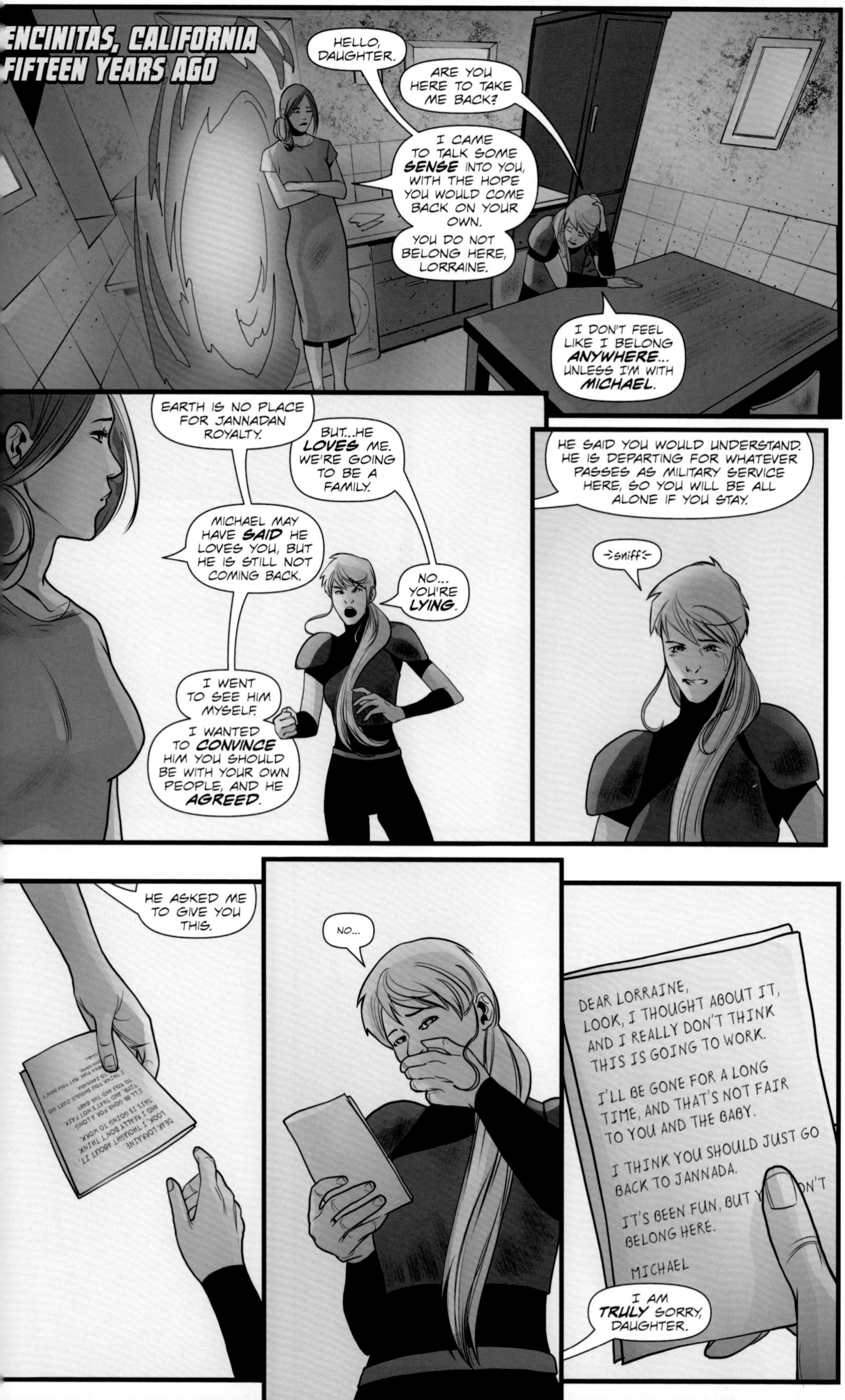

ENCINITAS, CALIFORNIA
FIFTEEN YEARS AGO
HELLO, DAUGHTER.
ARE YOU HERE TO TAKE ME BACK?
I CAME TO TALK SOME SENSE INTO YOU, WITH THE HOPE YOU WOULD COME BACK ON YOUR OWN.
YOU DO NOT BELONG HERE, LORRAINE.
I DON'T FEEL LIKE I BELONG ANYWHERE... UNLESS I'M WITH MICHAEL.
EARTH IS NO PLACE FOR JANNADAN ROYALTY.
BUT...HE LOVES ME. WE'RE GOING TO BE A FAMILY.
MICHAEL MAY HAVE SAID HE LOVES YOU, BUT HE IS STILL NOT COMING BACK.
NO... YOU'RE LYING.
I WENT TO SEE HIM MYSELF.
I WANTED TO CONVINCE HIM YOU SHOULD BE WITH YOUR OWN PEOPLE, AND HE AGREED.
HE SAID YOU WOULD UNDERSTAND. HE IS DEPARTING FOR WHATEVER PASSES AS MILITARY SERVICE HERE, SO YOU WILL BE ALL ALONE IF YOU STAY.
sniff
HE ASKED ME TO GIVE YOU THIS.
NO...
DEAR LORRAINE,
LOOK, I THOUGHT ABOUT IT, AND I REALLY DON'T THINK THIS IS GOING TO WORK.
I'LL BE GONE FOR A LONG TIME, AND THAT'S NOT FAIR TO YOU AND THE BABY.
I THINK YOU SHOULD JUST GO BACK TO JANNADA.
IT'S BEEN FUN, BUT Y ON'T BELONG HERE.
MICHAEL
I AM TRULY SORRY, DAUGHTER.

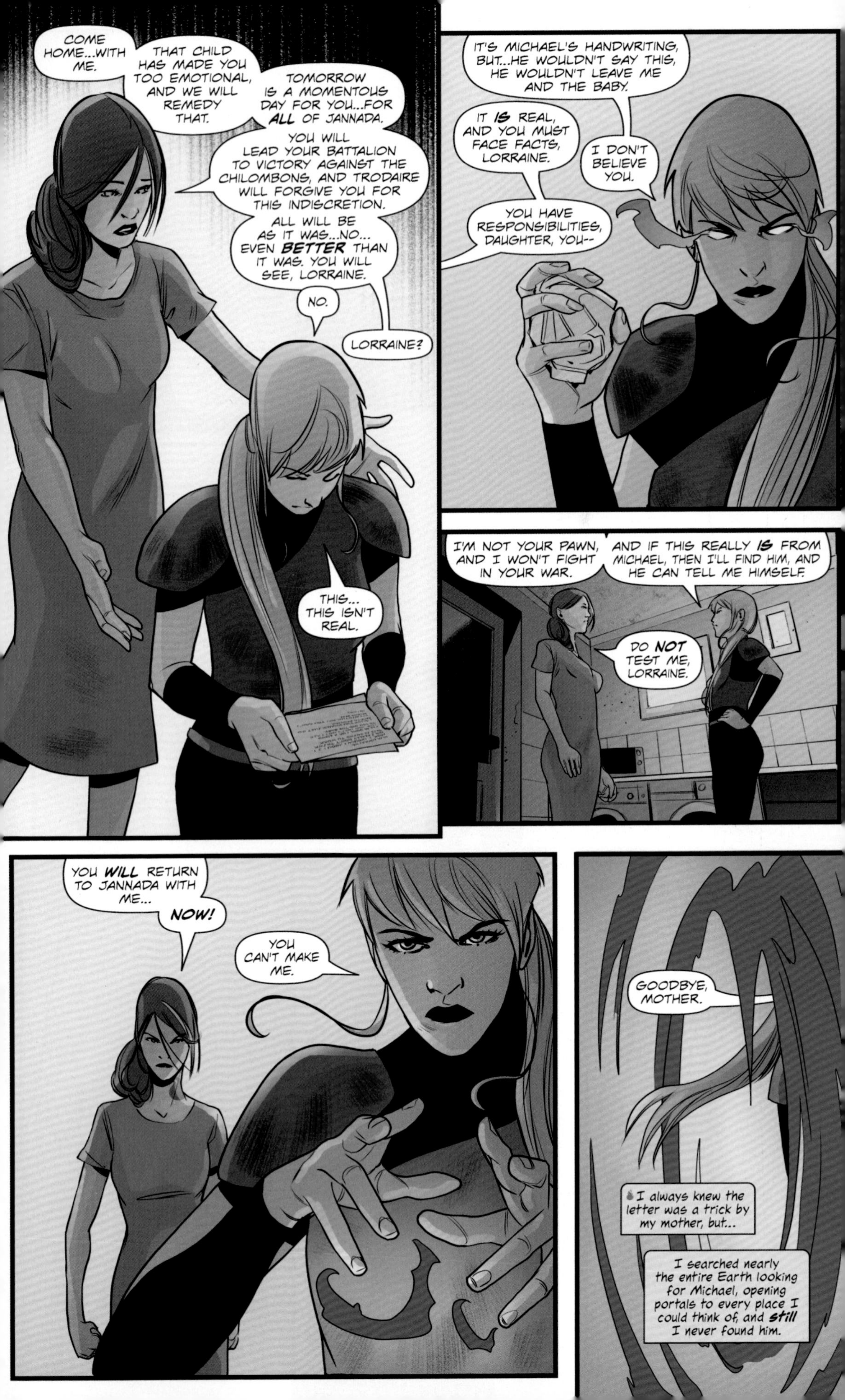
COME HOME...WITH ME.
THAT CHILD HAS MADE YOU TOO EMOTIONAL, AND WE WILL REMEDY THAT.
TOMORROW IS A MOMENTOUS DAY FOR YOU...FOR ALL OF JANNADA.
YOU WILL LEAD YOUR BATTALION TO VICTORY AGAINST THE CHILOMBONS, AND TRODAIRE WILL FORGIVE YOU FOR THIS INDISCRETION.
ALL WILL BE AS IT WAS...NO... EVEN BETTER THAN IT WAS. YOU WILL SEE, LORRAINE.
NO.
LORRAINE?
THIS... THIS ISN'T REAL.
IT'S MICHAEL'S HANDWRITING, BUT...HE WOULDN'T SAY THIS, HE WOULDN'T LEAVE ME AND THE BABY.
IT IS REAL, AND YOU MUST FACE FACTS, LORRAINE.
I DON'T BELIEVE YOU.
YOU HAVE RESPONSIBILITIES, DAUGHTER, YOU--
I'M NOT YOUR PAWN, AND I WON'T FIGHT IN YOUR WAR.
AND IF THIS REALLY IS FROM MICHAEL, THEN I'LL FIND HIM, AND HE CAN TELL ME HIMSELF.
DO NOT TEST ME, LORRAINE.
YOU WILL RETURN TO JANNADA WITH ME... NOW!
YOU CAN'T MAKE ME.
GOODBYE, MOTHER.
I always knew the letter was a trick by my mother, but...
I searched nearly the entire Earth looking for Michael, opening portals to every place I could think of, and still I never found him.

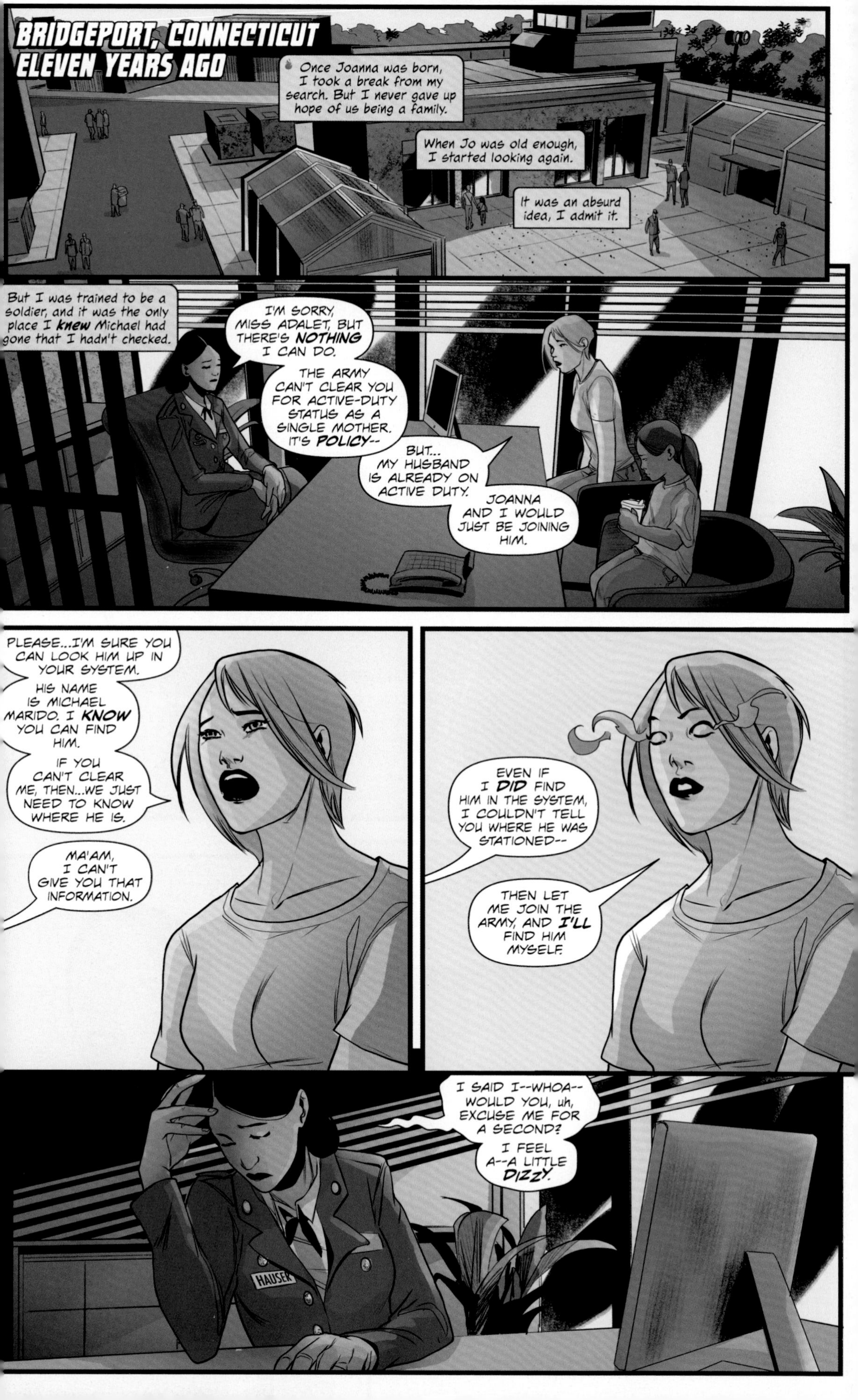
BRIDGEPORT, CONNECTICUT
ELEVEN YEARS AGO
Once Joanna was born, I took a break from my search. But I never gave up hope of us being a family.
When Jo was old enough, I started looking again.
It was an absurd idea, I admit it.
But I was trained to be a soldier, and it was the only place I knew Michael had gone that I hadn't checked.
I'M SORRY, MISS ADALET, BUT THERE'S NOTHING I CAN DO.
THE ARMY CAN'T CLEAR YOU FOR ACTIVE-DUTY STATUS AS A SINGLE MOTHER. IT'S POLICY--
BUT... MY HUSBAND IS ALREADY ON ACTIVE DUTY.
JOANNA AND I WOULD JUST BE JOINING HIM.
PLEASE...I'M SURE YOU CAN LOOK HIM UP IN YOUR SYSTEM.
HIS NAME IS MICHAEL MARIDO. I KNOW YOU CAN FIND HIM.
IF YOU CAN'T CLEAR ME, THEN...WE JUST NEED TO KNOW WHERE HE IS.
MA'AM, I CAN'T GIVE YOU THAT INFORMATION.
EVEN IF I DID FIND HIM IN THE SYSTEM, I COULDN'T TELL YOU WHERE HE WAS STATIONED--
THEN LET ME JOIN THE ARMY, AND I'LL FIND HIM MYSELF.
I SAID I--WHOA--WOULD YOU, uh, EXCUSE ME FOR A SECOND?
I FEEL A--A LITTLE DIZZY.
HAUSER

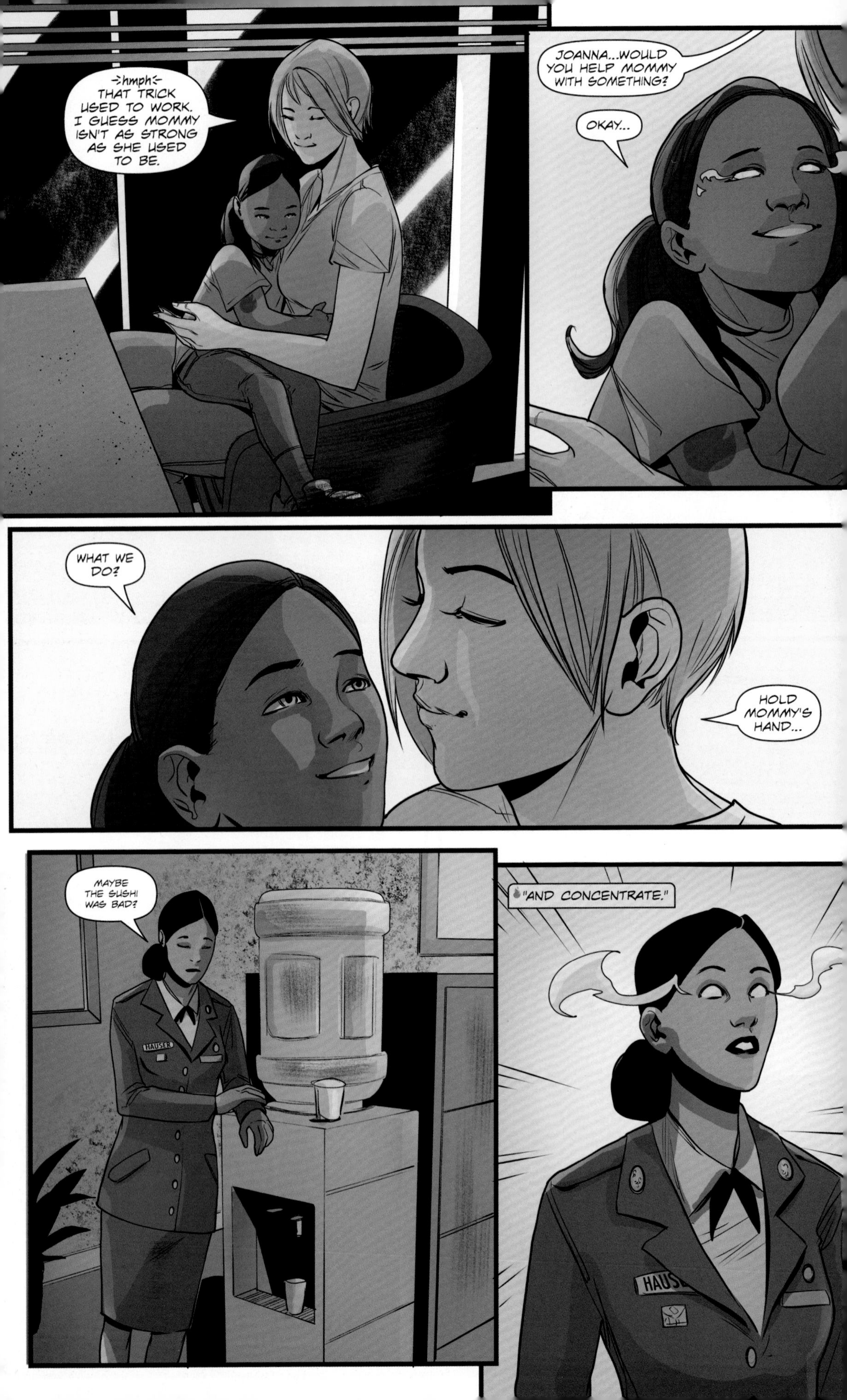

hmph
THAT TRICK USED TO WORK. I GUESS MOMMY ISN'T AS STRONG AS SHE USED TO BE.
JOANNA...WOULD YOU HELP MOMMY WITH SOMETHING?
OKAY...
WHAT WE DO?
HOLD MOMMY'S HAND...
MAYBE THE SUSHI WAS BAD?
HAUSER
"AND CONCENTRATE."
HAUSE

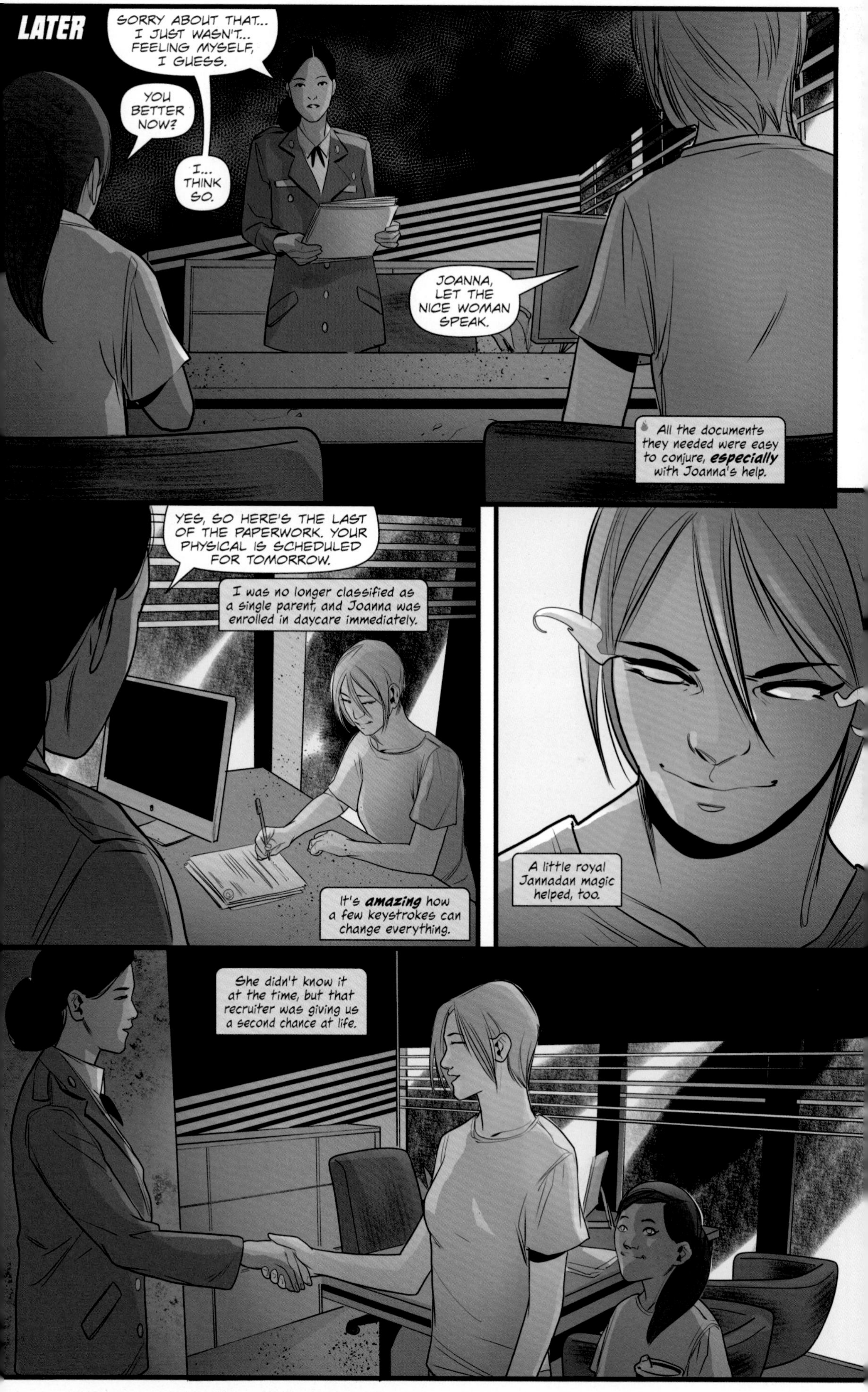
LATER
SORRY ABOUT THAT... I JUST WASN'T... FEELING MYSELF, I GUESS.
YOU BETTER NOW?
I... THINK SO.
JOANNA, LET THE NICE WOMAN SPEAK.
All the documents they needed were easy to conjure, especially with Joanna's help.
YES, SO HERE'S THE LAST OF THE PAPERWORK. YOUR PHYSICAL IS SCHEDULED FOR TOMORROW.
I was no longer classified as a single parent, and Joanna was enrolled in daycare immediately.
It's amazing how a few keystrokes can change everything.
A little royal Jannadan magic helped, too.
She didn't know it at the time, but that recruiter was giving us a second chance at life.

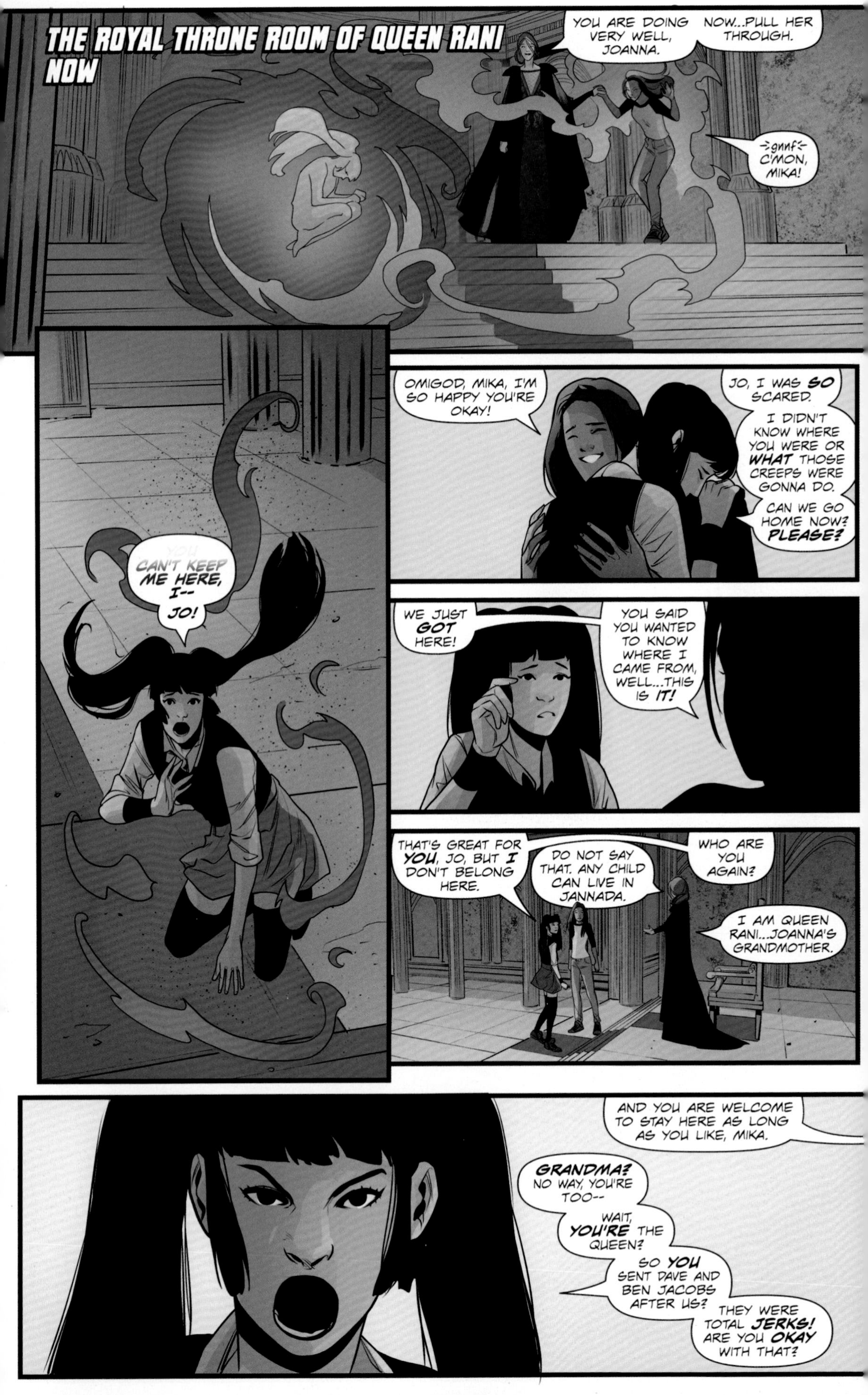
THE ROYAL THRONE ROOM OF QUEEN RANI
NOW
YOU ARE DOING VERY WELL, JOANNA.
NOW...PULL HER THROUGH.
-gnnf- C'MON, MIKA!
YOU CAN'T KEEP ME HERE, I--
JO!
OMIGOD, MIKA, I'M SO HAPPY YOU'RE OKAY!
JO, I WAS SO SCARED.
I DIDN'T KNOW WHERE YOU WERE OR WHAT THOSE CREEPS WERE GONNA DO.
CAN WE GO HOME NOW? PLEASE?
WE JUST GOT HERE!
YOU SAID YOU WANTED TO KNOW WHERE I CAME FROM, WELL...THIS IS IT!
THAT'S GREAT FOR YOU, JO, BUT I DON'T BELONG HERE.
DO NOT SAY THAT. ANY CHILD CAN LIVE IN JANNADA.
WHO ARE YOU AGAIN?
I AM QUEEN RANI...JOANNA'S GRANDMOTHER.
AND YOU ARE WELCOME TO STAY HERE AS LONG AS YOU LIKE, MIKA.
GRANDMA? NO WAY, YOU'RE TOO--
WAIT, YOU'RE THE QUEEN?
SO YOU SENT DAVE AND BEN JACOBS AFTER US?
THEY WERE TOTAL JERKS! ARE YOU OKAY WITH THAT?

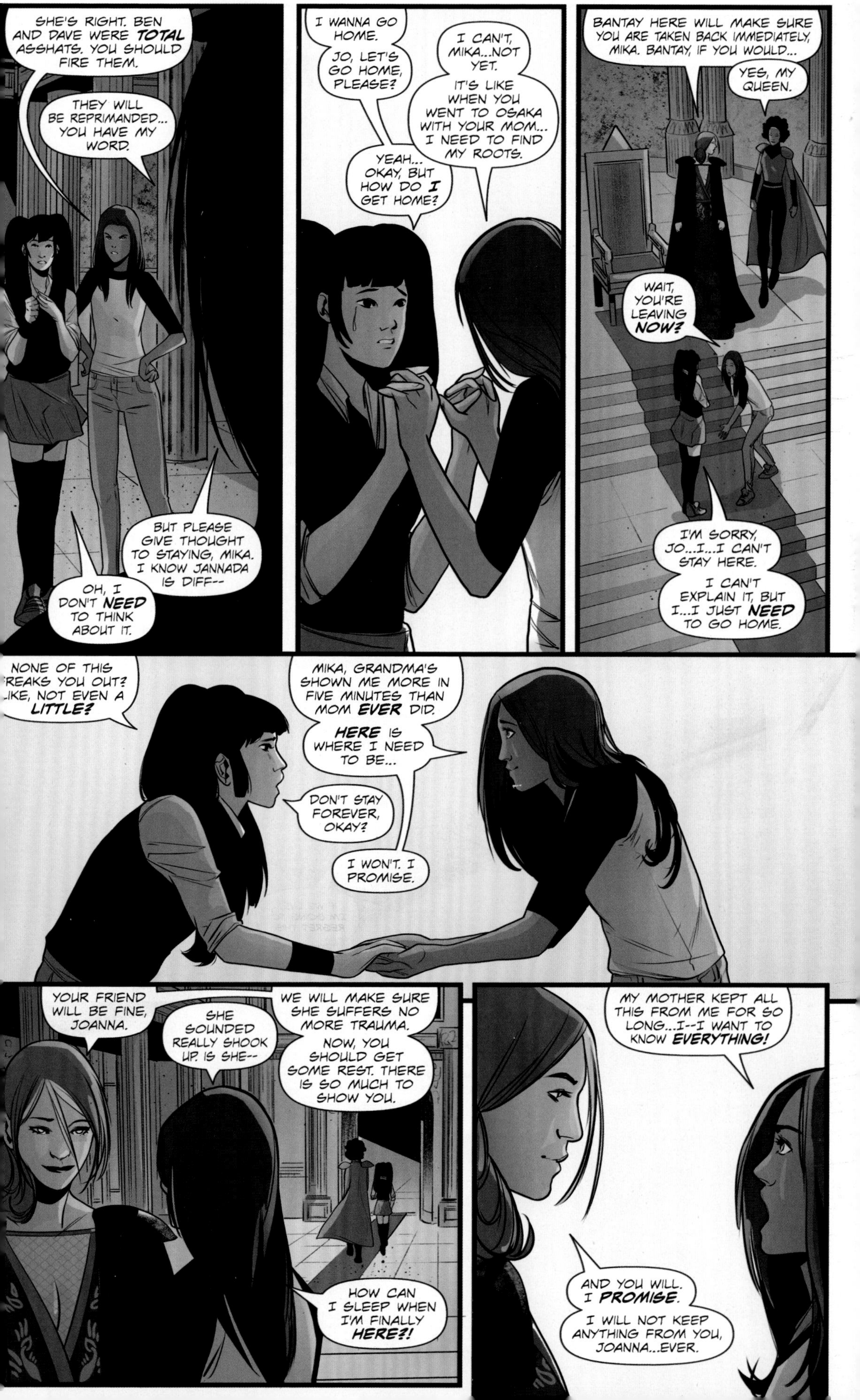
SHE'S RIGHT. BEN AND DAVE WERE TOTAL ASSHATS. YOU SHOULD FIRE THEM.
THEY WILL BE REPRIMANDED... YOU HAVE MY WORD.
BUT PLEASE GIVE THOUGHT TO STAYING, MIKA. I KNOW JANNADA IS DIFF--
OH, I DON'T NEED TO THINK ABOUT IT.
I WANNA GO HOME.
JO, LET'S GO HOME, PLEASE?
I CAN'T, MIKA...NOT YET.
IT'S LIKE WHEN YOU WENT TO OSAKA WITH YOUR MOM... I NEED TO FIND MY ROOTS.
YEAH... OKAY, BUT HOW DO I GET HOME?
BANTAY HERE WILL MAKE SURE YOU ARE TAKEN BACK IMMEDIATELY, MIKA. BANTAY, IF YOU WOULD...
YES, MY QUEEN.
WAIT, YOU'RE LEAVING NOW?
I'M SORRY, JO...I...I CAN'T STAY HERE.
I CAN'T EXPLAIN IT, BUT I...I JUST NEED TO GO HOME.
NONE OF THIS FREAKS YOU OUT? LIKE, NOT EVEN A LITTLE?
MIKA, GRANDMA'S SHOWN ME MORE IN FIVE MINUTES THAN MOM EVER DID.
HERE IS WHERE I NEED TO BE...
DON'T STAY FOREVER, OKAY?
I WON'T. I PROMISE.
YOUR FRIEND WILL BE FINE, JOANNA.
SHE SOUNDED REALLY SHOOK UP. IS SHE--
WE WILL MAKE SURE SHE SUFFERS NO MORE TRAUMA.
NOW, YOU SHOULD GET SOME REST. THERE IS SO MUCH TO SHOW YOU.
HOW CAN I SLEEP WHEN I'M FINALLY HERE?!
MY MOTHER KEPT ALL THIS FROM ME FOR SO LONG...I--I WANT TO KNOW EVERYTHING!
AND YOU WILL. I PROMISE.
I WILL NOT KEEP ANYTHING FROM YOU, JOANNA...EVER.

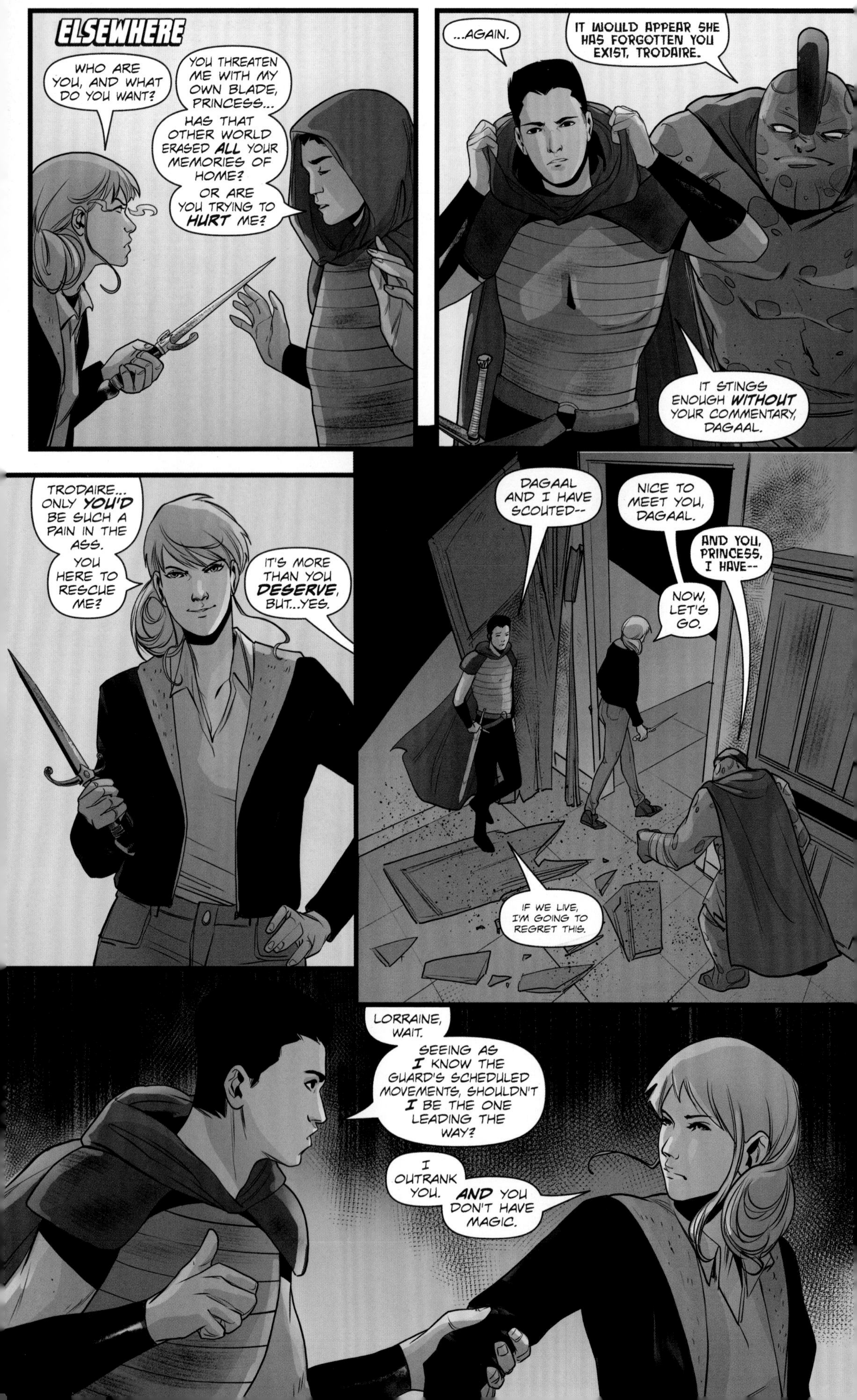
ELSEWHERE
WHO ARE YOU, AND WHAT DO YOU WANT?
YOU THREATEN ME WITH MY OWN BLADE, PRINCESS...
HAS THAT OTHER WORLD ERASED ALL YOUR MEMORIES OF HOME?
OR ARE YOU TRYING TO HURT ME?
...AGAIN.
IT WOULD APPEAR SHE HAS FORGOTTEN YOU EXIST, TRODAIRE.
IT STINGS ENOUGH WITHOUT YOUR COMMENTARY, DAGAAL.
TRODAIRE... ONLY YOU'D BE SUCH A PAIN IN THE ASS.
YOU HERE TO RESCUE ME?
IT'S MORE THAN YOU DESERVE, BUT...YES.
DAGAAL AND I HAVE SCOUTED--
NICE TO MEET YOU, DAGAAL.
AND YOU, PRINCESS, I HAVE--
NOW, LET'S GO.
IF WE LIVE, I'M GOING TO REGRET THIS.
LORRAINE, WAIT.
SEEING AS I KNOW THE GUARD'S SCHEDULED MOVEMENTS, SHOULDN'T I BE THE ONE LEADING THE WAY?
I OUTRANK YOU.
AND YOU DON'T HAVE MAGIC.

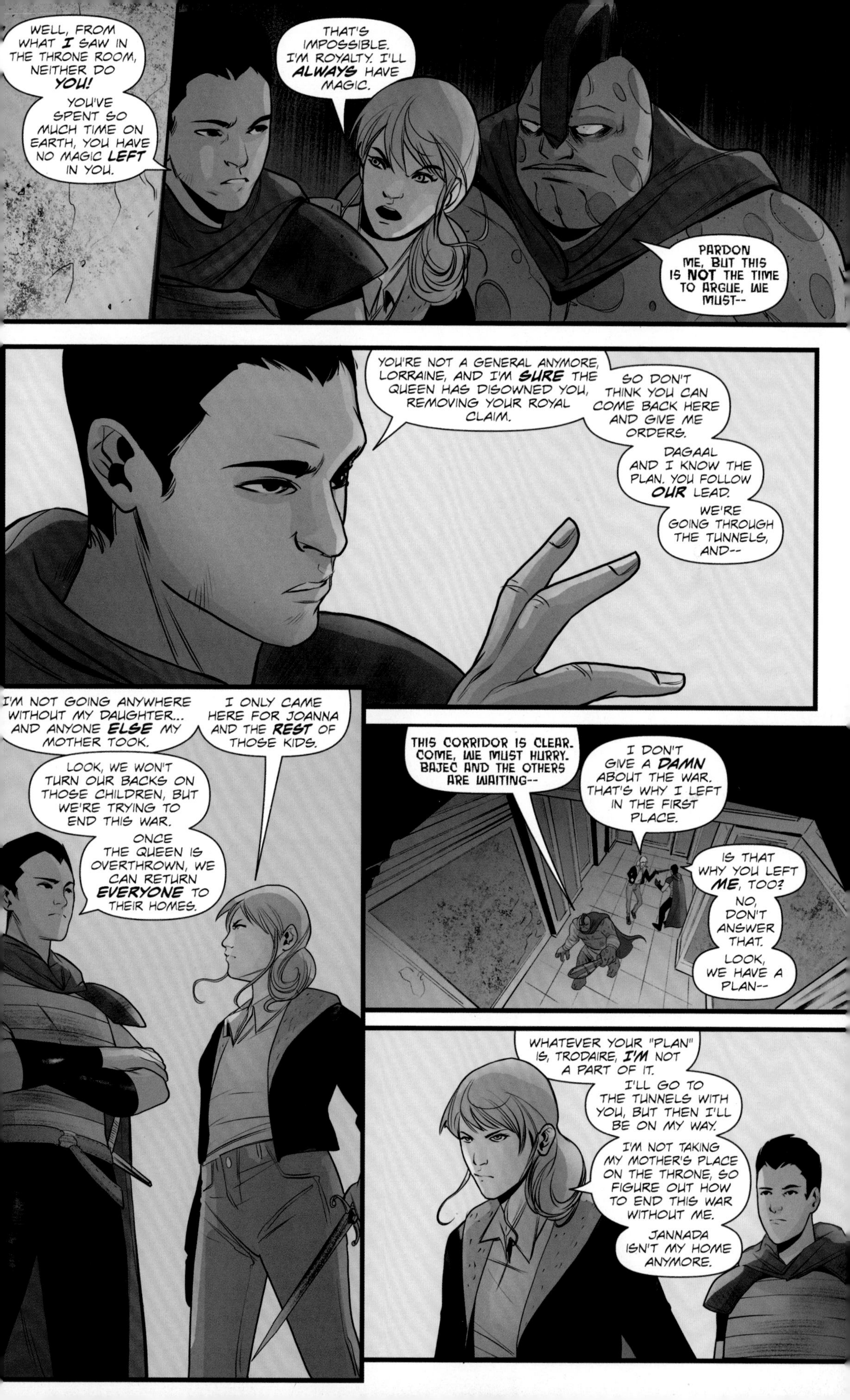
WELL, FROM WHAT I SAW IN THE THRONE ROOM, NEITHER DO YOU!
YOU'VE SPENT SO MUCH TIME ON EARTH, YOU HAVE NO MAGIC LEFT IN YOU.
THAT'S IMPOSSIBLE. I'M ROYALTY. I'LL ALWAYS HAVE MAGIC.
PARDON ME, BUT THIS IS NOT THE TIME TO ARGUE. WE MUST--
YOU'RE NOT A GENERAL ANYMORE, LORRAINE, AND I'M SURE THE QUEEN HAS DISOWNED YOU, REMOVING YOUR ROYAL CLAIM.
SO DON'T THINK YOU CAN COME BACK HERE AND GIVE ME ORDERS.
DAGAAL AND I KNOW THE PLAN. YOU FOLLOW OUR LEAD.
WE'RE GOING THROUGH THE TUNNELS, AND--
I'M NOT GOING ANYWHERE WITHOUT MY DAUGHTER... AND ANYONE ELSE MY MOTHER TOOK.
I ONLY CAME HERE FOR JOANNA AND THE REST OF THOSE KIDS.
LOOK, WE WON'T TURN OUR BACKS ON THOSE CHILDREN, BUT WE'RE TRYING TO END THIS WAR.
ONCE THE QUEEN IS OVERTHROWN, WE CAN RETURN EVERYONE TO THEIR HOMES.
THIS CORRIDOR IS CLEAR. COME, WE MUST HURRY. BAJEC AND THE OTHERS ARE WAITING--
I DON'T GIVE A DAMN ABOUT THE WAR. THAT'S WHY I LEFT IN THE FIRST PLACE.
IS THAT WHY YOU LEFT ME, TOO?
NO, DON'T ANSWER THAT.
LOOK, WE HAVE A PLAN--
WHATEVER YOUR "PLAN" IS, TRODAIRE, I'M NOT A PART OF IT.
I'LL GO TO THE TUNNELS WITH YOU, BUT THEN I'LL BE ON MY WAY.
I'M NOT TAKING MY MOTHER'S PLACE ON THE THRONE, SO FIGURE OUT HOW TO END THIS WAR WITHOUT ME.
JANNADA ISN'T MY HOME ANYMORE.

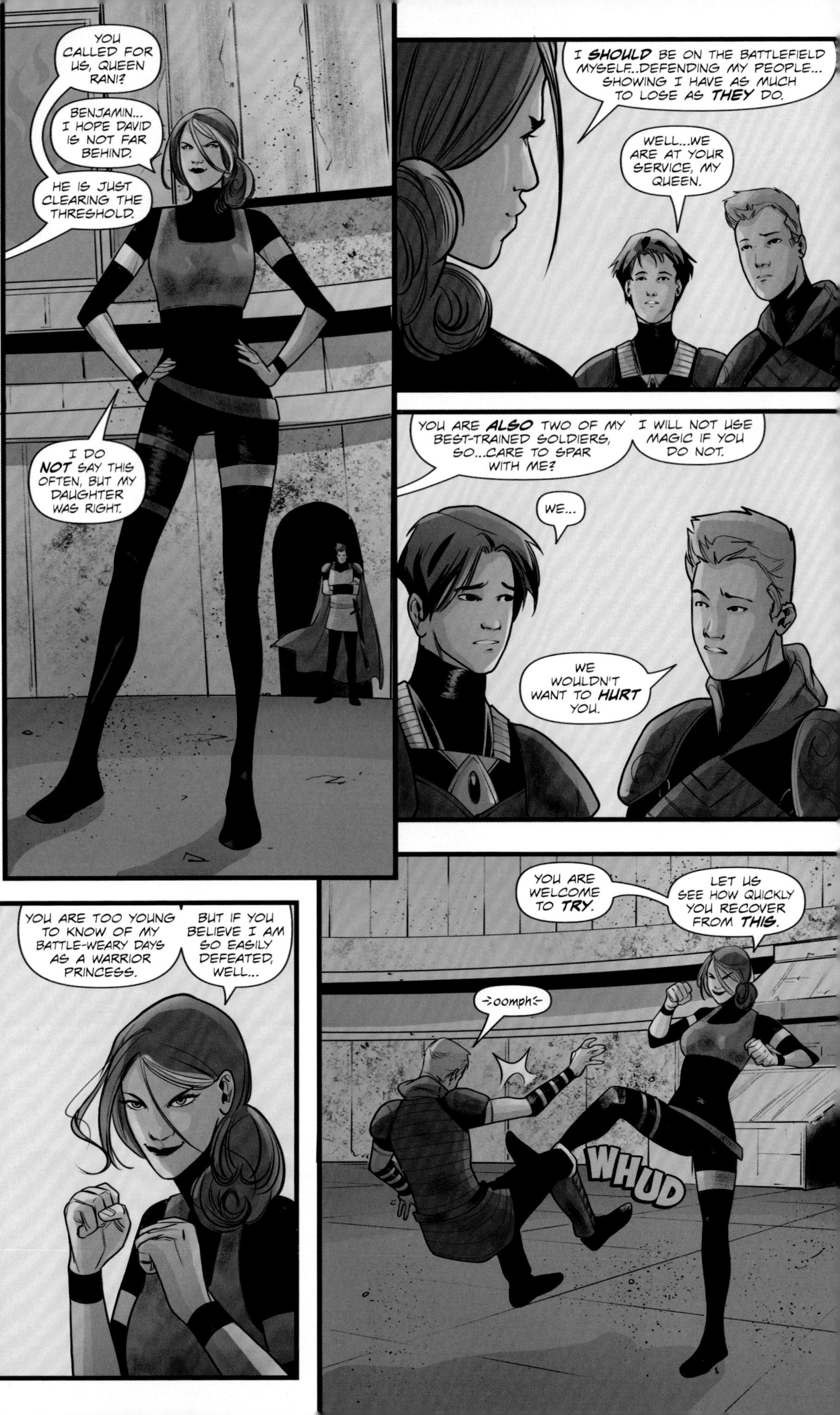
YOU CALLED FOR US, QUEEN RANI?
BENJAMIN... I HOPE DAVID IS NOT FAR BEHIND.
HE IS JUST CLEARING THE THRESHOLD.
I DO NOT SAY THIS OFTEN, BUT MY DAUGHTER WAS RIGHT.
I SHOULD BE ON THE BATTLEFIELD MYSELF..DEFENDING MY PEOPLE... SHOWING I HAVE AS MUCH TO LOSE AS THEY DO.
WELL...WE ARE AT YOUR SERVICE, MY QUEEN.
YOU ARE ALSO TWO OF MY BEST-TRAINED SOLDIERS, SO...CARE TO SPAR WITH ME?
I WILL NOT USE MAGIC IF YOU DO NOT.
WE...
WE WOULDN'T WANT TO HURT YOU.
YOU ARE TOO YOUNG TO KNOW OF MY BATTLE-WEARY DAYS AS A WARRIOR PRINCESS.
BUT IF YOU BELIEVE I AM SO EASILY DEFEATED, WELL...
YOU ARE WELCOME TO TRY.
LET US SEE HOW QUICKLY YOU RECOVER FROM THIS.
-oomph-
WHUD

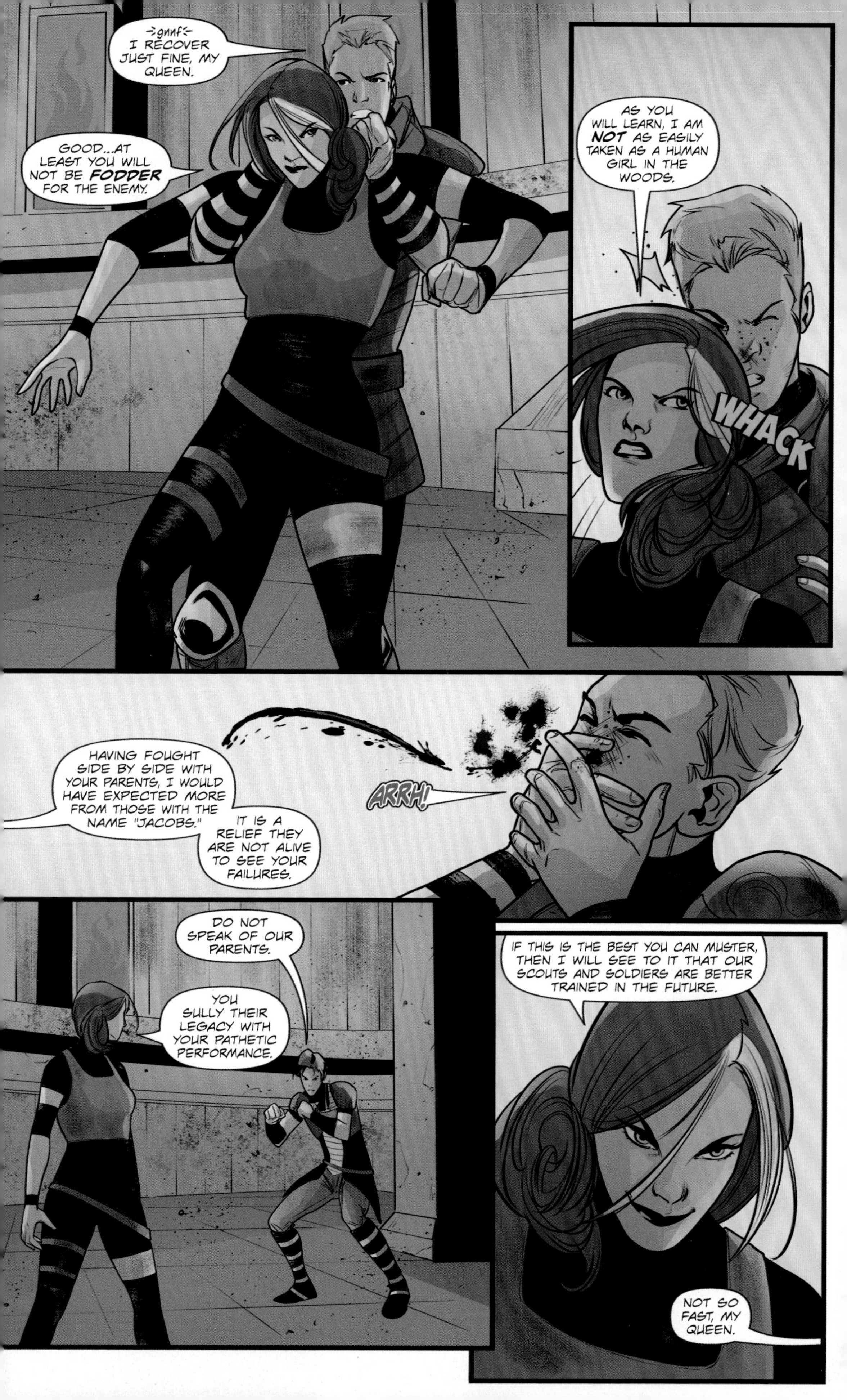

-gnnf- I RECOVER JUST FINE, MY QUEEN.
GOOD...AT LEAST YOU WILL NOT BE FODDER FOR THE ENEMY.
AS YOU WILL LEARN, I AM NOT AS EASILY TAKEN AS A HUMAN GIRL IN THE WOODS.
WHACK
HAVING FOUGHT SIDE BY SIDE WITH YOUR PARENTS, I WOULD HAVE EXPECTED MORE FROM THOSE WITH THE NAME "JACOBS."
IT IS A RELIEF THEY ARE NOT ALIVE TO SEE YOUR FAILURES.
ARRH!
DO NOT SPEAK OF OUR PARENTS.
YOU SULLY THEIR LEGACY WITH YOUR PATHETIC PERFORMANCE.
IF THIS IS THE BEST YOU CAN MUSTER, THEN I WILL SEE TO IT THAT OUR SCOUTS AND SOLDIERS ARE BETTER TRAINED IN THE FUTURE.
NOT SO FAST, MY QUEEN.

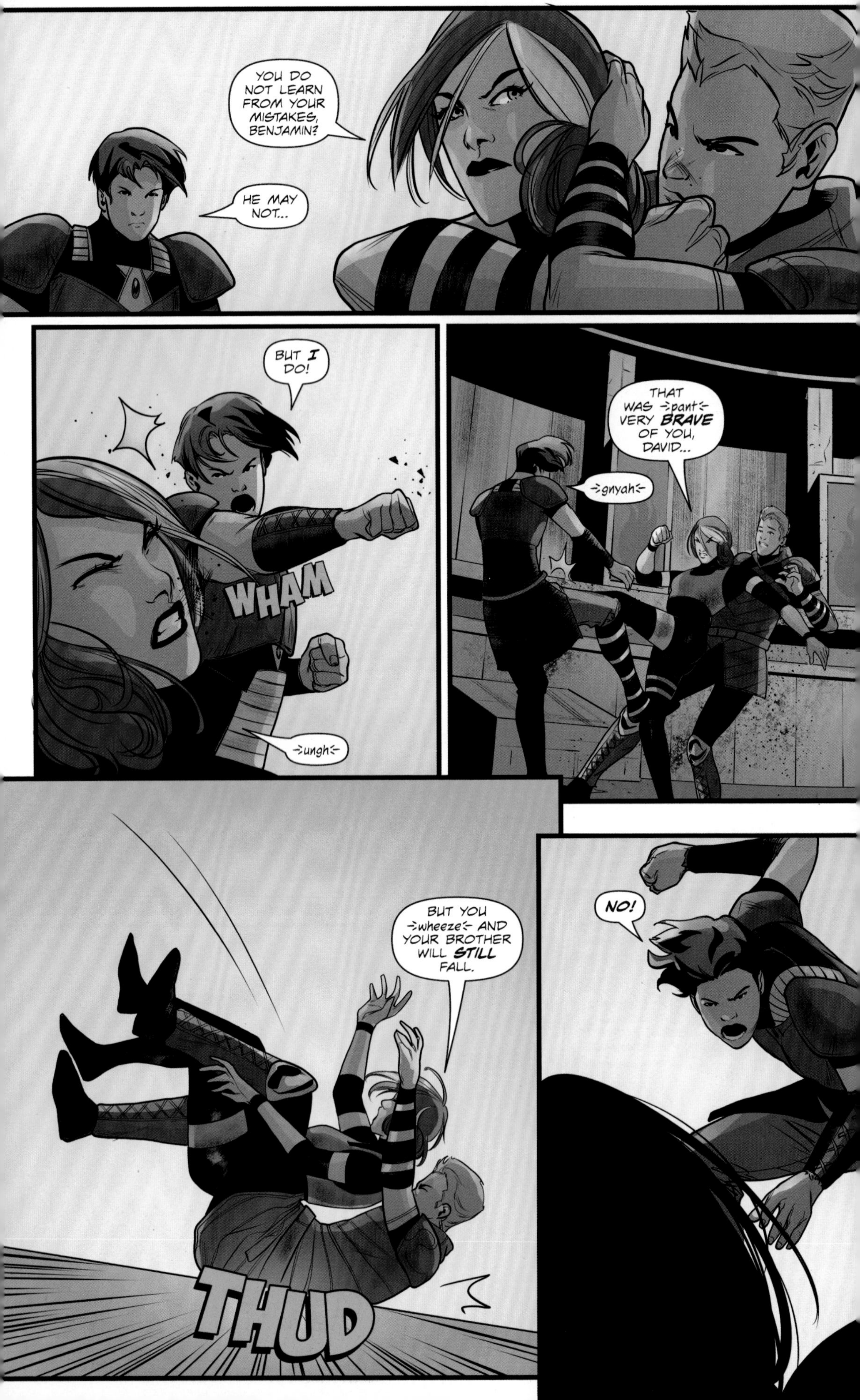
YOU DO NOT LEARN FROM YOUR MISTAKES, BENJAMIN?
HE MAY NOT...
BUT I DO!
WHAM
-ungh-
THAT WAS -pant- VERY BRAVE OF YOU, DAVID...
-gnyah-
BUT YOU -wheeze- AND YOUR BROTHER WILL STILL FALL.
THUD
NO!

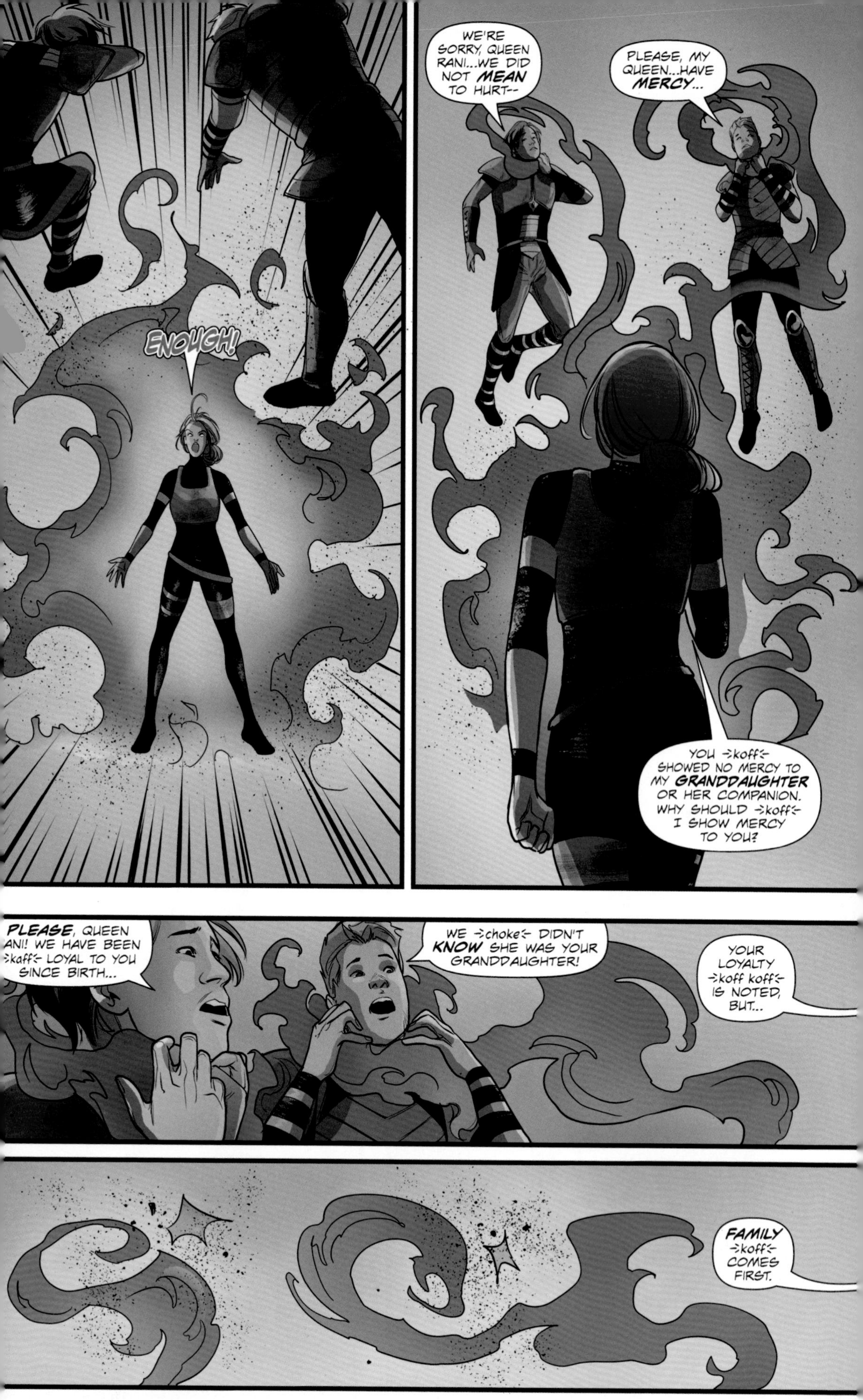
ENOUGH!
WE'RE SORRY, QUEEN RANI...WE DID NOT MEAN TO HURT--
PLEASE, MY QUEEN...HAVE MERCY...
YOU ->koff<- SHOWED NO MERCY TO MY GRANDDAUGHTER OR HER COMPANION. WHY SHOULD ->koff<- I SHOW MERCY TO YOU?
PLEASE, QUEEN RANI! WE HAVE BEEN ->kaff<- LOYAL TO YOU SINCE BIRTH...
WE ->choke<- DIDN'T KNOW SHE WAS YOUR GRANDDAUGHTER!
YOUR LOYALTY ->koff koff<- IS NOTED, BUT...
FAMILY ->koff<- COMES FIRST.

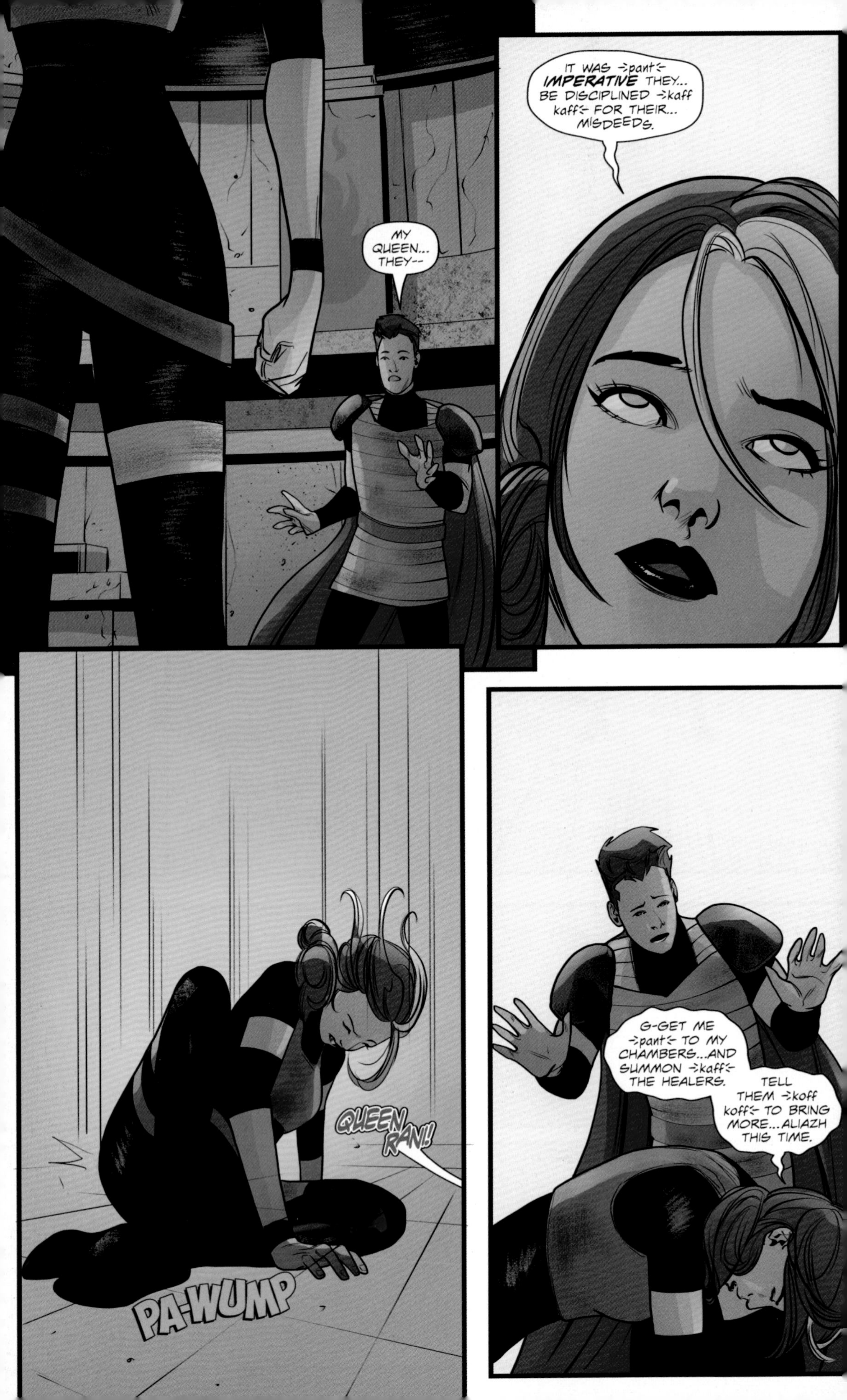
MY QUEEN... THEY--
IT WAS →pant← IMPERATIVE THEY... BE DISCIPLINED →kaff kaff← FOR THEIR... MISDEEDS.
QUEEN RAN!!
PA-WUMP
G-GET ME →pant← TO MY CHAMBERS...AND SUMMON →kaff← THE HEALERS.
TELL THEM →koff koff← TO BRING MORE...ALIAZH THIS TIME.

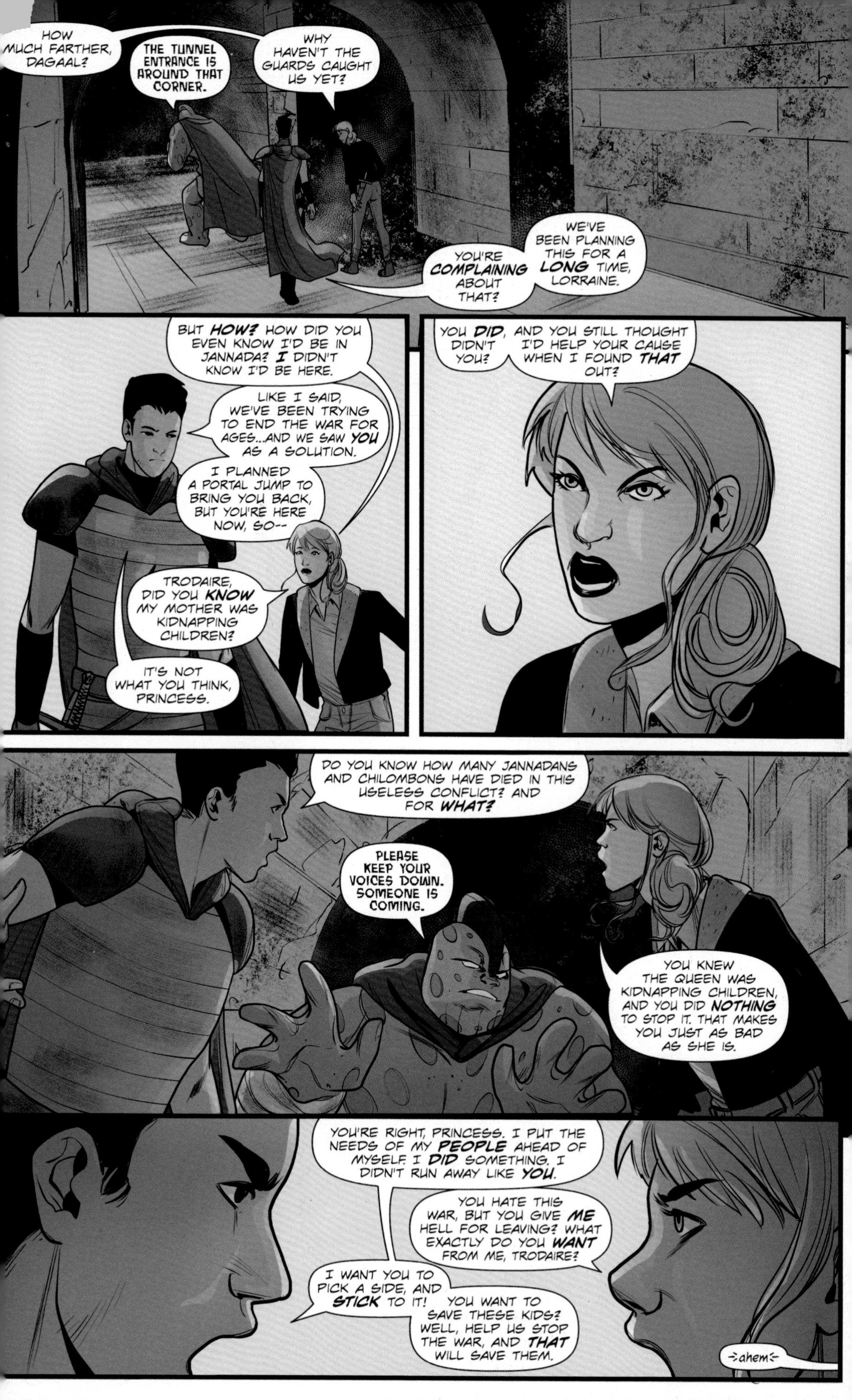
HOW MUCH FARTHER, DAGAAL?
THE TUNNEL ENTRANCE IS AROUND THAT CORNER.
WHY HAVEN'T THE GUARDS CAUGHT US YET?
YOU'RE COMPLAINING ABOUT THAT?
WE'VE BEEN PLANNING THIS FOR A LONG TIME, LORRAINE.
BUT HOW? HOW DID YOU EVEN KNOW I'D BE IN JANNADA? I DIDN'T KNOW I'D BE HERE.
LIKE I SAID, WE'VE BEEN TRYING TO END THE WAR FOR AGES...AND WE SAW YOU AS A SOLUTION.
I PLANNED A PORTAL JUMP TO BRING YOU BACK, BUT YOU'RE HERE NOW, SO--
TRODAIRE, DID YOU KNOW MY MOTHER WAS KIDNAPPING CHILDREN?
IT'S NOT WHAT YOU THINK, PRINCESS.
YOU DID, DIDN'T YOU?
AND YOU STILL THOUGHT I'D HELP YOUR CAUSE WHEN I FOUND THAT OUT?
DO YOU KNOW HOW MANY JANNADANS AND CHILOMBONS HAVE DIED IN THIS USELESS CONFLICT? AND FOR WHAT?
PLEASE KEEP YOUR VOICES DOWN. SOMEONE IS COMING.
YOU KNEW THE QUEEN WAS KIDNAPPING CHILDREN, AND YOU DID NOTHING TO STOP IT. THAT MAKES YOU JUST AS BAD AS SHE IS.
YOU'RE RIGHT, PRINCESS. I PUT THE NEEDS OF MY PEOPLE AHEAD OF MYSELF. I DID SOMETHING. I DIDN'T RUN AWAY LIKE YOU.
YOU HATE THIS WAR, BUT YOU GIVE ME HELL FOR LEAVING? WHAT EXACTLY DO YOU WANT FROM ME, TRODAIRE?
I WANT YOU TO PICK A SIDE, AND STICK TO IT!
YOU WANT TO SAVE THESE KIDS? WELL, HELP US STOP THE WAR, AND THAT WILL SAVE THEM.
ahem

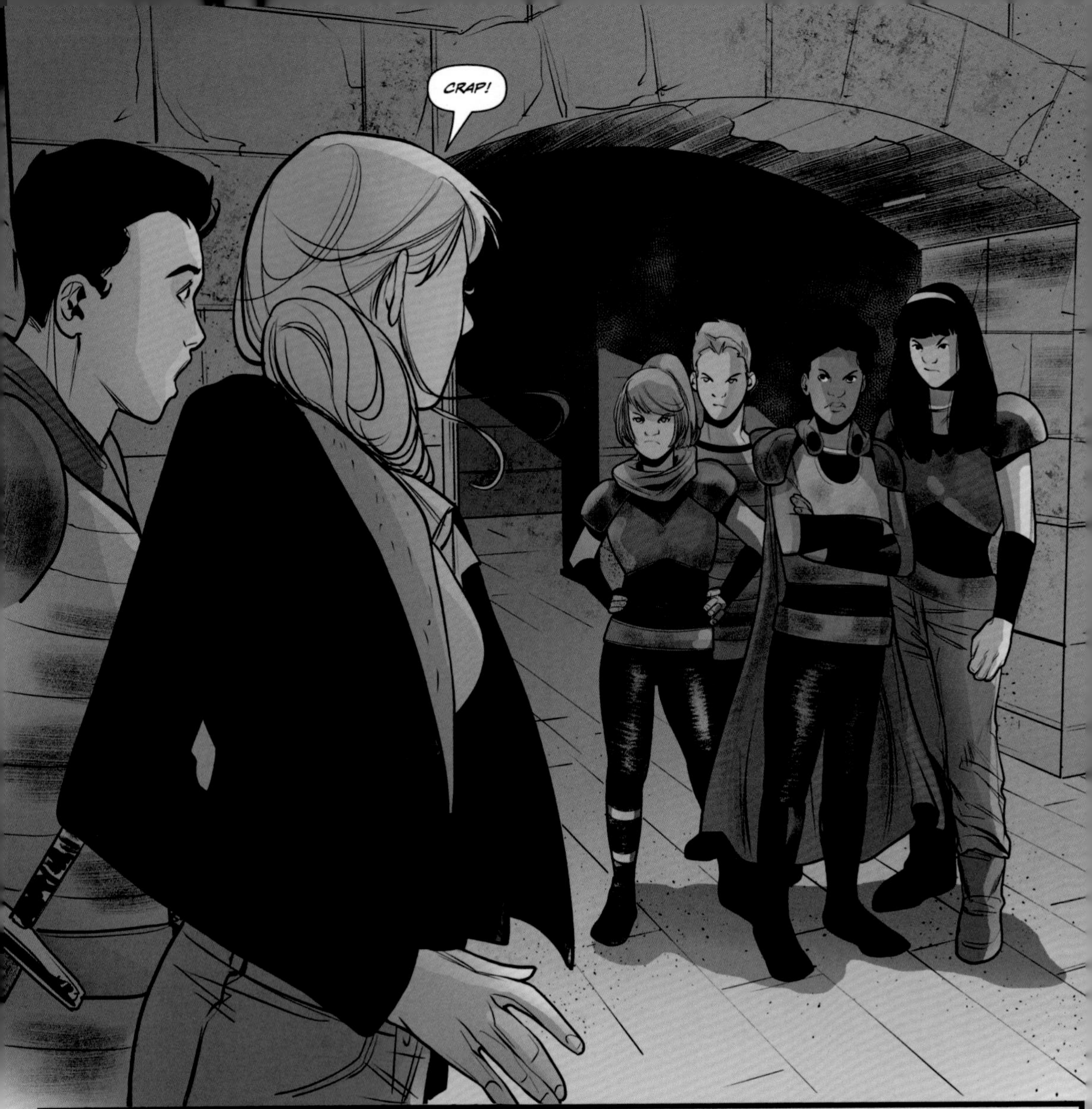
CRAP!

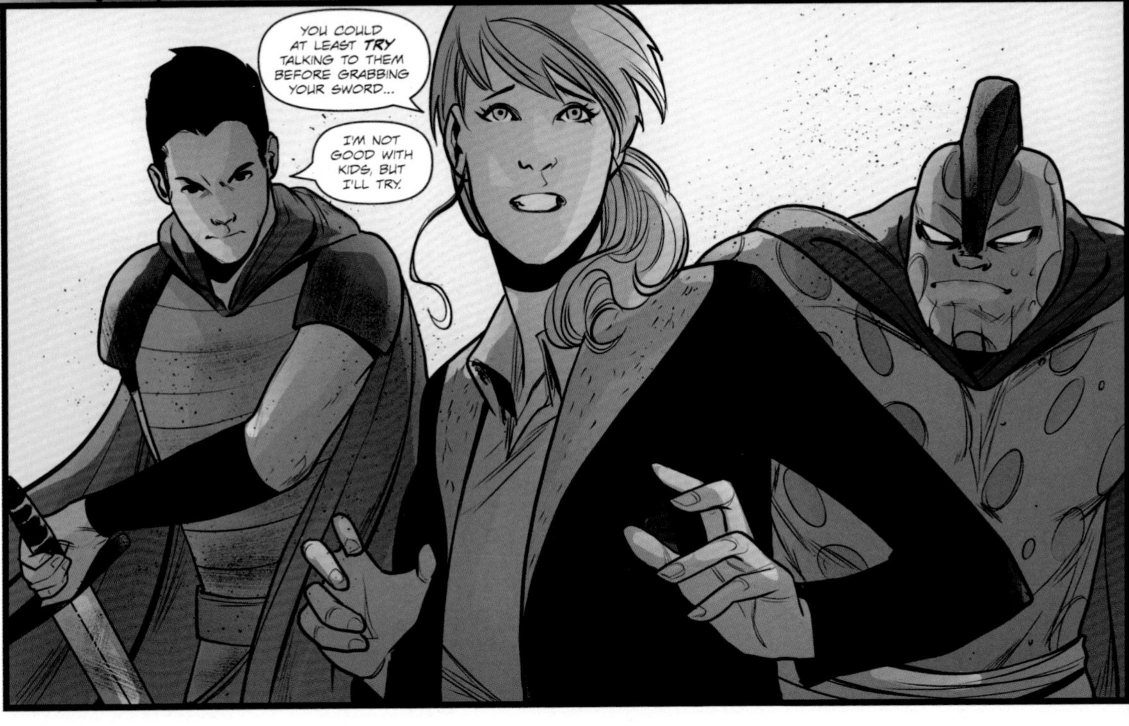
YOU COULD AT LEAST TRY TALKING TO THEM BEFORE GRABBING YOUR SWORD...
I'M NOT GOOD WITH KIDS, BUT I'LL TRY.

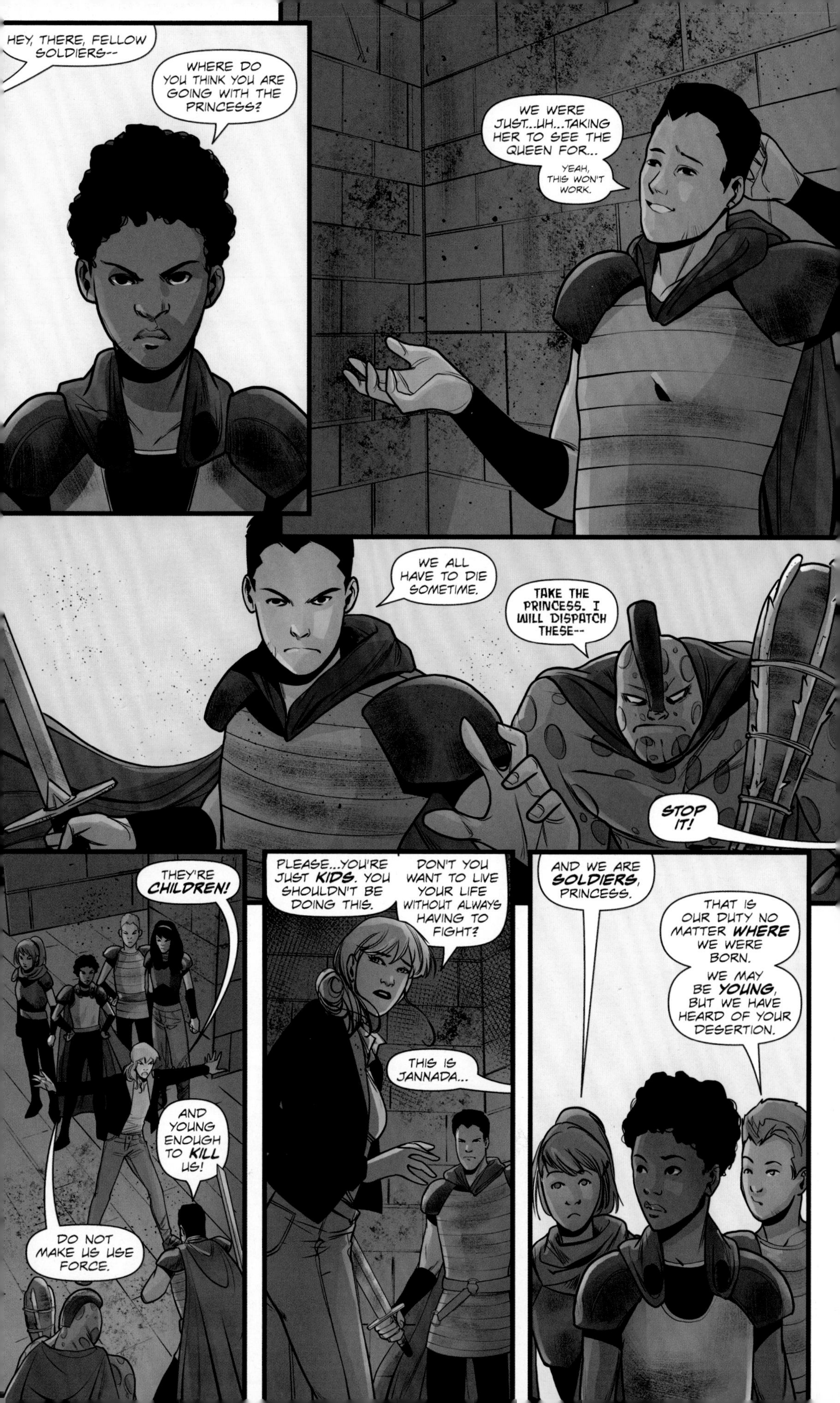
HEY, THERE, FELLOW SOLDIERS--
WHERE DO YOU THINK YOU ARE GOING WITH THE PRINCESS?
WE WERE JUST...UH...TAKING HER TO SEE THE QUEEN FOR...
YEAH, THIS WON'T WORK.
WE ALL HAVE TO DIE SOMETIME.
TAKE THE PRINCESS. I WILL DISPATCH THESE--
STOP IT!
THEY'RE CHILDREN!
AND YOUNG ENOUGH TO KILL US!
DO NOT MAKE US USE FORCE.
PLEASE...YOU'RE JUST KIDS. YOU SHOULDN'T BE DOING THIS.
DON'T YOU WANT TO LIVE YOUR LIFE WITHOUT ALWAYS HAVING TO FIGHT?
THIS IS JANNADA...
AND WE ARE SOLDIERS, PRINCESS.
THAT IS OUR DUTY NO MATTER WHERE WE WERE BORN.
WE MAY BE YOUNG, BUT WE HAVE HEARD OF YOUR DESERTION.

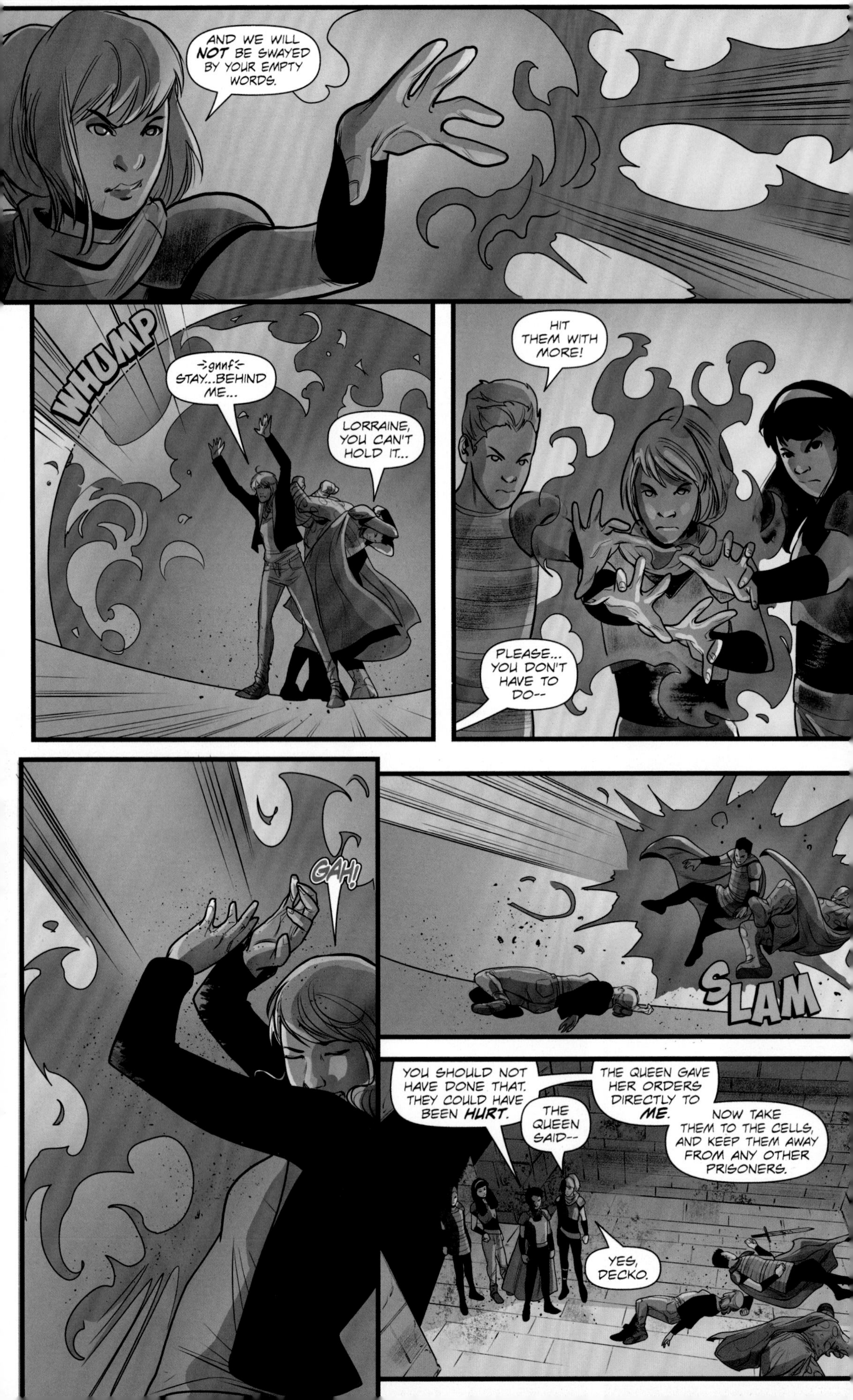
AND WE WILL NOT BE SWAYED BY YOUR EMPTY WORDS.
WHUMP
-gnnf- STAY...BEHIND ME...
LORRAINE, YOU CAN'T HOLD IT...
HIT THEM WITH MORE!
PLEASE... YOU DON'T HAVE TO DO--
GAH!
SLAM
YOU SHOULD NOT HAVE DONE THAT. THEY COULD HAVE BEEN HURT.
THE QUEEN SAID--
THE QUEEN GAVE HER ORDERS DIRECTLY TO ME.
NOW TAKE THEM TO THE CELLS, AND KEEP THEM AWAY FROM ANY OTHER PRISONERS.
YES, DECKO.

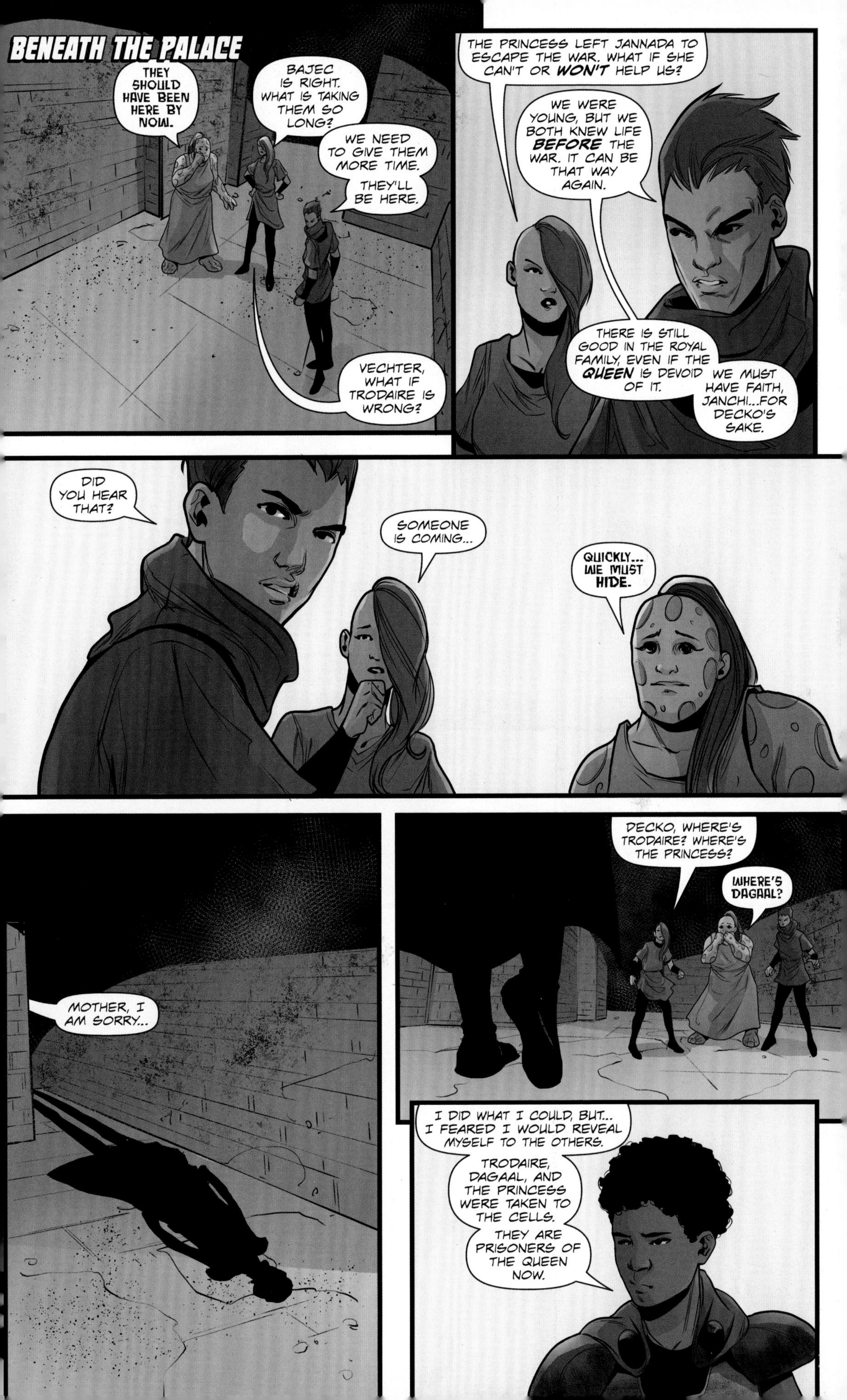
BENEATH THE PALACE
THEY SHOULD HAVE BEEN HERE BY NOW.
BAJEC IS RIGHT. WHAT IS TAKING THEM SO LONG?
WE NEED TO GIVE THEM MORE TIME.
THEY'LL BE HERE.
VECHTER, WHAT IF TRODAIRE IS WRONG?
THE PRINCESS LEFT JANNADA TO ESCAPE THE WAR. WHAT IF SHE CAN'T OR WON'T HELP US?
WE WERE YOUNG, BUT WE BOTH KNEW LIFE BEFORE THE WAR. IT CAN BE THAT WAY AGAIN.
THERE IS STILL GOOD IN THE ROYAL FAMILY, EVEN IF THE QUEEN IS DEVOID OF IT.
WE MUST HAVE FAITH, JANCHI...FOR DECKO'S SAKE.
DID YOU HEAR THAT?
SOMEONE IS COMING...
QUICKLY... WE MUST HIDE.
MOTHER, I AM SORRY...
DECKO, WHERE'S TRODAIRE? WHERE'S THE PRINCESS?
WHERE'S DAGAAL?
I DID WHAT I COULD, BUT... I FEARED I WOULD REVEAL MYSELF TO THE OTHERS.
TRODAIRE, DAGAAL, AND THE PRINCESS WERE TAKEN TO THE CELLS.
THEY ARE PRISONERS OF THE QUEEN NOW.

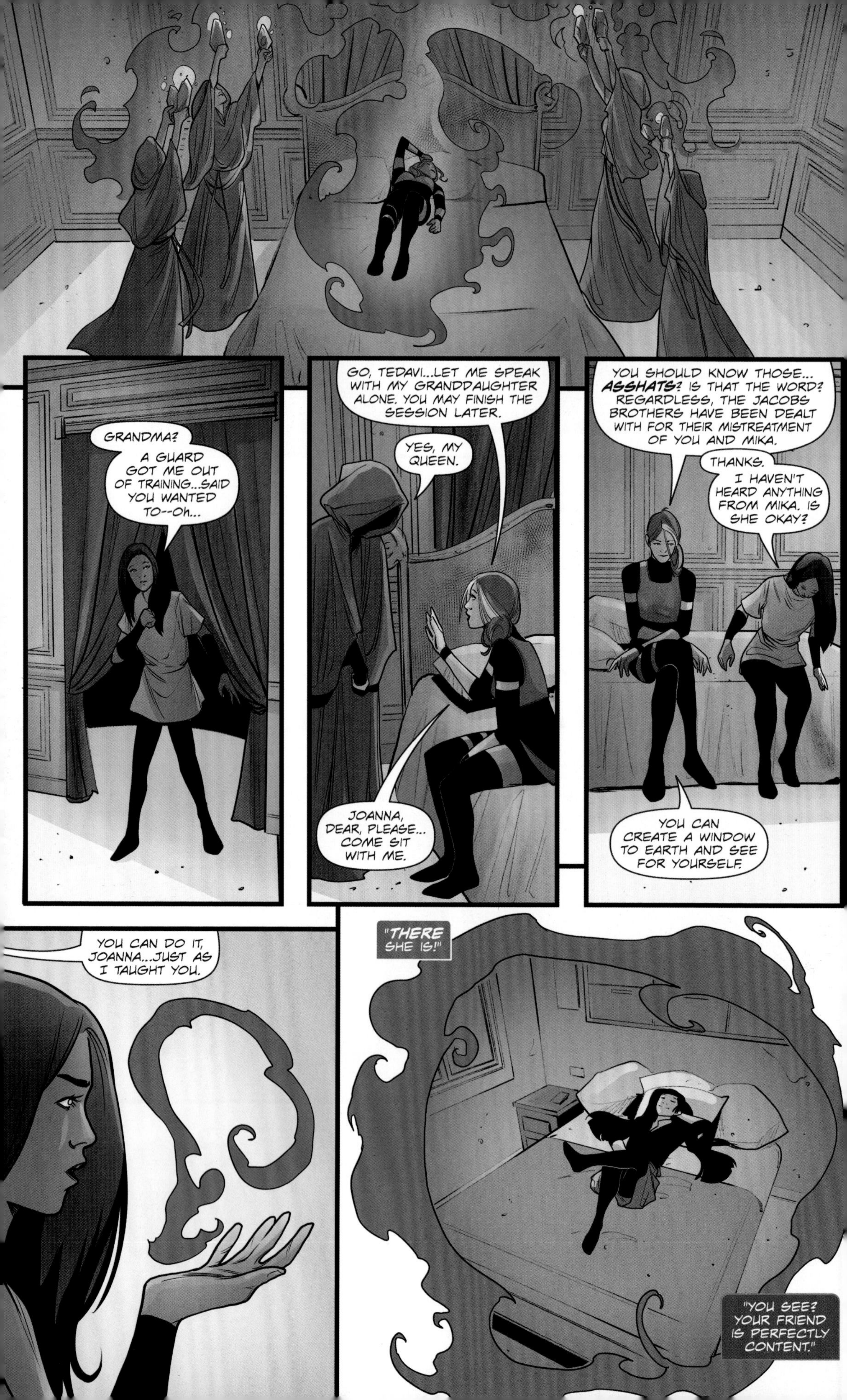
GRANDMA?
A GUARD GOT ME OUT OF TRAINING...SAID YOU WANTED TO--Oh...
GO, TEDAVI...LET ME SPEAK WITH MY GRANDDAUGHTER ALONE. YOU MAY FINISH THE SESSION LATER.
YES, MY QUEEN.
JOANNA, DEAR, PLEASE... COME SIT WITH ME.
YOU SHOULD KNOW THOSE... ASSHATS? IS THAT THE WORD? REGARDLESS, THE JACOBS BROTHERS HAVE BEEN DEALT WITH FOR THEIR MISTREATMENT OF YOU AND MIKA.
THANKS.
I HAVEN'T HEARD ANYTHING FROM MIKA. IS SHE OKAY?
YOU CAN CREATE A WINDOW TO EARTH AND SEE FOR YOURSELF.
YOU CAN DO IT, JOANNA...JUST AS I TAUGHT YOU.
"THERE SHE IS!"
"YOU SEE? YOUR FRIEND IS PERFECTLY CONTENT."

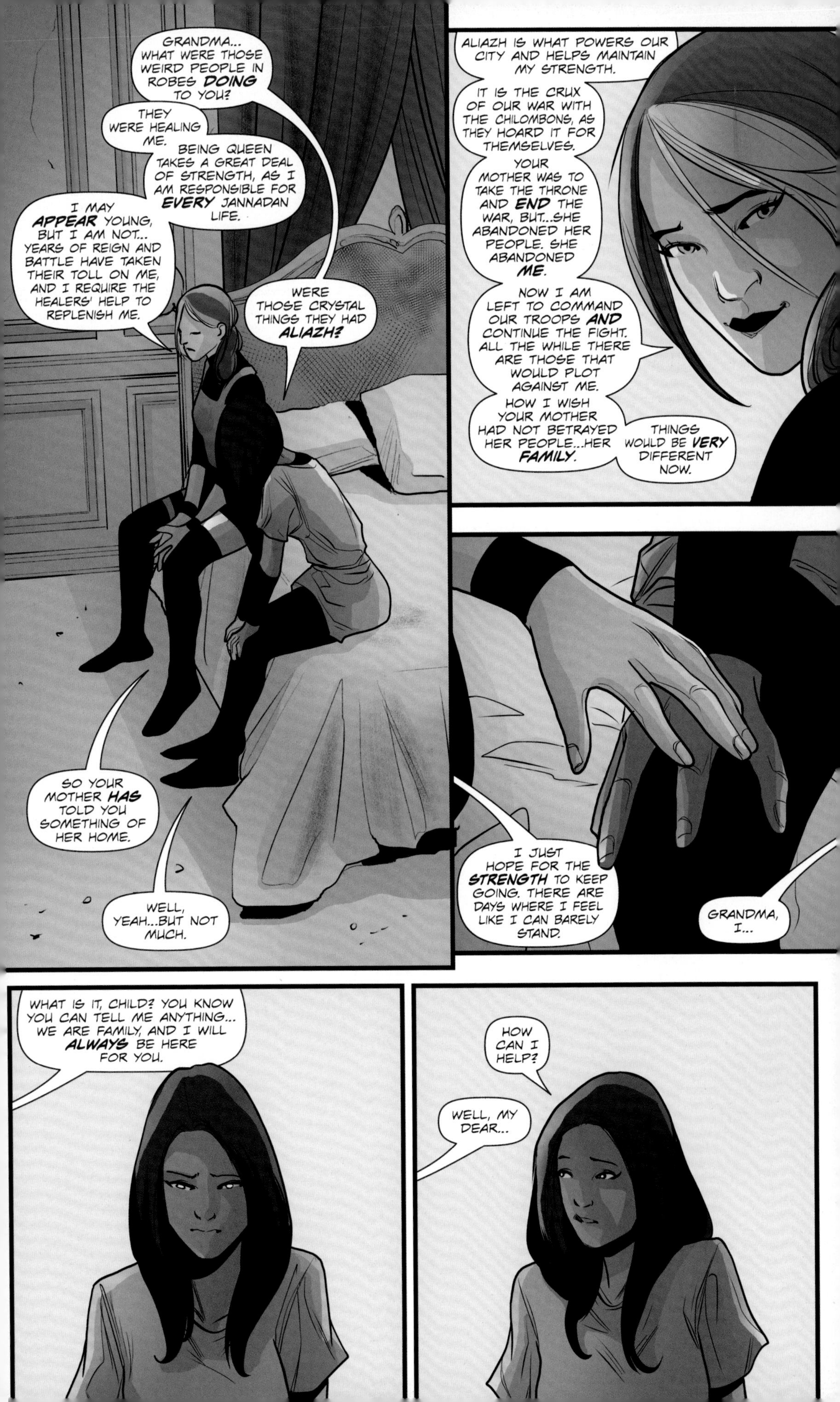
GRANDMA... WHAT WERE THOSE WEIRD PEOPLE IN ROBES DOING TO YOU?
THEY WERE HEALING ME.
BEING QUEEN TAKES A GREAT DEAL OF STRENGTH, AS I AM RESPONSIBLE FOR EVERY JANNADAN LIFE.
I MAY APPEAR YOUNG, BUT I AM NOT... YEARS OF REIGN AND BATTLE HAVE TAKEN THEIR TOLL ON ME, AND I REQUIRE THE HEALERS' HELP TO REPLENISH ME.
WERE THOSE CRYSTAL THINGS THEY HAD ALIAZH?
SO YOUR MOTHER HAS TOLD YOU SOMETHING OF HER HOME.
WELL, YEAH...BUT NOT MUCH.
ALIAZH IS WHAT POWERS OUR CITY AND HELPS MAINTAIN MY STRENGTH.
IT IS THE CRUX OF OUR WAR WITH THE CHILOMBONS, AS THEY HOARD IT FOR THEMSELVES.
YOUR MOTHER WAS TO TAKE THE THRONE AND END THE WAR, BUT...SHE ABANDONED HER PEOPLE. SHE ABANDONED ME.
NOW I AM LEFT TO COMMAND OUR TROOPS AND CONTINUE THE FIGHT. ALL THE WHILE THERE ARE THOSE THAT WOULD PLOT AGAINST ME.
HOW I WISH YOUR MOTHER HAD NOT BETRAYED HER PEOPLE...HER FAMILY.
THINGS WOULD BE VERY DIFFERENT NOW.
I JUST HOPE FOR THE STRENGTH TO KEEP GOING. THERE ARE DAYS WHERE I FEEL LIKE I CAN BARELY STAND.
GRANDMA, I...
WHAT IS IT, CHILD? YOU KNOW YOU CAN TELL ME ANYTHING... WE ARE FAMILY, AND I WILL ALWAYS BE HERE FOR YOU.
HOW CAN I HELP?
WELL, MY DEAR...

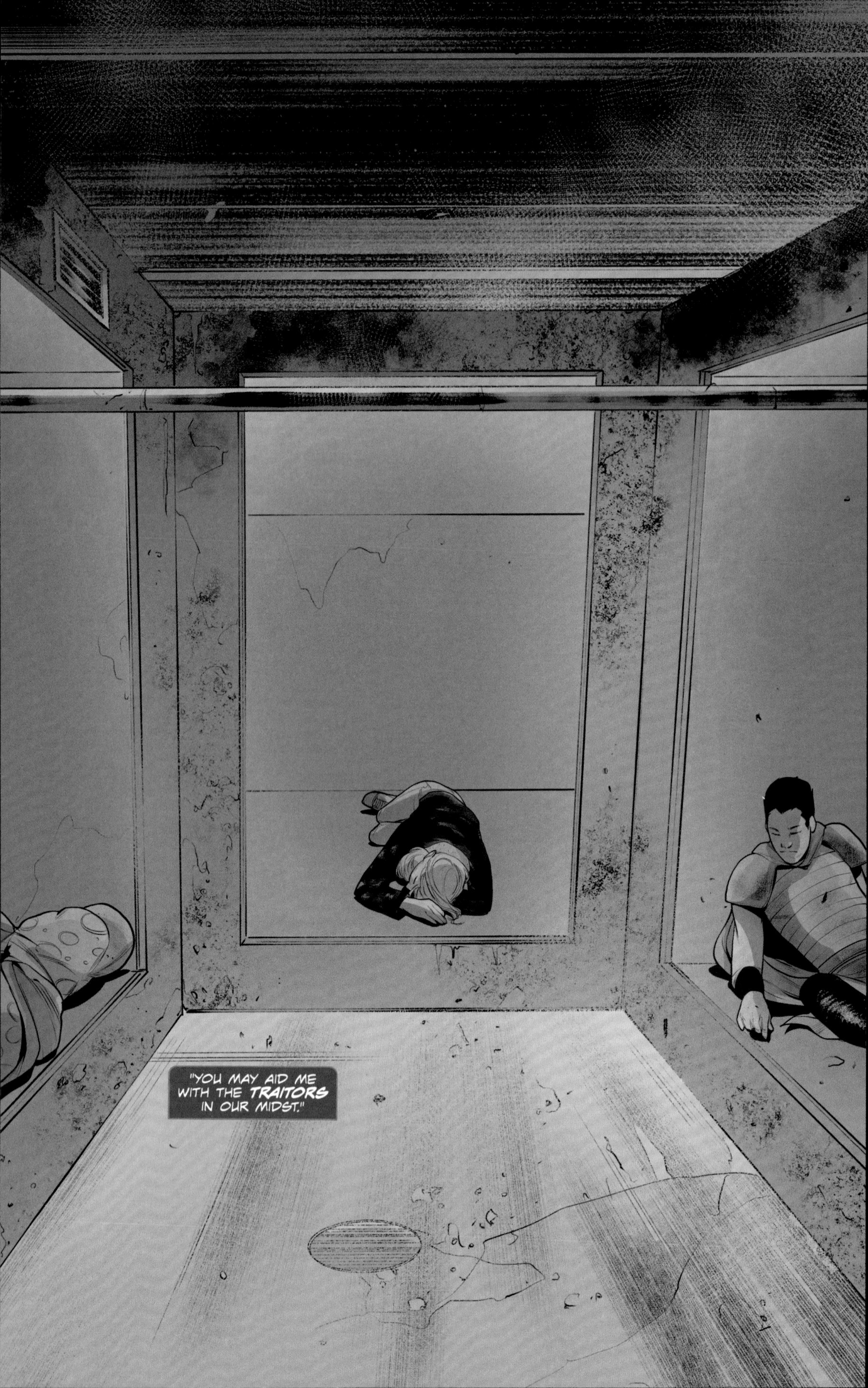
"YOU MAY AID ME WITH THE TRAITORS IN OUR MIDST."

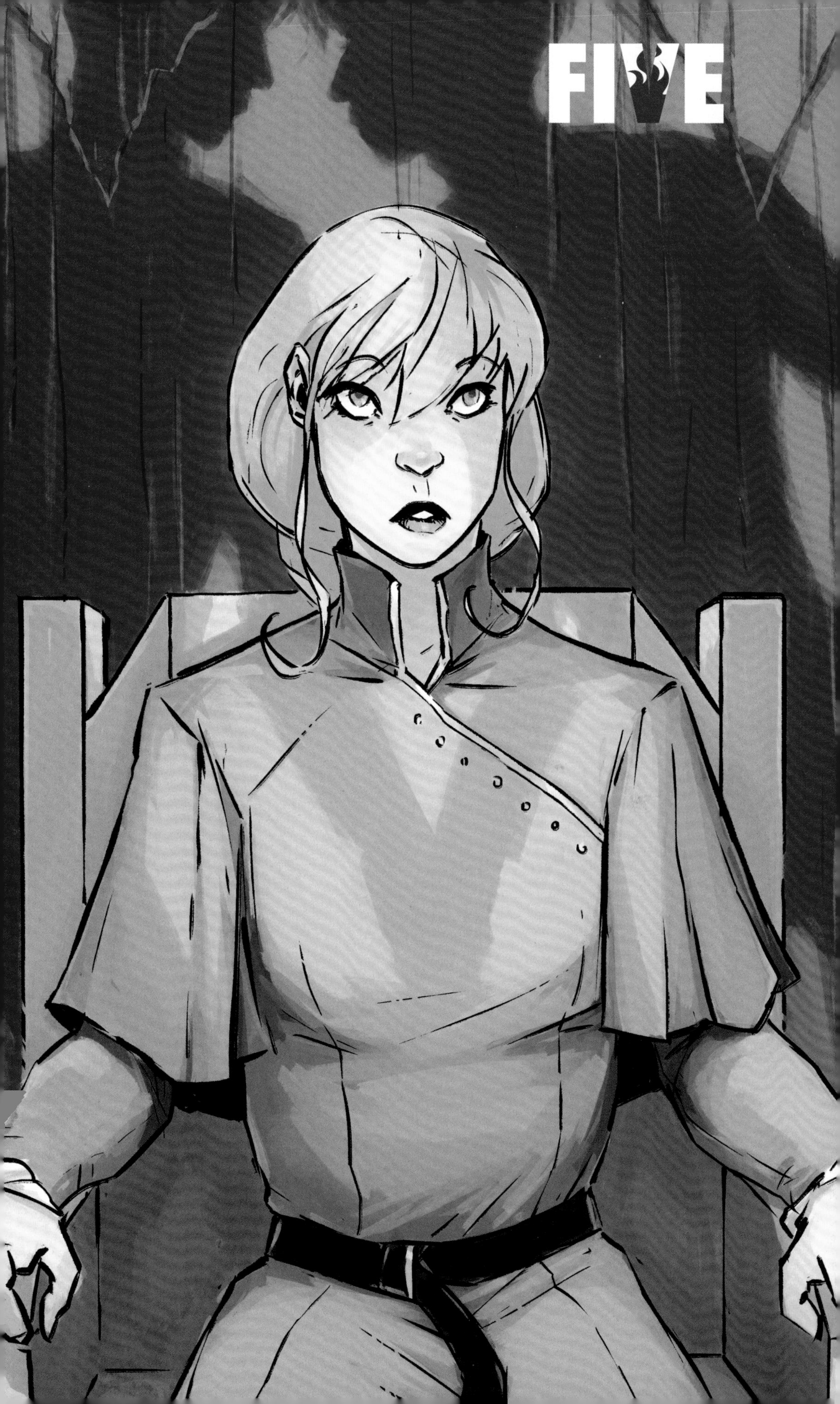
FIVE

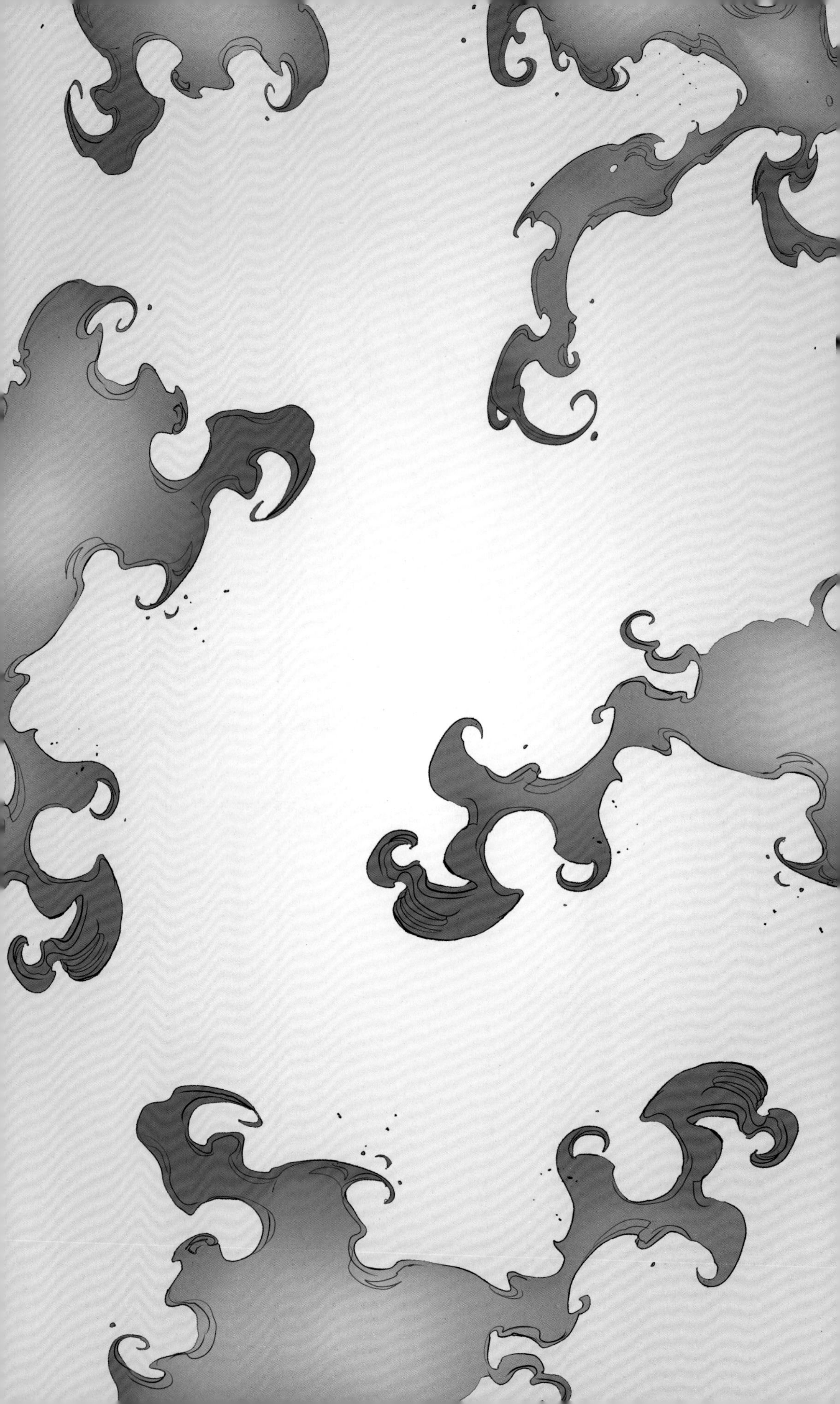

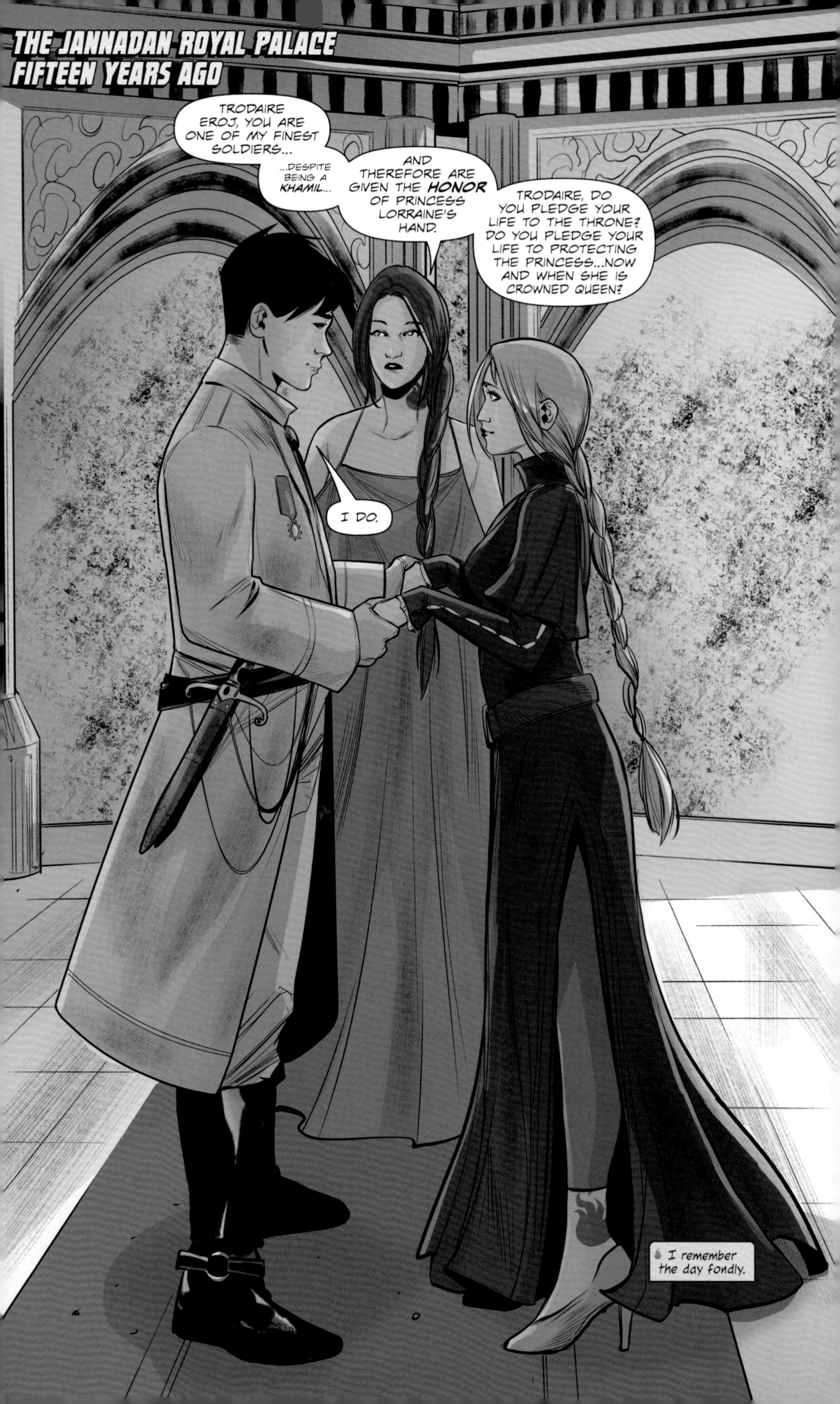

THE JANNADAN ROYAL PALACE
FIFTEEN YEARS AGO
TRODAIRE EROJ, YOU ARE ONE OF MY FINEST SOLDIERS...
...DESPITE BEING A KHAMIL...
AND THEREFORE ARE GIVEN THE HONOR OF PRINCESS LORRAINE'S HAND.
TRODAIRE, DO YOU PLEDGE YOUR LIFE TO THE THRONE? DO YOU PLEDGE YOUR LIFE TO PROTECTING THE PRINCESS...NOW AND WHEN SHE IS CROWNED QUEEN?
I DO.
I remember the day fondly.

I SWEAR TO ALWAYS HONOR AND PROTECT PRINCESS LORRAINE... TO FIGHT AT HER SIDE...

Trodaire looked so handsome.

AND I WILL LOVE HER AND GIVE HER AN **HEIR** TO THE GREAT THRONE OF JANNADA.

TRODAIRE...

And I was so nervous.

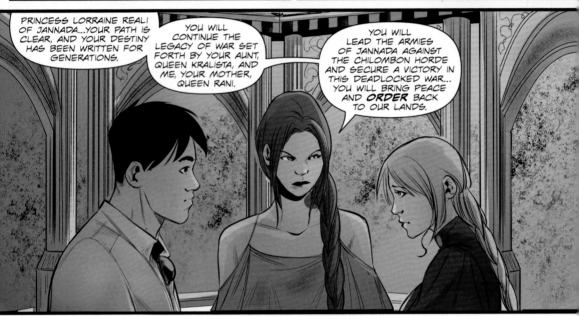

PRINCESS LORRAINE REALI OF JANNADA...YOUR PATH IS CLEAR, AND YOUR DESTINY HAS BEEN WRITTEN FOR GENERATIONS.

YOU WILL CONTINUE THE LEGACY OF WAR SET FORTH BY YOUR AUNT, QUEEN KRALISTA, AND ME, YOUR MOTHER, QUEEN RANI.

YOU WILL LEAD THE ARMIES OF JANNADA AGAINST THE CHILOMBON HORDE AND SECURE A VICTORY IN THIS DEADLOCKED WAR... YOU WILL BRING PEACE AND **ORDER** BACK TO OUR LANDS.

DO YOU ACCEPT THESE RESPONSIBILITIES, PRINCESS?

I WILL.

LOUDER, CHILD.

It was a pledge I never wanted to make.

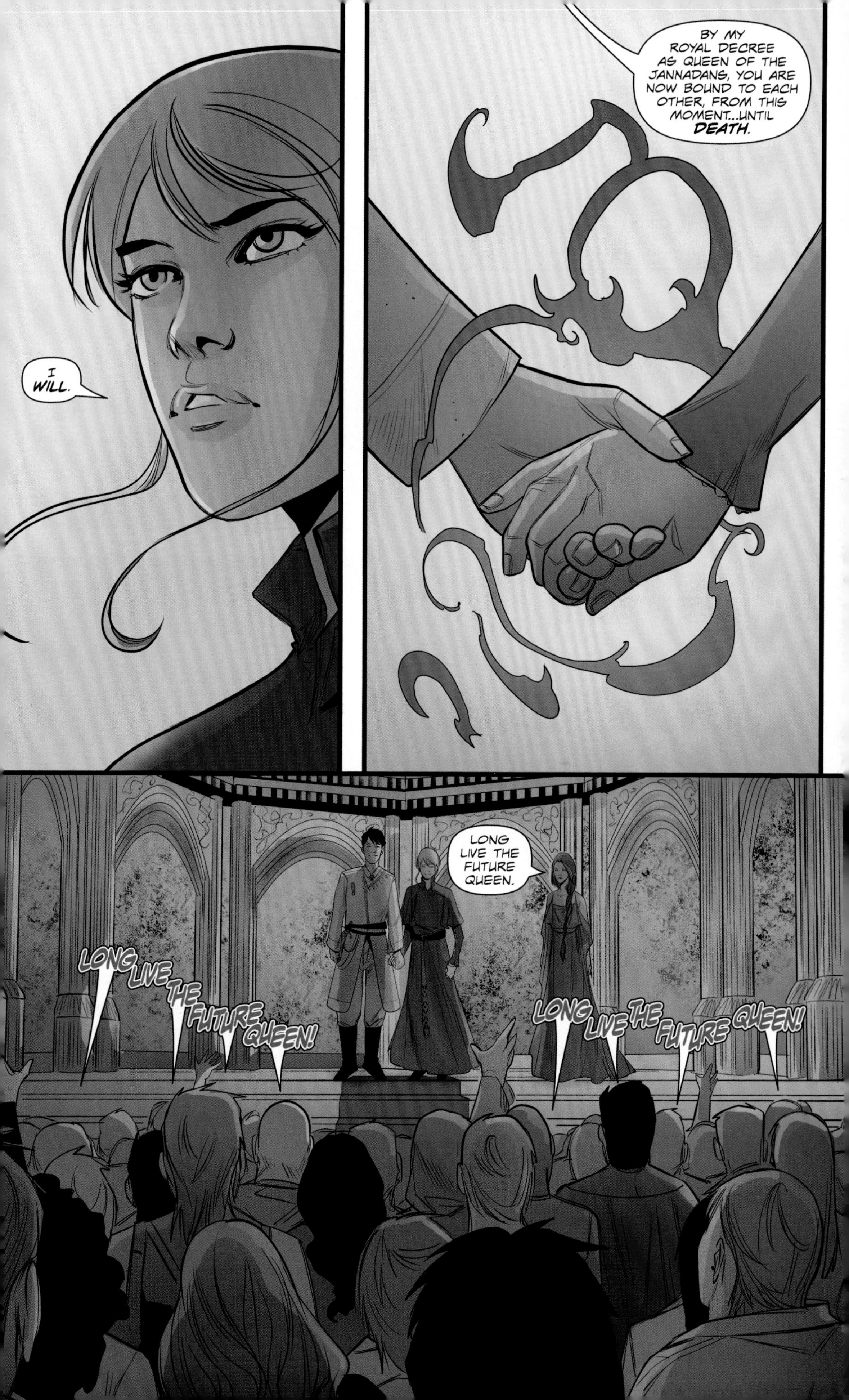
I WILL.
BY MY ROYAL DECREE AS QUEEN OF THE JANNADANS, YOU ARE NOW BOUND TO EACH OTHER, FROM THIS MOMENT...UNTIL DEATH.
LONG LIVE THE FUTURE QUEEN.
LONG LIVE THE FUTURE QUEEN!
LONG LIVE THE FUTURE QUEEN!

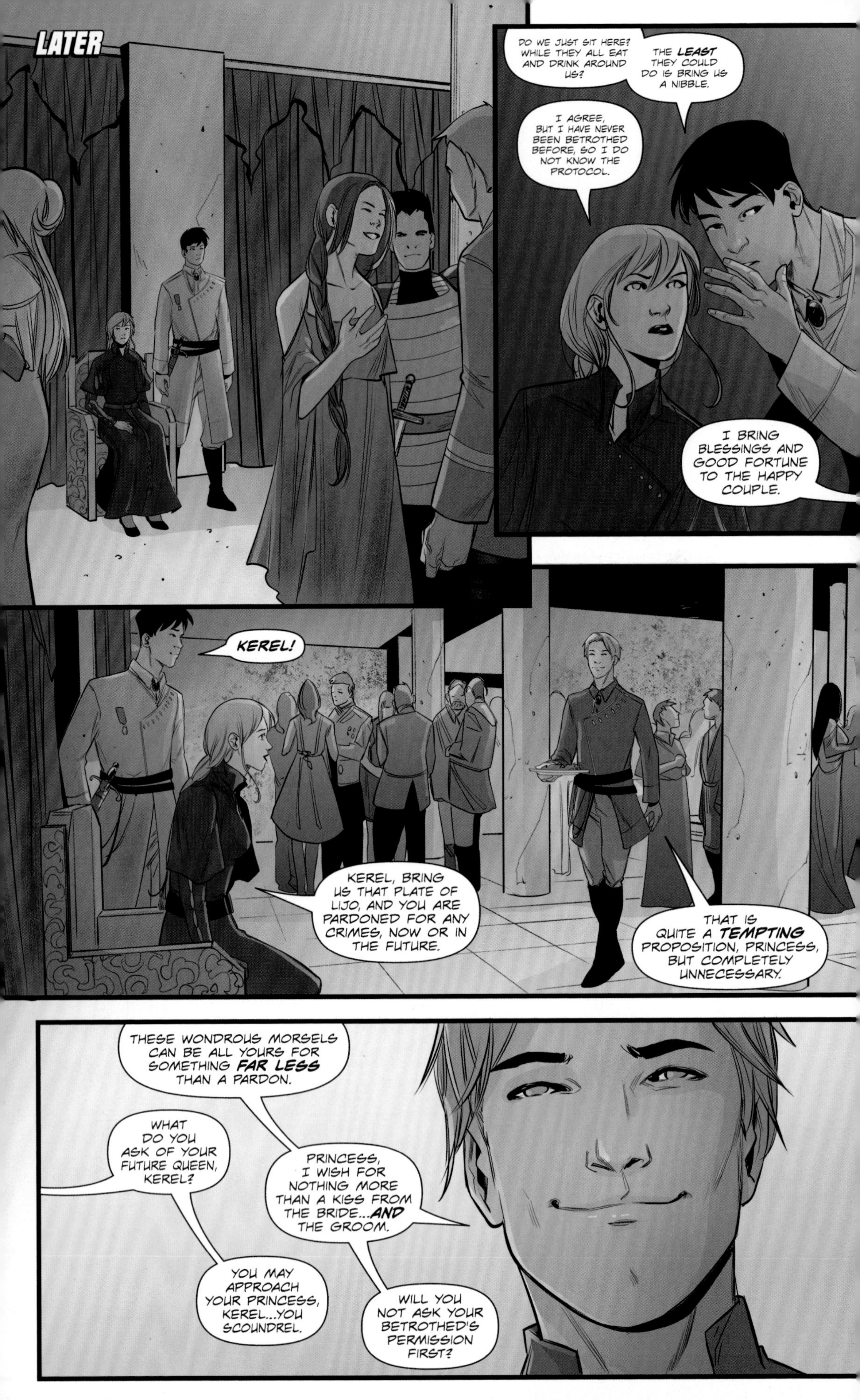
LATER
DO WE JUST SIT HERE? WHILE THEY ALL EAT AND DRINK AROUND US?
THE LEAST THEY COULD DO IS BRING US A NIBBLE.
I AGREE, BUT I HAVE NEVER BEEN BETROTHED BEFORE, SO I DO NOT KNOW THE PROTOCOL.
I BRING BLESSINGS AND GOOD FORTUNE TO THE HAPPY COUPLE.
KEREL!
KEREL, BRING US THAT PLATE OF LIJO, AND YOU ARE PARDONED FOR ANY CRIMES, NOW OR IN THE FUTURE.
THAT IS QUITE A TEMPTING PROPOSITION, PRINCESS, BUT COMPLETELY UNNECESSARY.
THESE WONDROUS MORSELS CAN BE ALL YOURS FOR SOMETHING FAR LESS THAN A PARDON.
WHAT DO YOU ASK OF YOUR FUTURE QUEEN, KEREL?
PRINCESS, I WISH FOR NOTHING MORE THAN A KISS FROM THE BRIDE...AND THE GROOM.
YOU MAY APPROACH YOUR PRINCESS, KEREL...YOU SCOUNDREL.
WILL YOU NOT ASK YOUR BETROTHED'S PERMISSION FIRST?

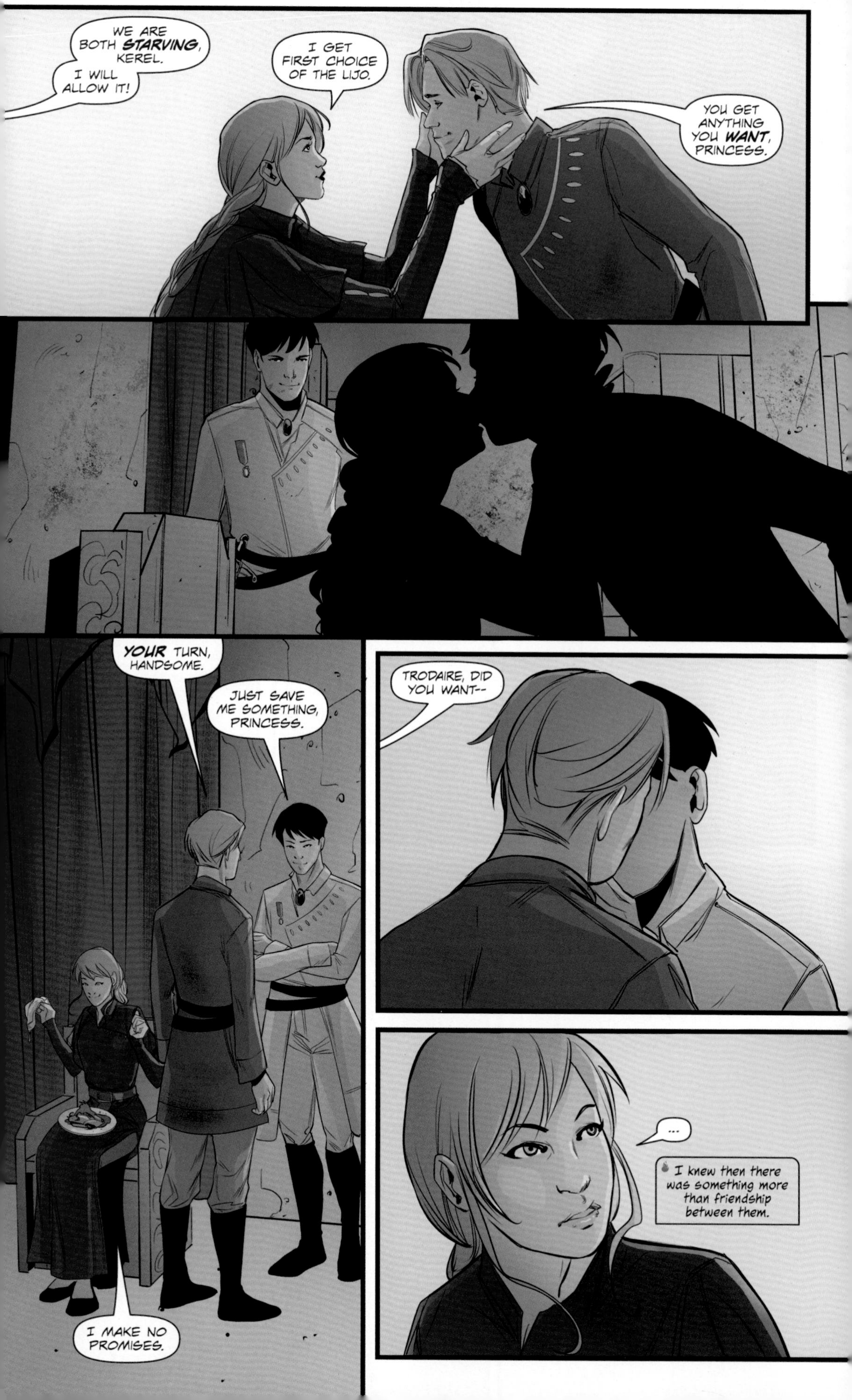
WE ARE BOTH STARVING, KEREL.
I WILL ALLOW IT!
I GET FIRST CHOICE OF THE LIJO.
YOU GET ANYTHING YOU WANT, PRINCESS.
YOUR TURN, HANDSOME.
JUST SAVE ME SOMETHING, PRINCESS.
I MAKE NO PROMISES.
TRODAIRE, DID YOU WANT--
...
I knew then there was something more than friendship between them.

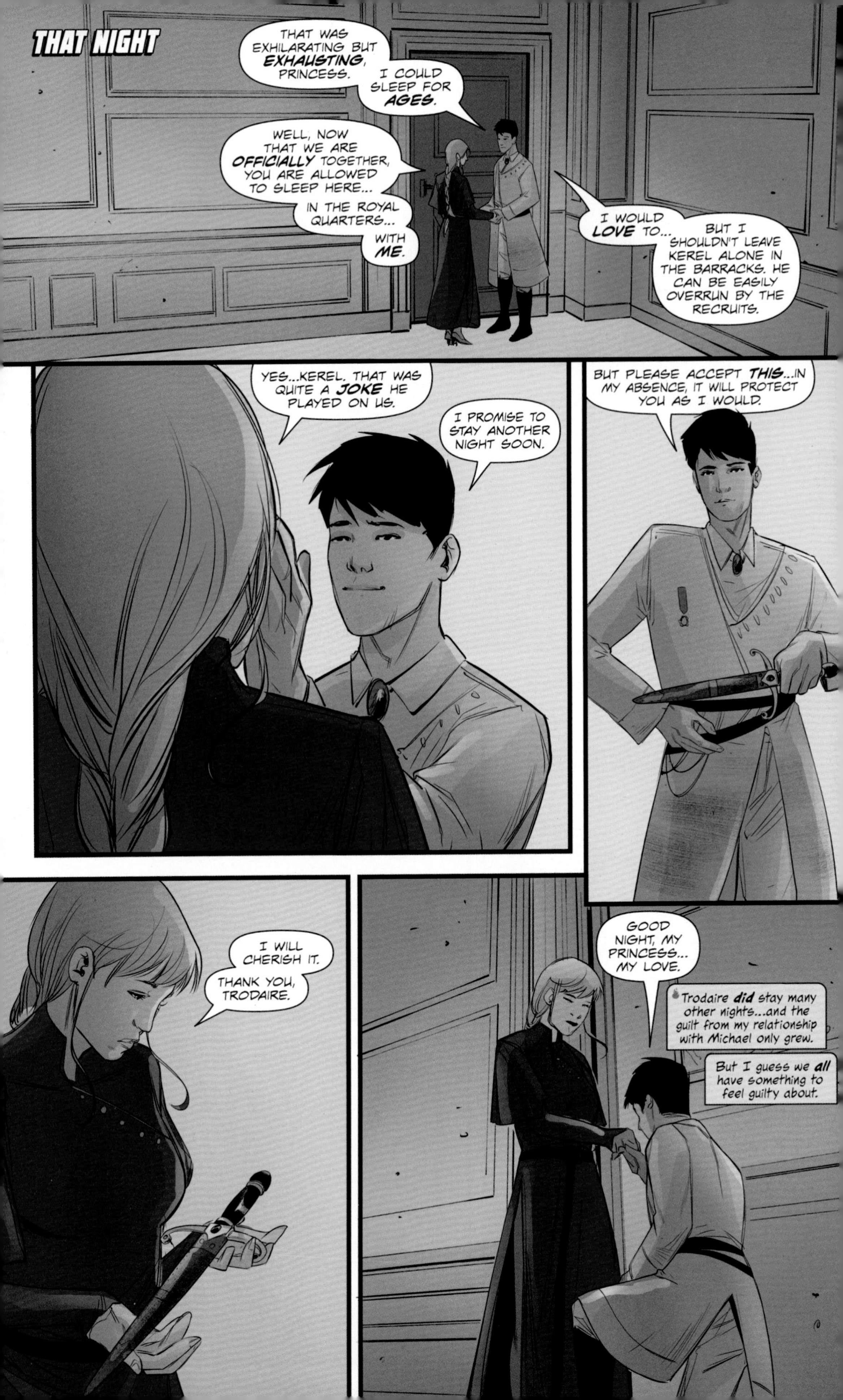
THAT NIGHT
THAT WAS EXHILARATING BUT EXHAUSTING, PRINCESS.
I COULD SLEEP FOR AGES.
WELL, NOW THAT WE ARE OFFICIALLY TOGETHER, YOU ARE ALLOWED TO SLEEP HERE...
IN THE ROYAL QUARTERS...
WITH ME.
I WOULD LOVE TO...
BUT I SHOULDN'T LEAVE KEREL ALONE IN THE BARRACKS. HE CAN BE EASILY OVERRUN BY THE RECRUITS.
YES...KEREL. THAT WAS QUITE A JOKE HE PLAYED ON US.
I PROMISE TO STAY ANOTHER NIGHT SOON.
BUT PLEASE ACCEPT THIS...IN MY ABSENCE, IT WILL PROTECT YOU AS I WOULD.
I WILL CHERISH IT.
THANK YOU, TRODAIRE.
GOOD NIGHT, MY PRINCESS... MY LOVE.
Trodaire did stay many other nights...and the guilt from my relationship with Michael only grew.
But I guess we all have something to feel guilty about.

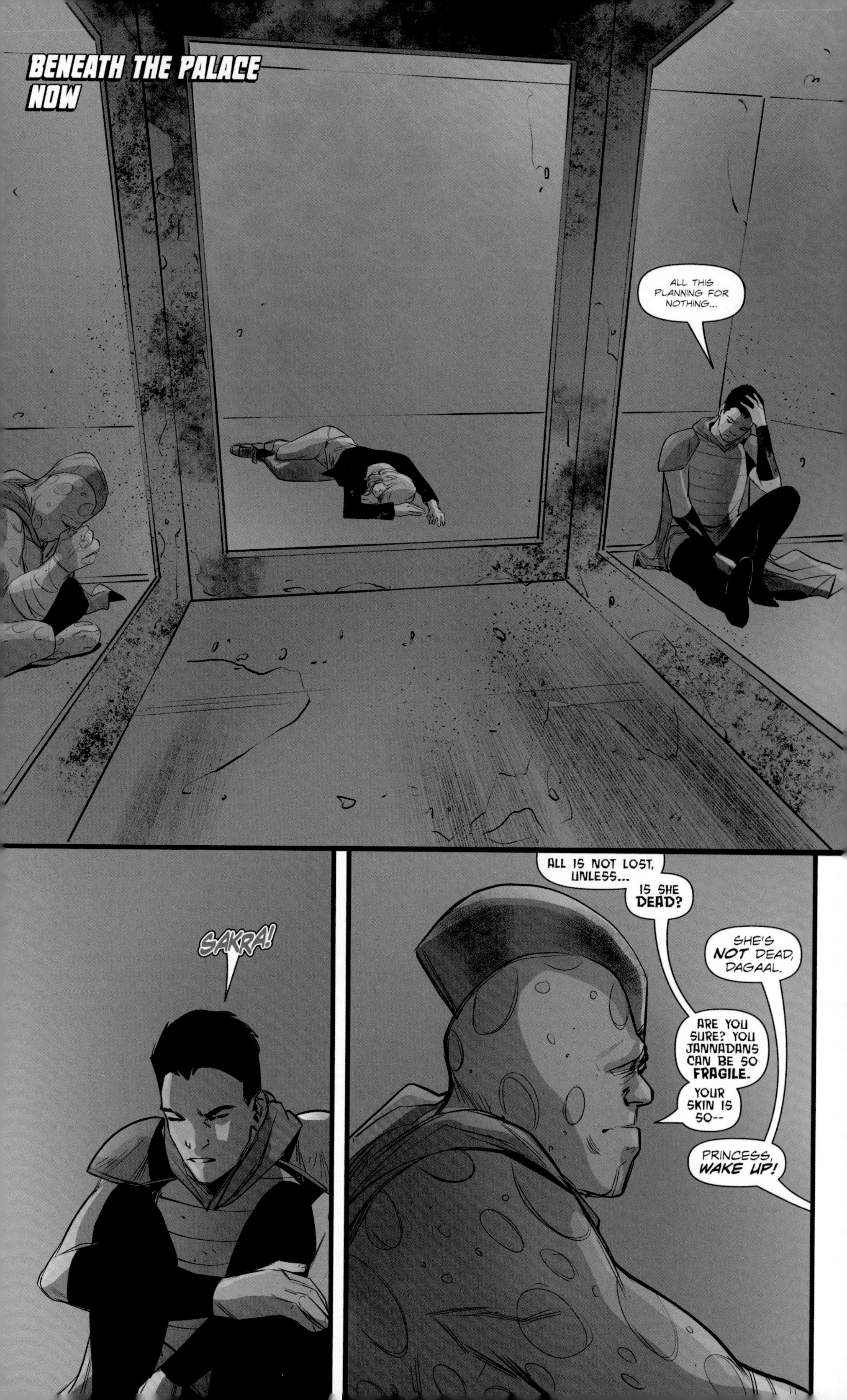
BENEATH THE PALACE
NOW
ALL THIS PLANNING FOR NOTHING...
SAKRA!
ALL IS NOT LOST, UNLESS... IS SHE DEAD?
SHE'S NOT DEAD, DAGAAL.
ARE YOU SURE? YOU JANNADANS CAN BE SO FRAGILE.
YOUR SKIN IS SO--
PRINCESS, WAKE UP!

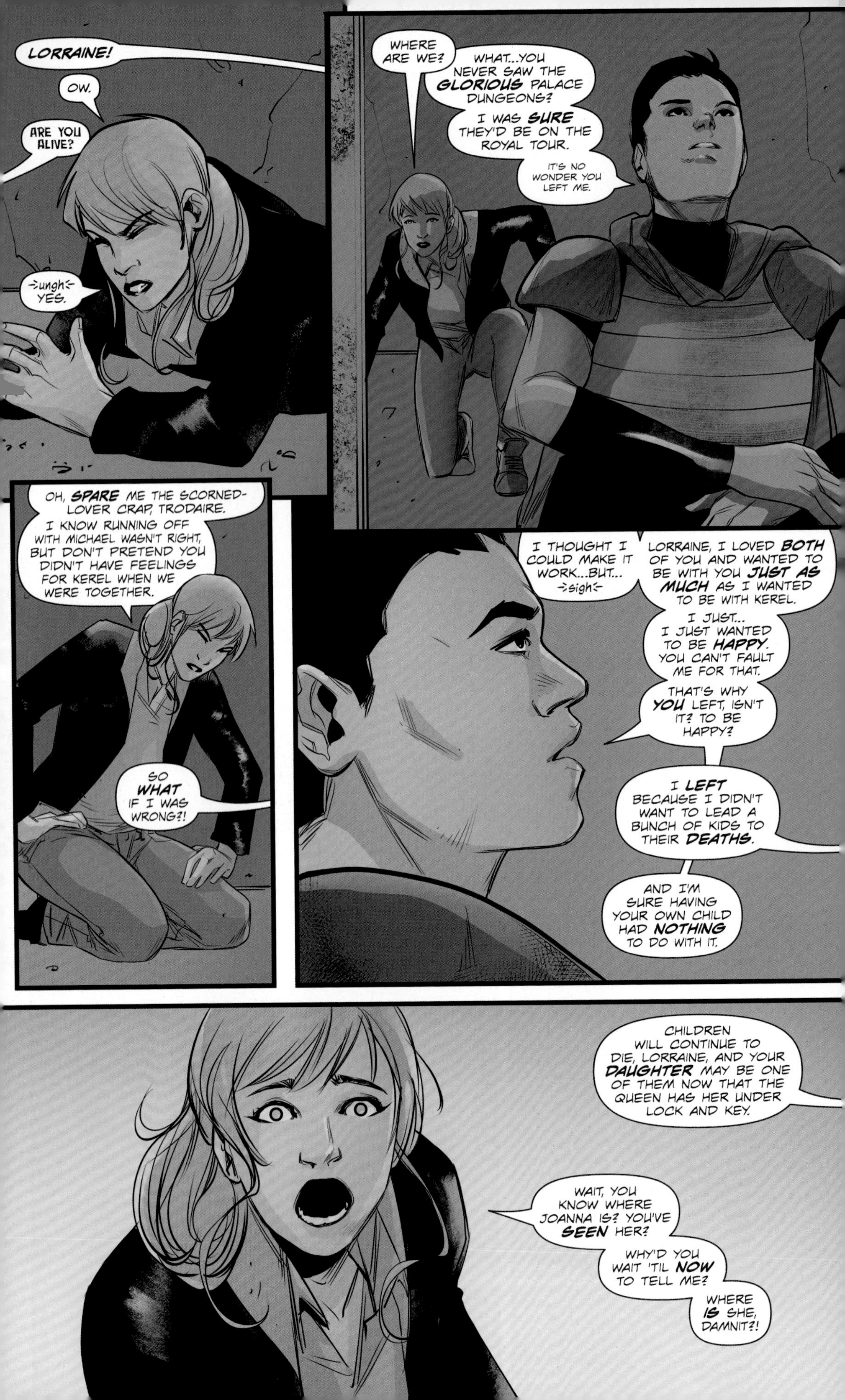
LORRAINE!
OW.
ARE YOU ALIVE?
-ungh- YES.
WHERE ARE WE?
WHAT...YOU NEVER SAW THE GLORIOUS PALACE DUNGEONS?
I WAS SURE THEY'D BE ON THE ROYAL TOUR.
IT'S NO WONDER YOU LEFT ME.
OH, SPARE ME THE SCORNED-LOVER CRAP, TRODAIRE.
I KNOW RUNNING OFF WITH MICHAEL WASN'T RIGHT, BUT DON'T PRETEND YOU DIDN'T HAVE FEELINGS FOR KEREL WHEN WE WERE TOGETHER.
SO WHAT IF I WAS WRONG?!
I THOUGHT I COULD MAKE IT WORK...BUT... -sigh-
LORRAINE, I LOVED BOTH OF YOU AND WANTED TO BE WITH YOU JUST AS MUCH AS I WANTED TO BE WITH KEREL.
I JUST... I JUST WANTED TO BE HAPPY. YOU CAN'T FAULT ME FOR THAT.
THAT'S WHY YOU LEFT, ISN'T IT? TO BE HAPPY?
I LEFT BECAUSE I DIDN'T WANT TO LEAD A BUNCH OF KIDS TO THEIR DEATHS.
AND I'M SURE HAVING YOUR OWN CHILD HAD NOTHING TO DO WITH IT.
CHILDREN WILL CONTINUE TO DIE, LORRAINE, AND YOUR DAUGHTER MAY BE ONE OF THEM NOW THAT THE QUEEN HAS HER UNDER LOCK AND KEY.
WAIT, YOU KNOW WHERE JOANNA IS? YOU'VE SEEN HER?
WHY'D YOU WAIT 'TIL NOW TO TELL ME?
WHERE IS SHE, DAMNIT?!

THE DECEPTION WAS NOT MEANT TO HARM YOU, PRINCESS, BUT THE TRUTH OF THE MATTER IS THIS...

THE QUEEN WILL NOT RELEASE YOUR DAUGHTER WILLINGLY.

THE ONLY WAY TO GET HER BACK IS TO HELP US OVERTHROW RANI.

DAGAAL, WHOEVER'S ON THE THRONE... THIS WAR WILL GO ON FOREVER.

THAT IS NOT TRUE.

YOU ARE TOO YOUNG TO KNOW OF THE TIME WHEN ALL THOSE IN JANNADA LIVED IN HARMONY.

WE CHILOMBONS WISH TO RETURN TO THAT AS DO MANY JANNADANS. SO MANY HAVE URGED YOUR MOTHER TO SIGN THE PEACE TREATY WE HAVE BEEN OFFERING FOR YEARS.

WE HAD HOPED THAT YOU COULD INFLUENCE HER.

THE QUEEN WAS DISMISSIVE OF ME AS A CHILD, AND SHE CERTAINLY WON'T TAKE MY ADVICE NOW.

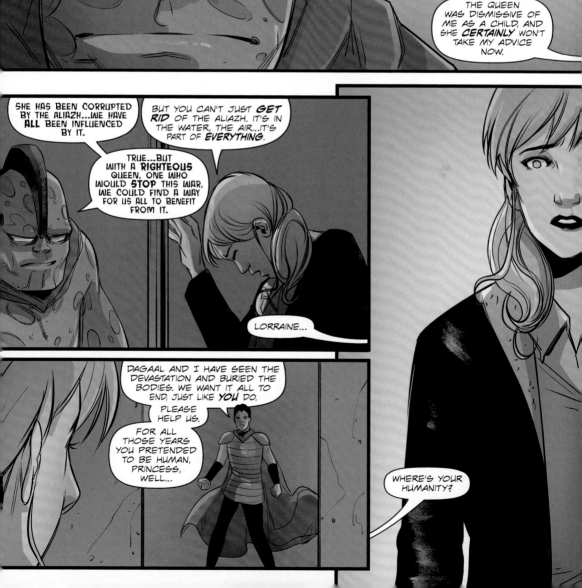

SHE HAS BEEN CORRUPTED BY THE ALIAZH...WE HAVE ALL BEEN INFLUENCED BY IT.

BUT YOU CAN'T JUST GET RID OF THE ALIAZH. IT'S IN THE WATER, THE AIR...IT'S PART OF EVERYTHING.

TRUE....BUT WITH A RIGHTEOUS QUEEN, ONE WHO WOULD STOP THIS WAR, WE COULD FIND A WAY FOR US ALL TO BENEFIT FROM IT.

LORRAINE...

DAGAAL AND I HAVE SEEN THE DEVASTATION AND BURIED THE BODIES. WE WANT IT ALL TO END, JUST LIKE YOU DO.

PLEASE HELP US.

FOR ALL THOSE YEARS YOU PRETENDED TO BE HUMAN, PRINCESS, WELL...

WHERE'S YOUR HUMANITY?

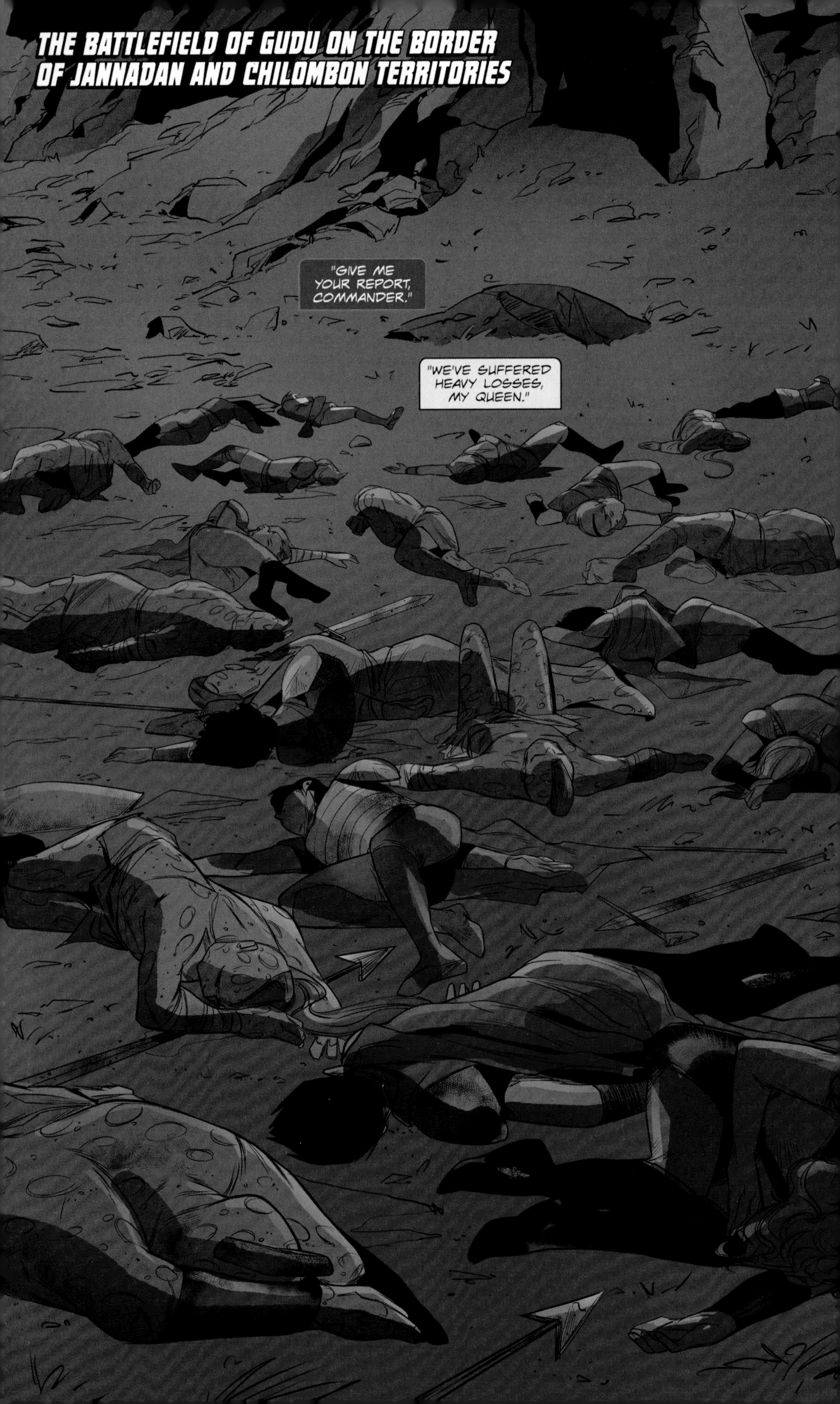
THE BATTLEFIELD OF GUDU ON THE BORDER OF JANNADAN AND CHILOMBON TERRITORIES
"GIVE ME YOUR REPORT, COMMANDER."
"WE'VE SUFFERED HEAVY LOSSES, MY QUEEN."

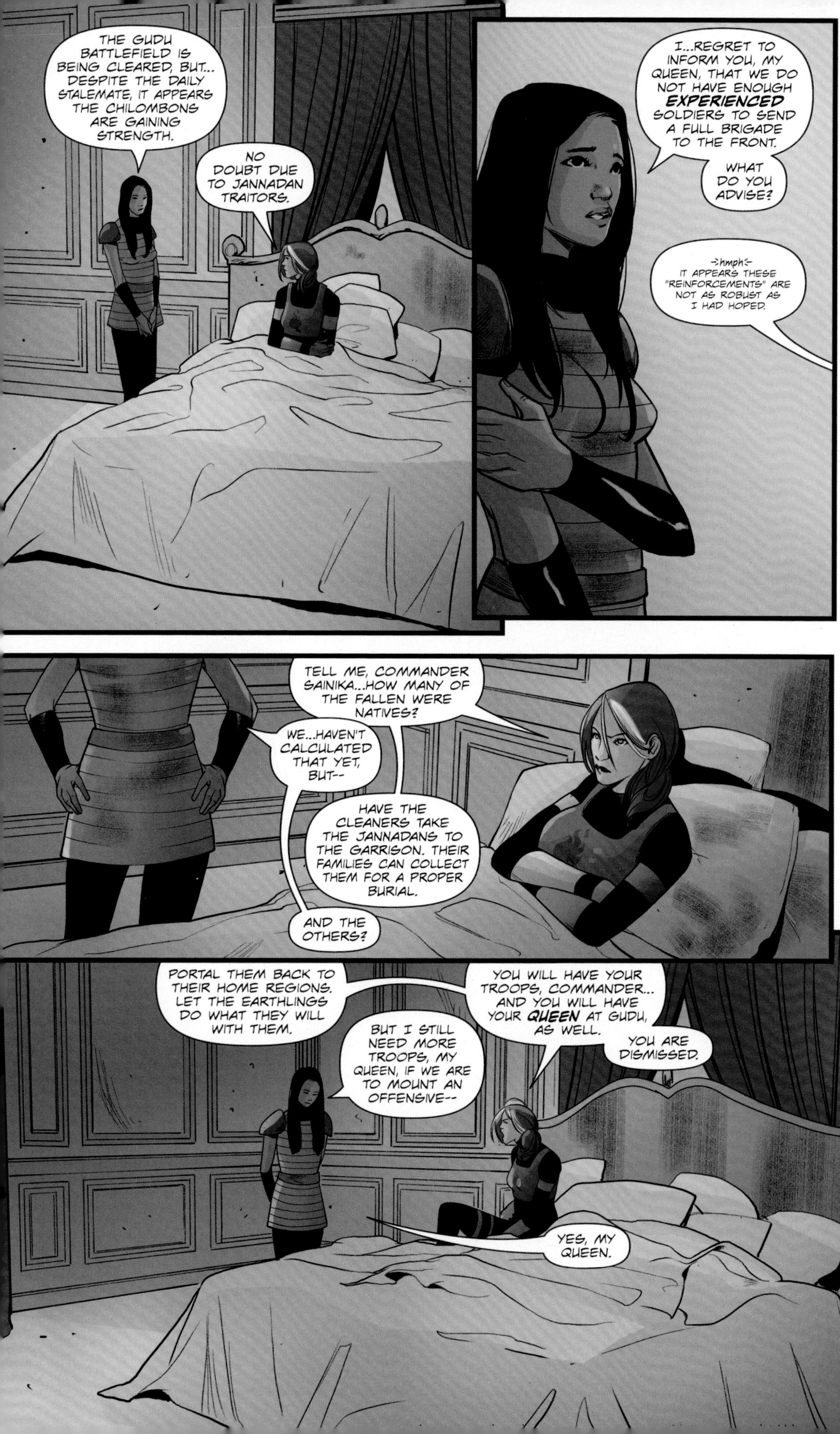
THE GUDU BATTLEFIELD IS BEING CLEARED, BUT... DESPITE THE DAILY STALEMATE, IT APPEARS THE CHILOMBONS ARE GAINING STRENGTH.
NO DOUBT DUE TO JANNADAN TRAITORS.
I...REGRET TO INFORM YOU, MY QUEEN, THAT WE DO NOT HAVE ENOUGH **EXPERIENCED** SOLDIERS TO SEND A FULL BRIGADE TO THE FRONT.
WHAT DO YOU ADVISE?
hmph
IT APPEARS THESE "REINFORCEMENTS" ARE NOT AS ROBUST AS I HAD HOPED.
TELL ME, COMMANDER SAINIKA...HOW MANY OF THE FALLEN WERE NATIVES?
WE...HAVEN'T CALCULATED THAT YET, BUT--
HAVE THE CLEANERS TAKE THE JANNADANS TO THE GARRISON. THEIR FAMILIES CAN COLLECT THEM FOR A PROPER BURIAL.
AND THE OTHERS?
PORTAL THEM BACK TO THEIR HOME REGIONS. LET THE EARTHLINGS DO WHAT THEY WILL WITH THEM.
BUT I STILL NEED MORE TROOPS, MY QUEEN, IF WE ARE TO MOUNT AN OFFENSIVE--
YOU WILL HAVE YOUR TROOPS, COMMANDER... AND YOU WILL HAVE YOUR **QUEEN** AT GUDU, AS WELL.
YOU ARE DISMISSED.
YES, MY QUEEN.

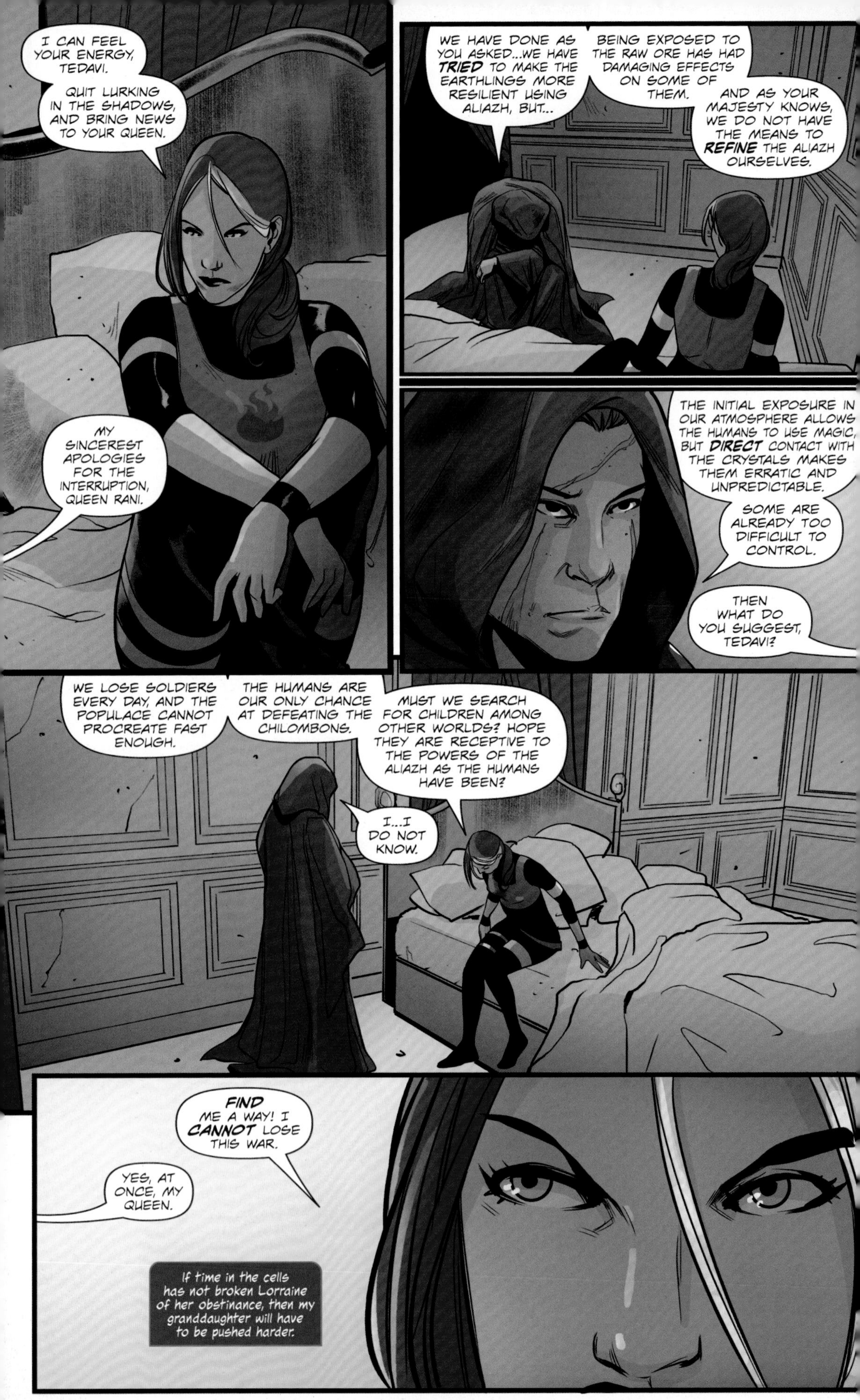

I CAN FEEL YOUR ENERGY, TEDAVI.
QUIT LURKING IN THE SHADOWS, AND BRING NEWS TO YOUR QUEEN.
MY SINCEREST APOLOGIES FOR THE INTERRUPTION, QUEEN RANI.
WE HAVE DONE AS YOU ASKED...WE HAVE TRIED TO MAKE THE EARTHLINGS MORE RESILIENT USING ALIAZH, BUT...
BEING EXPOSED TO THE RAW ORE HAS HAD DAMAGING EFFECTS ON SOME OF THEM.
AND AS YOUR MAJESTY KNOWS, WE DO NOT HAVE THE MEANS TO REFINE THE ALIAZH OURSELVES.
THE INITIAL EXPOSURE IN OUR ATMOSPHERE ALLOWS THE HUMANS TO USE MAGIC, BUT DIRECT CONTACT WITH THE CRYSTALS MAKES THEM ERRATIC AND UNPREDICTABLE.
SOME ARE ALREADY TOO DIFFICULT TO CONTROL.
THEN WHAT DO YOU SUGGEST, TEDAVI?
WE LOSE SOLDIERS EVERY DAY, AND THE POPULACE CANNOT PROCREATE FAST ENOUGH.
THE HUMANS ARE OUR ONLY CHANCE AT DEFEATING THE CHILOMBONS.
MUST WE SEARCH FOR CHILDREN AMONG OTHER WORLDS? HOPE THEY ARE RECEPTIVE TO THE POWERS OF THE ALIAZH AS THE HUMANS HAVE BEEN?
I...I DO NOT KNOW.
FIND ME A WAY! I CANNOT LOSE THIS WAR.
YES, AT ONCE, MY QUEEN.
If time in the cells has not broken Lorraine of her obstinance, then my granddaughter will have to be pushed harder.

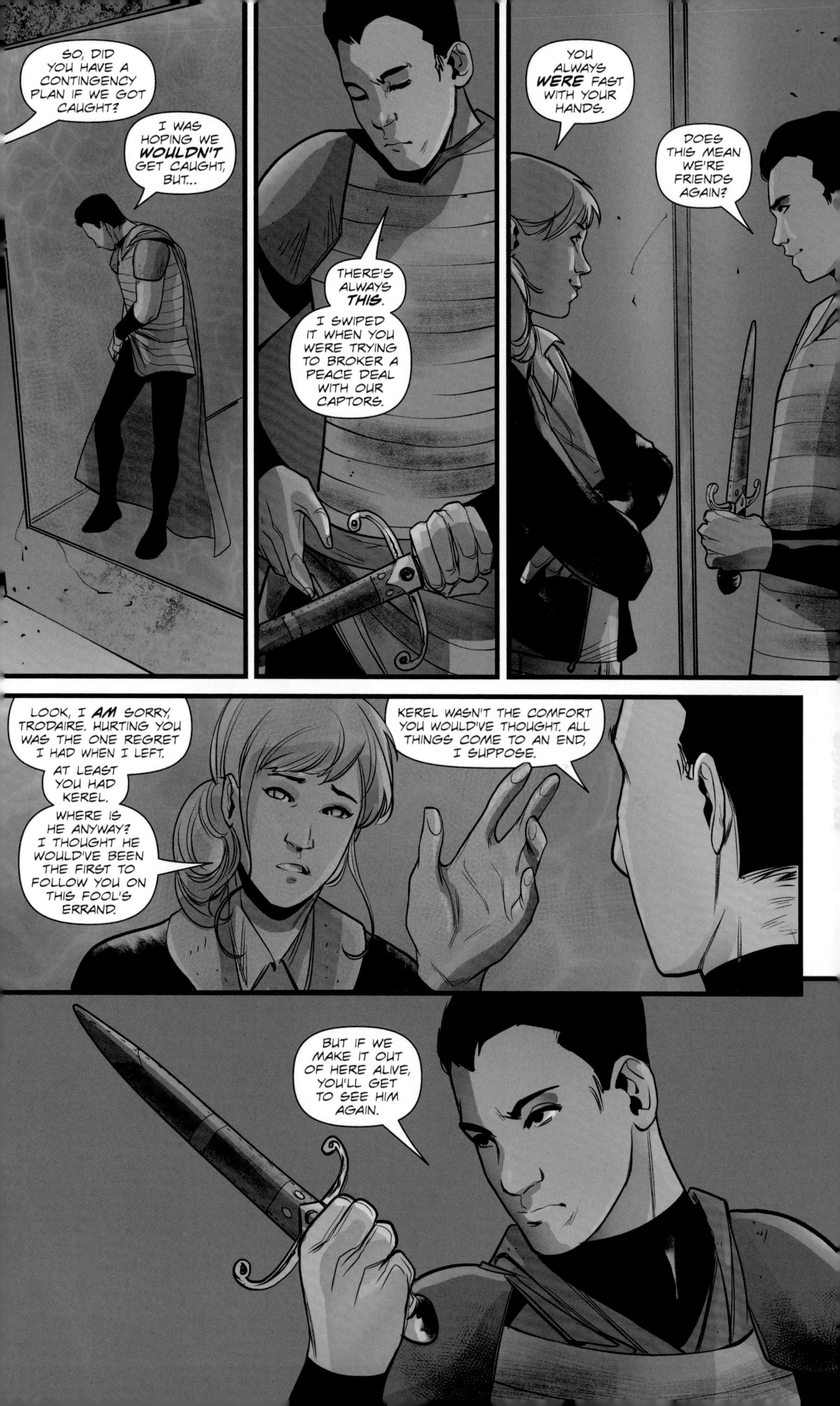
SO, DID YOU HAVE A CONTINGENCY PLAN IF WE GOT CAUGHT?
I WAS HOPING WE WOULDN'T GET CAUGHT, BUT...
THERE'S ALWAYS THIS.
I SWIPED IT WHEN YOU WERE TRYING TO BROKER A PEACE DEAL WITH OUR CAPTORS.
YOU ALWAYS WERE FAST WITH YOUR HANDS.
DOES THIS MEAN WE'RE FRIENDS AGAIN?
LOOK, I AM SORRY, TRODAIRE. HURTING YOU WAS THE ONE REGRET I HAD WHEN I LEFT.
AT LEAST YOU HAD KEREL.
WHERE IS HE ANYWAY? I THOUGHT HE WOULD'VE BEEN THE FIRST TO FOLLOW YOU ON THIS FOOL'S ERRAND.
KEREL WASN'T THE COMFORT YOU WOULD'VE THOUGHT. ALL THINGS COME TO AN END, I SUPPOSE.
BUT IF WE MAKE IT OUT OF HERE ALIVE, YOU'LL GET TO SEE HIM AGAIN.

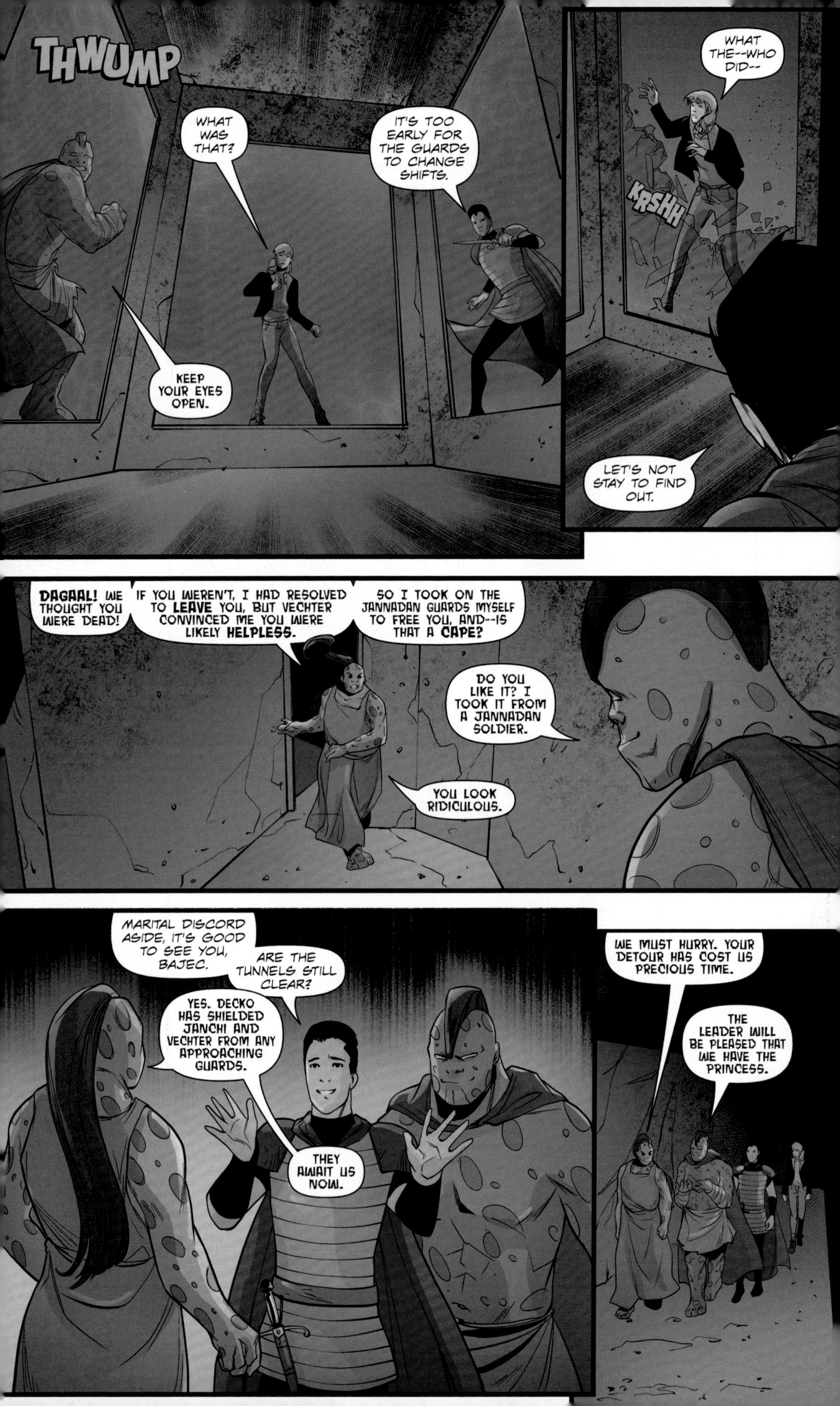
THWUMP
WHAT WAS THAT?
IT'S TOO EARLY FOR THE GUARDS TO CHANGE SHIFTS.
KEEP YOUR EYES OPEN.
WHAT THE--WHO DID--
KRSHH
LET'S NOT STAY TO FIND OUT.
DAGAAL! WE THOUGHT YOU WERE DEAD!
IF YOU WEREN'T, I HAD RESOLVED TO LEAVE YOU, BUT VECHTER CONVINCED ME YOU WERE LIKELY HELPLESS.
SO I TOOK ON THE JANNADAN GUARDS MYSELF TO FREE YOU, AND--IS THAT A CAPE?
DO YOU LIKE IT? I TOOK IT FROM A JANNADAN SOLDIER.
YOU LOOK RIDICULOUS.
MARITAL DISCORD ASIDE, IT'S GOOD TO SEE YOU, BAJEC.
ARE THE TUNNELS STILL CLEAR?
YES. DECKO HAS SHIELDED JANCHI AND VECHTER FROM ANY APPROACHING GUARDS.
THEY AWAIT US NOW.
WE MUST HURRY. YOUR DETOUR HAS COST US PRECIOUS TIME.
THE LEADER WILL BE PLEASED THAT WE HAVE THE PRINCESS.

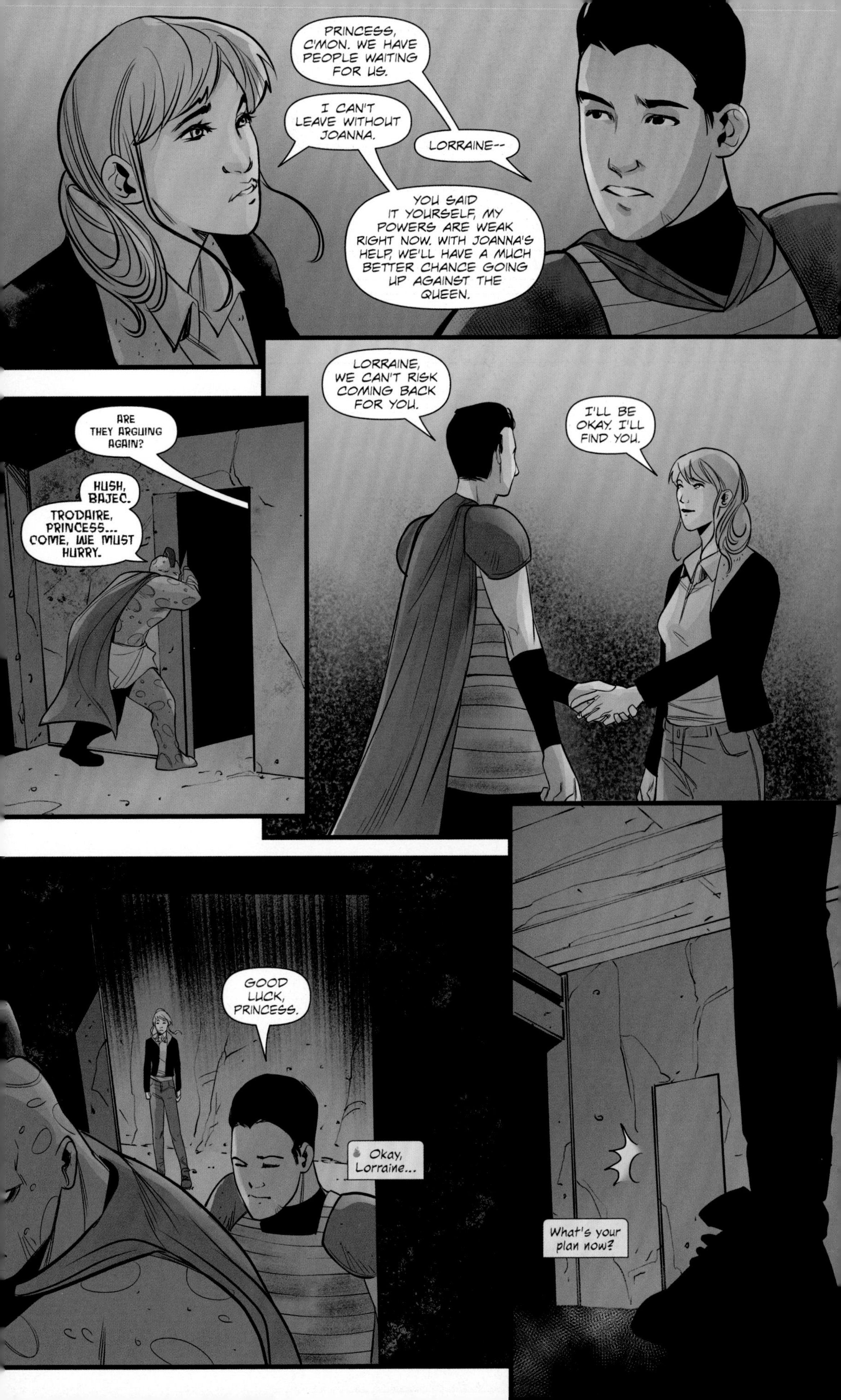
PRINCESS, C'MON. WE HAVE PEOPLE WAITING FOR US.
I CAN'T LEAVE WITHOUT JOANNA.
LORRAINE--
YOU SAID IT YOURSELF, MY POWERS ARE WEAK RIGHT NOW. WITH JOANNA'S HELP, WE'LL HAVE A MUCH BETTER CHANCE GOING UP AGAINST THE QUEEN.
ARE THEY ARGUING AGAIN?
HUSH, BAJEC.
TRODAIRE, PRINCESS... COME, WE MUST HURRY.
LORRAINE, WE CAN'T RISK COMING BACK FOR YOU.
I'LL BE OKAY. I'LL FIND YOU.
GOOD LUCK, PRINCESS.
Okay, Lorraine...
What's your plan now?

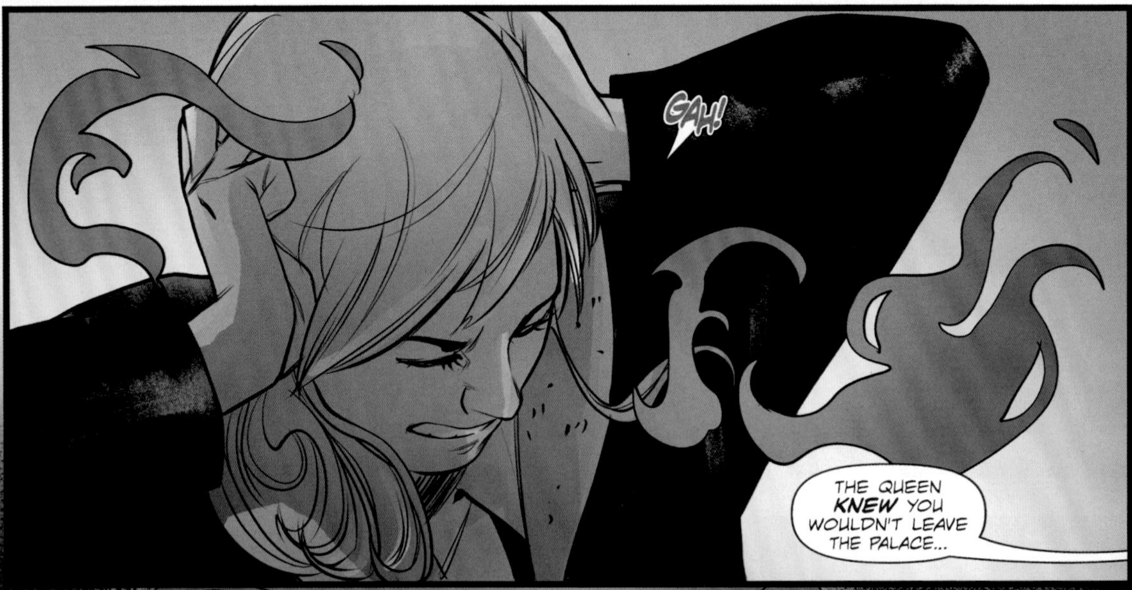
GAH!
THE QUEEN KNEW YOU WOULDN'T LEAVE THE PALACE...

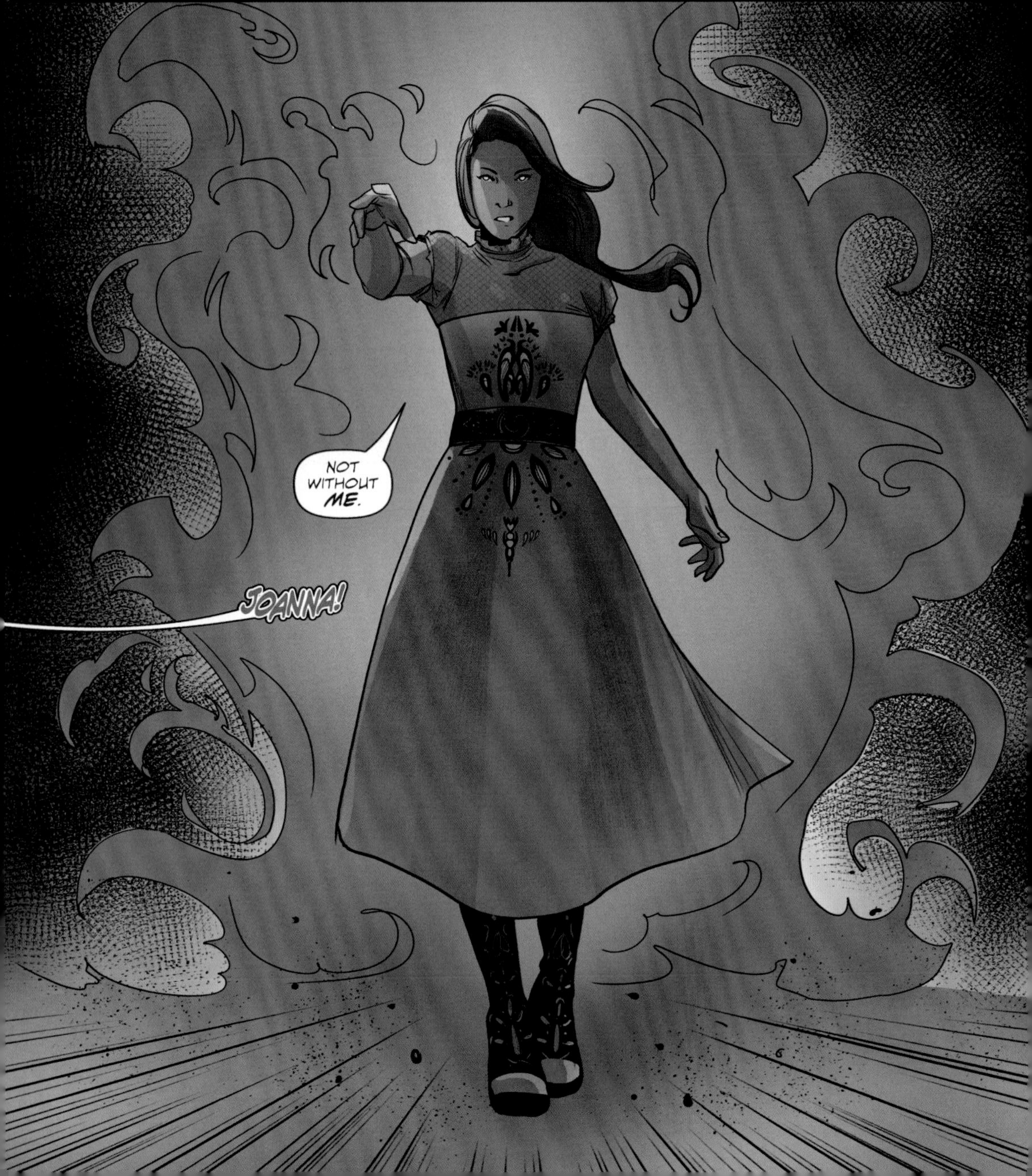
NOT WITHOUT ME.
JOANNA!

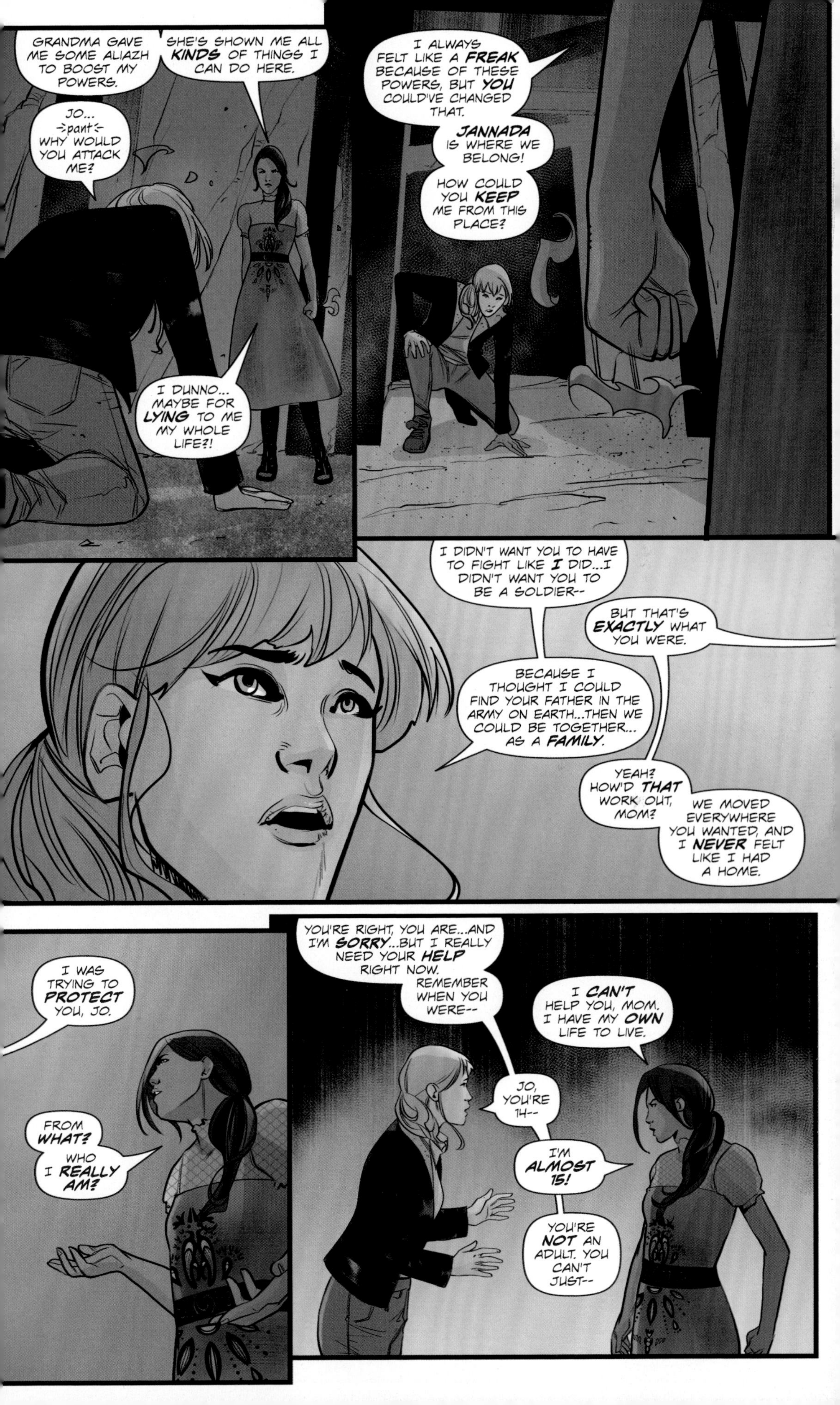
GRANDMA GAVE ME SOME ALIAZH TO BOOST MY POWERS.
SHE'S SHOWN ME ALL KINDS OF THINGS I CAN DO HERE.
JO... ~pant~ WHY WOULD YOU ATTACK ME?
I DUNNO... MAYBE FOR LYING TO ME MY WHOLE LIFE?!
I ALWAYS FELT LIKE A FREAK BECAUSE OF THESE POWERS, BUT YOU COULD'VE CHANGED THAT.
JANNADA IS WHERE WE BELONG!
HOW COULD YOU KEEP ME FROM THIS PLACE?
I DIDN'T WANT YOU TO HAVE TO FIGHT LIKE I DID...I DIDN'T WANT YOU TO BE A SOLDIER--
BUT THAT'S EXACTLY WHAT YOU WERE.
BECAUSE I THOUGHT I COULD FIND YOUR FATHER IN THE ARMY ON EARTH...THEN WE COULD BE TOGETHER... AS A FAMILY.
YEAH? HOW'D THAT WORK OUT, MOM?
WE MOVED EVERYWHERE YOU WANTED, AND I NEVER FELT LIKE I HAD A HOME.
I WAS TRYING TO PROTECT YOU, JO.
FROM WHAT?
WHO I REALLY AM?
YOU'RE RIGHT, YOU ARE...AND I'M SORRY...BUT I REALLY NEED YOUR HELP RIGHT NOW.
REMEMBER WHEN YOU WERE--
I CAN'T HELP YOU, MOM. I HAVE MY OWN LIFE TO LIVE.
JO, YOU'RE 14--
I'M ALMOST 15!
YOU'RE NOT AN ADULT. YOU CAN'T JUST--

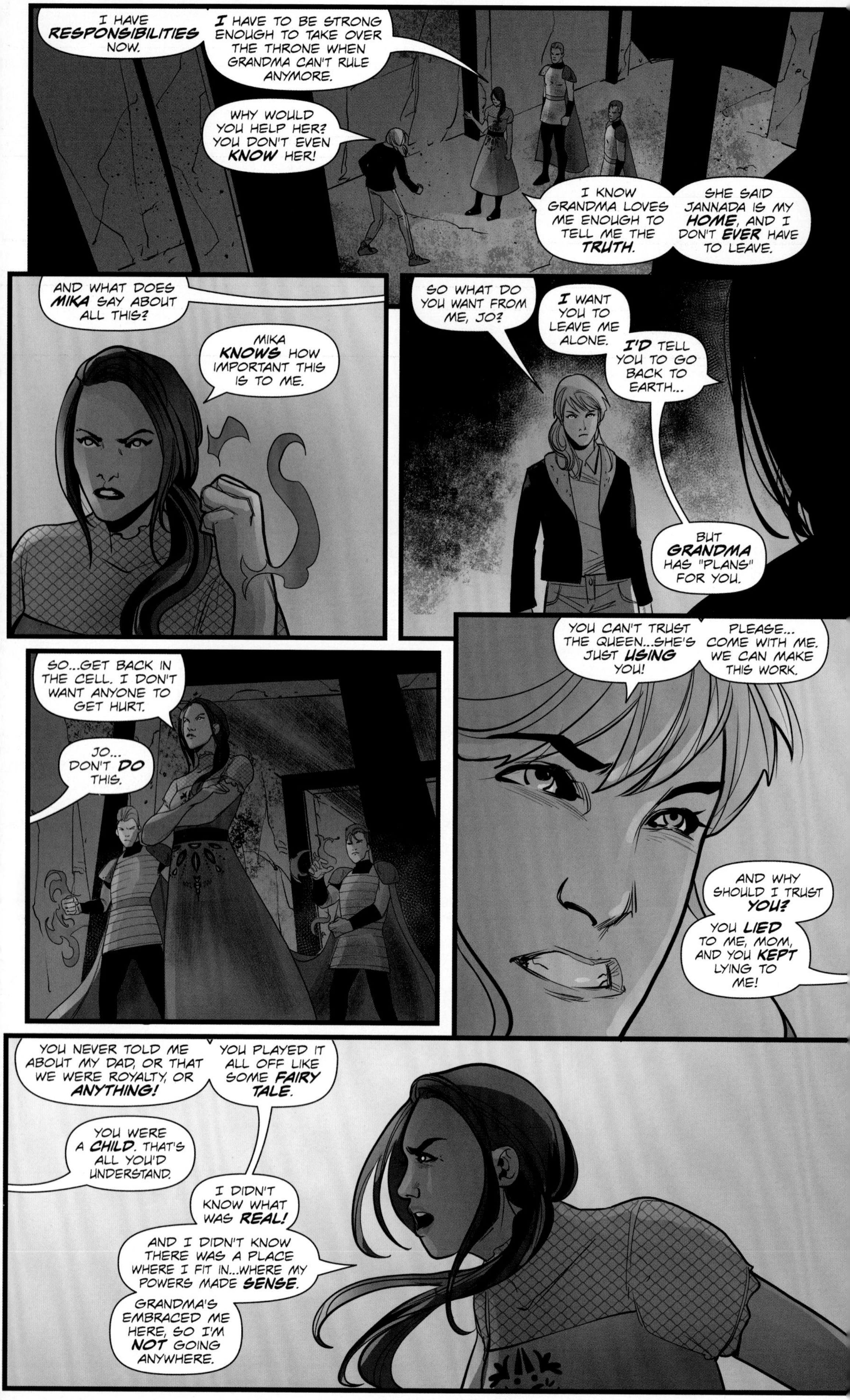
I HAVE RESPONSIBILITIES NOW.
I HAVE TO BE STRONG ENOUGH TO TAKE OVER THE THRONE WHEN GRANDMA CAN'T RULE ANYMORE.
WHY WOULD YOU HELP HER? YOU DON'T EVEN KNOW HER!
I KNOW GRANDMA LOVES ME ENOUGH TO TELL ME THE TRUTH.
SHE SAID JANNADA IS MY HOME, AND I DON'T EVER HAVE TO LEAVE.
AND WHAT DOES MIKA SAY ABOUT ALL THIS?
MIKA KNOWS HOW IMPORTANT THIS IS TO ME.
SO WHAT DO YOU WANT FROM ME, JO?
I WANT YOU TO LEAVE ME ALONE.
I'D TELL YOU TO GO BACK TO EARTH...
BUT GRANDMA HAS "PLANS" FOR YOU.
SO...GET BACK IN THE CELL. I DON'T WANT ANYONE TO GET HURT.
JO... DON'T DO THIS.
YOU CAN'T TRUST THE QUEEN...SHE'S JUST USING YOU!
PLEASE... COME WITH ME. WE CAN MAKE THIS WORK.
AND WHY SHOULD I TRUST YOU?
YOU LIED TO ME, MOM, AND YOU KEPT LYING TO ME!
YOU NEVER TOLD ME ABOUT MY DAD, OR THAT WE WERE ROYALTY, OR ANYTHING!
YOU PLAYED IT ALL OFF LIKE SOME FAIRY TALE.
YOU WERE A CHILD. THAT'S ALL YOU'D UNDERSTAND.
I DIDN'T KNOW WHAT WAS REAL!
AND I DIDN'T KNOW THERE WAS A PLACE WHERE I FIT IN...WHERE MY POWERS MADE SENSE.
GRANDMA'S EMBRACED ME HERE, SO I'M NOT GOING ANYWHERE.

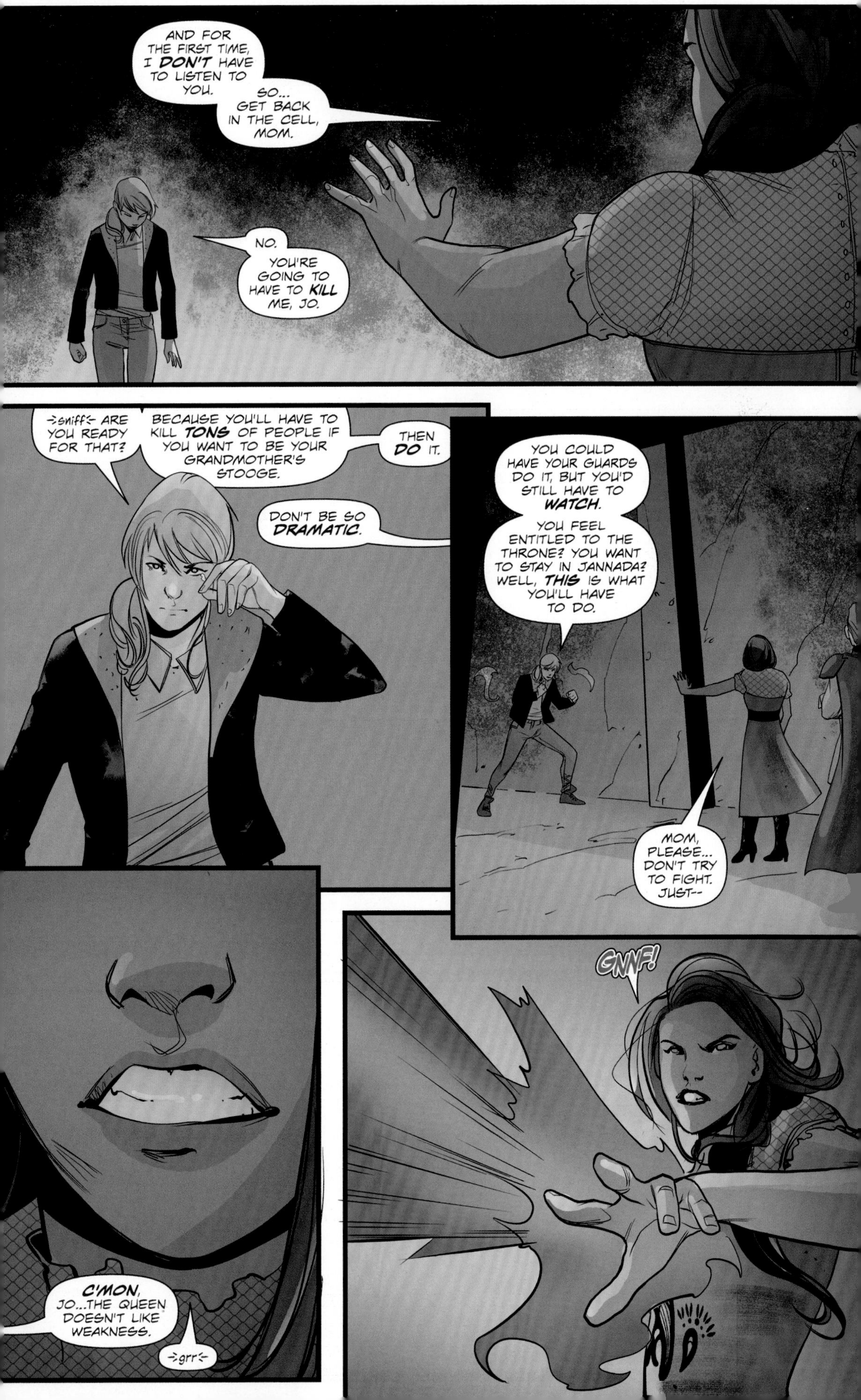
AND FOR THE FIRST TIME, I DON'T HAVE TO LISTEN TO YOU.
SO... GET BACK IN THE CELL, MOM.
NO. YOU'RE GOING TO HAVE TO KILL ME, JO.
-sniff- ARE YOU READY FOR THAT?
BECAUSE YOU'LL HAVE TO KILL TONS OF PEOPLE IF YOU WANT TO BE YOUR GRANDMOTHER'S STOOGE.
THEN DO IT.
DON'T BE SO DRAMATIC.
YOU COULD HAVE YOUR GUARDS DO IT, BUT YOU'D STILL HAVE TO WATCH.
YOU FEEL ENTITLED TO THE THRONE? YOU WANT TO STAY IN JANNADA? WELL, THIS IS WHAT YOU'LL HAVE TO DO.
MOM, PLEASE... DON'T TRY TO FIGHT. JUST--
C'MON, JO...THE QUEEN DOESN'T LIKE WEAKNESS.
-grr-
GNNF!

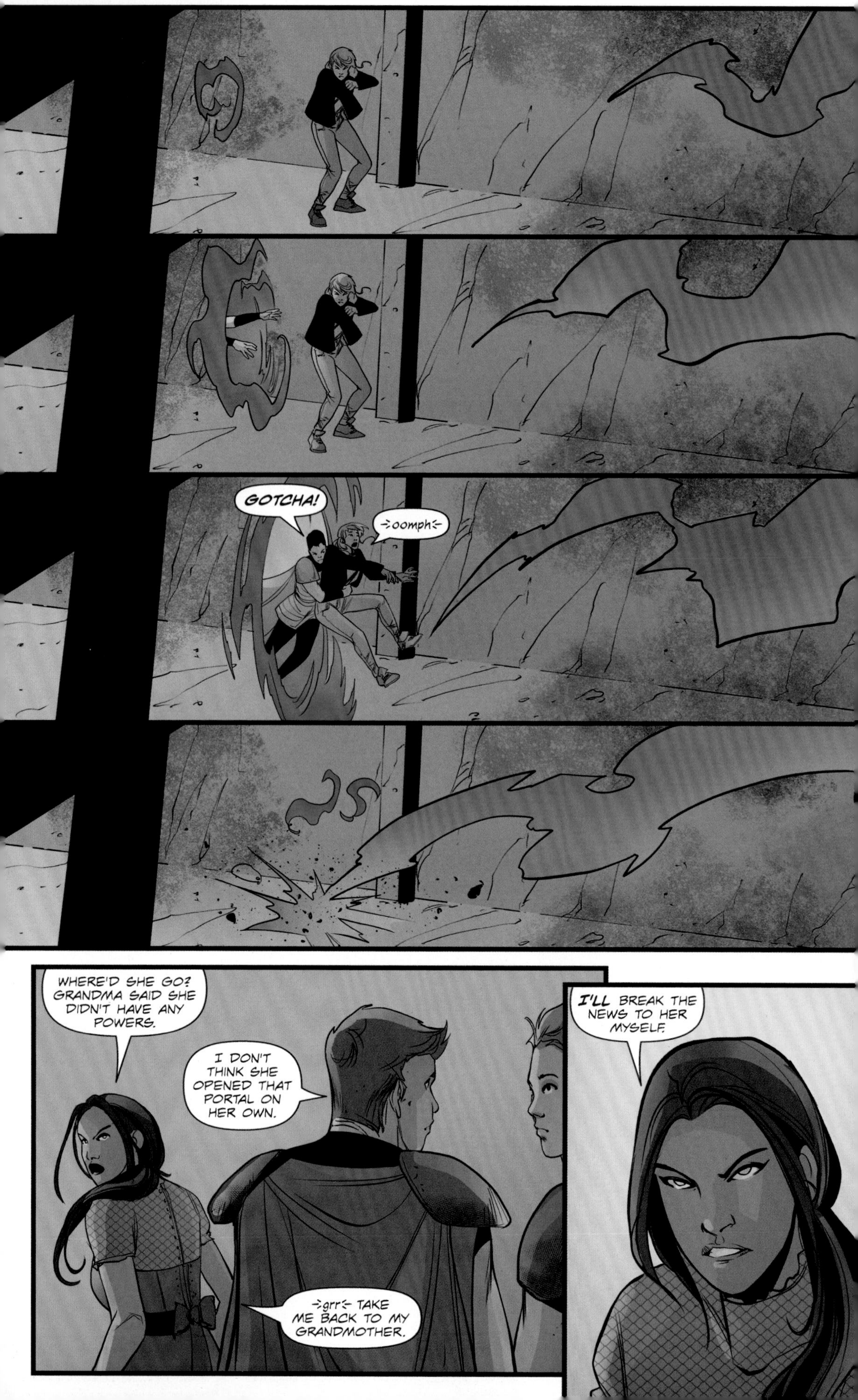
GOTCHA!
oomph
WHERE'D SHE GO? GRANDMA SAID SHE DIDN'T HAVE ANY POWERS.
I DON'T THINK SHE OPENED THAT PORTAL ON HER OWN.
grr TAKE ME BACK TO MY GRANDMOTHER.
I'LL BREAK THE NEWS TO HER MYSELF.

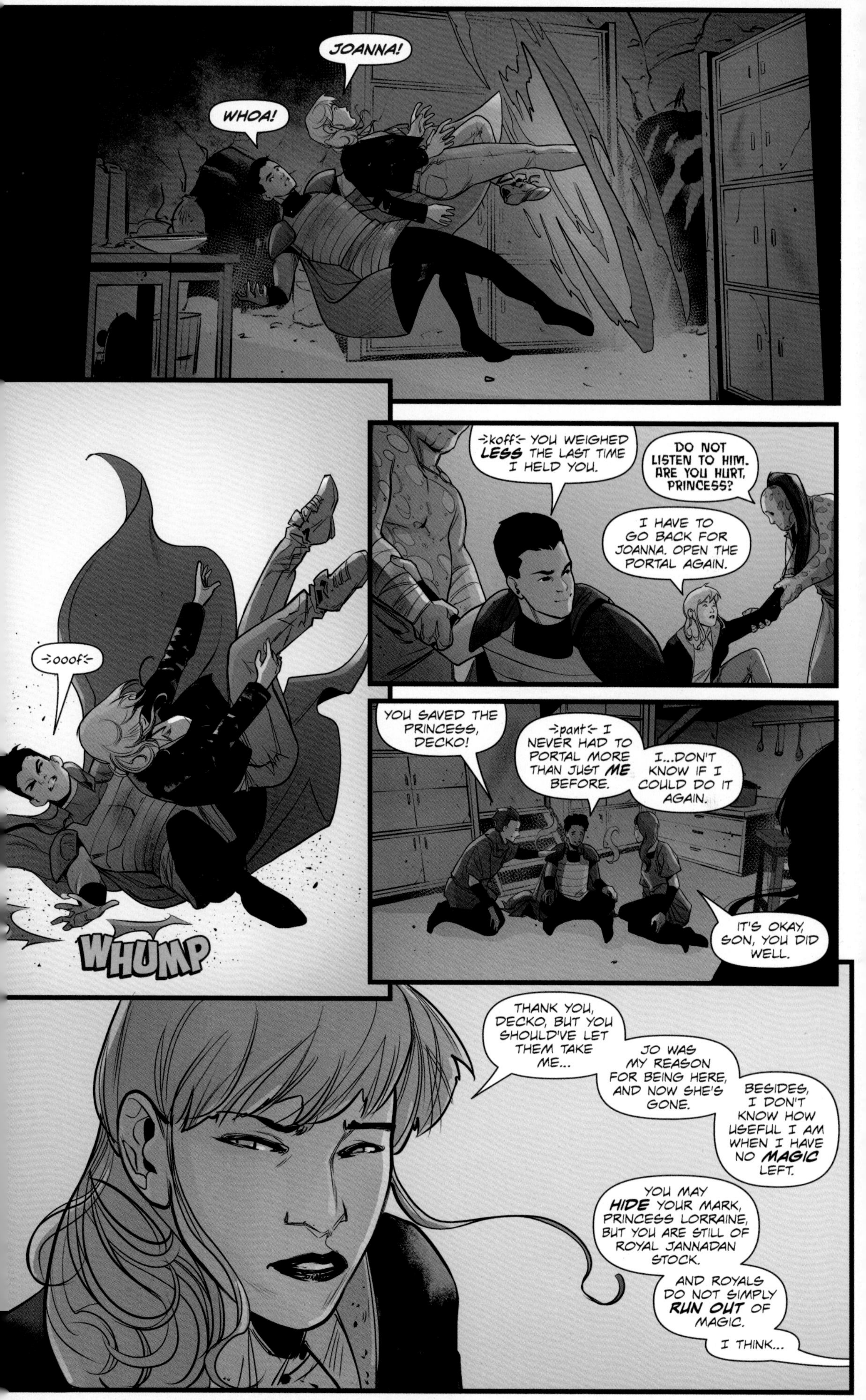
JOANNA!
WHOA!
>ooof<
WHUMP
>koff< YOU WEIGHED LESS THE LAST TIME I HELD YOU.
DO NOT LISTEN TO HIM. ARE YOU HURT, PRINCESS?
I HAVE TO GO BACK FOR JOANNA. OPEN THE PORTAL AGAIN.
YOU SAVED THE PRINCESS, DECKO!
>pant< I NEVER HAD TO PORTAL MORE THAN JUST ME BEFORE.
I...DON'T KNOW IF I COULD DO IT AGAIN.
IT'S OKAY, SON, YOU DID WELL.
THANK YOU, DECKO, BUT YOU SHOULD'VE LET THEM TAKE ME...
JO WAS MY REASON FOR BEING HERE, AND NOW SHE'S GONE.
BESIDES, I DON'T KNOW HOW USEFUL I AM WHEN I HAVE NO MAGIC LEFT.
YOU MAY HIDE YOUR MARK, PRINCESS LORRAINE, BUT YOU ARE STILL OF ROYAL JANNADAN STOCK.
AND ROYALS DO NOT SIMPLY RUN OUT OF MAGIC.
I THINK...

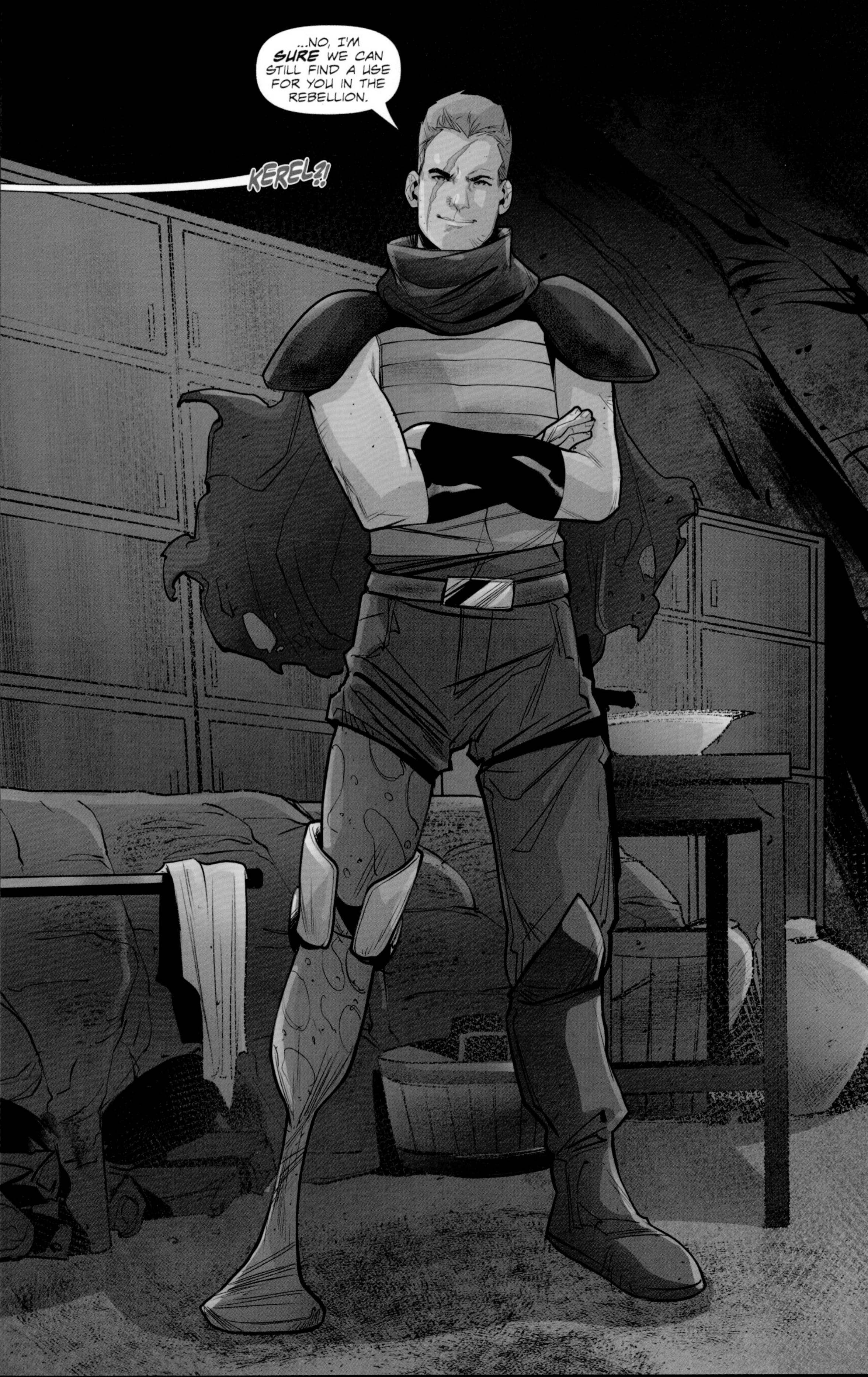
KEREL?!
...NO, I'M SURE WE CAN STILL FIND A USE FOR YOU IN THE REBELLION.

SIX

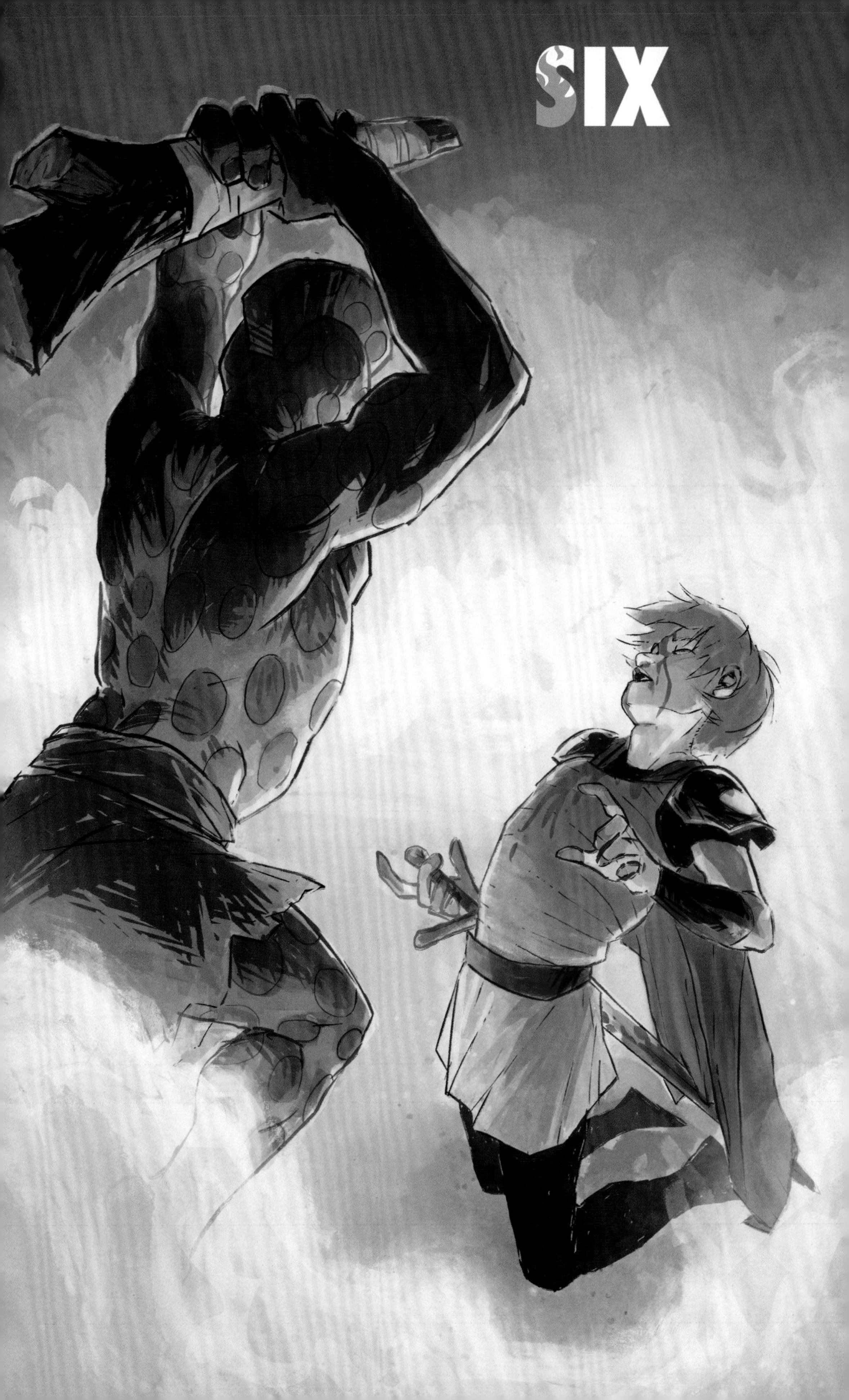

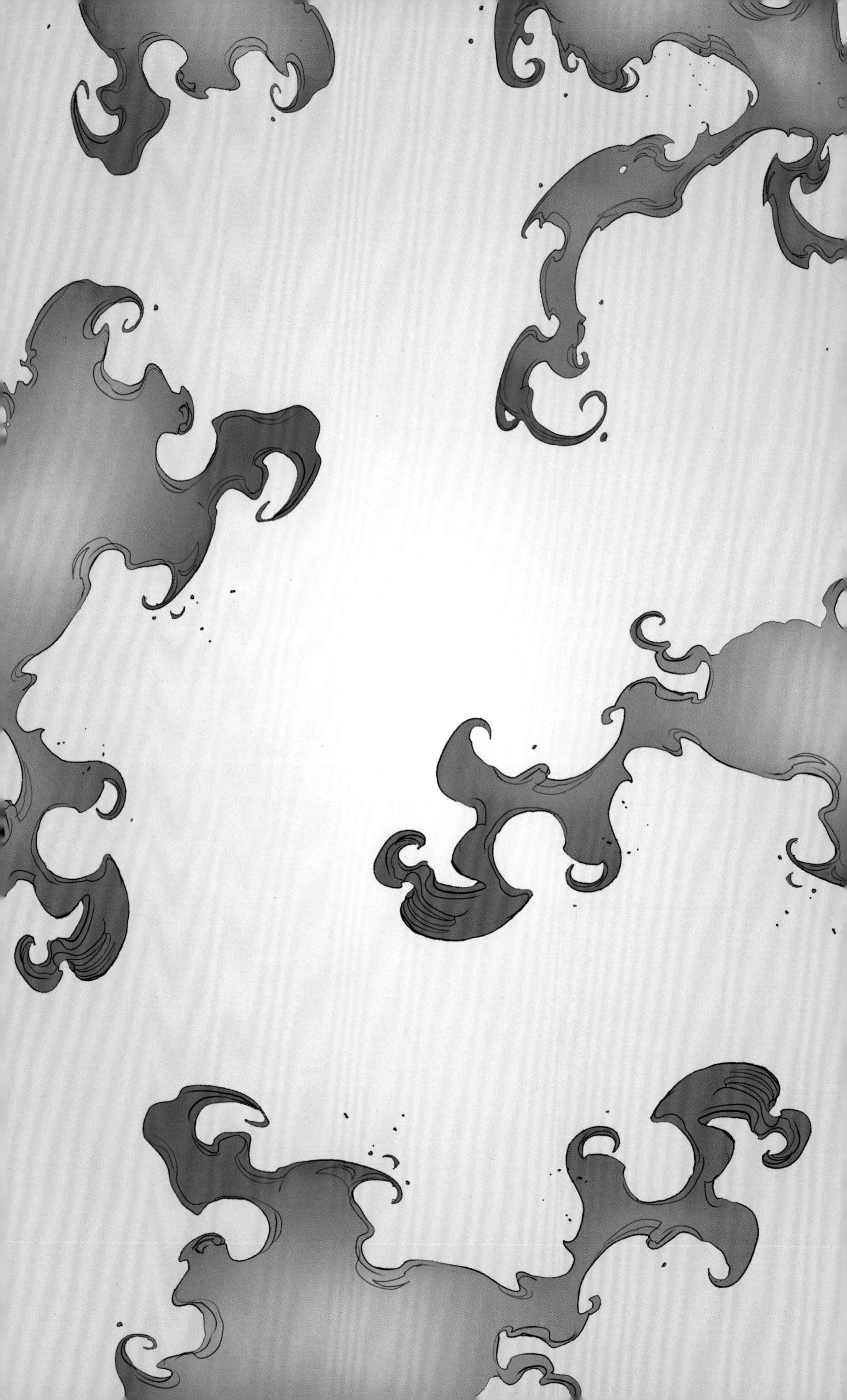

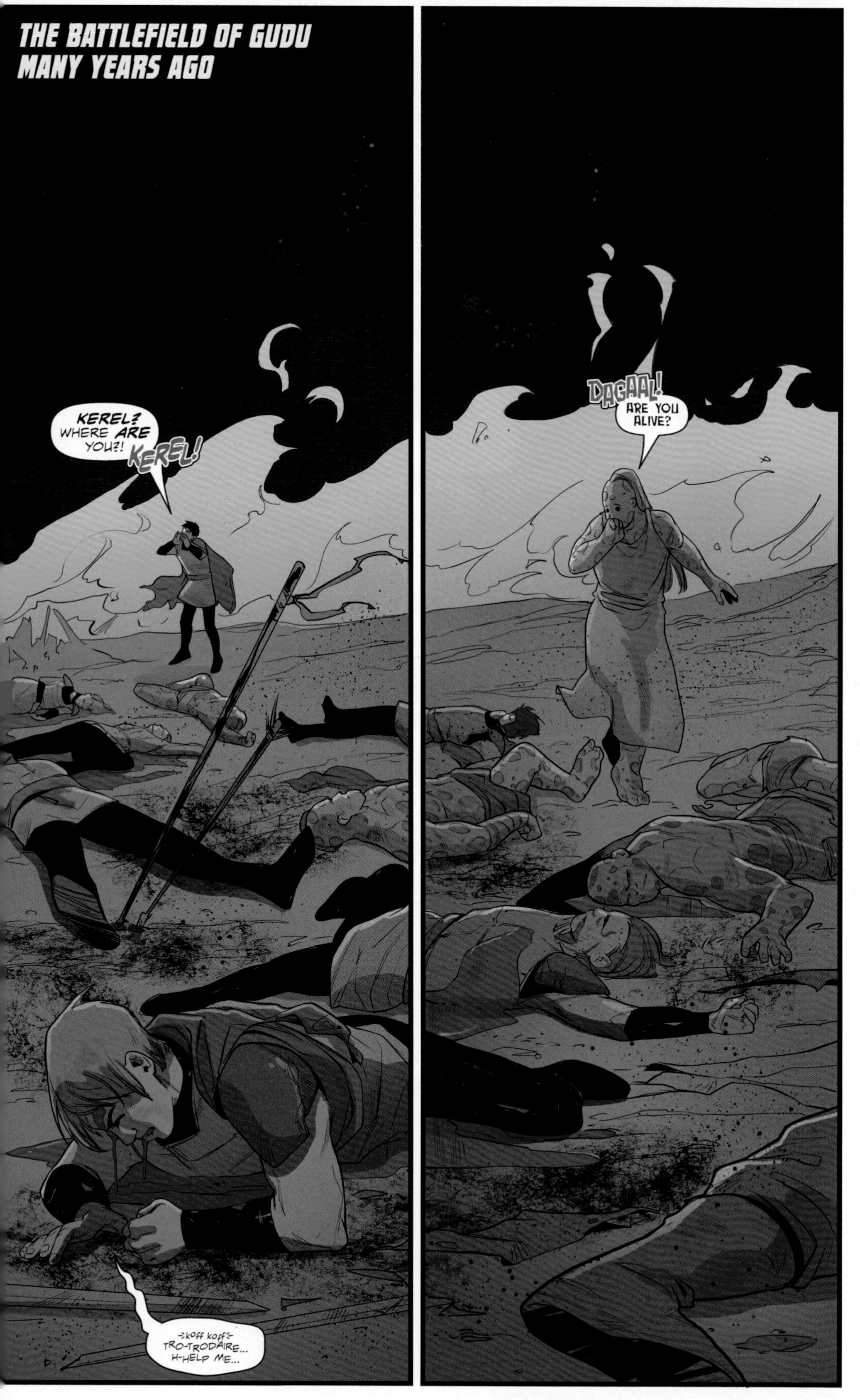
THE BATTLEFIELD OF GUDU
MANY YEARS AGO
KEREL? WHERE ARE YOU?! KEREL!
DAGAAL! ARE YOU ALIVE?
koff koff TRO-TRODAIRE... H-HELP ME...

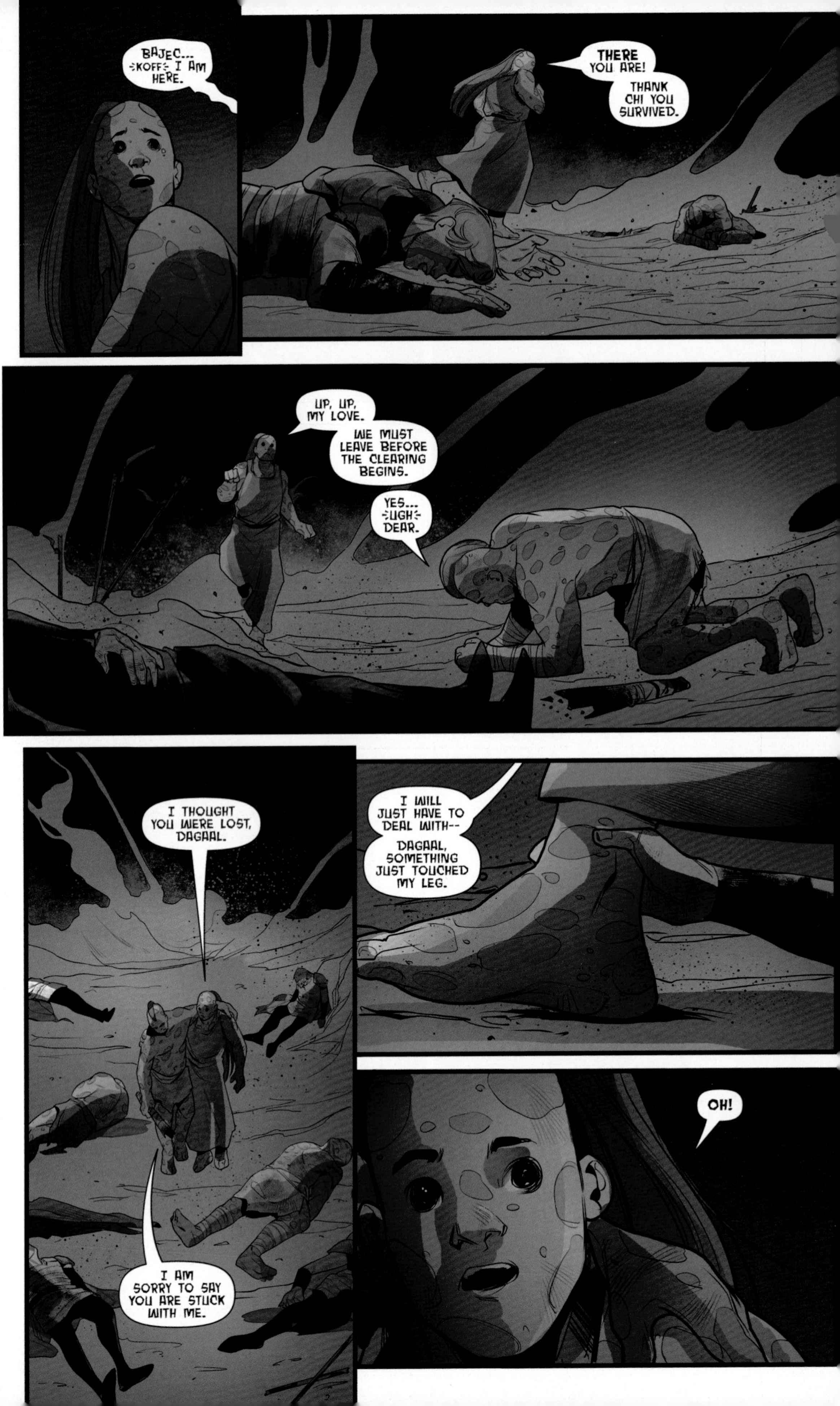
BAJEC... ≠KOFF≠ I AM HERE.
THERE YOU ARE!
THANK CHI YOU SURVIVED.
UP, UP, MY LOVE.
WE MUST LEAVE BEFORE THE CLEARING BEGINS.
YES... ≠UGH≠ DEAR.
I THOUGHT YOU WERE LOST, DAGAAL.
I AM SORRY TO SAY YOU ARE STUCK WITH ME.
I WILL JUST HAVE TO DEAL WITH--
DAGAAL, SOMETHING JUST TOUCHED MY LEG.
OH!

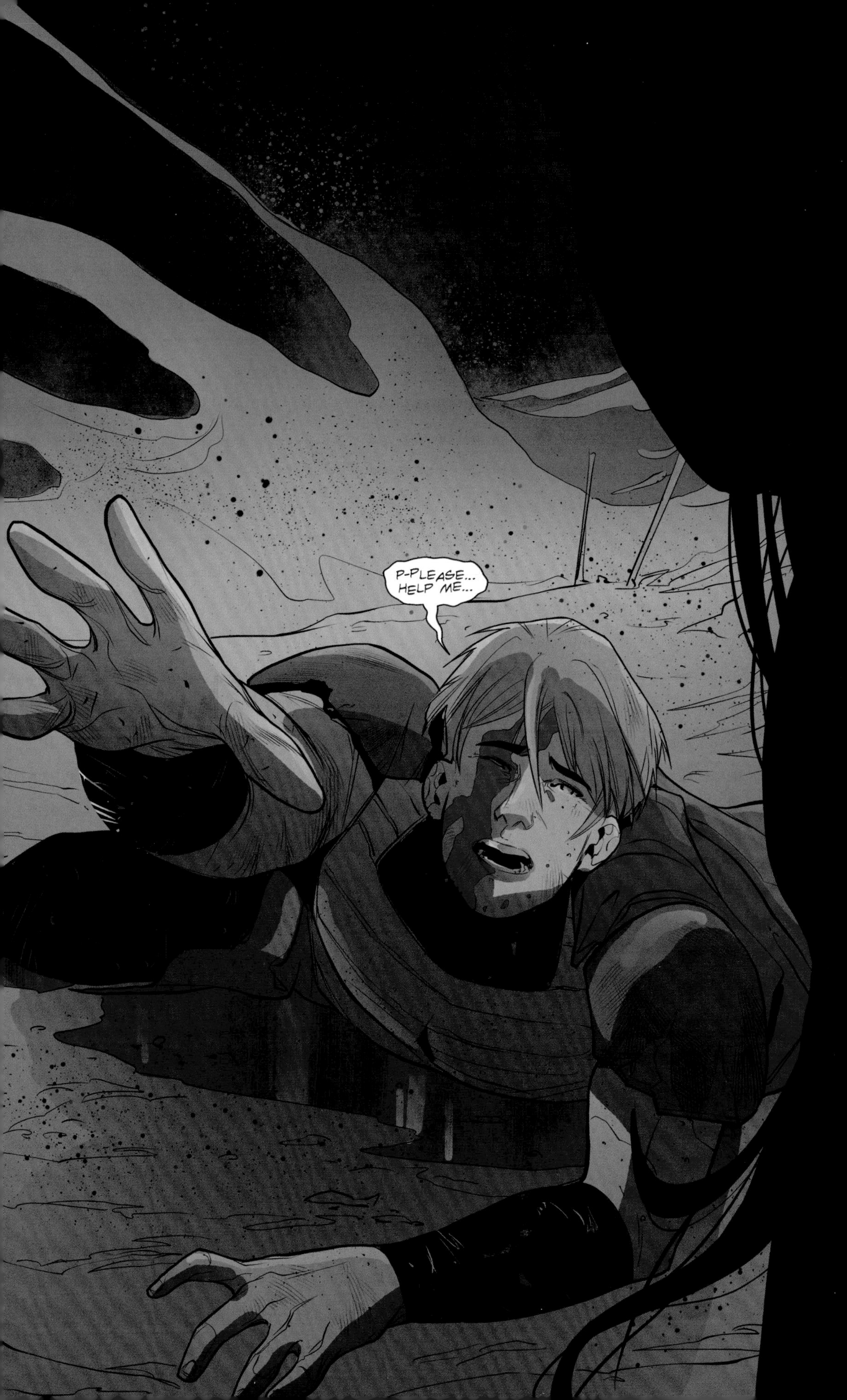
P-PLEASE... HELP ME...

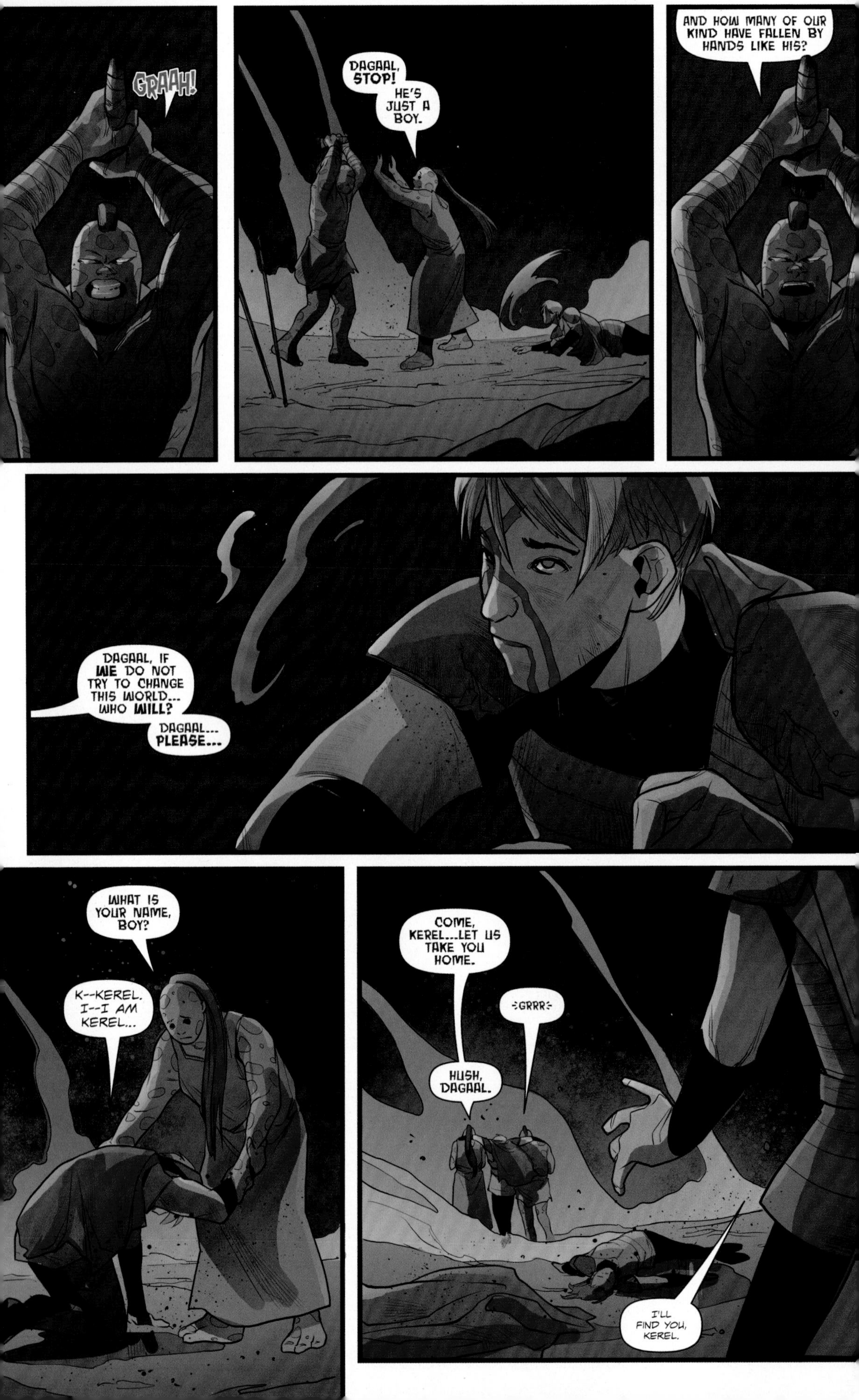
GRAAH!
DAGAAL, STOP!
HE'S JUST A BOY.
AND HOW MANY OF OUR KIND HAVE FALLEN BY HANDS LIKE HIS?
DAGAAL, IF WE DO NOT TRY TO CHANGE THIS WORLD... WHO WILL?
DAGAAL... PLEASE...
WHAT IS YOUR NAME, BOY?
K--KEREL. I--I AM KEREL...
COME, KEREL...LET US TAKE YOU HOME.
GRRR
HUSH, DAGAAL.
I'LL FIND YOU, KEREL.

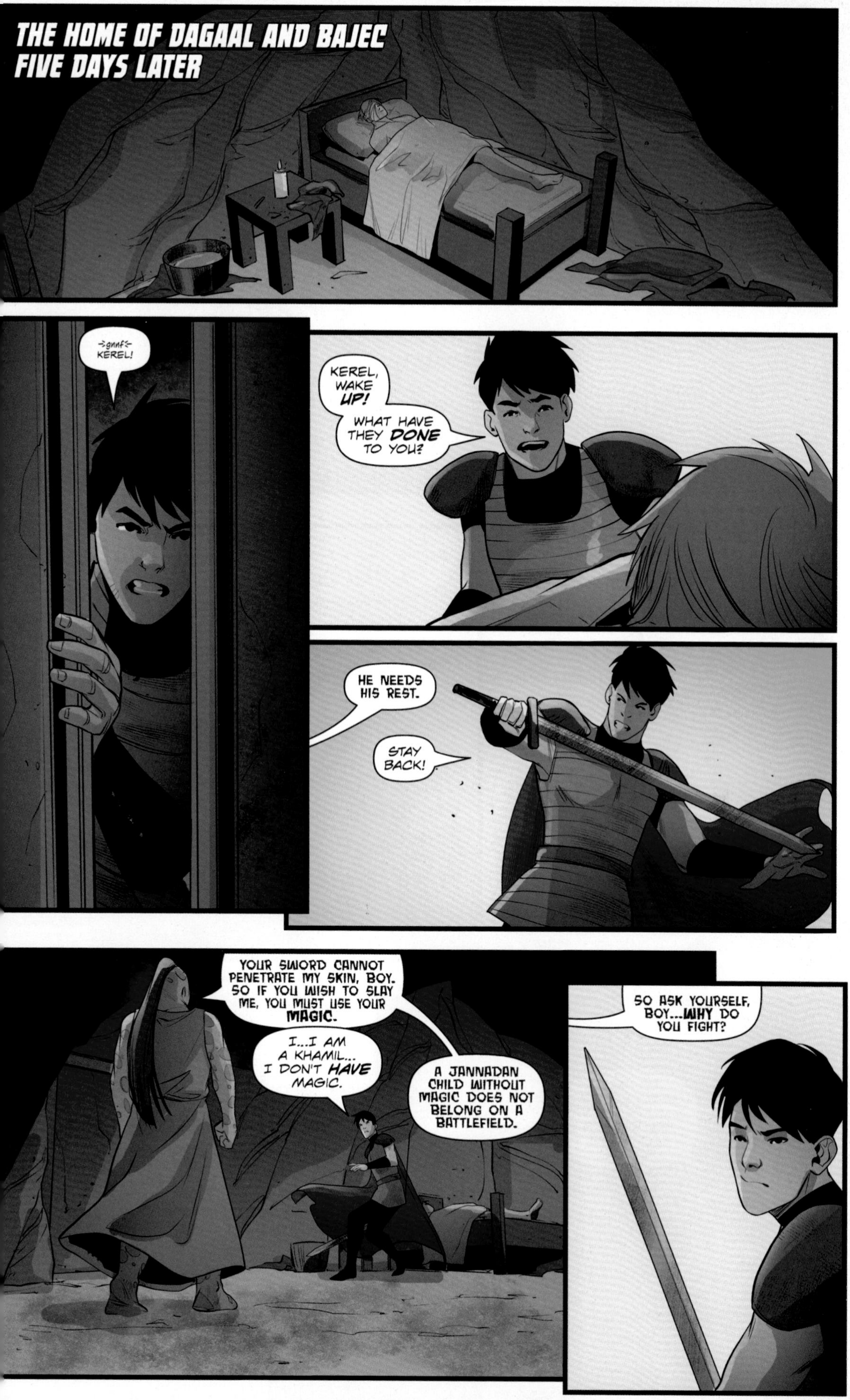
THE HOME OF DAGAAL AND BAJEC
FIVE DAYS LATER
-gnnf- KEREL!
KEREL, WAKE UP!
WHAT HAVE THEY DONE TO YOU?
HE NEEDS HIS REST.
STAY BACK!
YOUR SWORD CANNOT PENETRATE MY SKIN, BOY. SO IF YOU WISH TO SLAY ME, YOU MUST USE YOUR MAGIC.
I...I AM A KHAMIL... I DON'T HAVE MAGIC.
A JANNADAN CHILD WITHOUT MAGIC DOES NOT BELONG ON A BATTLEFIELD.
SO ASK YOURSELF, BOY...WHY DO YOU FIGHT?

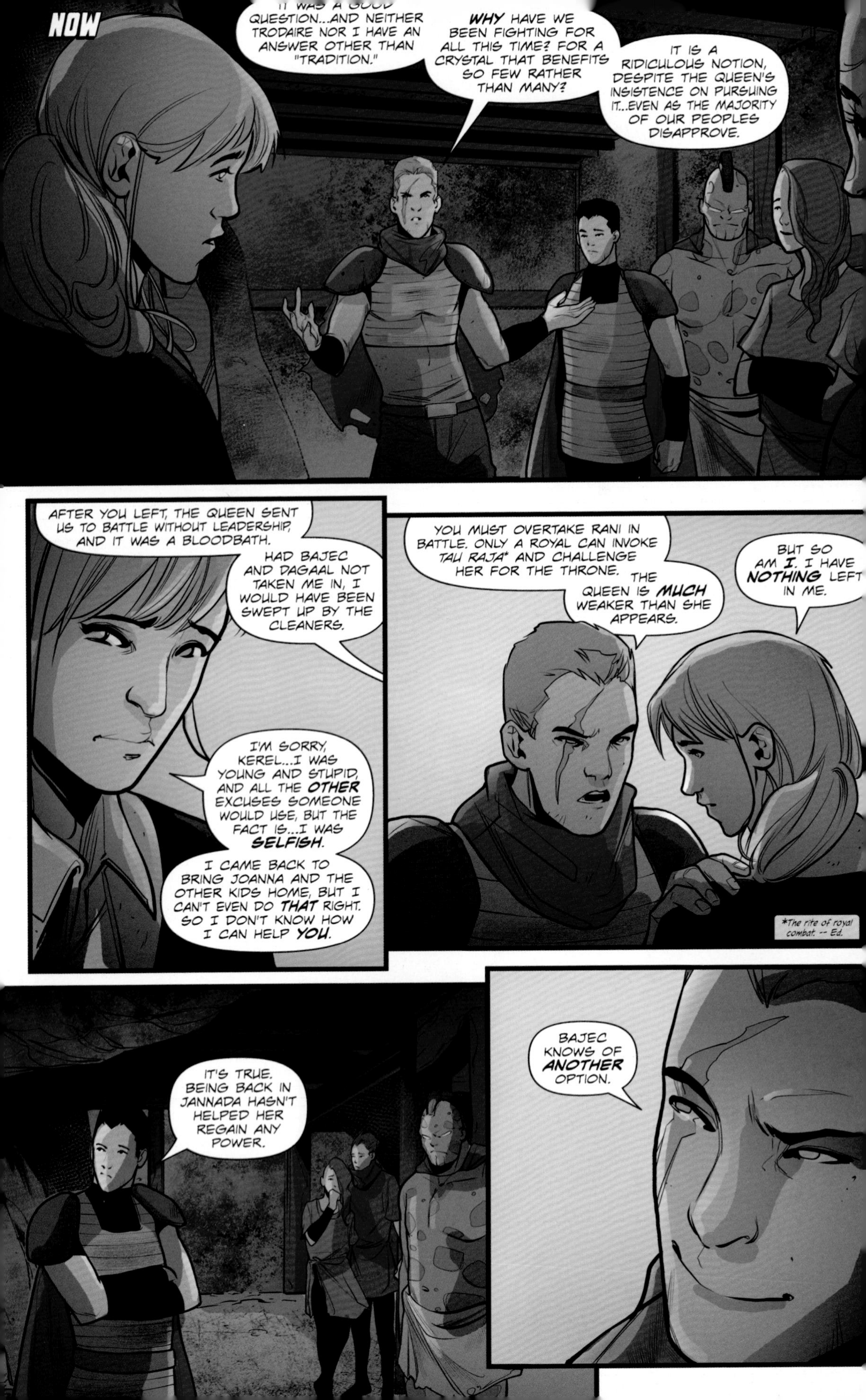
NOW
IT WAS A GOOD QUESTION...AND NEITHER TRODAIRE NOR I HAVE AN ANSWER OTHER THAN "TRADITION."
WHY HAVE WE BEEN FIGHTING FOR ALL THIS TIME? FOR A CRYSTAL THAT BENEFITS SO FEW RATHER THAN MANY?
IT IS A RIDICULOUS NOTION, DESPITE THE QUEEN'S INSISTENCE ON PURSUING IT...EVEN AS THE MAJORITY OF OUR PEOPLES DISAPPROVE.
AFTER YOU LEFT, THE QUEEN SENT US TO BATTLE WITHOUT LEADERSHIP, AND IT WAS A BLOODBATH.
HAD BAJEC AND DAGAAL NOT TAKEN ME IN, I WOULD HAVE BEEN SWEPT UP BY THE CLEANERS.
I'M SORRY, KEREL...I WAS YOUNG AND STUPID, AND ALL THE OTHER EXCUSES SOMEONE WOULD USE, BUT THE FACT IS...I WAS SELFISH.
I CAME BACK TO BRING JOANNA AND THE OTHER KIDS HOME, BUT I CAN'T EVEN DO THAT RIGHT. SO I DON'T KNOW HOW I CAN HELP YOU.
YOU MUST OVERTAKE RANI IN BATTLE. ONLY A ROYAL CAN INVOKE TAU RAJA* AND CHALLENGE HER FOR THE THRONE.
THE QUEEN IS MUCH WEAKER THAN SHE APPEARS.
BUT SO AM I. I HAVE NOTHING LEFT IN ME.
*The rite of royal combat. -- Ed.
IT'S TRUE. BEING BACK IN JANNADA HASN'T HELPED HER REGAIN ANY POWER.
BAJEC KNOWS OF ANOTHER OPTION.

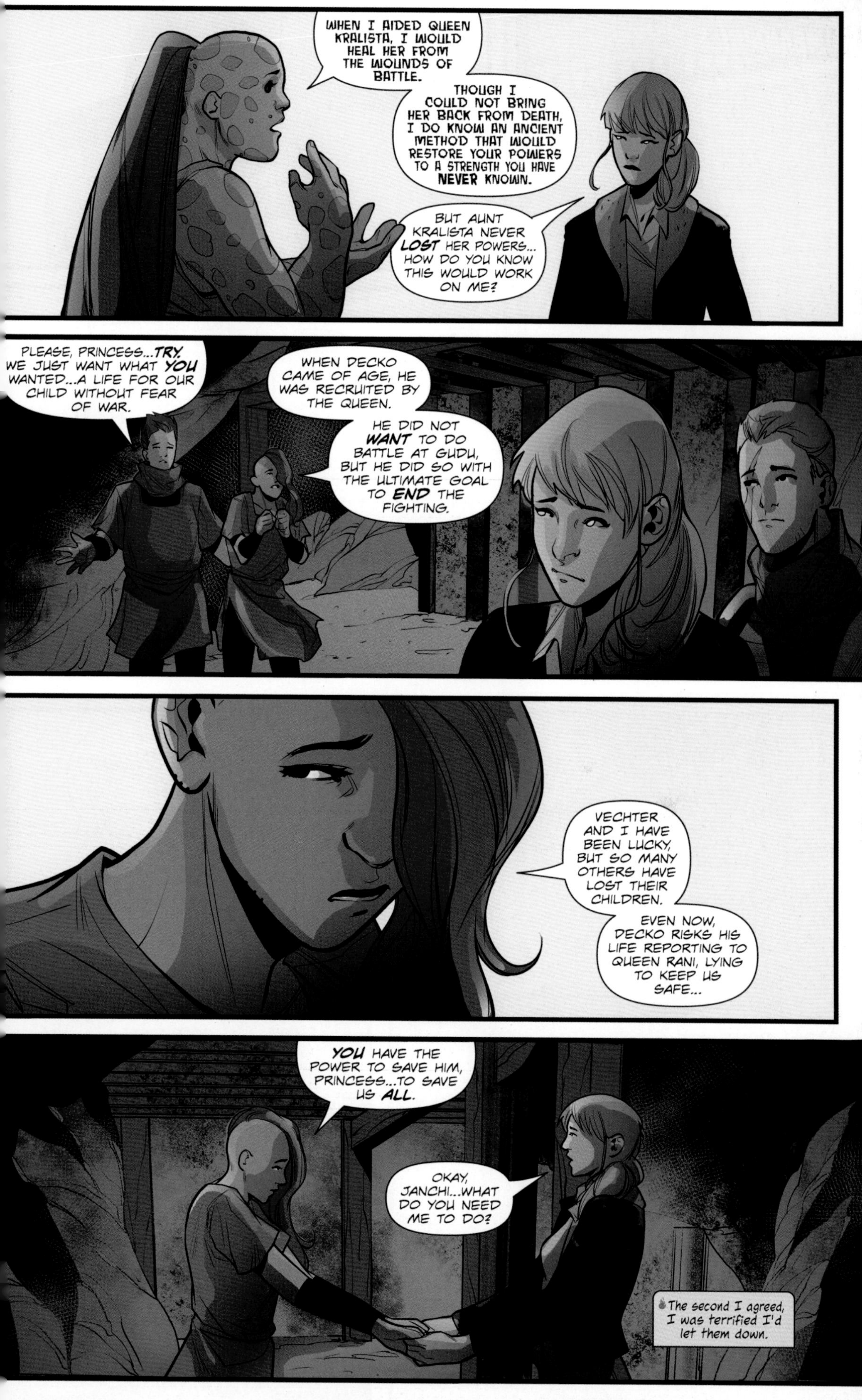
WHEN I AIDED QUEEN KRALISTA, I WOULD HEAL HER FROM THE WOUNDS OF BATTLE.
THOUGH I COULD NOT BRING HER BACK FROM DEATH, I DO KNOW AN ANCIENT METHOD THAT WOULD RESTORE YOUR POWERS TO A STRENGTH YOU HAVE **NEVER** KNOWN.
BUT AUNT KRALISTA NEVER ***LOST*** HER POWERS... HOW DO YOU KNOW THIS WOULD WORK ON ME?
PLEASE, PRINCESS...***TRY.*** WE JUST WANT WHAT ***YOU*** WANTED...A LIFE FOR OUR CHILD WITHOUT FEAR OF WAR.
WHEN DECKO CAME OF AGE, HE WAS RECRUITED BY THE QUEEN.
HE DID NOT ***WANT*** TO DO BATTLE AT GUDU, BUT HE DID SO WITH THE ULTIMATE GOAL TO ***END*** THE FIGHTING.
VECHTER AND I HAVE BEEN LUCKY, BUT SO MANY OTHERS HAVE LOST THEIR CHILDREN.
EVEN NOW, DECKO RISKS HIS LIFE REPORTING TO QUEEN RANI, LYING TO KEEP US SAFE...
YOU HAVE THE POWER TO SAVE HIM, PRINCESS...TO SAVE US ***ALL***.
OKAY, JANCHI...WHAT DO YOU NEED ME TO DO?
The second I agreed, I was terrified I'd let them down.

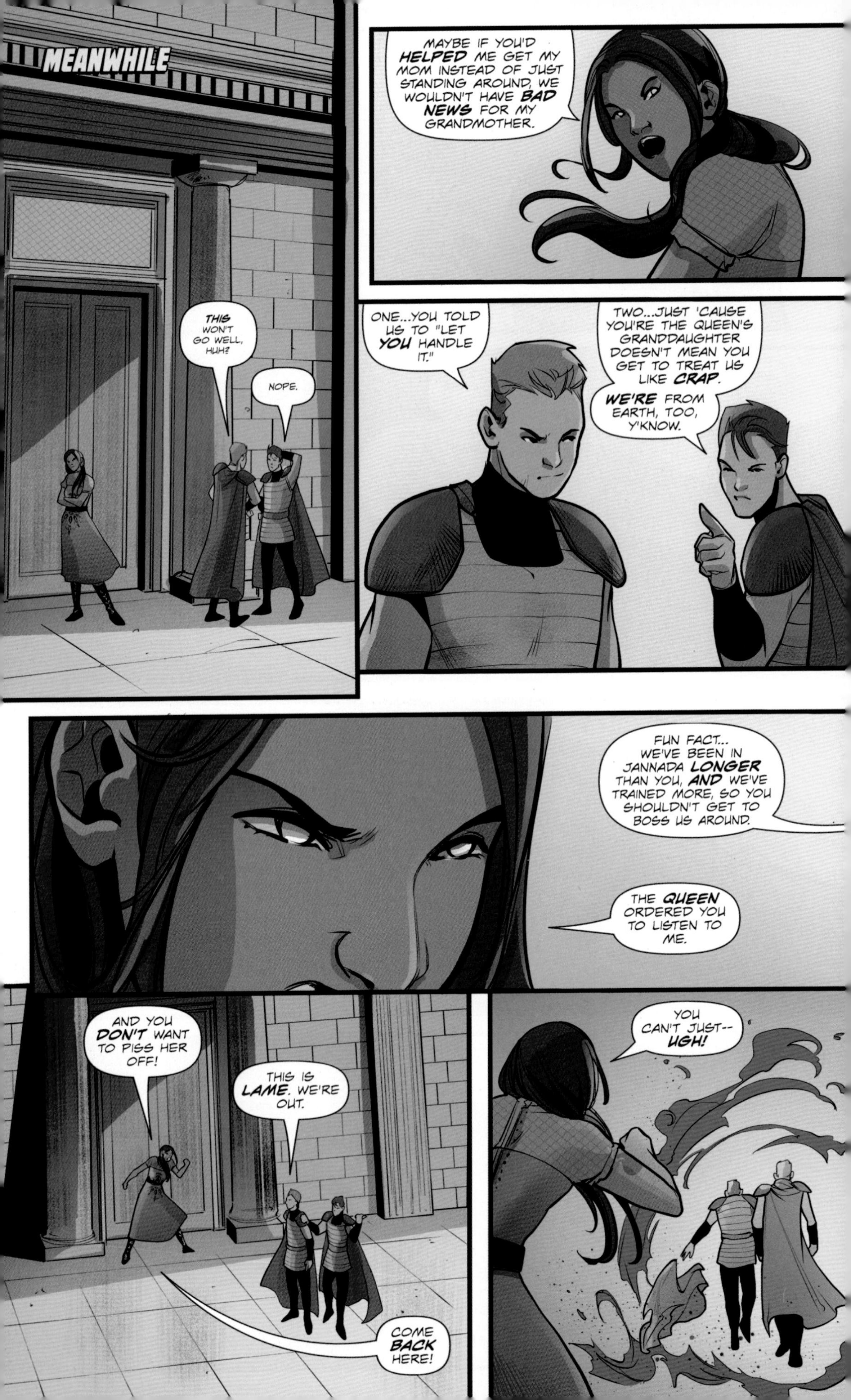
MEANWHILE
THIS WON'T GO WELL, HUH?
NOPE.
MAYBE IF YOU'D HELPED ME GET MY MOM INSTEAD OF JUST STANDING AROUND, WE WOULDN'T HAVE BAD NEWS FOR MY GRANDMOTHER.
ONE...YOU TOLD US TO "LET YOU HANDLE IT."
TWO...JUST 'CAUSE YOU'RE THE QUEEN'S GRANDDAUGHTER DOESN'T MEAN YOU GET TO TREAT US LIKE CRAP.
WE'RE FROM EARTH, TOO, Y'KNOW.
FUN FACT... WE'VE BEEN IN JANNADA LONGER THAN YOU, AND WE'VE TRAINED MORE, SO YOU SHOULDN'T GET TO BOSS US AROUND.
THE QUEEN ORDERED YOU TO LISTEN TO ME.
AND YOU DON'T WANT TO PISS HER OFF!
THIS IS LAME. WE'RE OUT.
COME BACK HERE!
YOU CAN'T JUST-- UGH!

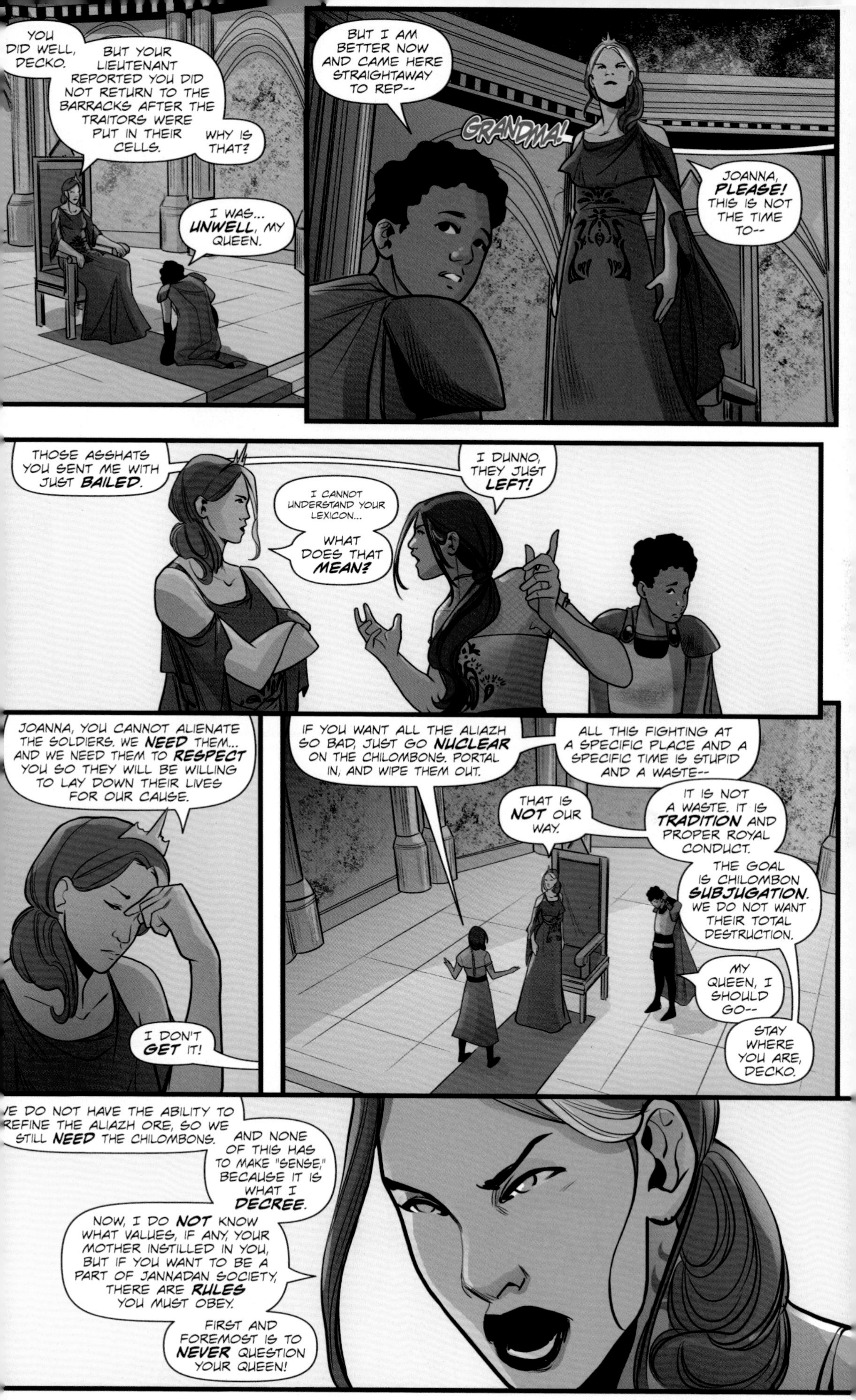

YOU DID WELL, DECKO.
BUT YOUR LIEUTENANT REPORTED YOU DID NOT RETURN TO THE BARRACKS AFTER THE TRAITORS WERE PUT IN THEIR CELLS.
WHY IS THAT?
I WAS... UNWELL, MY QUEEN.
BUT I AM BETTER NOW AND CAME HERE STRAIGHTAWAY TO REP--
GRANDMA!
JOANNA, PLEASE! THIS IS NOT THE TIME TO--
THOSE ASSHATS YOU SENT ME WITH JUST BAILED.
I CANNOT UNDERSTAND YOUR LEXICON...
WHAT DOES THAT MEAN?
I DUNNO, THEY JUST LEFT!
JOANNA, YOU CANNOT ALIENATE THE SOLDIERS. WE NEED THEM... AND WE NEED THEM TO RESPECT YOU SO THEY WILL BE WILLING TO LAY DOWN THEIR LIVES FOR OUR CAUSE.
I DON'T GET IT!
IF YOU WANT ALL THE ALIAZH SO BAD, JUST GO NUCLEAR ON THE CHILOMBONS. PORTAL IN, AND WIPE THEM OUT.
ALL THIS FIGHTING AT A SPECIFIC PLACE AND A SPECIFIC TIME IS STUPID AND A WASTE--
THAT IS NOT OUR WAY.
IT IS NOT A WASTE. IT IS TRADITION AND PROPER ROYAL CONDUCT.
THE GOAL IS CHILOMBON SUBJUGATION. WE DO NOT WANT THEIR TOTAL DESTRUCTION.
MY QUEEN, I SHOULD GO--
STAY WHERE YOU ARE, DECKO.
WE DO NOT HAVE THE ABILITY TO REFINE THE ALIAZH ORE, SO WE STILL NEED THE CHILOMBONS.
AND NONE OF THIS HAS TO MAKE "SENSE," BECAUSE IT IS WHAT I DECREE.
NOW, I DO NOT KNOW WHAT VALUES, IF ANY, YOUR MOTHER INSTILLED IN YOU, BUT IF YOU WANT TO BE A PART OF JANNADAN SOCIETY, THERE ARE RULES YOU MUST OBEY.
FIRST AND FOREMOST IS TO NEVER QUESTION YOUR QUEEN!

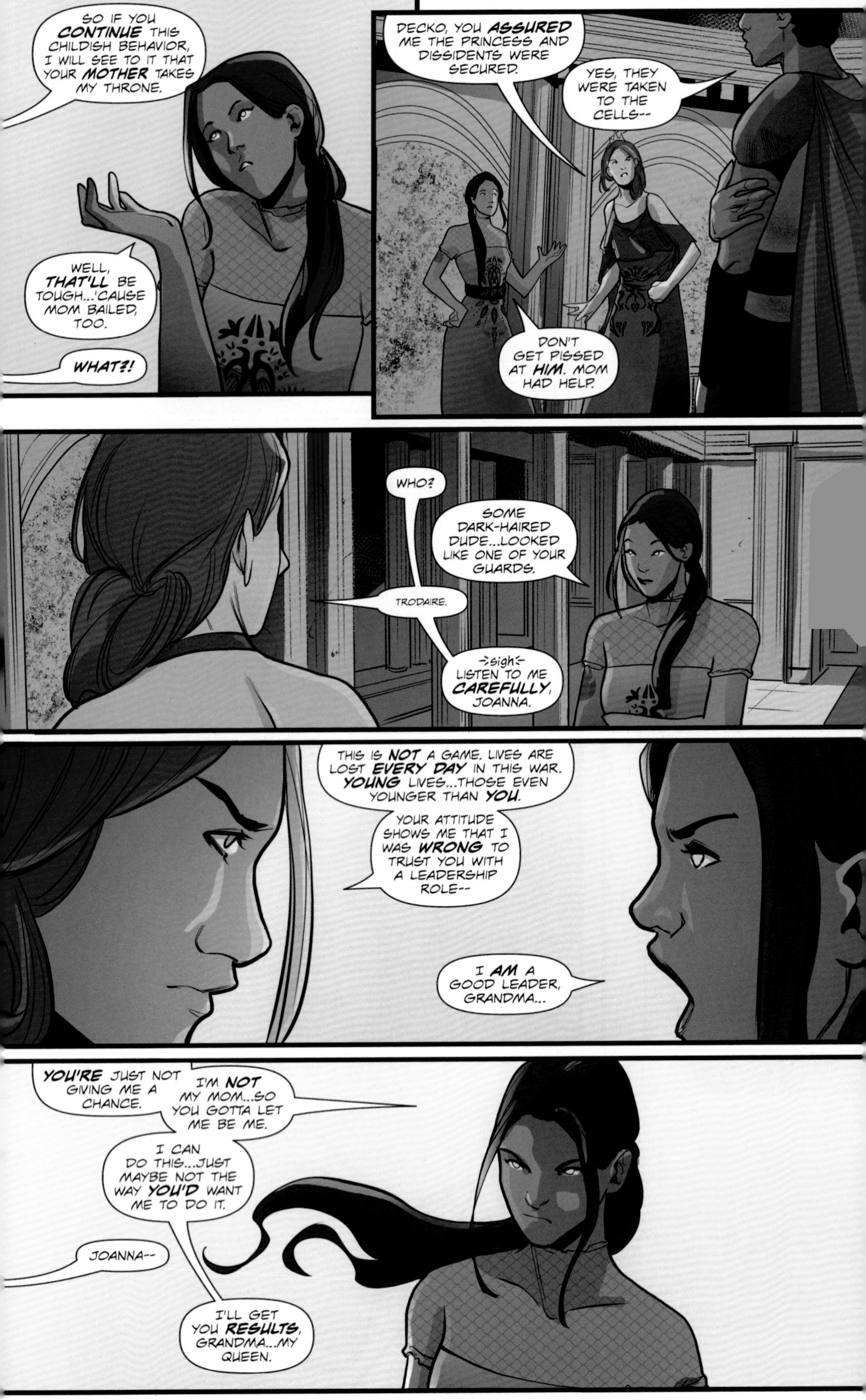
SO IF YOU CONTINUE THIS CHILDISH BEHAVIOR, I WILL SEE TO IT THAT YOUR MOTHER TAKES MY THRONE.
WELL, THAT'LL BE TOUGH...'CAUSE MOM BAILED, TOO.
WHAT?!
DECKO, YOU ASSURED ME THE PRINCESS AND DISSIDENTS WERE SECURED.
YES, THEY WERE TAKEN TO THE CELLS--
DON'T GET PISSED AT HIM. MOM HAD HELP.
WHO?
SOME DARK-HAIRED DUDE...LOOKED LIKE ONE OF YOUR GUARDS.
TRODAIRE.
-sigh- LISTEN TO ME CAREFULLY, JOANNA.
THIS IS NOT A GAME. LIVES ARE LOST EVERY DAY IN THIS WAR. YOUNG LIVES...THOSE EVEN YOUNGER THAN YOU.
YOUR ATTITUDE SHOWS ME THAT I WAS WRONG TO TRUST YOU WITH A LEADERSHIP ROLE--
I AM A GOOD LEADER, GRANDMA...
YOU'RE JUST NOT GIVING ME A CHANCE.
I'M NOT MY MOM...SO YOU GOTTA LET ME BE ME.
I CAN DO THIS...JUST MAYBE NOT THE WAY YOU'D WANT ME TO DO IT.
JOANNA--
I'LL GET YOU RESULTS, GRANDMA...MY QUEEN.

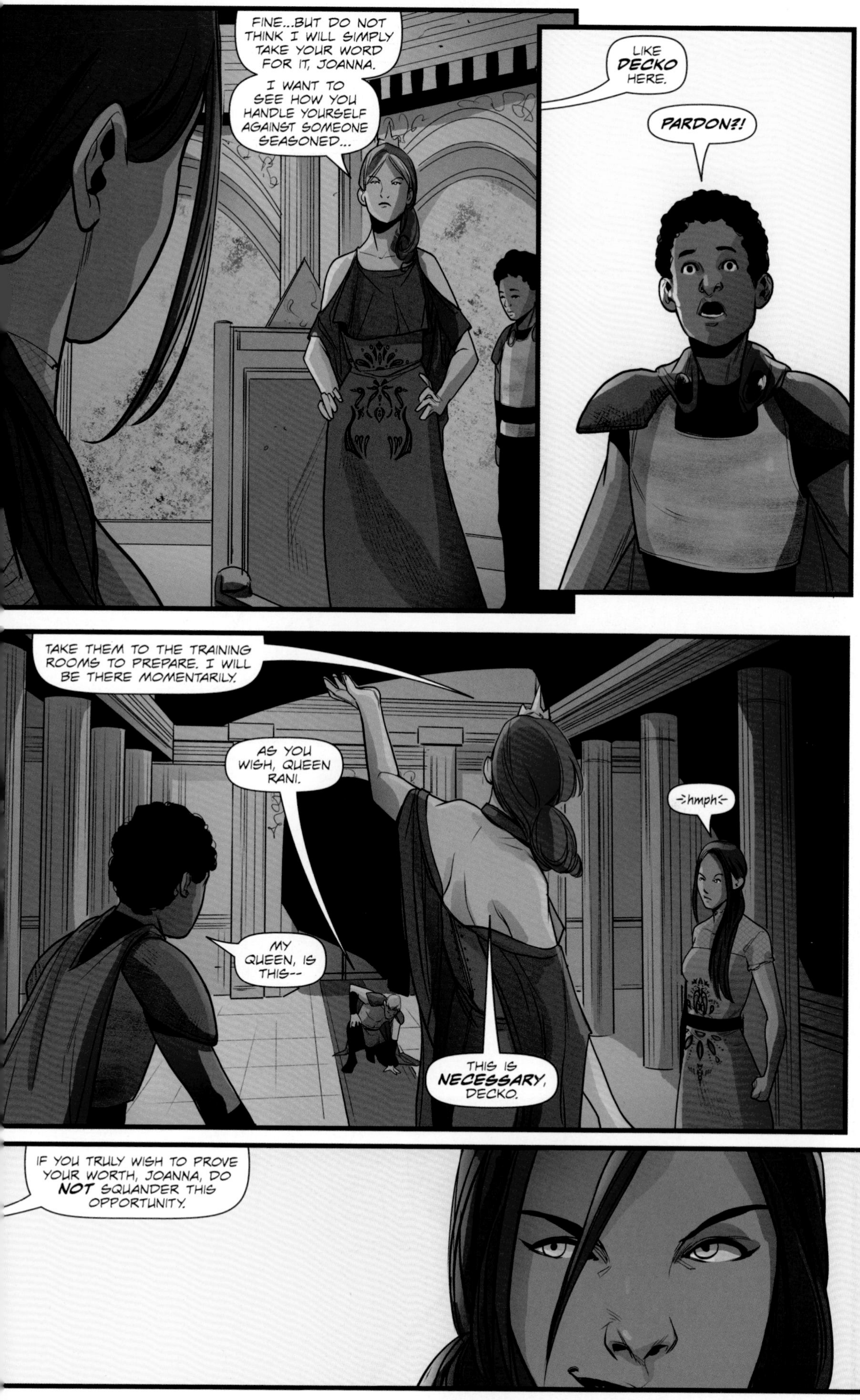
FINE...BUT DO NOT THINK I WILL SIMPLY TAKE YOUR WORD FOR IT, JOANNA.
I WANT TO SEE HOW YOU HANDLE YOURSELF AGAINST SOMEONE SEASONED...
LIKE DECKO HERE.
PARDON?!
TAKE THEM TO THE TRAINING ROOMS TO PREPARE. I WILL BE THERE MOMENTARILY.
AS YOU WISH, QUEEN RANI.
hmph
MY QUEEN, IS THIS--
THIS IS NECESSARY, DECKO.
IF YOU TRULY WISH TO PROVE YOUR WORTH, JOANNA, DO NOT SQUANDER THIS OPPORTUNITY.

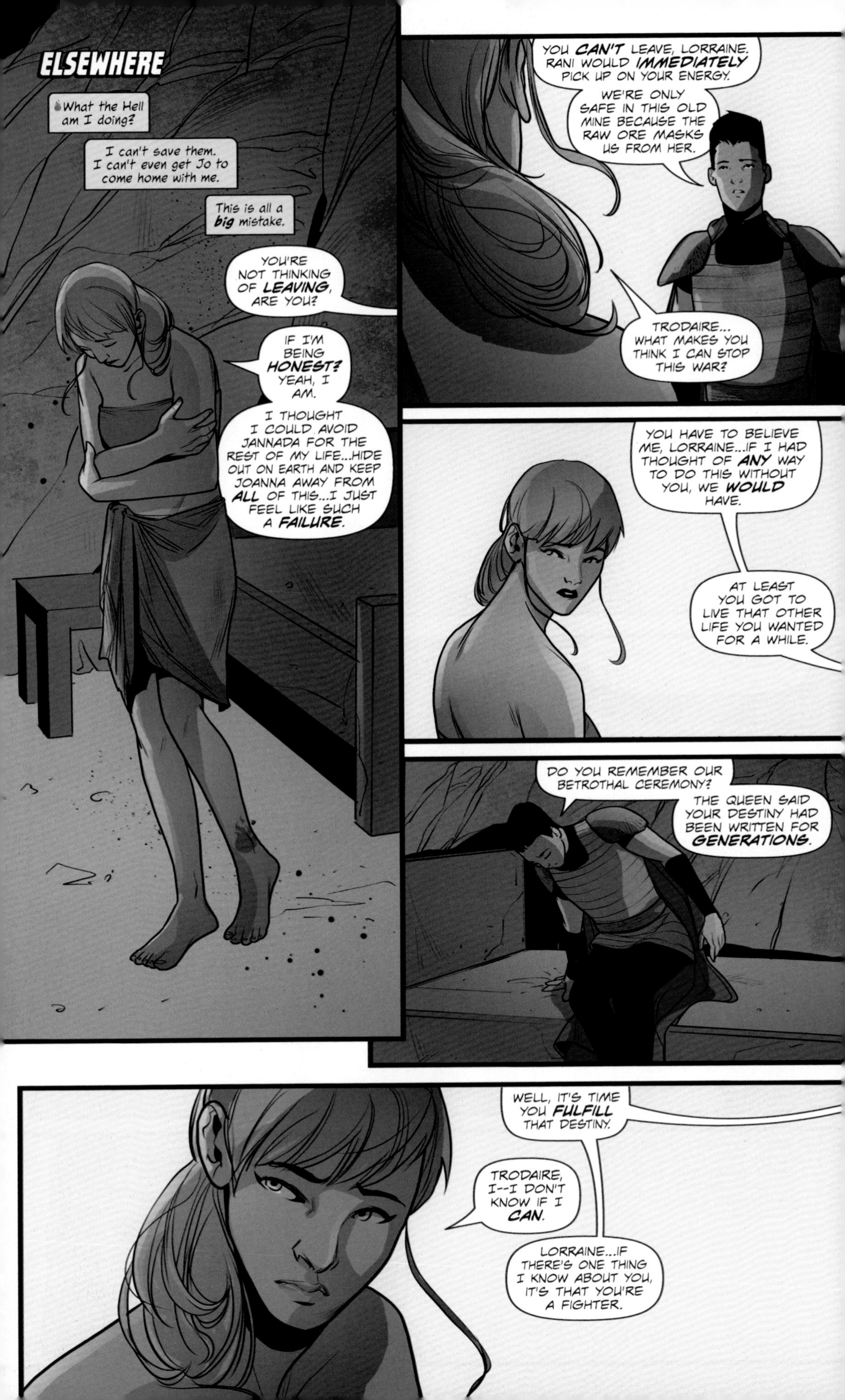
ELSEWHERE
What the Hell am I doing?
I can't save them. I can't even get Jo to come home with me.
This is all a big mistake.
YOU'RE NOT THINKING OF LEAVING, ARE YOU?
IF I'M BEING HONEST? YEAH, I AM.
I THOUGHT I COULD AVOID JANNADA FOR THE REST OF MY LIFE...HIDE OUT ON EARTH AND KEEP JOANNA AWAY FROM ALL OF THIS...I JUST FEEL LIKE SUCH A FAILURE.
YOU CAN'T LEAVE, LORRAINE. RANI WOULD IMMEDIATELY PICK UP ON YOUR ENERGY.
WE'RE ONLY SAFE IN THIS OLD MINE BECAUSE THE RAW ORE MASKS US FROM HER.
TRODAIRE... WHAT MAKES YOU THINK I CAN STOP THIS WAR?
YOU HAVE TO BELIEVE ME, LORRAINE...IF I HAD THOUGHT OF ANY WAY TO DO THIS WITHOUT YOU, WE WOULD HAVE.
AT LEAST YOU GOT TO LIVE THAT OTHER LIFE YOU WANTED FOR A WHILE.
DO YOU REMEMBER OUR BETROTHAL CEREMONY?
THE QUEEN SAID YOUR DESTINY HAD BEEN WRITTEN FOR GENERATIONS.
WELL, IT'S TIME YOU FULFILL THAT DESTINY.
TRODAIRE, I--I DON'T KNOW IF I CAN.
LORRAINE...IF THERE'S ONE THING I KNOW ABOUT YOU, IT'S THAT YOU'RE A FIGHTER.

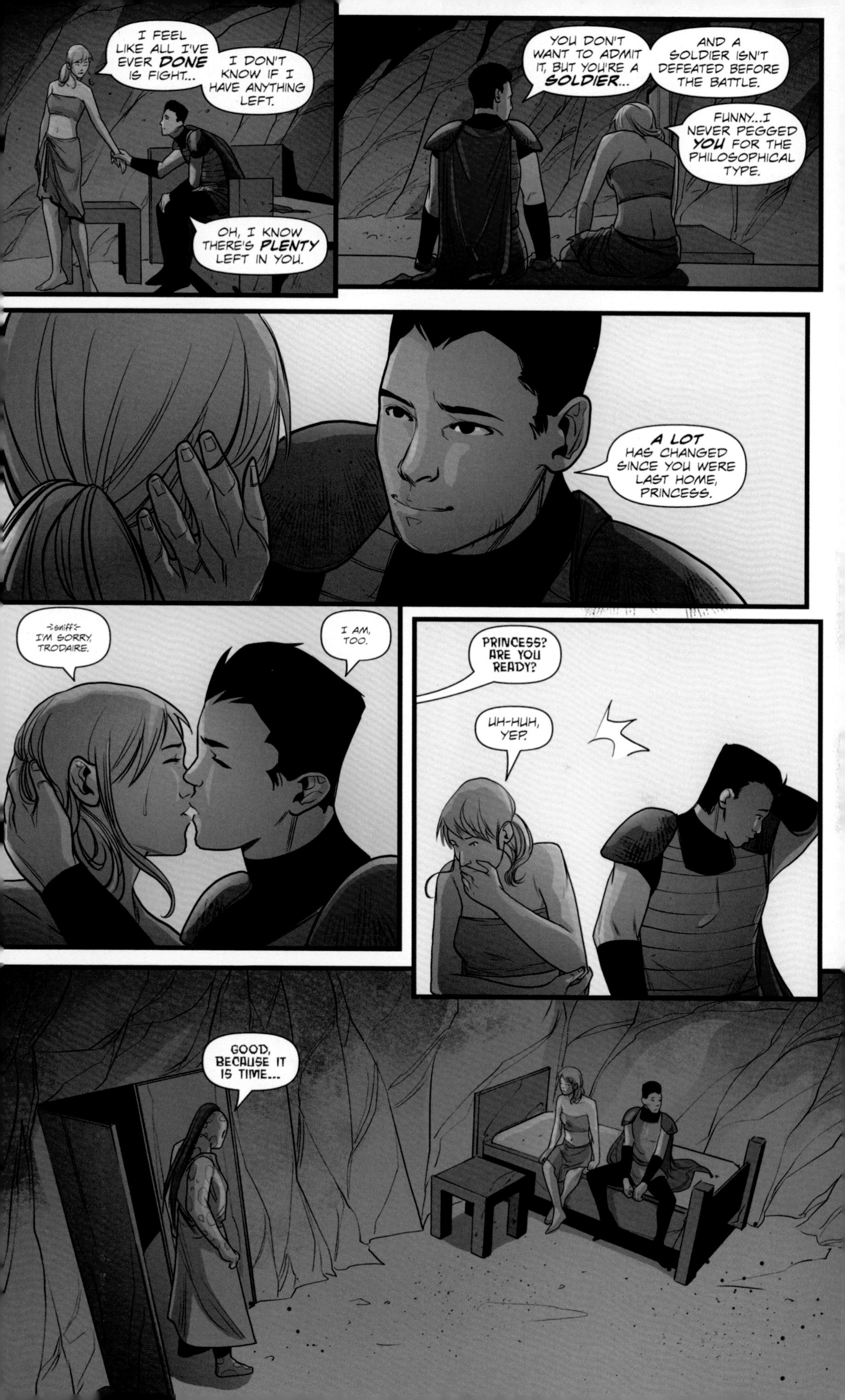
I FEEL LIKE ALL I'VE EVER **DONE** IS FIGHT...
I DON'T KNOW IF I HAVE ANYTHING LEFT.
OH, I KNOW THERE'S **PLENTY** LEFT IN YOU.
YOU DON'T WANT TO ADMIT IT, BUT YOU'RE A **SOLDIER**...
AND A SOLDIER ISN'T DEFEATED BEFORE THE BATTLE.
FUNNY...I NEVER PEGGED **YOU** FOR THE PHILOSOPHICAL TYPE.
A LOT HAS CHANGED SINCE YOU WERE LAST HOME, PRINCESS.
sniff I'M SORRY, TRODAIRE.
I AM, TOO.
PRINCESS? ARE YOU READY?
UH-HUH, YEP.
GOOD, BECAUSE IT IS TIME...

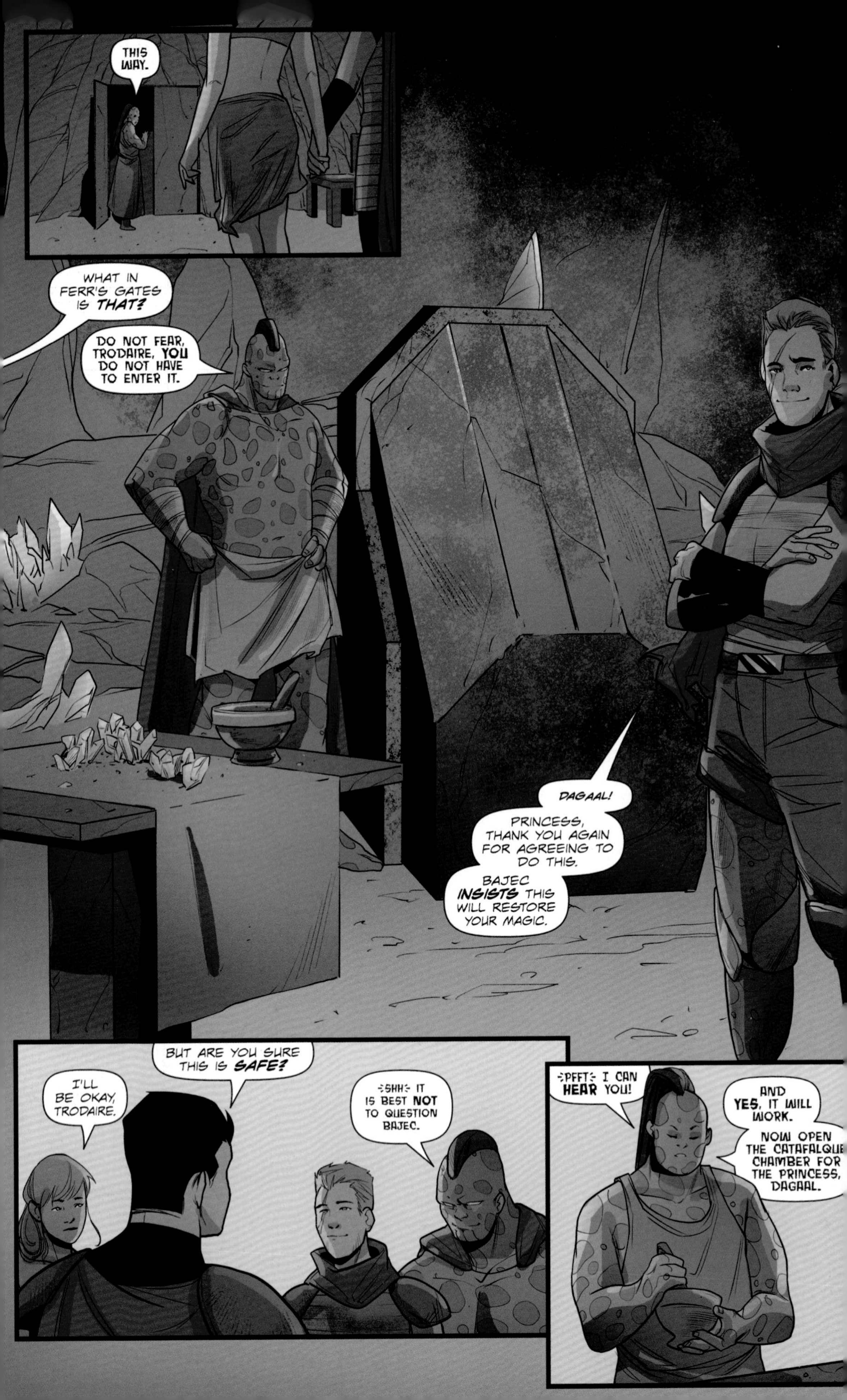
THIS WAY.
WHAT IN FERR'S GATES IS THAT?
DO NOT FEAR, TRODAIRE, YOU DO NOT HAVE TO ENTER IT.
DAGAAL!
PRINCESS, THANK YOU AGAIN FOR AGREEING TO DO THIS.
BAJEC INSISTS THIS WILL RESTORE YOUR MAGIC.
BUT ARE YOU SURE THIS IS SAFE?
I'LL BE OKAY, TRODAIRE.
SHH IT IS BEST NOT TO QUESTION BAJEC.
PFFT I CAN HEAR YOU!
AND YES, IT WILL WORK.
NOW OPEN THE CATAFALQUE CHAMBER FOR THE PRINCESS, DAGAAL.

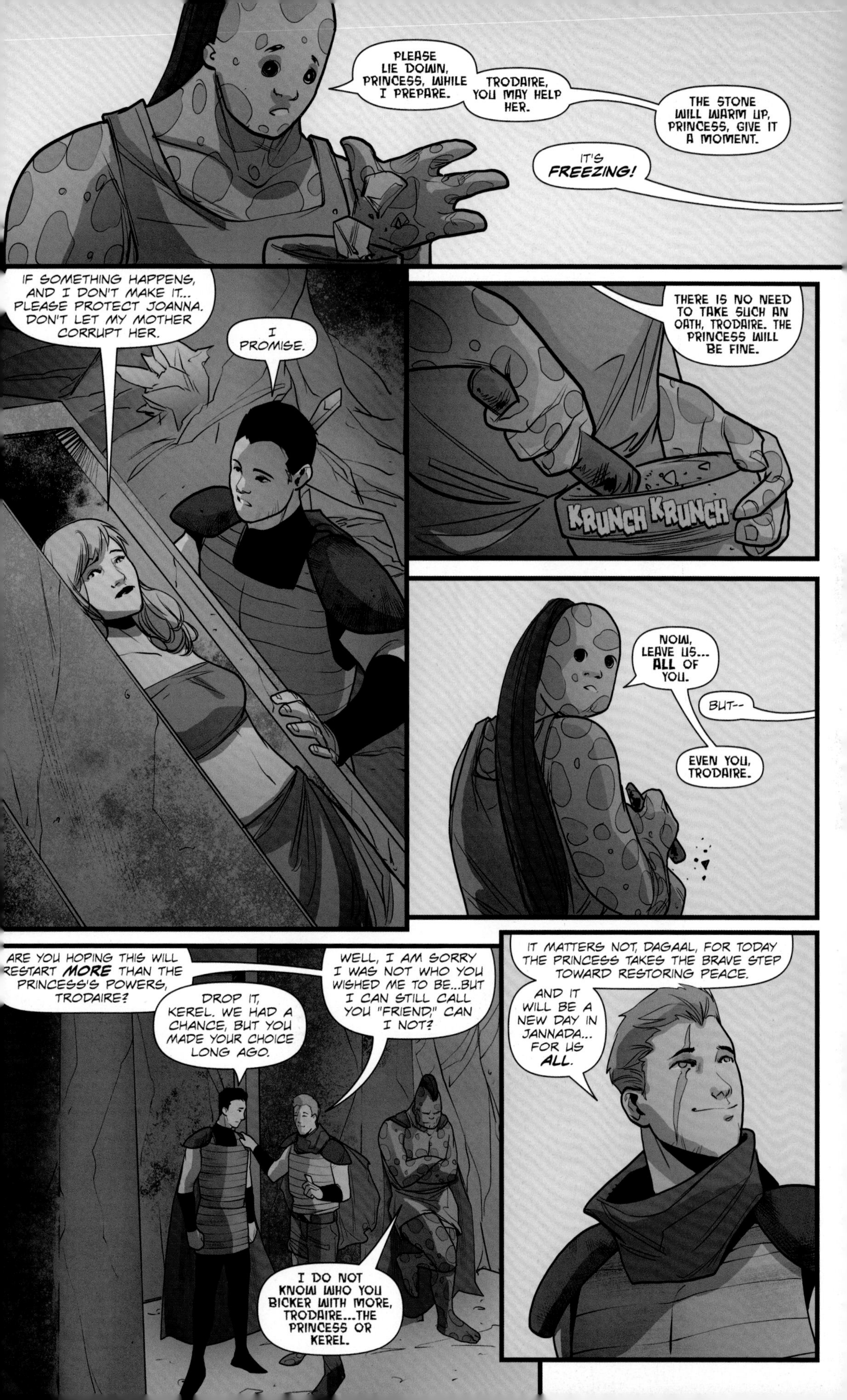
PLEASE LIE DOWN, PRINCESS, WHILE I PREPARE.
TRODAIRE, YOU MAY HELP HER.
THE STONE WILL WARM UP, PRINCESS, GIVE IT A MOMENT.
IT'S FREEZING!
IF SOMETHING HAPPENS, AND I DON'T MAKE IT... PLEASE PROTECT JOANNA. DON'T LET MY MOTHER CORRUPT HER.
I PROMISE.
THERE IS NO NEED TO TAKE SUCH AN OATH, TRODAIRE. THE PRINCESS WILL BE FINE.
KRUNCH KRUNCH
NOW, LEAVE US... ALL OF YOU.
BUT--
EVEN YOU, TRODAIRE.
ARE YOU HOPING THIS WILL RESTART MORE THAN THE PRINCESS'S POWERS, TRODAIRE?
DROP IT, KEREL. WE HAD A CHANCE, BUT YOU MADE YOUR CHOICE LONG AGO.
WELL, I AM SORRY I WAS NOT WHO YOU WISHED ME TO BE...BUT I CAN STILL CALL YOU "FRIEND," CAN I NOT?
I DO NOT KNOW WHO YOU BICKER WITH MORE, TRODAIRE...THE PRINCESS OR KEREL.
IT MATTERS NOT, DAGAAL, FOR TODAY THE PRINCESS TAKES THE BRAVE STEP TOWARD RESTORING PEACE.
AND IT WILL BE A NEW DAY IN JANNADA... FOR US ALL.

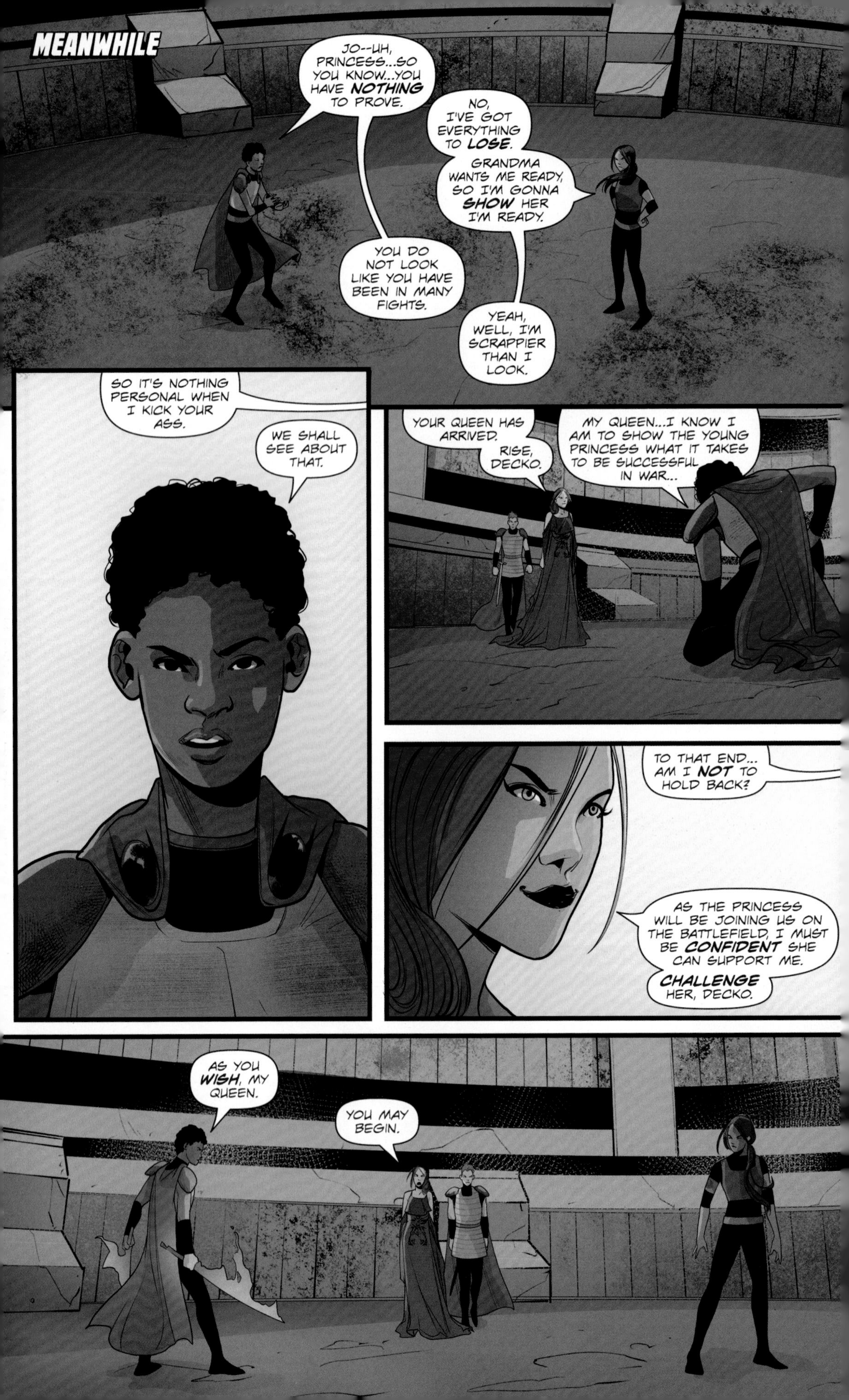
MEANWHILE
JO--UH, PRINCESS...SO YOU KNOW...YOU HAVE NOTHING TO PROVE.
NO, I'VE GOT EVERYTHING TO LOSE.
GRANDMA WANTS ME READY, SO I'M GONNA SHOW HER I'M READY.
YOU DO NOT LOOK LIKE YOU HAVE BEEN IN MANY FIGHTS.
YEAH, WELL, I'M SCRAPPIER THAN I LOOK.
SO IT'S NOTHING PERSONAL WHEN I KICK YOUR ASS.
WE SHALL SEE ABOUT THAT.
YOUR QUEEN HAS ARRIVED.
RISE, DECKO.
MY QUEEN...I KNOW I AM TO SHOW THE YOUNG PRINCESS WHAT IT TAKES TO BE SUCCESSFUL IN WAR...
TO THAT END... AM I NOT TO HOLD BACK?
AS THE PRINCESS WILL BE JOINING US ON THE BATTLEFIELD, I MUST BE CONFIDENT SHE CAN SUPPORT ME.
CHALLENGE HER, DECKO.
AS YOU WISH, MY QUEEN.
YOU MAY BEGIN.

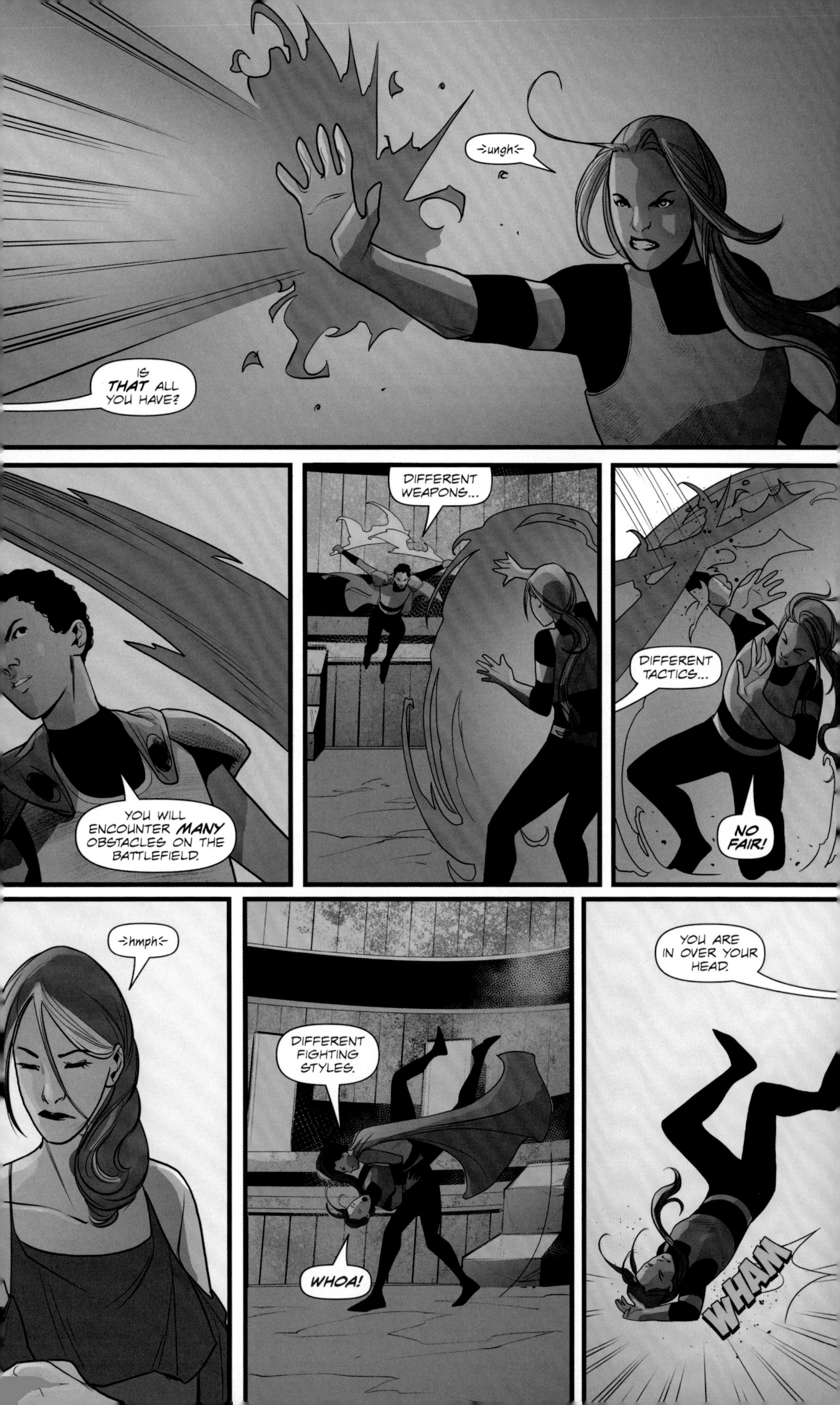

-ungh-
IS THAT ALL YOU HAVE?
YOU WILL ENCOUNTER MANY OBSTACLES ON THE BATTLEFIELD.
DIFFERENT WEAPONS...
DIFFERENT TACTICS...
NO FAIR!
-hmph-
DIFFERENT FIGHTING STYLES.
WHOA!
YOU ARE IN OVER YOUR HEAD.
WHAM

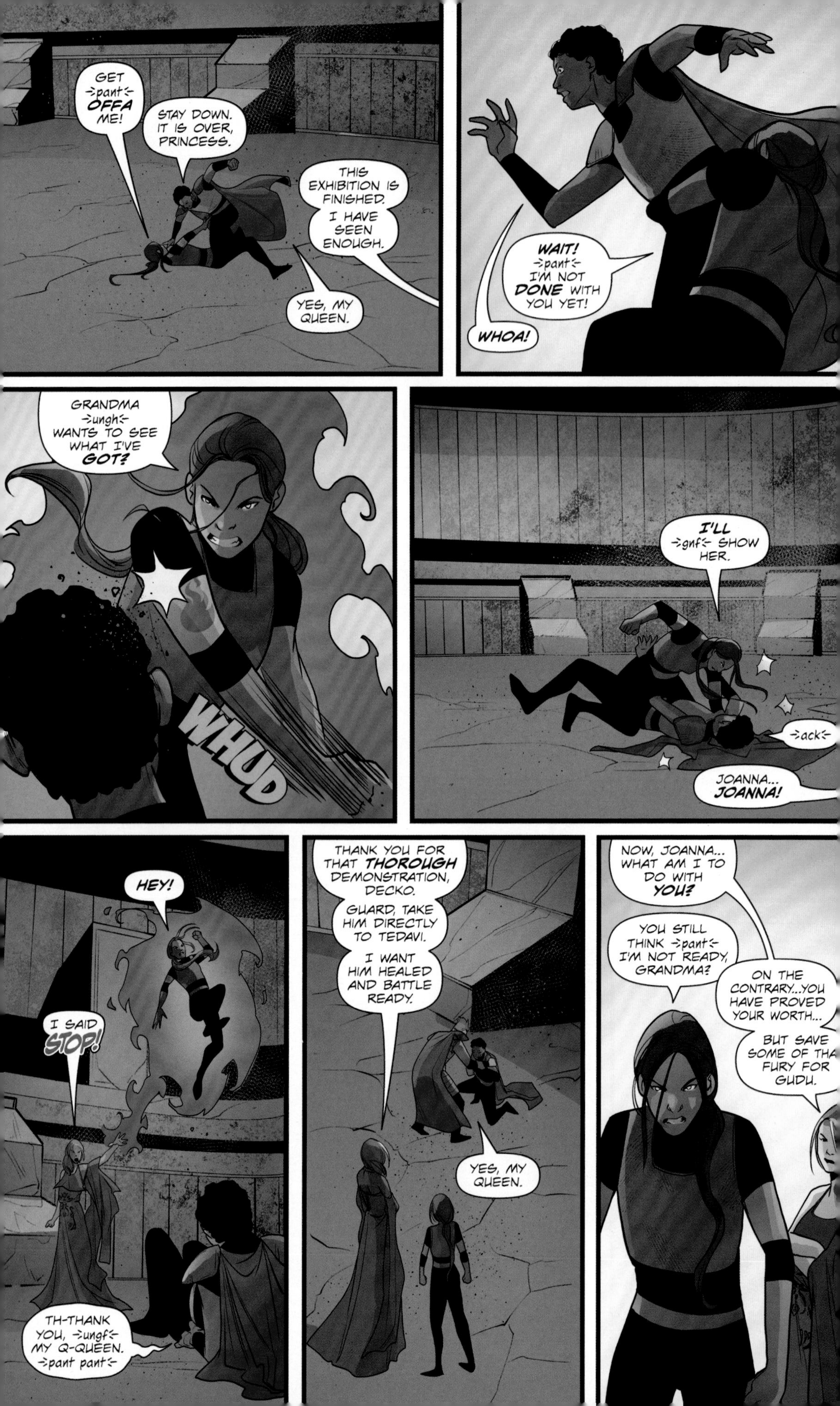
GET ⇢pant⇠ OFFA ME!
STAY DOWN. IT IS OVER, PRINCESS.
THIS EXHIBITION IS FINISHED.
I HAVE SEEN ENOUGH.
YES, MY QUEEN.
WAIT! ⇢pant⇠ I'M NOT DONE WITH YOU YET!
WHOA!
GRANDMA ⇢ungh⇠ WANTS TO SEE WHAT I'VE GOT?
WHUD
I'LL ⇢gnf⇠ SHOW HER.
⇢ack⇠
JOANNA... JOANNA!
HEY!
I SAID STOP!
TH-THANK YOU, ⇢ungf⇠ MY Q-QUEEN. ⇢pant pant⇠
THANK YOU FOR THAT THOROUGH DEMONSTRATION, DECKO.
GUARD, TAKE HIM DIRECTLY TO TEDAVI.
I WANT HIM HEALED AND BATTLE READY.
YES, MY QUEEN.
NOW, JOANNA... WHAT AM I TO DO WITH YOU?
YOU STILL THINK ⇢pant⇠ I'M NOT READY, GRANDMA?
ON THE CONTRARY...YOU HAVE PROVED YOUR WORTH...
BUT SAVE SOME OF THA FURY FOR GUDU.

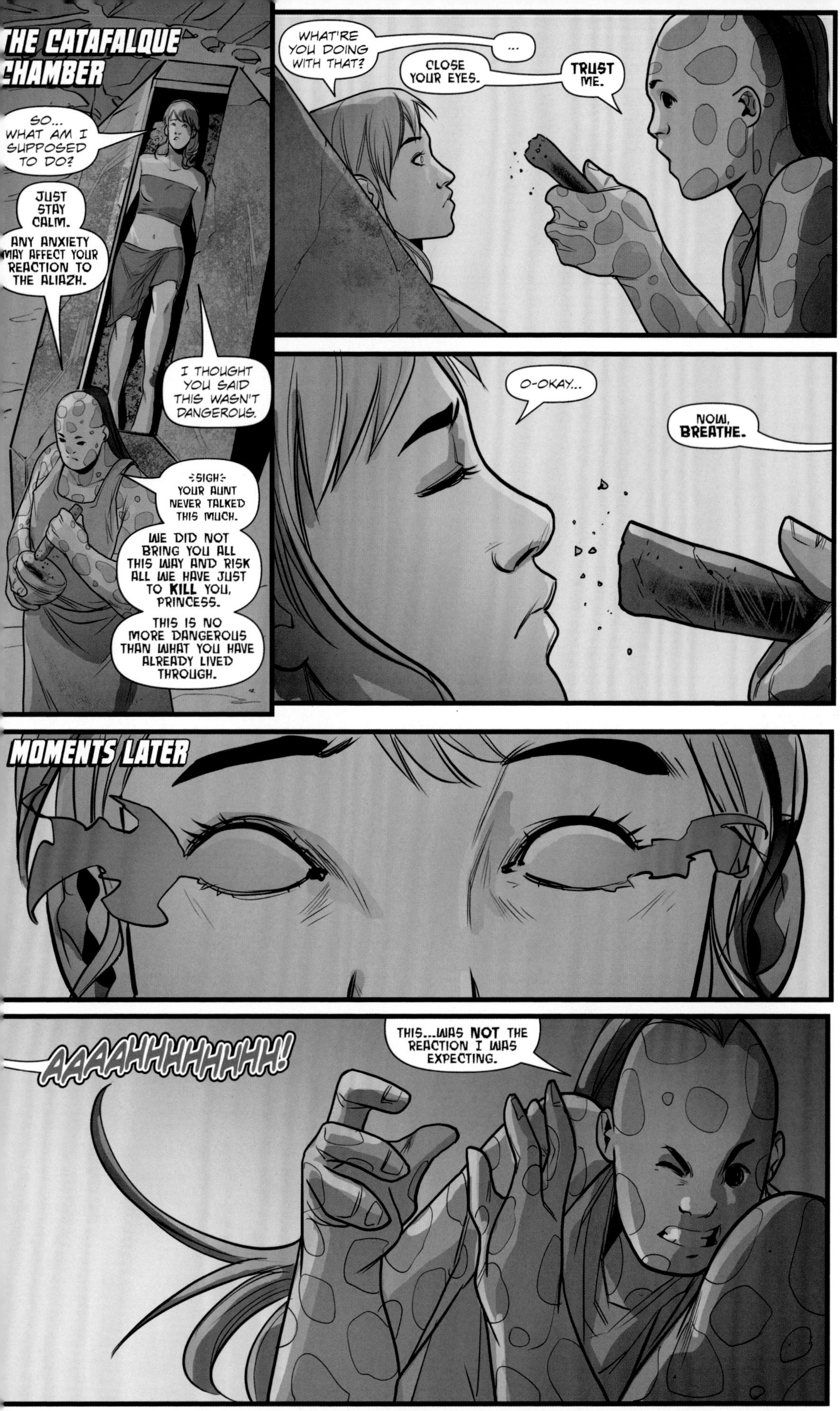
THE CATAFALQUE CHAMBER
SO... WHAT AM I SUPPOSED TO DO?
JUST STAY CALM.
ANY ANXIETY MAY AFFECT YOUR REACTION TO THE ALIAZH.
I THOUGHT YOU SAID THIS WASN'T DANGEROUS.
÷SIGH÷ YOUR AUNT NEVER TALKED THIS MUCH.
WE DID NOT BRING YOU ALL THIS WAY AND RISK ALL WE HAVE JUST TO KILL YOU, PRINCESS.
THIS IS NO MORE DANGEROUS THAN WHAT YOU HAVE ALREADY LIVED THROUGH.
WHAT'RE YOU DOING WITH THAT?
...
CLOSE YOUR EYES.
TRUST ME.
O-OKAY...
NOW, BREATHE.
MOMENTS LATER
AAAAHHHHHHH!
THIS...WAS NOT THE REACTION I WAS EXPECTING.

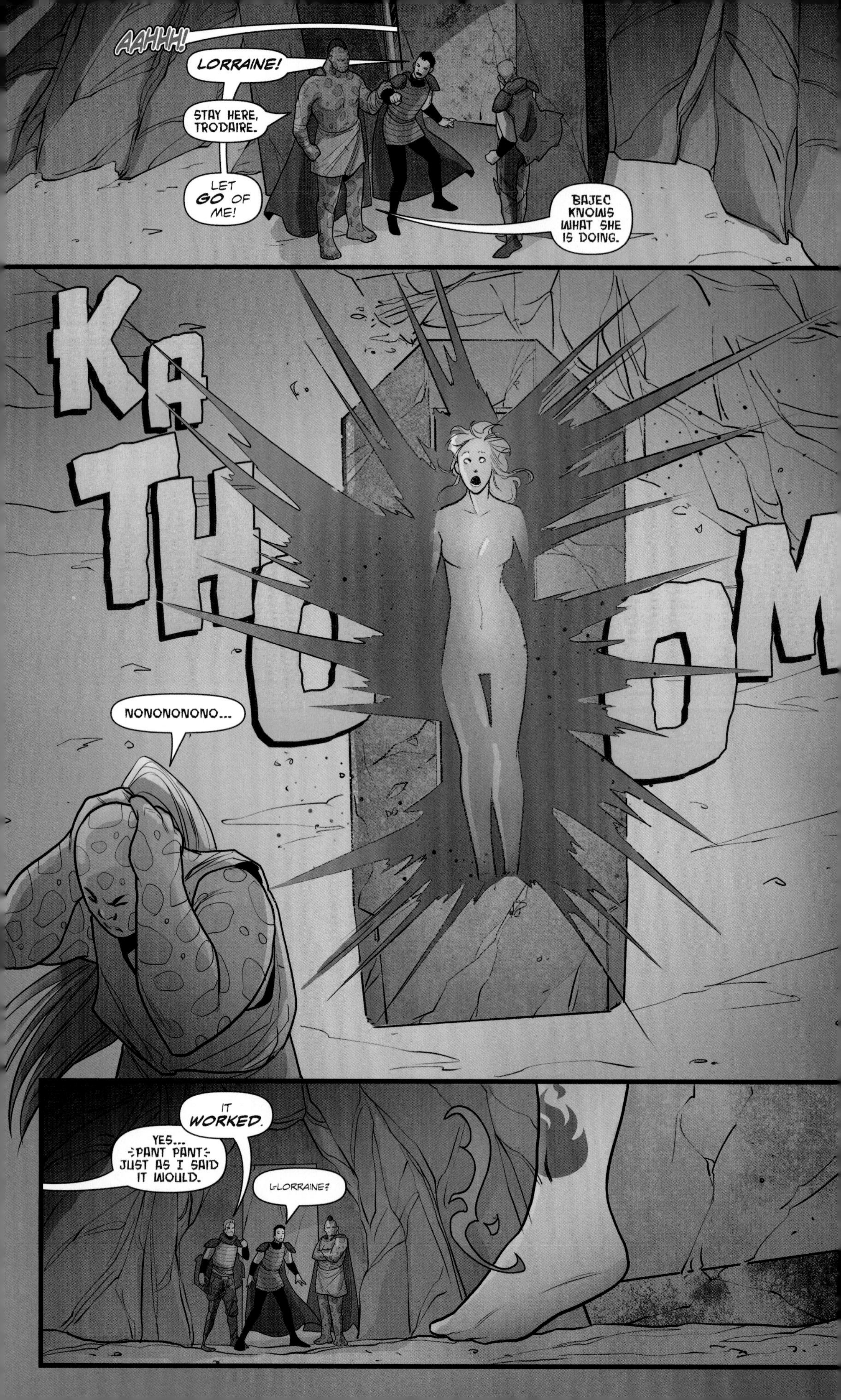
AAHHH!
LORRAINE!
STAY HERE, TRODAIRE.
LET GO OF ME!
BAJEC KNOWS WHAT SHE IS DOING.
KA THOOM
NONONONONO...
IT WORKED.
YES... =PANT PANT= JUST AS I SAID IT WOULD.
L-LORRAINE?

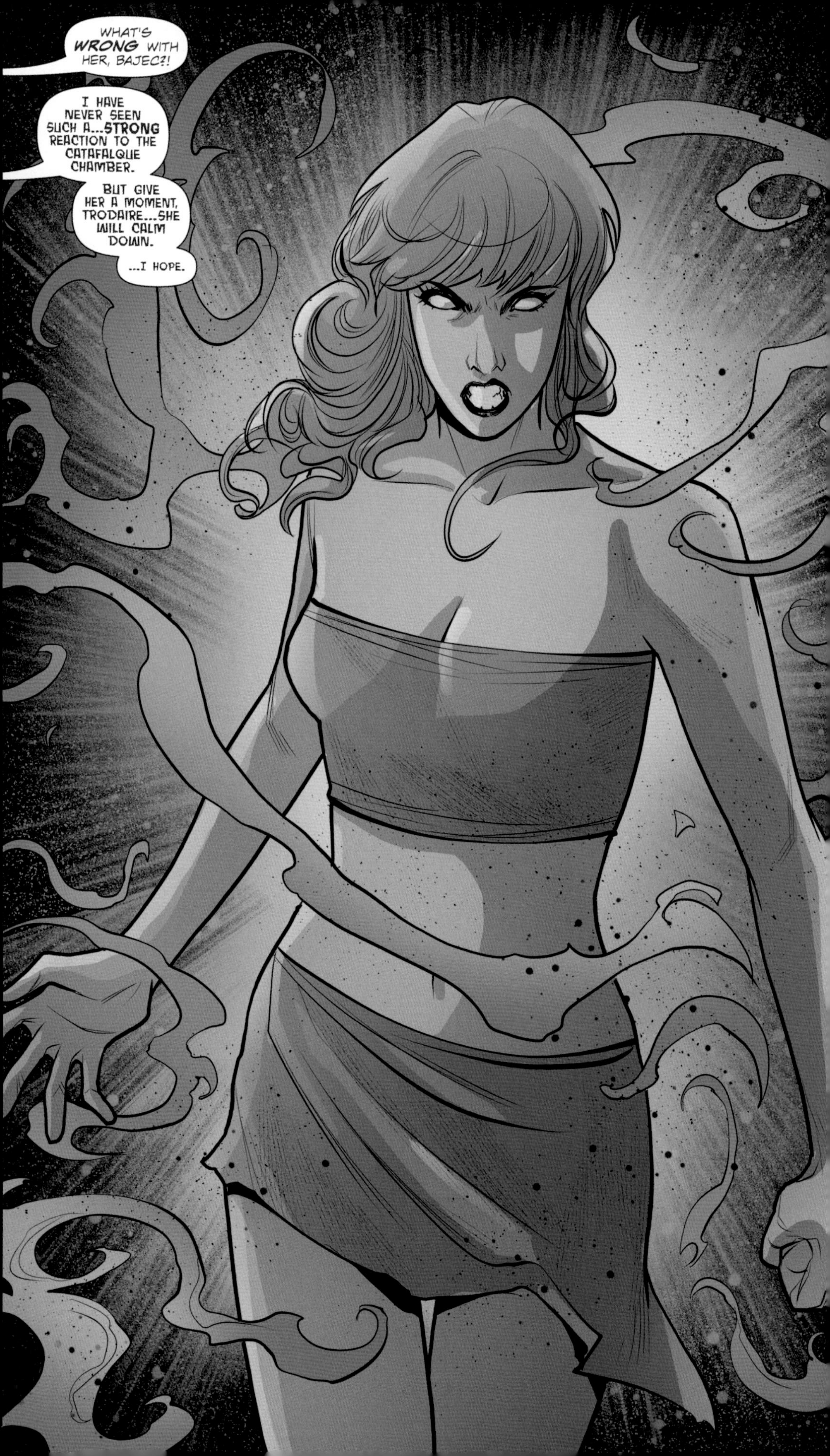
WHAT'S **WRONG** WITH HER, BAJEC?!
I HAVE NEVER SEEN SUCH A...**STRONG** REACTION TO THE CATAFALQUE CHAMBER.
BUT GIVE HER A MOMENT, TRODAIRE...SHE WILL CALM DOWN.
...I HOPE.

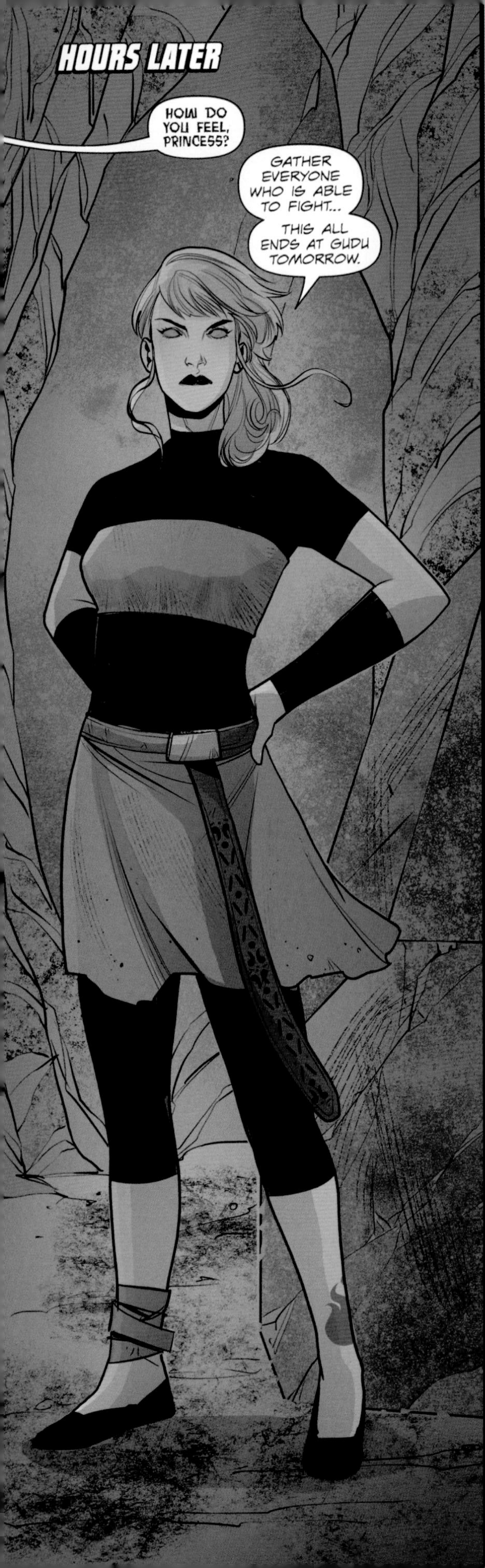
HOURS LATER
HOW DO YOU FEEL, PRINCESS?
GATHER EVERYONE WHO IS ABLE TO FIGHT...
THIS ALL ENDS AT GUDU TOMORROW.

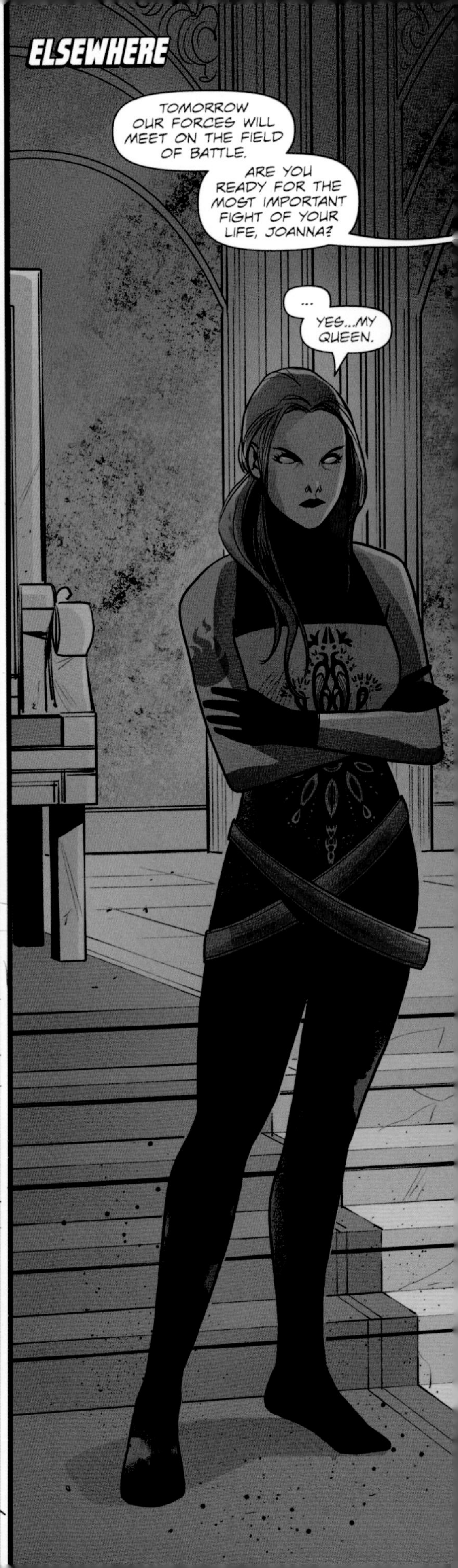
ELSEWHERE
TOMORROW OUR FORCES WILL MEET ON THE FIELD OF BATTLE.
ARE YOU READY FOR THE MOST IMPORTANT FIGHT OF YOUR LIFE, JOANNA?
...
YES...MY QUEEN.

SEVEN

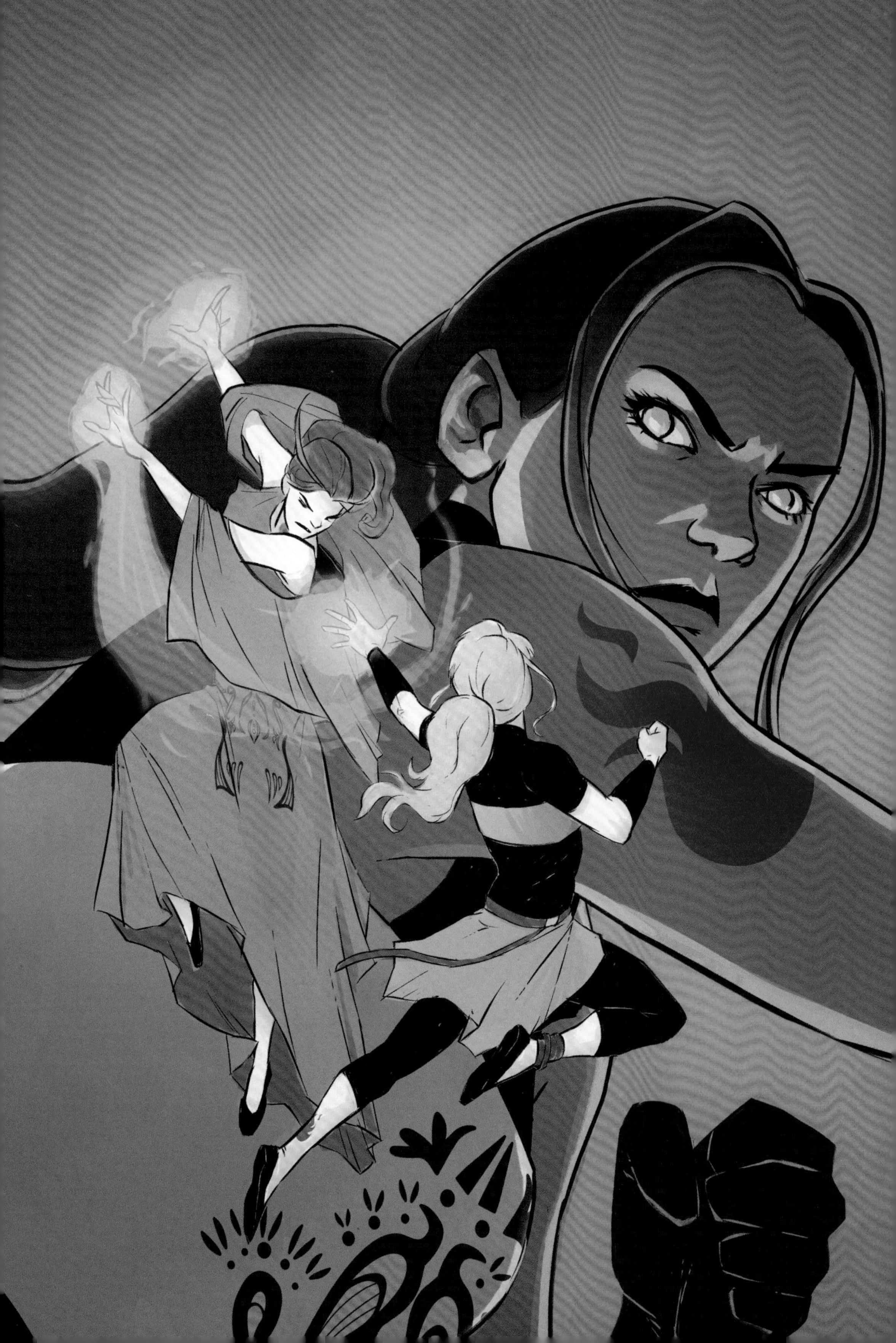

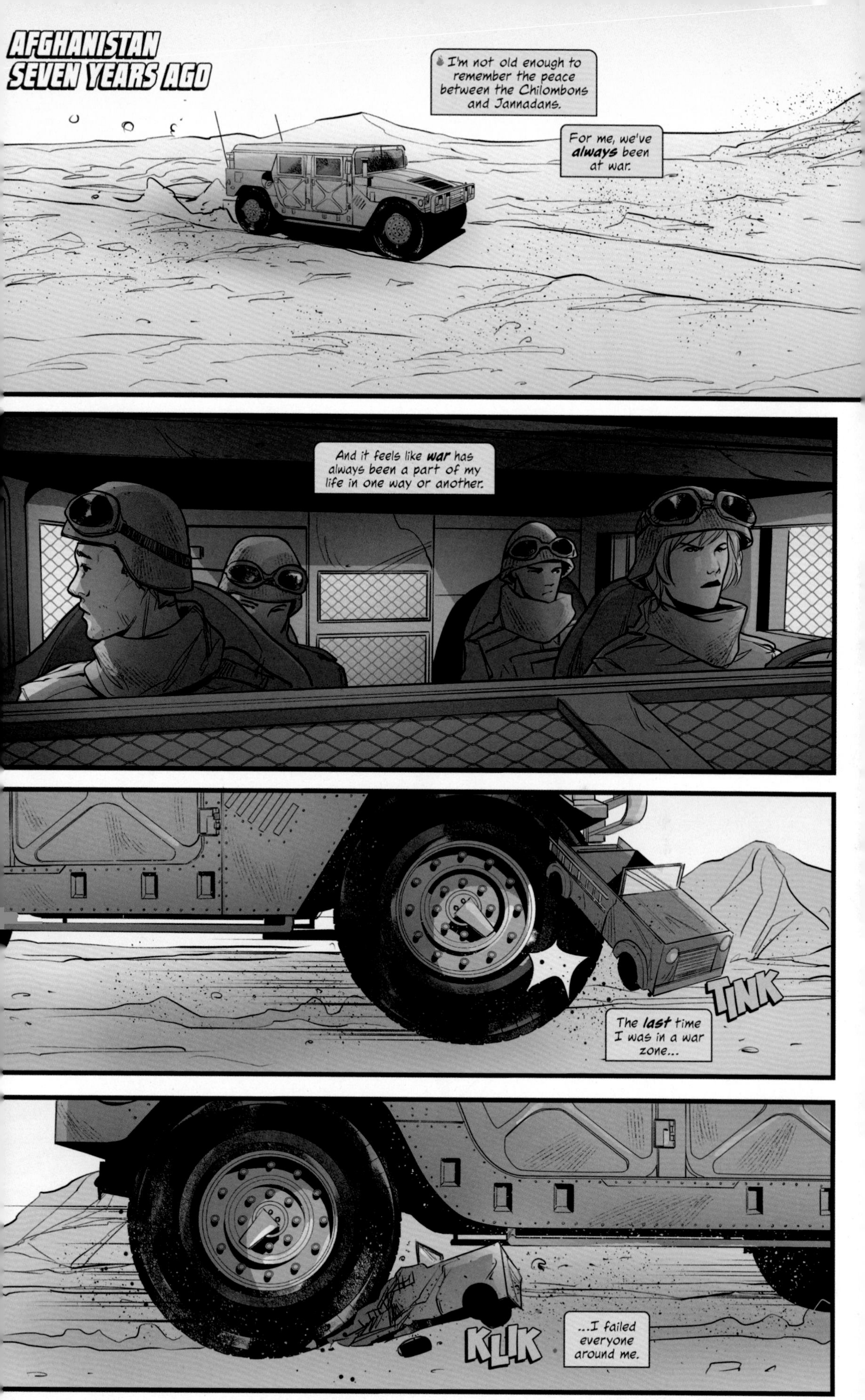
AFGHANISTAN
SEVEN YEARS AGO
I'm not old enough to remember the peace between the Chilombons and Jannadans.
For me, we've always been at war.
And it feels like war has always been a part of my life in one way or another.
TINK
The last time I was in a war zone...
KLIK
...I failed everyone around me.

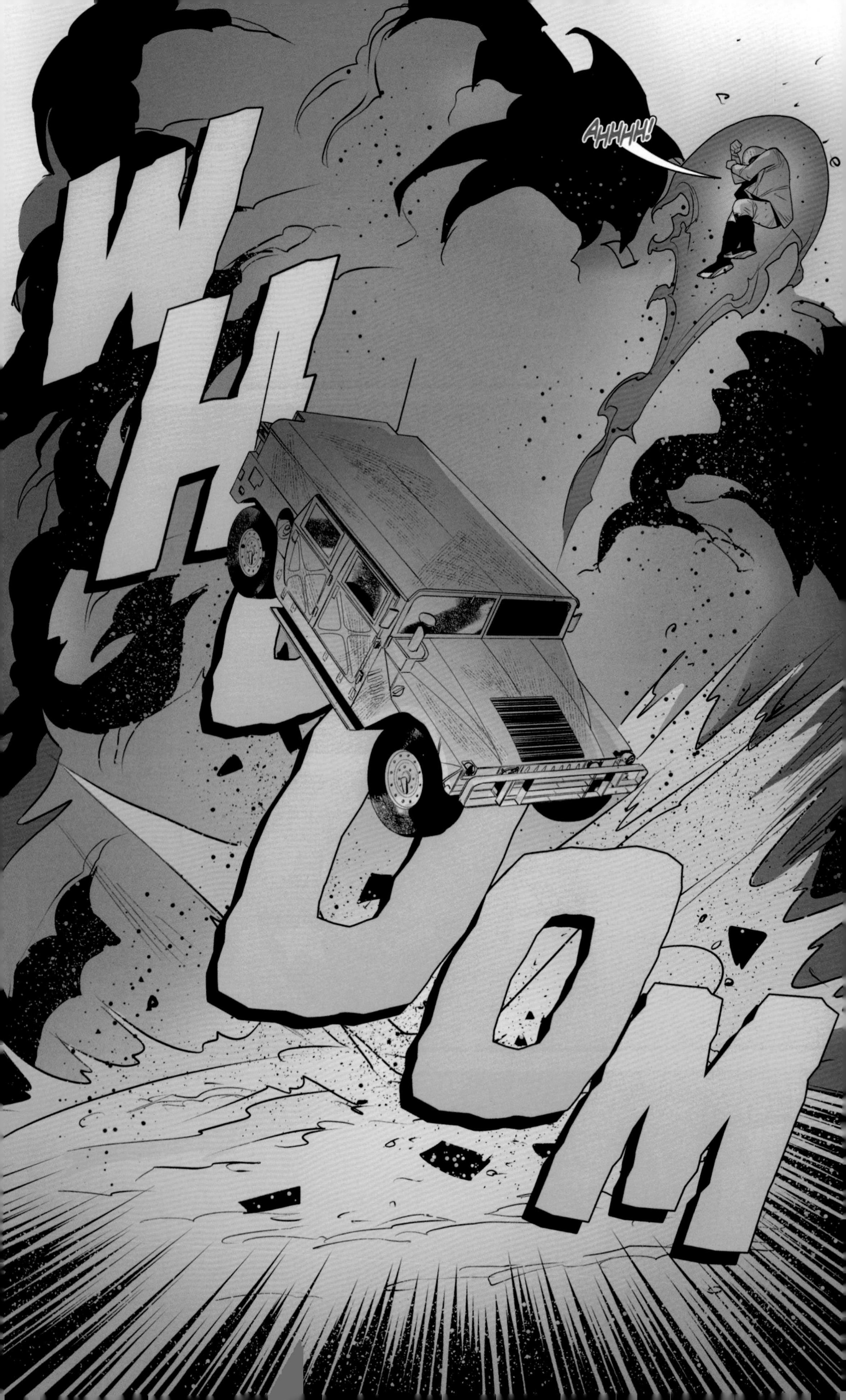
AHHHH!
WHOOM

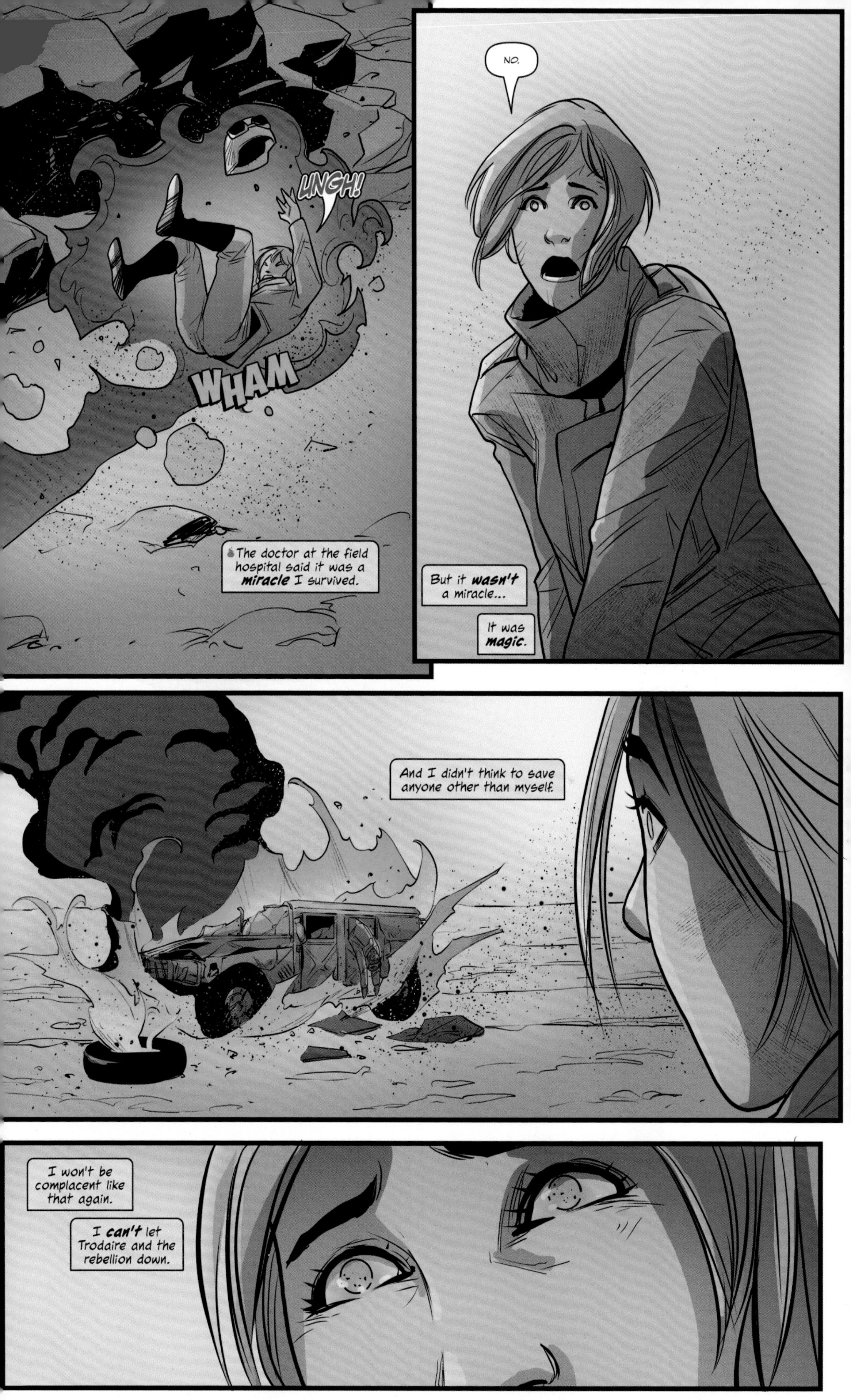
UNGH!
WHAM
The doctor at the field hospital said it was a miracle I survived.
NO.
But it wasn't a miracle...
It was magic.
And I didn't think to save anyone other than myself.
I won't be complacent like that again.
I can't let Trodaire and the rebellion down.

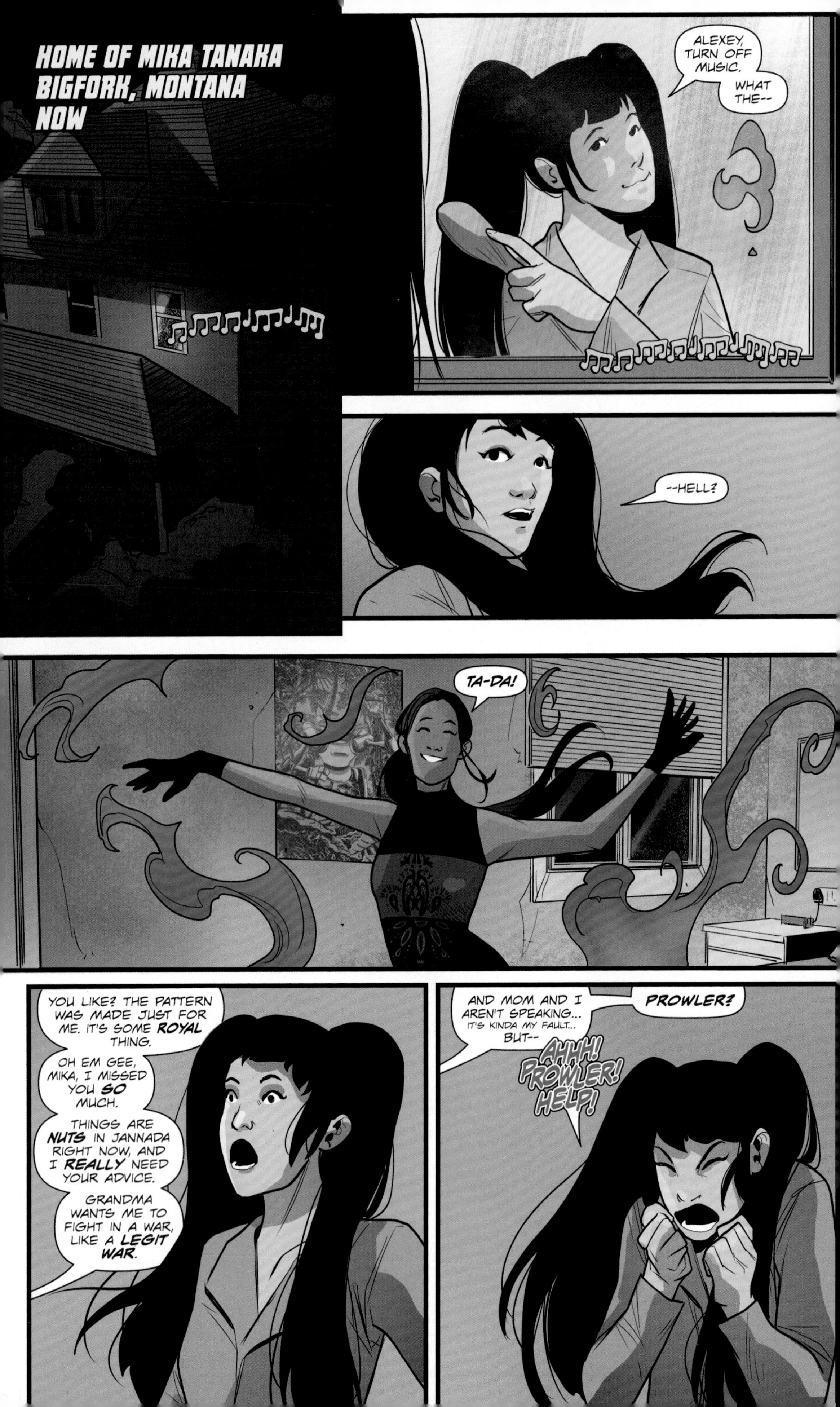
HOME OF MIKA TANAKA
BIGFORK, MONTANA
NOW
ALEXEY, TURN OFF MUSIC.
WHAT THE--
--HELL?
TA-DA!
YOU LIKE? THE PATTERN WAS MADE JUST FOR ME. IT'S SOME ROYAL THING.
OH EM GEE, MIKA, I MISSED YOU SO MUCH.
THINGS ARE NUTS IN JANNADA RIGHT NOW, AND I REALLY NEED YOUR ADVICE.
GRANDMA WANTS ME TO FIGHT IN A WAR, LIKE A LEGIT WAR.
AND MOM AND I AREN'T SPEAKING... IT'S KINDA MY FAULT... BUT--
PROWLER?
AHHH! PROWLER! HELP!

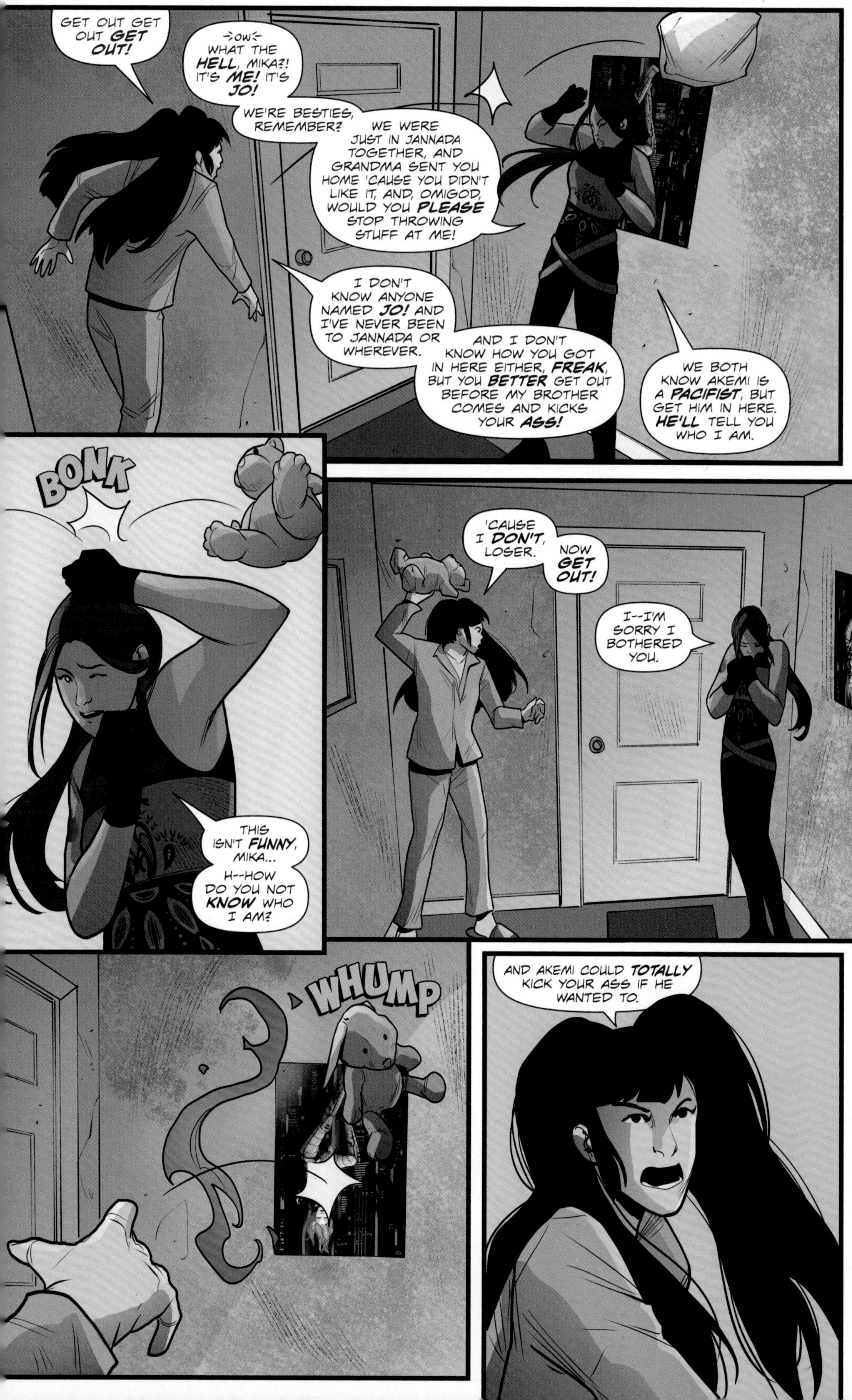
GET OUT GET OUT GET OUT!
>OW< WHAT THE HELL, MIKA?! IT'S ME! IT'S JO!
WE'RE BESTIES, REMEMBER?
WE WERE JUST IN JANNADA TOGETHER, AND GRANDMA SENT YOU HOME 'CAUSE YOU DIDN'T LIKE IT, AND, OMIGOD, WOULD YOU PLEASE STOP THROWING STUFF AT ME!
I DON'T KNOW ANYONE NAMED JO! AND I'VE NEVER BEEN TO JANNADA OR WHEREVER.
AND I DON'T KNOW HOW YOU GOT IN HERE EITHER, FREAK, BUT YOU BETTER GET OUT BEFORE MY BROTHER COMES AND KICKS YOUR ASS!
WE BOTH KNOW AKEMI IS A PACIFIST, BUT GET HIM IN HERE. HE'LL TELL YOU WHO I AM.
BONK
THIS ISN'T FUNNY, MIKA...
H--HOW DO YOU NOT KNOW WHO I AM?
'CAUSE I DON'T, LOSER.
NOW GET OUT!
I--I'M SORRY I BOTHERED YOU.
WHUMP
AND AKEMI COULD TOTALLY KICK YOUR ASS IF HE WANTED TO.

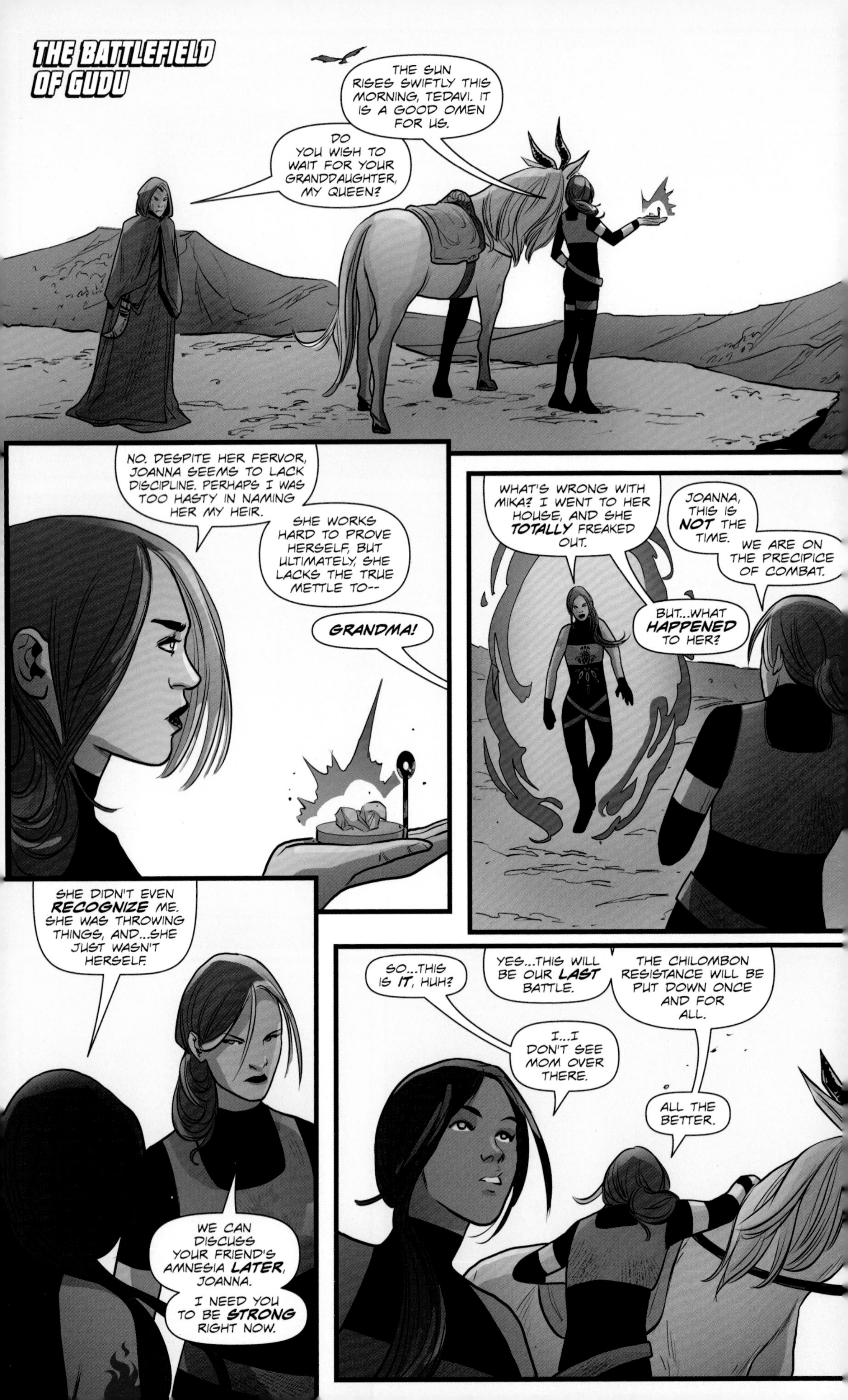
THE BATTLEFIELD OF GUDU
THE SUN RISES SWIFTLY THIS MORNING, TEDAVI. IT IS A GOOD OMEN FOR US.
DO YOU WISH TO WAIT FOR YOUR GRANDDAUGHTER, MY QUEEN?
NO. DESPITE HER FERVOR, JOANNA SEEMS TO LACK DISCIPLINE. PERHAPS I WAS TOO HASTY IN NAMING HER MY HEIR.
SHE WORKS HARD TO PROVE HERSELF, BUT ULTIMATELY, SHE LACKS THE TRUE METTLE TO--
GRANDMA!
WHAT'S WRONG WITH MIKA? I WENT TO HER HOUSE, AND SHE TOTALLY FREAKED OUT.
JOANNA, THIS IS NOT THE TIME.
WE ARE ON THE PRECIPICE OF COMBAT.
BUT...WHAT HAPPENED TO HER?
SHE DIDN'T EVEN RECOGNIZE ME. SHE WAS THROWING THINGS, AND...SHE JUST WASN'T HERSELF.
WE CAN DISCUSS YOUR FRIEND'S AMNESIA LATER, JOANNA.
I NEED YOU TO BE STRONG RIGHT NOW.
SO...THIS IS IT, HUH?
YES...THIS WILL BE OUR LAST BATTLE.
THE CHILOMBON RESISTANCE WILL BE PUT DOWN ONCE AND FOR ALL.
I...I DON'T SEE MOM OVER THERE.
ALL THE BETTER.

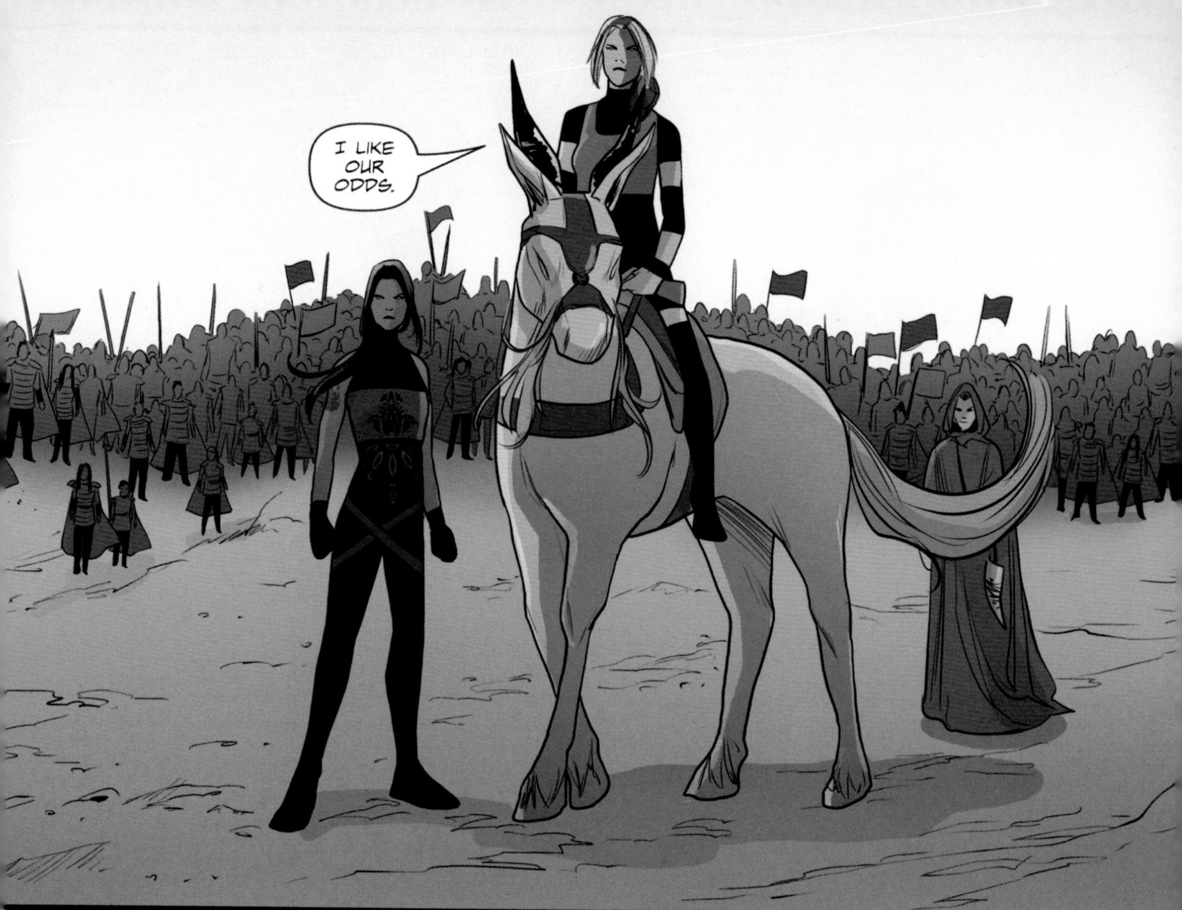
I LIKE OUR ODDS.

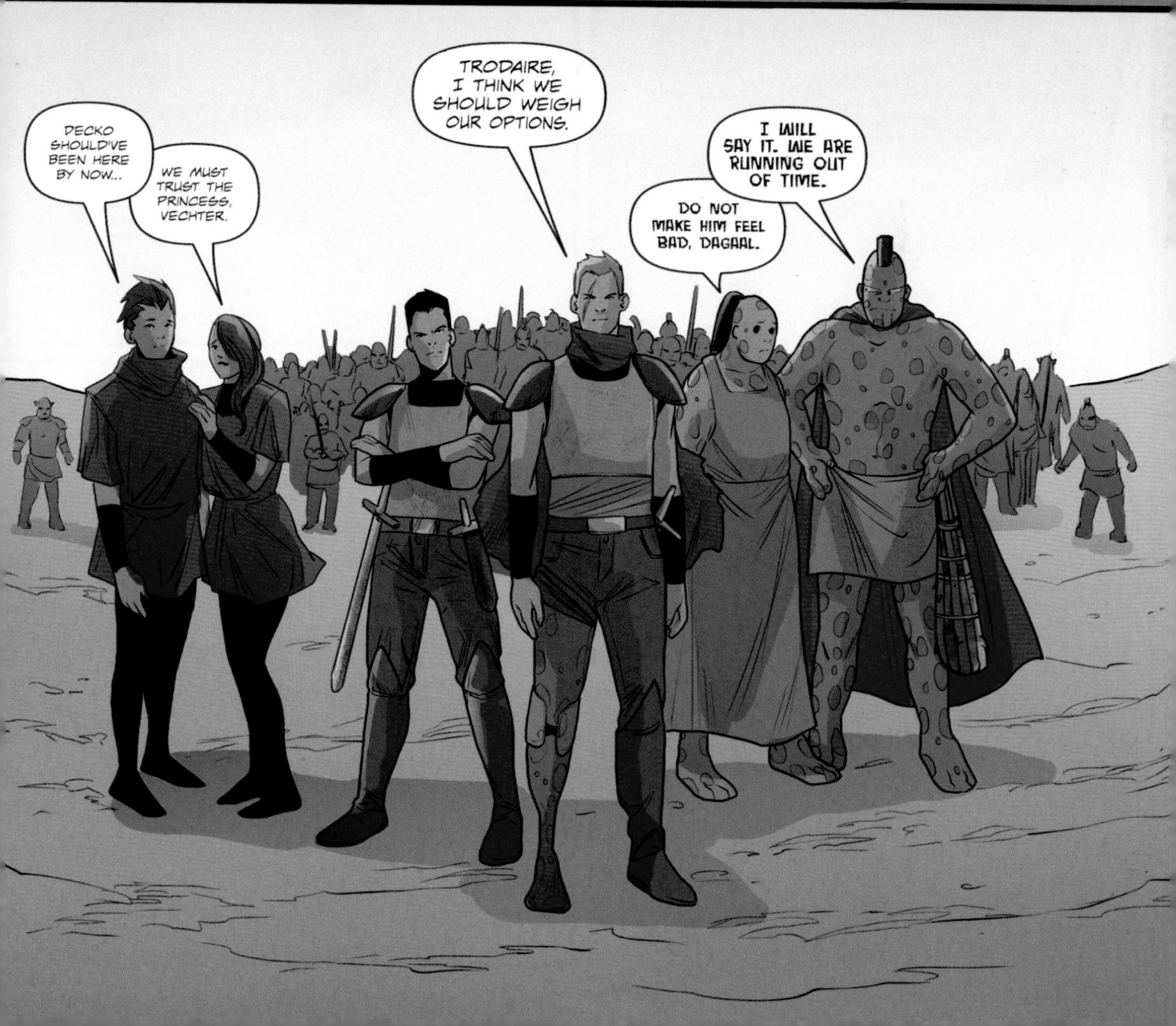
DECKO SHOULD'VE BEEN HERE BY NOW...
WE MUST TRUST THE PRINCESS, VECHTER.
TRODAIRE, I THINK WE SHOULD WEIGH OUR OPTIONS.
I WILL SAY IT. WE ARE RUNNING OUT OF TIME.
DO NOT MAKE HIM FEEL BAD, DAGAAL.

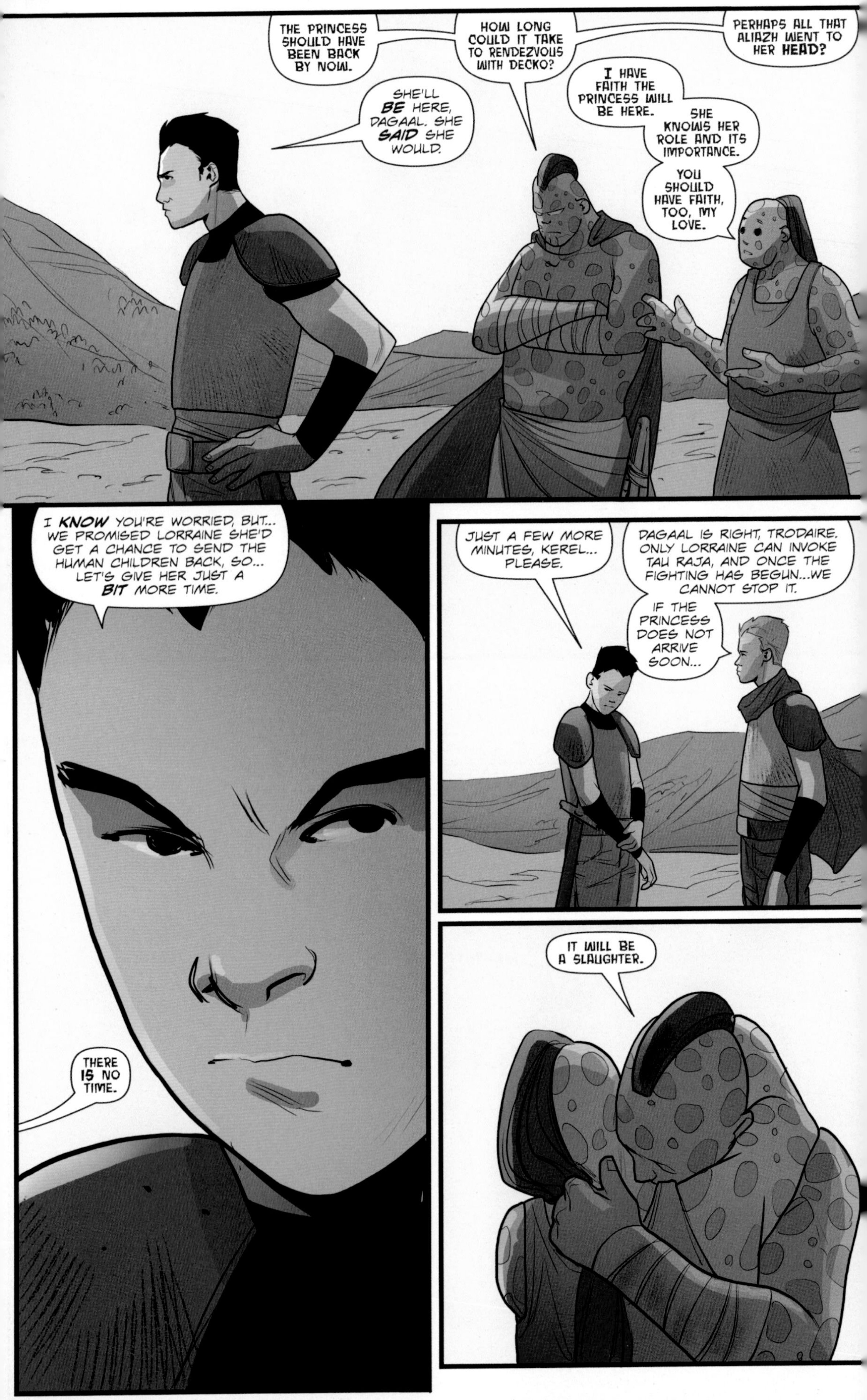
THE PRINCESS SHOULD HAVE BEEN BACK BY NOW.
HOW LONG COULD IT TAKE TO RENDEZVOUS WITH DECKO?
PERHAPS ALL THAT ALIAZH WENT TO HER HEAD?
SHE'LL BE HERE, DAGAAL. SHE SAID SHE WOULD.
I HAVE FAITH THE PRINCESS WILL BE HERE.
SHE KNOWS HER ROLE AND ITS IMPORTANCE.
YOU SHOULD HAVE FAITH, TOO, MY LOVE.
I KNOW YOU'RE WORRIED, BUT... WE PROMISED LORRAINE SHE'D GET A CHANCE TO SEND THE HUMAN CHILDREN BACK, SO... LET'S GIVE HER JUST A BIT MORE TIME.
THERE IS NO TIME.
JUST A FEW MORE MINUTES, KEREL... PLEASE.
DAGAAL IS RIGHT, TRODAIRE. ONLY LORRAINE CAN INVOKE TAU RAJA, AND ONCE THE FIGHTING HAS BEGUN...WE CANNOT STOP IT.
IF THE PRINCESS DOES NOT ARRIVE SOON...
IT WILL BE A SLAUGHTER.

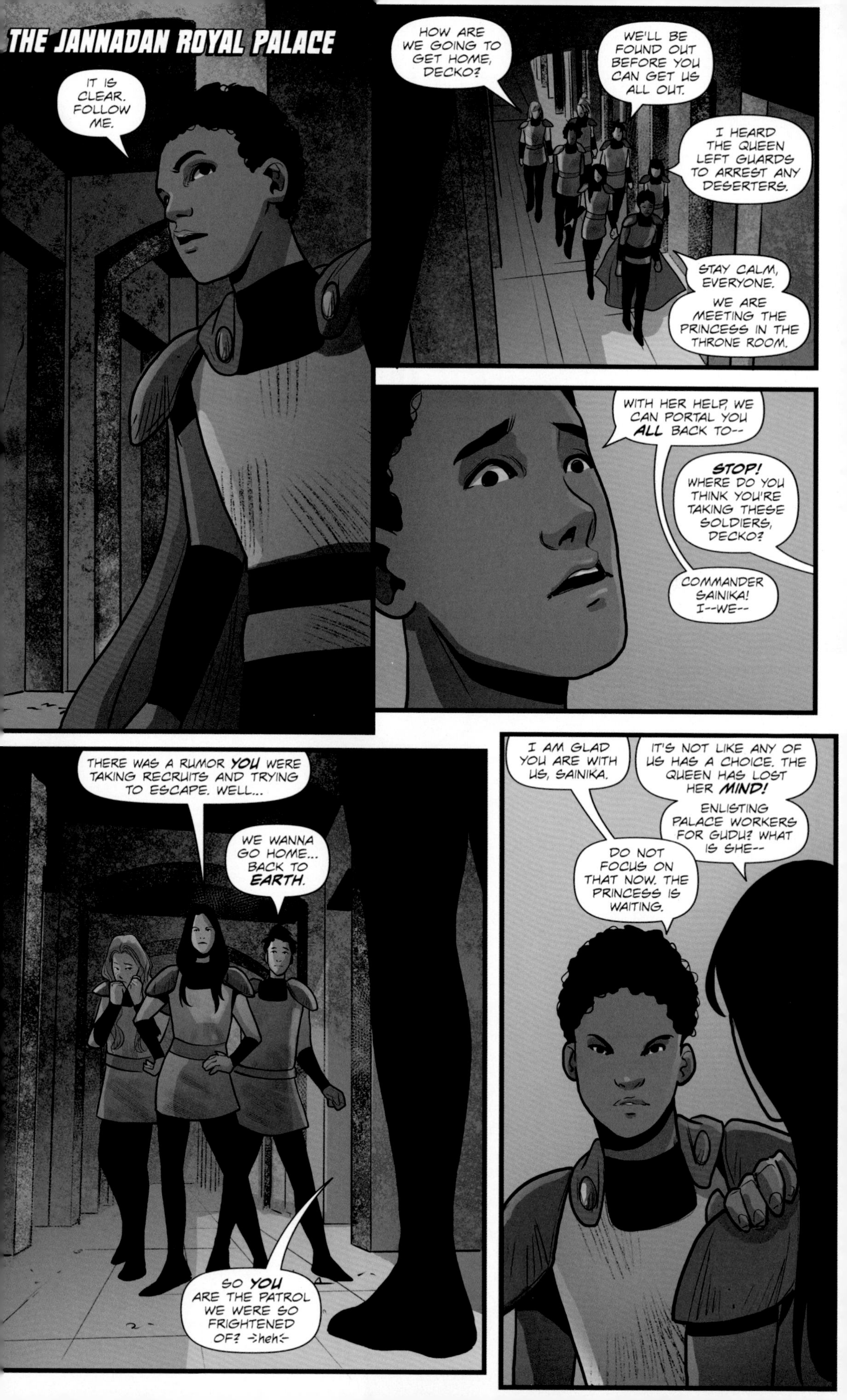
THE JANNADAN ROYAL PALACE
IT IS CLEAR. FOLLOW ME.
HOW ARE WE GOING TO GET HOME, DECKO?
WE'LL BE FOUND OUT BEFORE YOU CAN GET US ALL OUT.
I HEARD THE QUEEN LEFT GUARDS TO ARREST ANY DESERTERS.
STAY CALM, EVERYONE.
WE ARE MEETING THE PRINCESS IN THE THRONE ROOM.
WITH HER HELP, WE CAN PORTAL YOU ALL BACK TO--
STOP! WHERE DO YOU THINK YOU'RE TAKING THESE SOLDIERS, DECKO?
COMMANDER SAINIKA! I--WE--
THERE WAS A RUMOR YOU WERE TAKING RECRUITS AND TRYING TO ESCAPE. WELL...
WE WANNA GO HOME... BACK TO EARTH.
SO YOU ARE THE PATROL WE WERE SO FRIGHTENED OF? >heh<
I AM GLAD YOU ARE WITH US, SAINIKA.
IT'S NOT LIKE ANY OF US HAS A CHOICE. THE QUEEN HAS LOST HER MIND!
ENLISTING PALACE WORKERS FOR GUDU? WHAT IS SHE--
DO NOT FOCUS ON THAT NOW. THE PRINCESS IS WAITING.

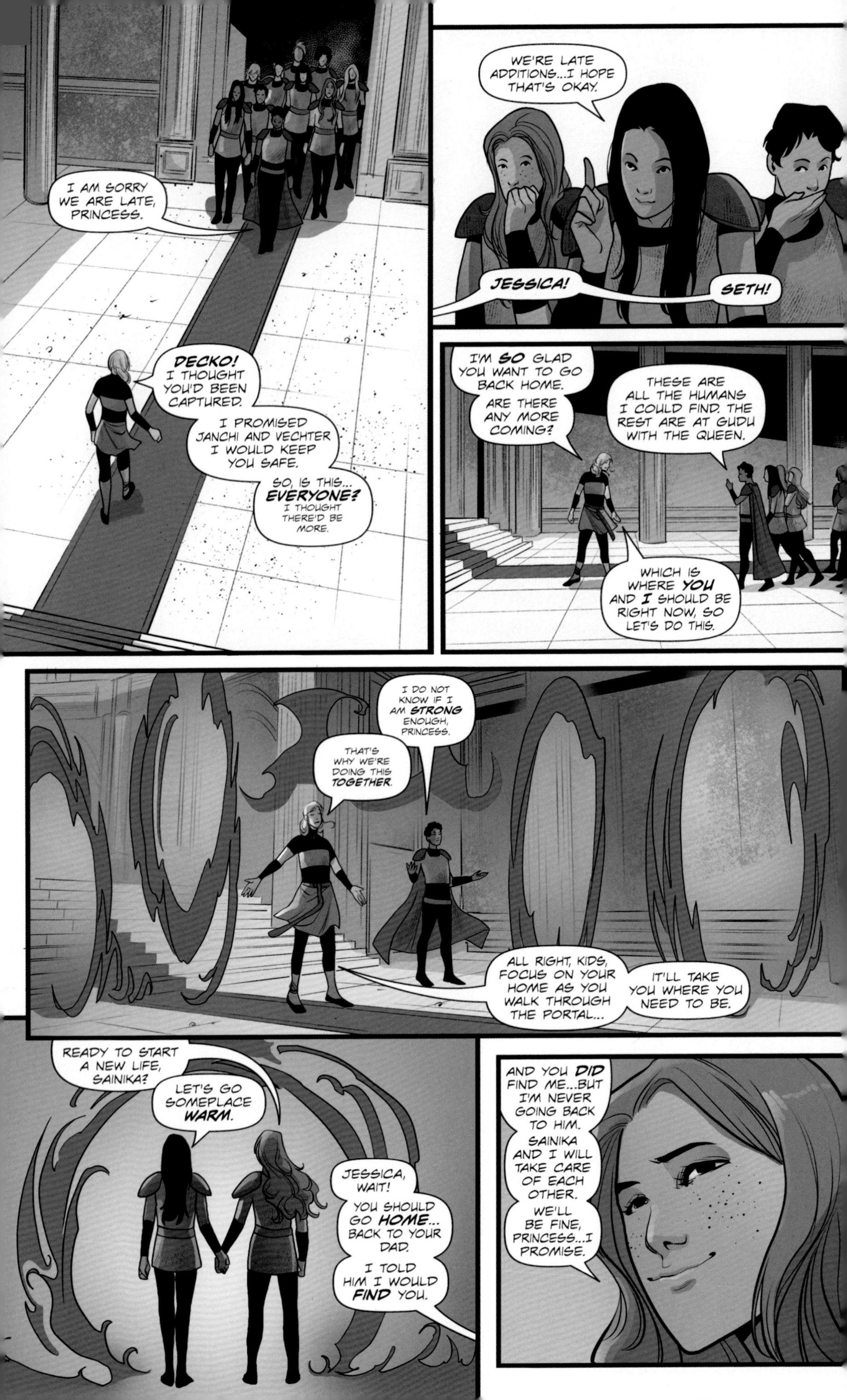
I AM SORRY WE ARE LATE, PRINCESS.
DECKO! I THOUGHT YOU'D BEEN CAPTURED.
I PROMISED JANCHI AND VECHTER I WOULD KEEP YOU SAFE.
SO, IS THIS... EVERYONE? I THOUGHT THERE'D BE MORE.
WE'RE LATE ADDITIONS...I HOPE THAT'S OKAY.
JESSICA!
SETH!
I'M SO GLAD YOU WANT TO GO BACK HOME.
ARE THERE ANY MORE COMING?
THESE ARE ALL THE HUMANS I COULD FIND. THE REST ARE AT GUDU WITH THE QUEEN.
WHICH IS WHERE YOU AND I SHOULD BE RIGHT NOW, SO LET'S DO THIS.
I DO NOT KNOW IF I AM STRONG ENOUGH, PRINCESS.
THAT'S WHY WE'RE DOING THIS TOGETHER.
ALL RIGHT, KIDS, FOCUS ON YOUR HOME AS YOU WALK THROUGH THE PORTAL...
IT'LL TAKE YOU WHERE YOU NEED TO BE.
READY TO START A NEW LIFE, SAINIKA?
LET'S GO SOMEPLACE WARM.
JESSICA, WAIT!
YOU SHOULD GO HOME... BACK TO YOUR DAD.
I TOLD HIM I WOULD FIND YOU.
AND YOU DID FIND ME...BUT I'M NEVER GOING BACK TO HIM.
SAINIKA AND I WILL TAKE CARE OF EACH OTHER.
WE'LL BE FINE, PRINCESS...I PROMISE.

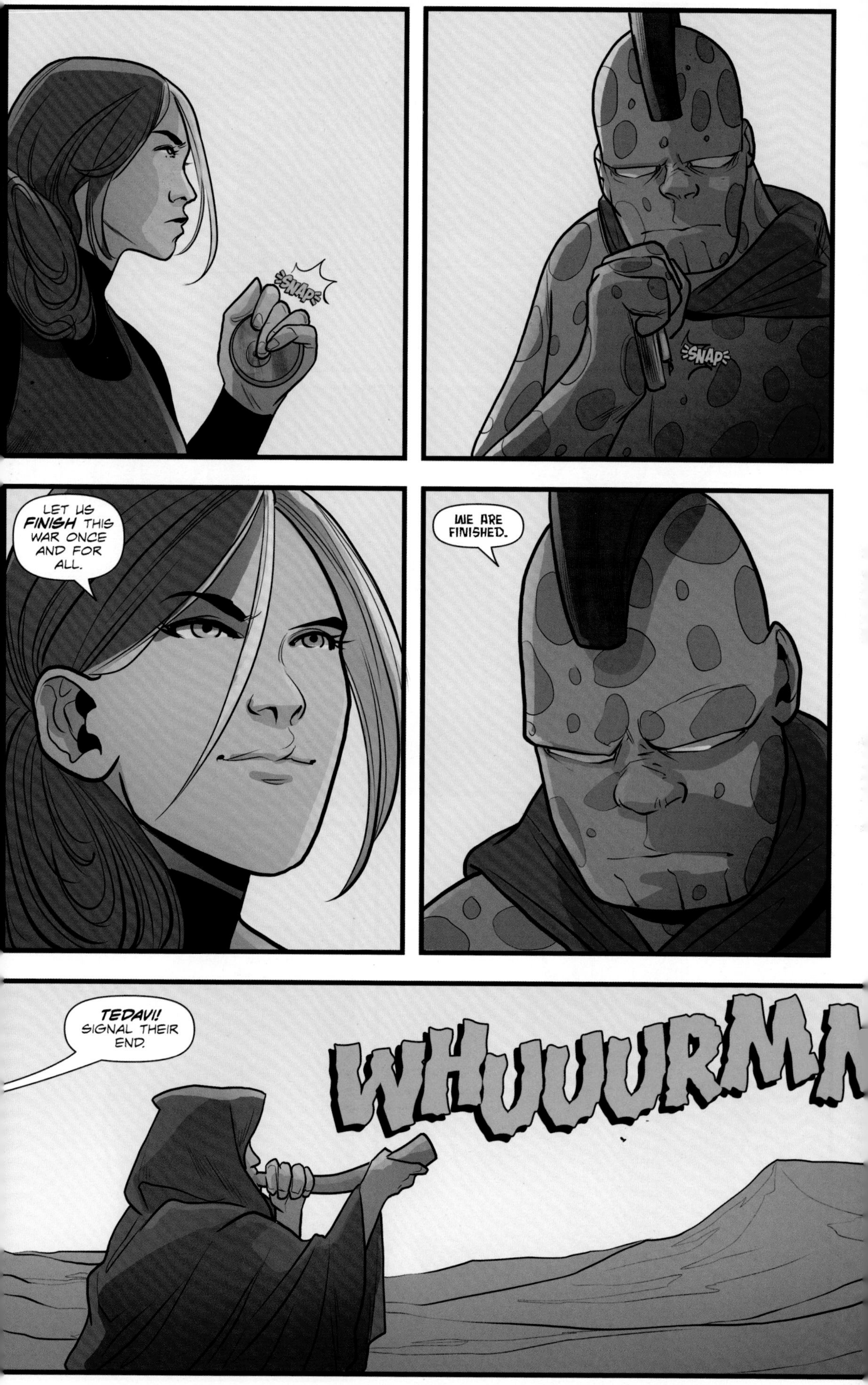
SNAP
SNAP
LET US FINISH THIS WAR ONCE AND FOR ALL.
WE ARE FINISHED.
TEDAVI! SIGNAL THEIR END.
WHUUURMM

I CAN'T WAIT TO SEE MY MOM.

HURRY, SETH.

WHUUUUUURRRMMM

CRAP! WE'RE TOO LATE!

WHAT NOW, PRINCESS?

WHUUUUUURKRMN

I REALLY THOUGHT LORRAINE WOULD COME THROUGH.

IT IS NOT YOUR FAULT THE PRINCESS HAD OTHER PRIORITIES, TRODAIRE.

WHAT SAY YOU, DAGAAL? IS IT A GOOD DAY TO DIE?

÷SIGH÷ LET US GET IT OVER WITH.

TODAY WE FINALLY PUT DOWN THE CHILOMBONS AND THEIR TRAITOROUS JANNADAN COLLABORATORS!

CRAP, MOM...WHERE ARE YOU?

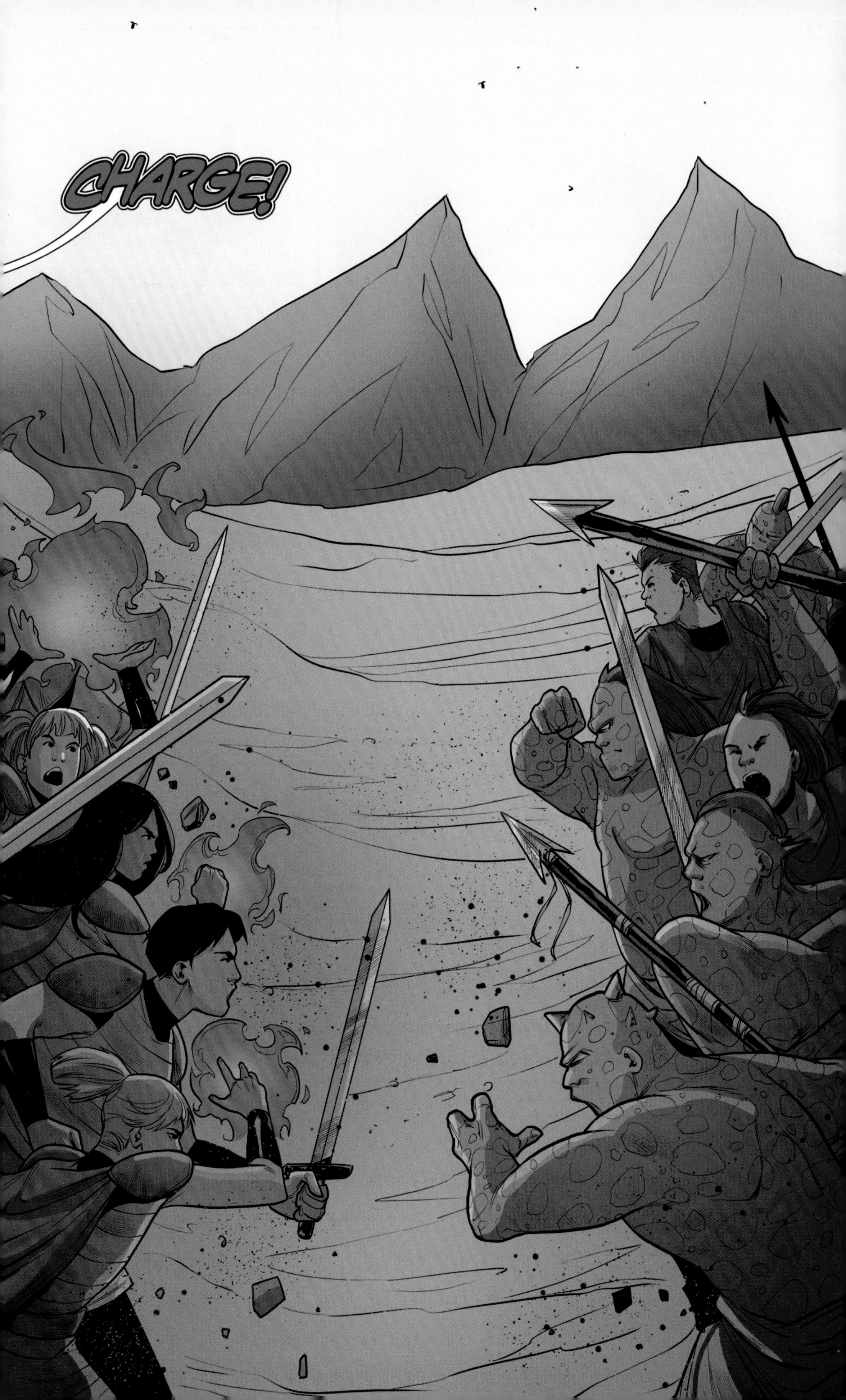
CHARGE!

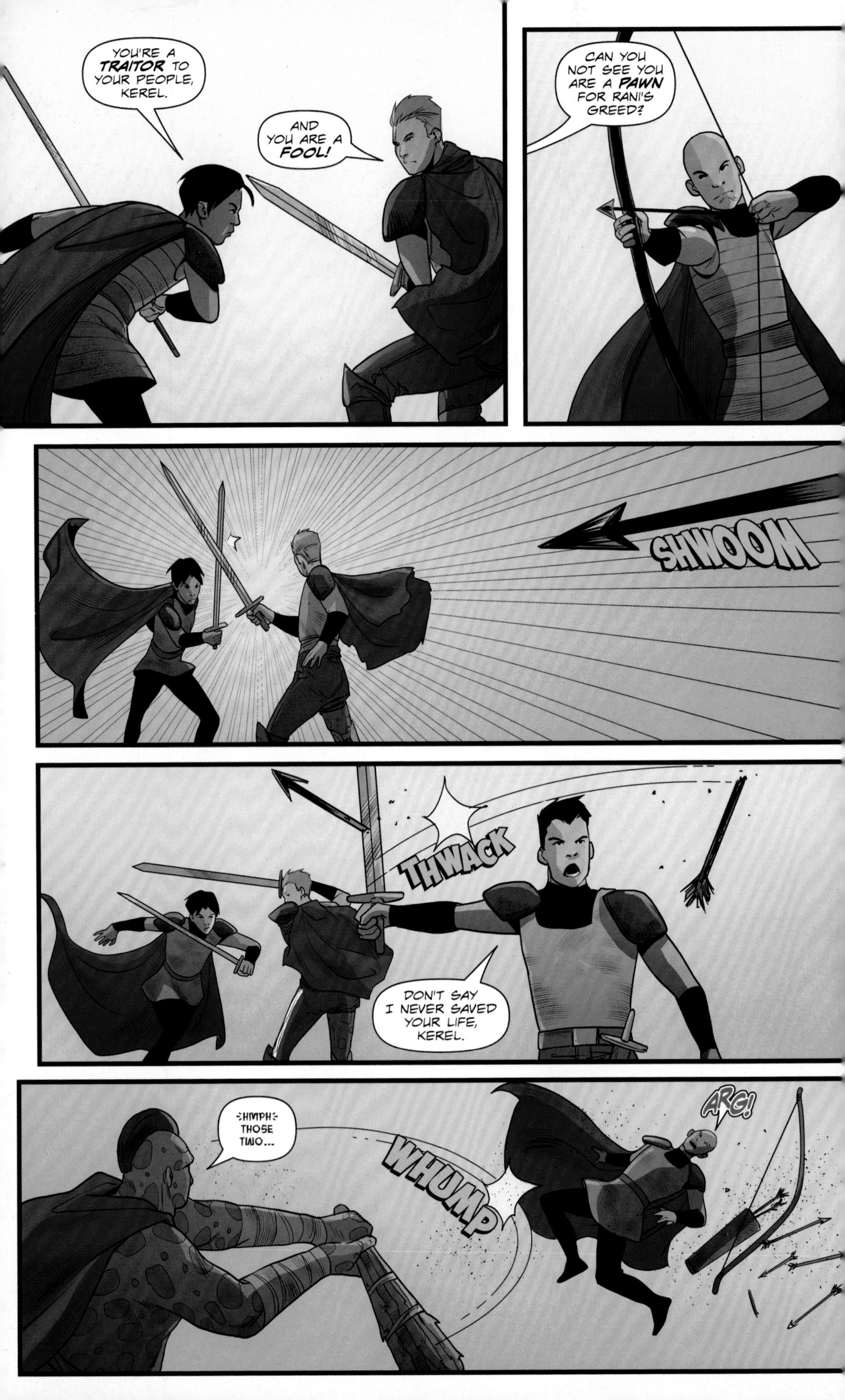
YOU'RE A TRAITOR TO YOUR PEOPLE, KEREL.
AND YOU ARE A FOOL!
CAN YOU NOT SEE YOU ARE A PAWN FOR RANI'S GREED?
SHWOOM
THWACK
DON'T SAY I NEVER SAVED YOUR LIFE, KEREL.
-HMPH- THOSE TWO...
WHUMP
ARG!

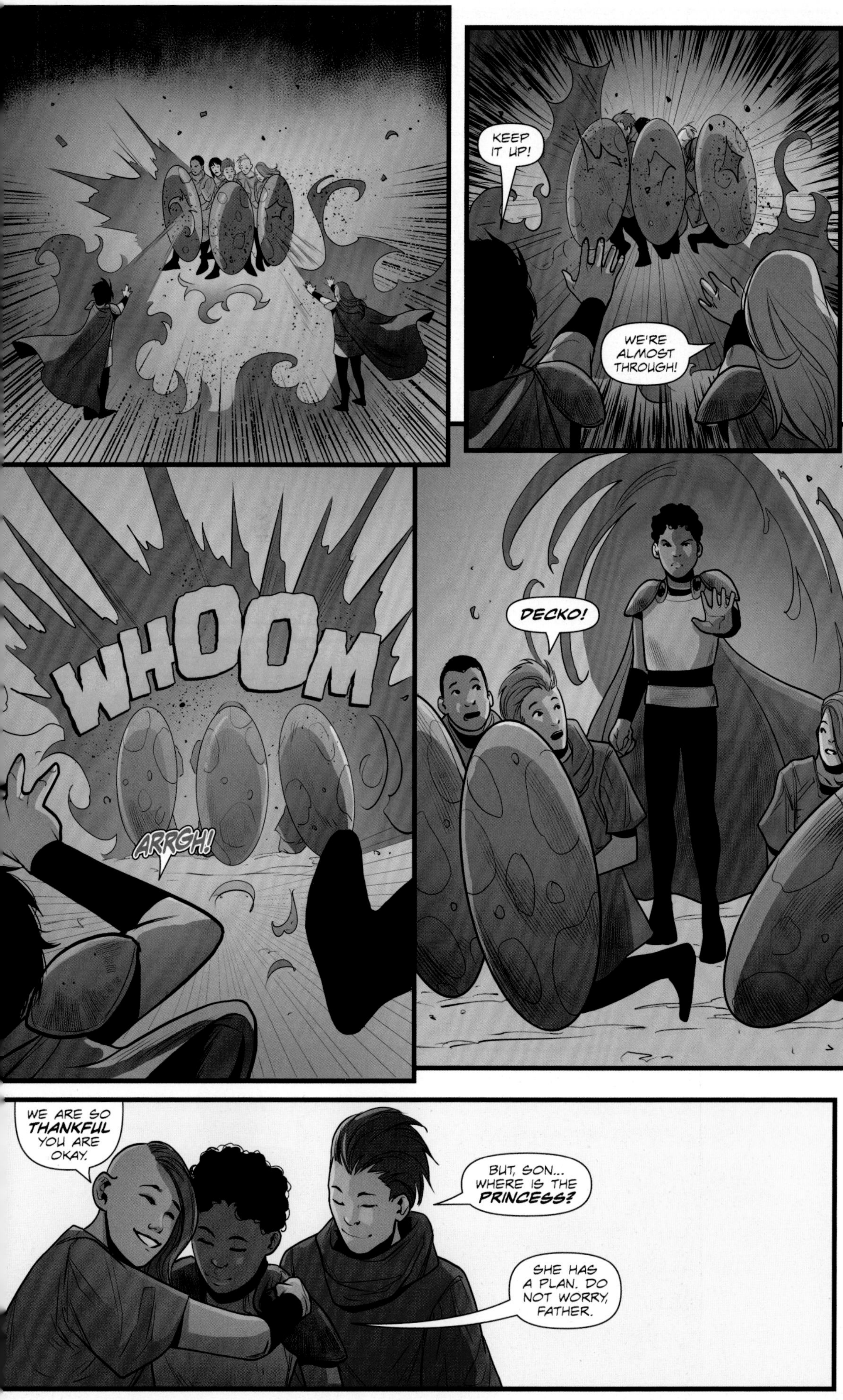
KEEP IT UP!
WE'RE ALMOST THROUGH!
WHOOM
ARRGH!
DECKO!
WE ARE SO THANKFUL YOU ARE OKAY.
BUT, SON... WHERE IS THE PRINCESS?
SHE HAS A PLAN. DO NOT WORRY, FATHER.

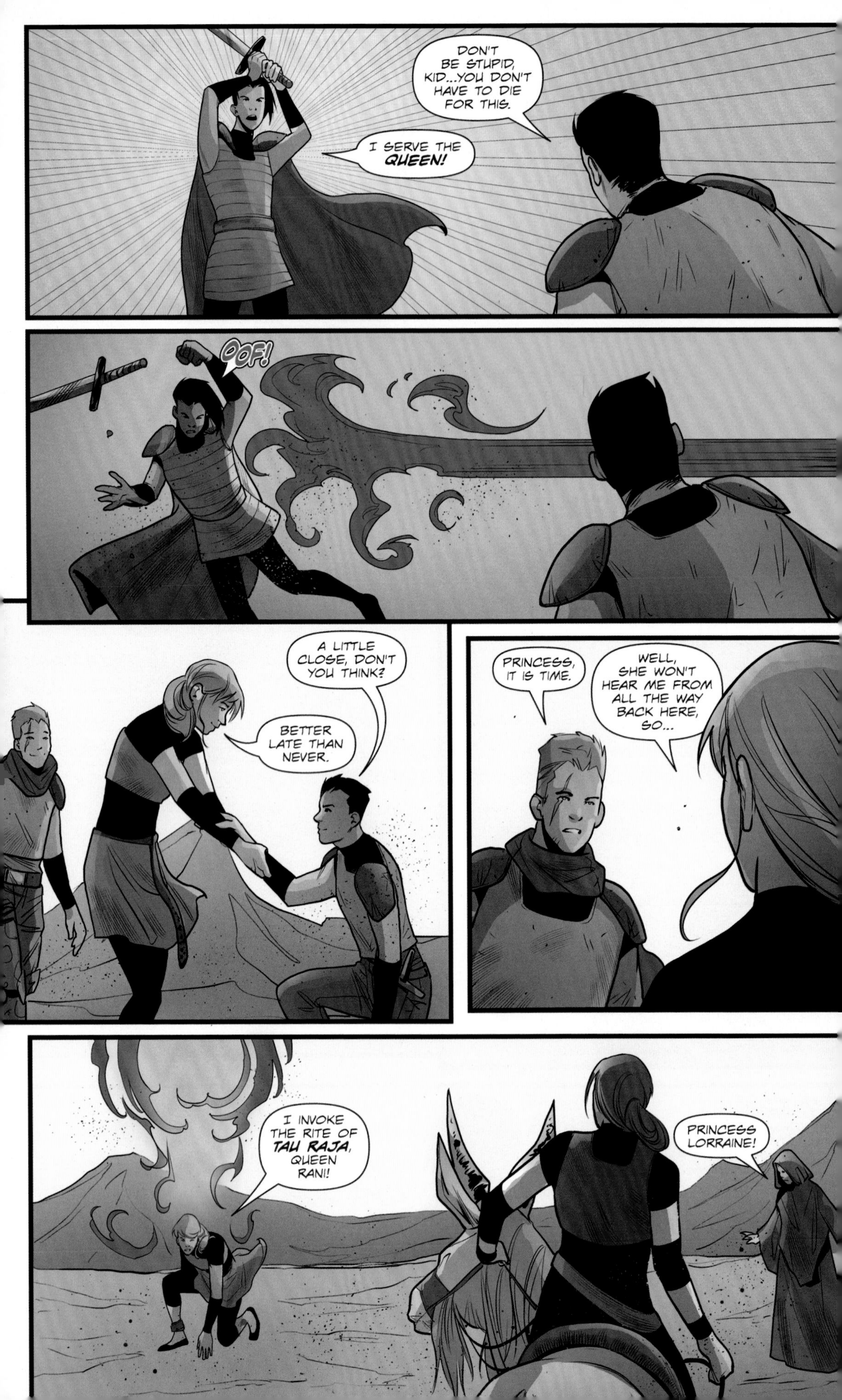
DON'T BE STUPID, KID...YOU DON'T HAVE TO DIE FOR THIS.
I SERVE THE QUEEN!
OOF!
A LITTLE CLOSE, DON'T YOU THINK?
BETTER LATE THAN NEVER.
PRINCESS, IT IS TIME.
WELL, SHE WON'T HEAR ME FROM ALL THE WAY BACK HERE, SO...
I INVOKE THE RITE OF TAU RAJA, QUEEN RANI!
PRINCESS LORRAINE!

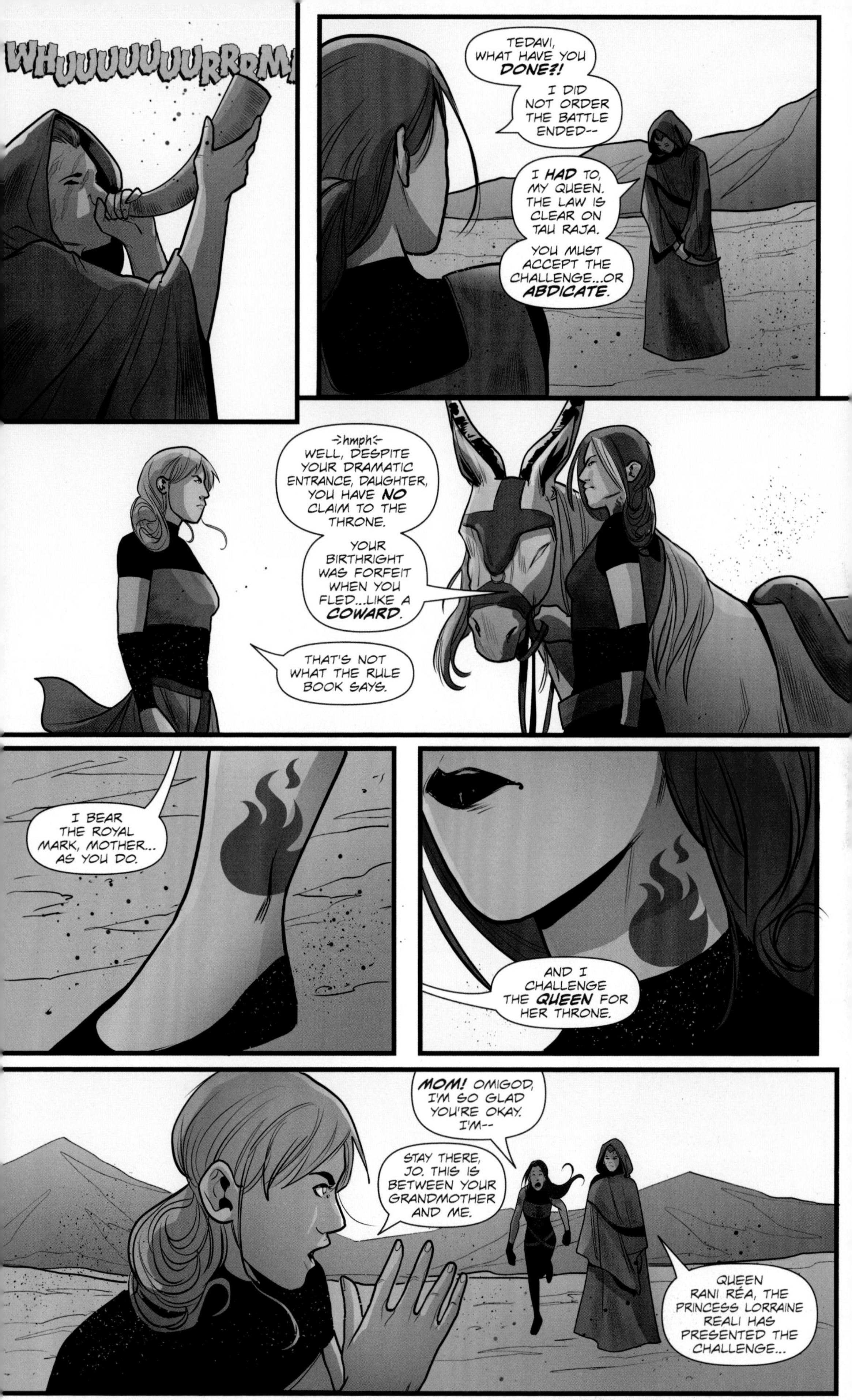

WHUUUUUUURRRM!
TEDAVI, WHAT HAVE YOU **DONE?!**
I DID NOT ORDER THE BATTLE ENDED--
I **HAD** TO, MY QUEEN. THE LAW IS CLEAR ON TAU RAJA.
YOU MUST ACCEPT THE CHALLENGE...OR ***ABDICATE***.
hmph
WELL, DESPITE YOUR DRAMATIC ENTRANCE, DAUGHTER, YOU HAVE **NO** CLAIM TO THE THRONE.
YOUR BIRTHRIGHT WAS FORFEIT WHEN YOU FLED...LIKE A ***COWARD***.
THAT'S NOT WHAT THE RULE BOOK SAYS.
I BEAR THE ROYAL MARK, MOTHER... AS YOU DO.
AND I CHALLENGE THE **QUEEN** FOR HER THRONE.
MOM! OMIGOD, I'M SO GLAD YOU'RE OKAY. I'M--
STAY THERE, JO. THIS IS BETWEEN YOUR GRANDMOTHER AND ME.
QUEEN RANI RÉA, THE PRINCESS LORRAINE REALI HAS PRESENTED THE CHALLENGE...

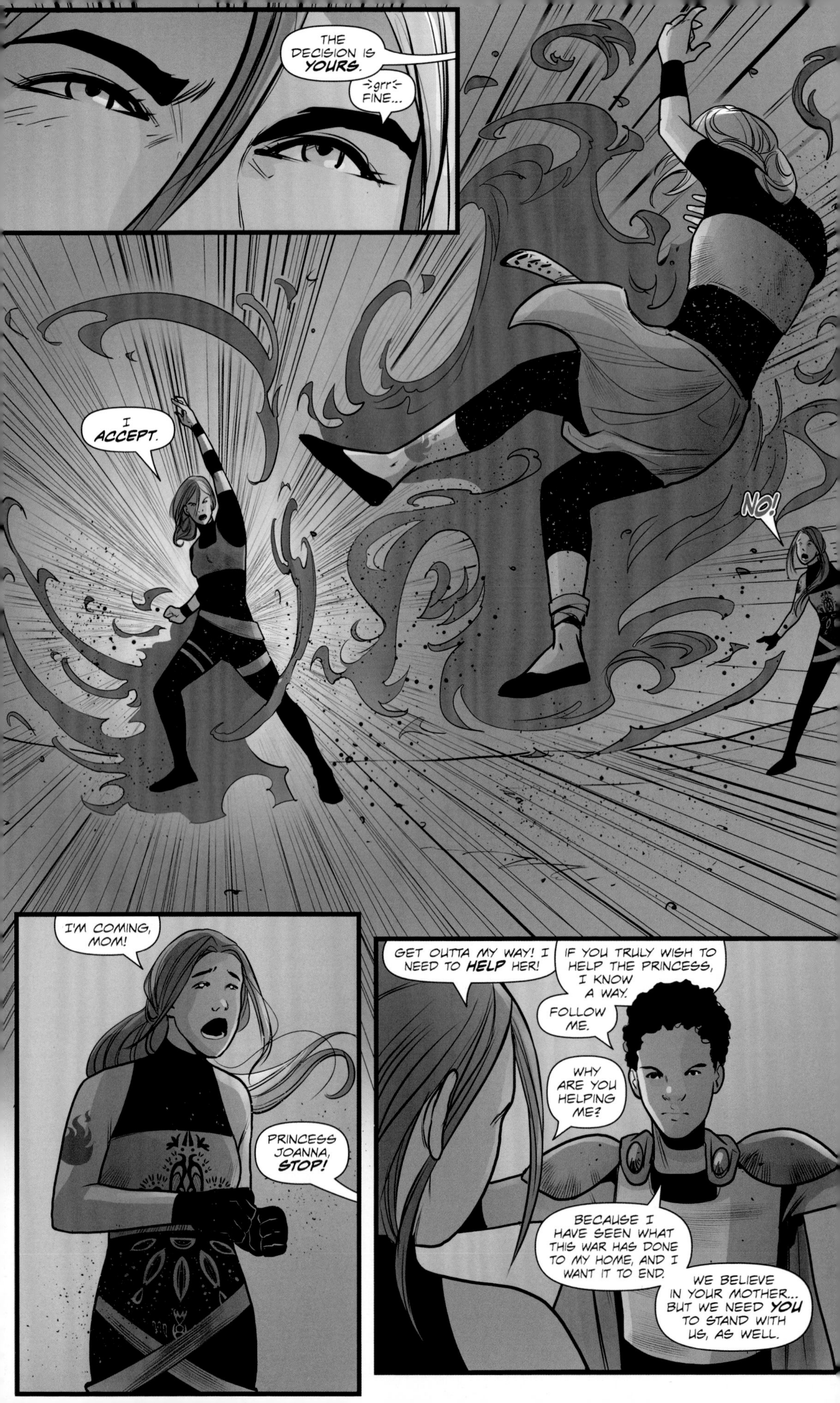

THE DECISION IS YOURS.
-grr- FINE...
I ACCEPT.
NO!
I'M COMING, MOM!
PRINCESS JOANNA, STOP!
GET OUTTA MY WAY! I NEED TO HELP HER!
IF YOU TRULY WISH TO HELP THE PRINCESS, I KNOW A WAY.
FOLLOW ME.
WHY ARE YOU HELPING ME?
BECAUSE I HAVE SEEN WHAT THIS WAR HAS DONE TO MY HOME, AND I WANT IT TO END.
WE BELIEVE IN YOUR MOTHER... BUT WE NEED YOU TO STAND WITH US, AS WELL.

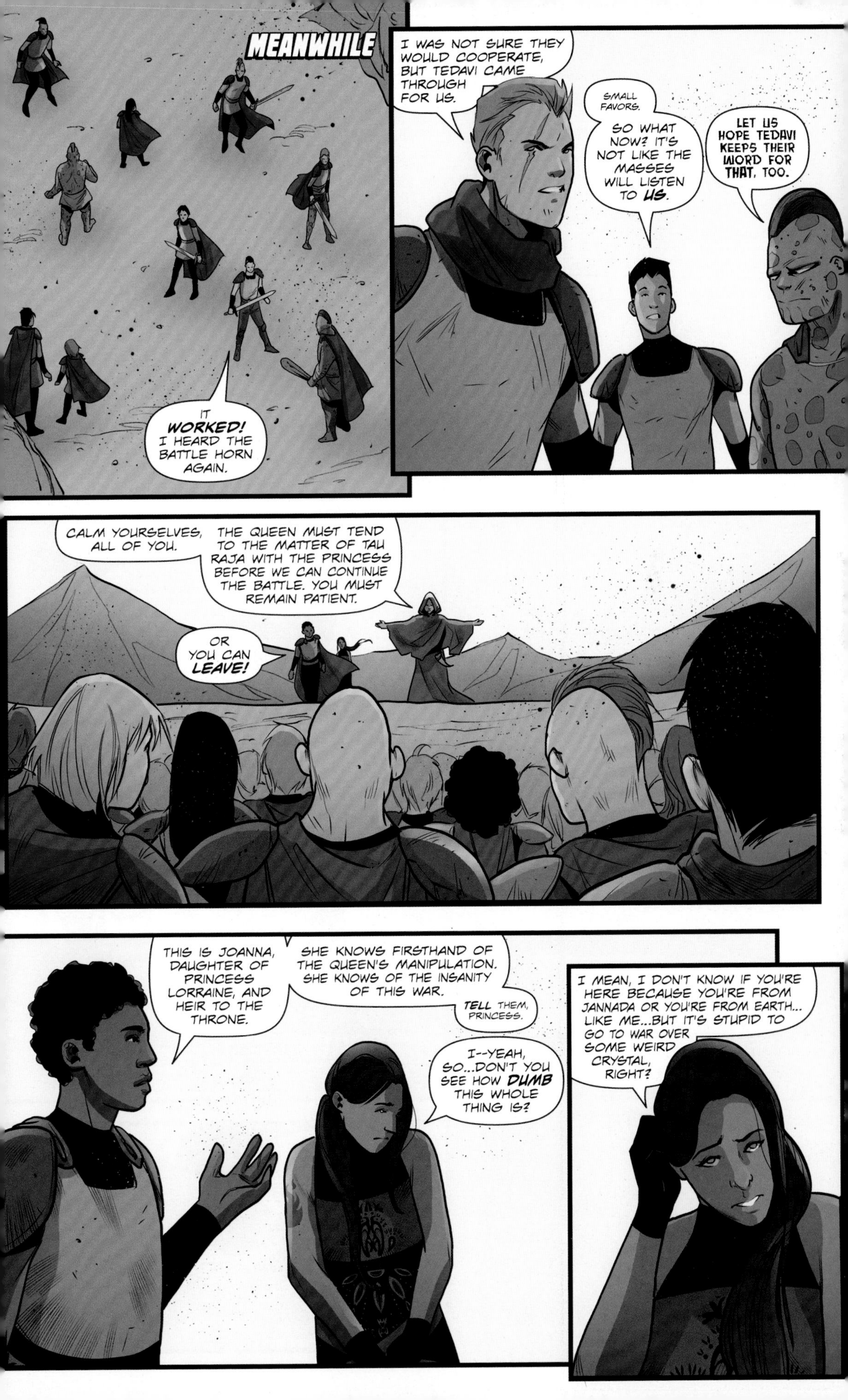
MEANWHILE
IT WORKED! I HEARD THE BATTLE HORN AGAIN.
I WAS NOT SURE THEY WOULD COOPERATE, BUT TEDAVI CAME THROUGH FOR US.
SMALL FAVORS.
SO WHAT NOW? IT'S NOT LIKE THE MASSES WILL LISTEN TO US.
LET US HOPE TEDAVI KEEPS THEIR WORD FOR THAT, TOO.
CALM YOURSELVES, ALL OF YOU.
THE QUEEN MUST TEND TO THE MATTER OF TAU RAJA WITH THE PRINCESS BEFORE WE CAN CONTINUE THE BATTLE. YOU MUST REMAIN PATIENT.
OR YOU CAN LEAVE!
THIS IS JOANNA, DAUGHTER OF PRINCESS LORRAINE, AND HEIR TO THE THRONE.
SHE KNOWS FIRSTHAND OF THE QUEEN'S MANIPULATION. SHE KNOWS OF THE INSANITY OF THIS WAR.
TELL THEM, PRINCESS.
I--YEAH, SO...DON'T YOU SEE HOW DUMB THIS WHOLE THING IS?
I MEAN, I DON'T KNOW IF YOU'RE HERE BECAUSE YOU'RE FROM JANNADA OR YOU'RE FROM EARTH... LIKE ME...BUT IT'S STUPID TO GO TO WAR OVER SOME WEIRD CRYSTAL, RIGHT?

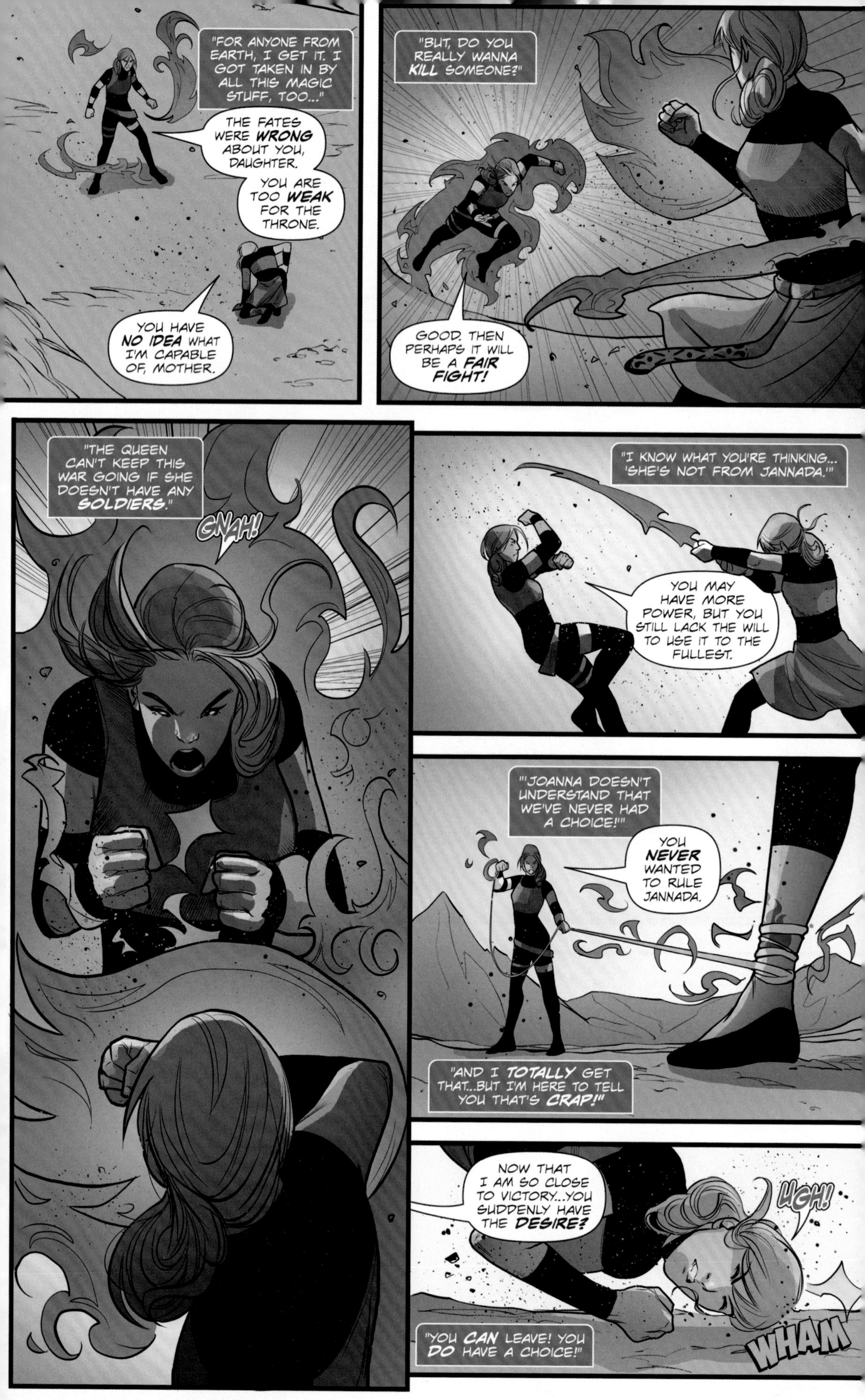
"FOR ANYONE FROM EARTH, I GET IT. I GOT TAKEN IN BY ALL THIS MAGIC STUFF, TOO..."
THE FATES WERE WRONG ABOUT YOU, DAUGHTER.
YOU ARE TOO WEAK FOR THE THRONE.
YOU HAVE NO IDEA WHAT I'M CAPABLE OF, MOTHER.
"BUT, DO YOU REALLY WANNA KILL SOMEONE?"
GOOD. THEN PERHAPS IT WILL BE A FAIR FIGHT!
"THE QUEEN CAN'T KEEP THIS WAR GOING IF SHE DOESN'T HAVE ANY SOLDIERS."
GNAH!
"I KNOW WHAT YOU'RE THINKING... 'SHE'S NOT FROM JANNADA.'"
YOU MAY HAVE MORE POWER, BUT YOU STILL LACK THE WILL TO USE IT TO THE FULLEST.
"'JOANNA DOESN'T UNDERSTAND THAT WE'VE NEVER HAD A CHOICE!'"
YOU NEVER WANTED TO RULE JANNADA.
"AND I TOTALLY GET THAT...BUT I'M HERE TO TELL YOU THAT'S CRAP!"
NOW THAT I AM SO CLOSE TO VICTORY...YOU SUDDENLY HAVE THE DESIRE?
UGH!
"YOU CAN LEAVE! YOU DO HAVE A CHOICE!"
WHAM

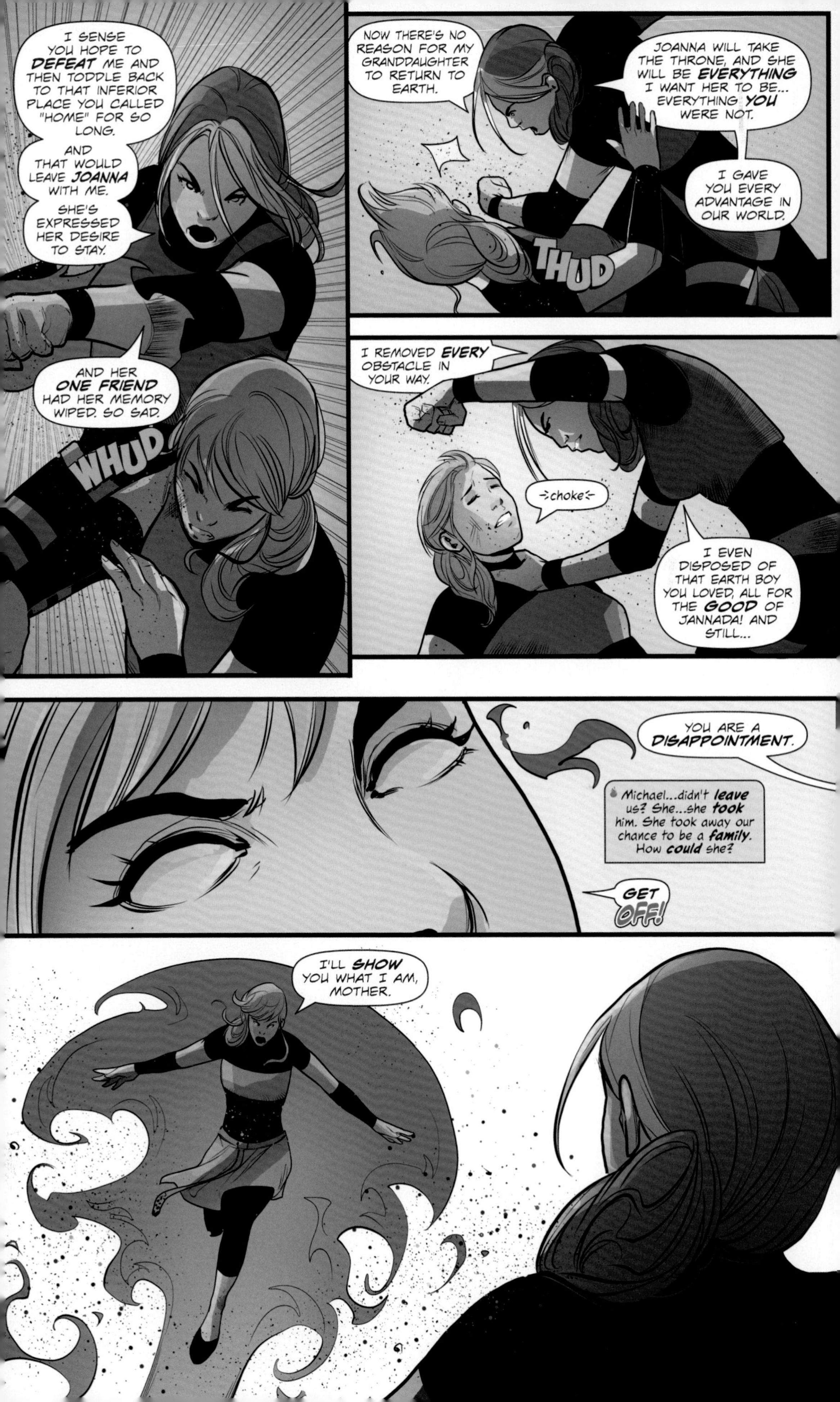

I SENSE YOU HOPE TO **DEFEAT** ME AND THEN TODDLE BACK TO THAT INFERIOR PLACE YOU CALLED "HOME" FOR SO LONG.
AND THAT WOULD LEAVE **JOANNA** WITH ME.
SHE'S EXPRESSED HER DESIRE TO STAY.
AND HER **ONE FRIEND** HAD HER MEMORY WIPED. SO SAD.
WHUD
NOW THERE'S NO REASON FOR MY GRANDDAUGHTER TO RETURN TO EARTH.
JOANNA WILL TAKE THE THRONE, AND SHE WILL BE **EVERYTHING** I WANT HER TO BE... EVERYTHING **YOU** WERE NOT.
I GAVE YOU EVERY ADVANTAGE IN OUR WORLD.
THUD
I REMOVED **EVERY** OBSTACLE IN YOUR WAY.
choke
I EVEN DISPOSED OF THAT EARTH BOY YOU LOVED, ALL FOR THE **GOOD** OF JANNADA! AND STILL...
YOU ARE A **DISAPPOINTMENT**.
Michael...didn't **leave** us? She...she **took** him. She took away our chance to be a **family**. How **could** she?
GET OFF!
I'LL **SHOW** YOU WHAT I AM, MOTHER.

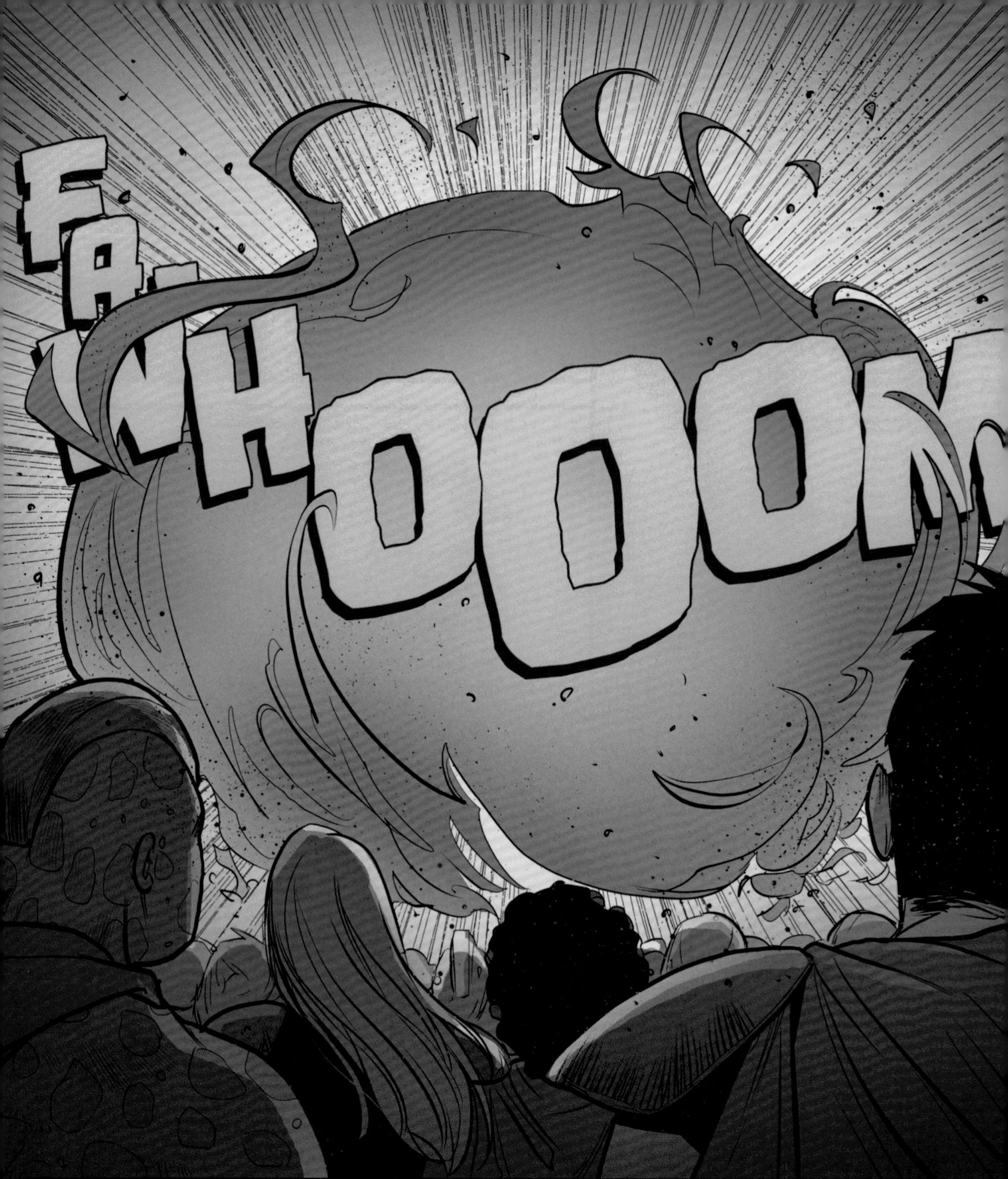
FA-WHOOOM
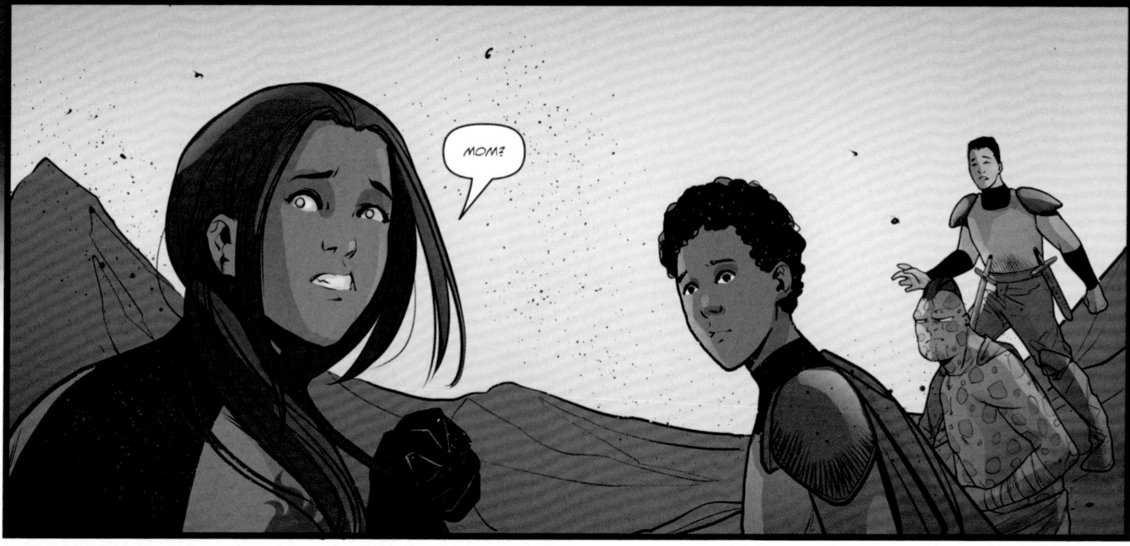
MOM?

EIGHT

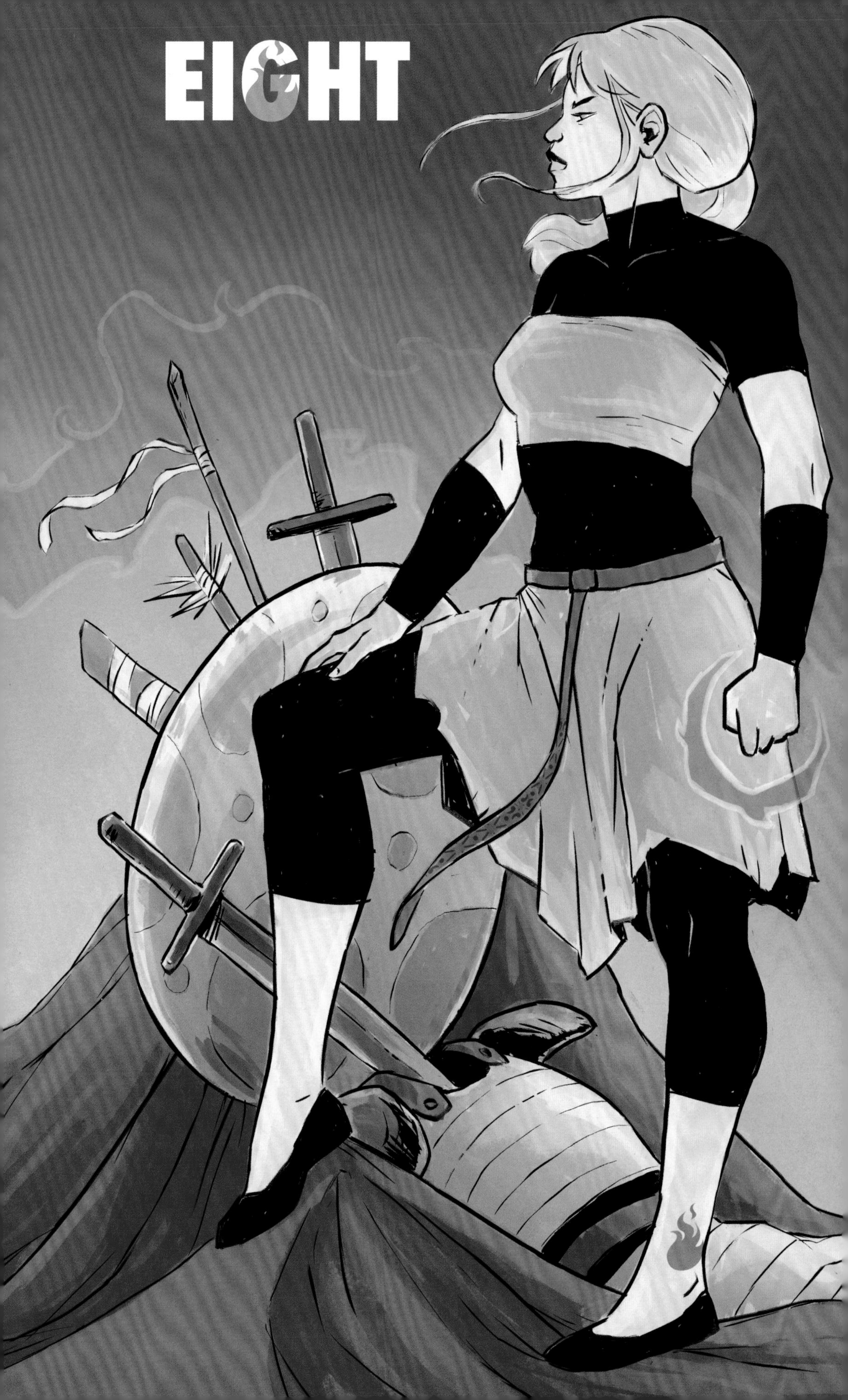

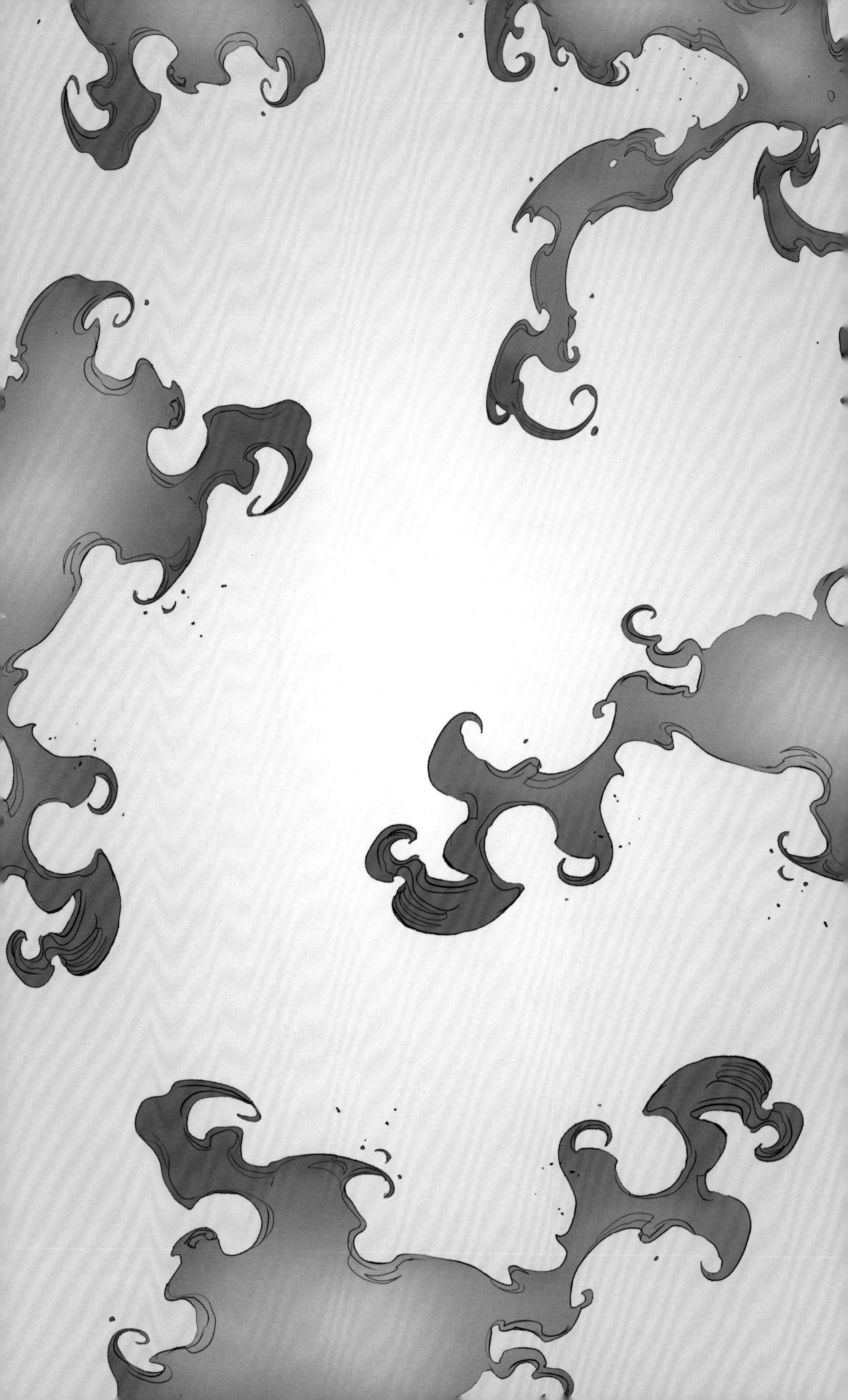

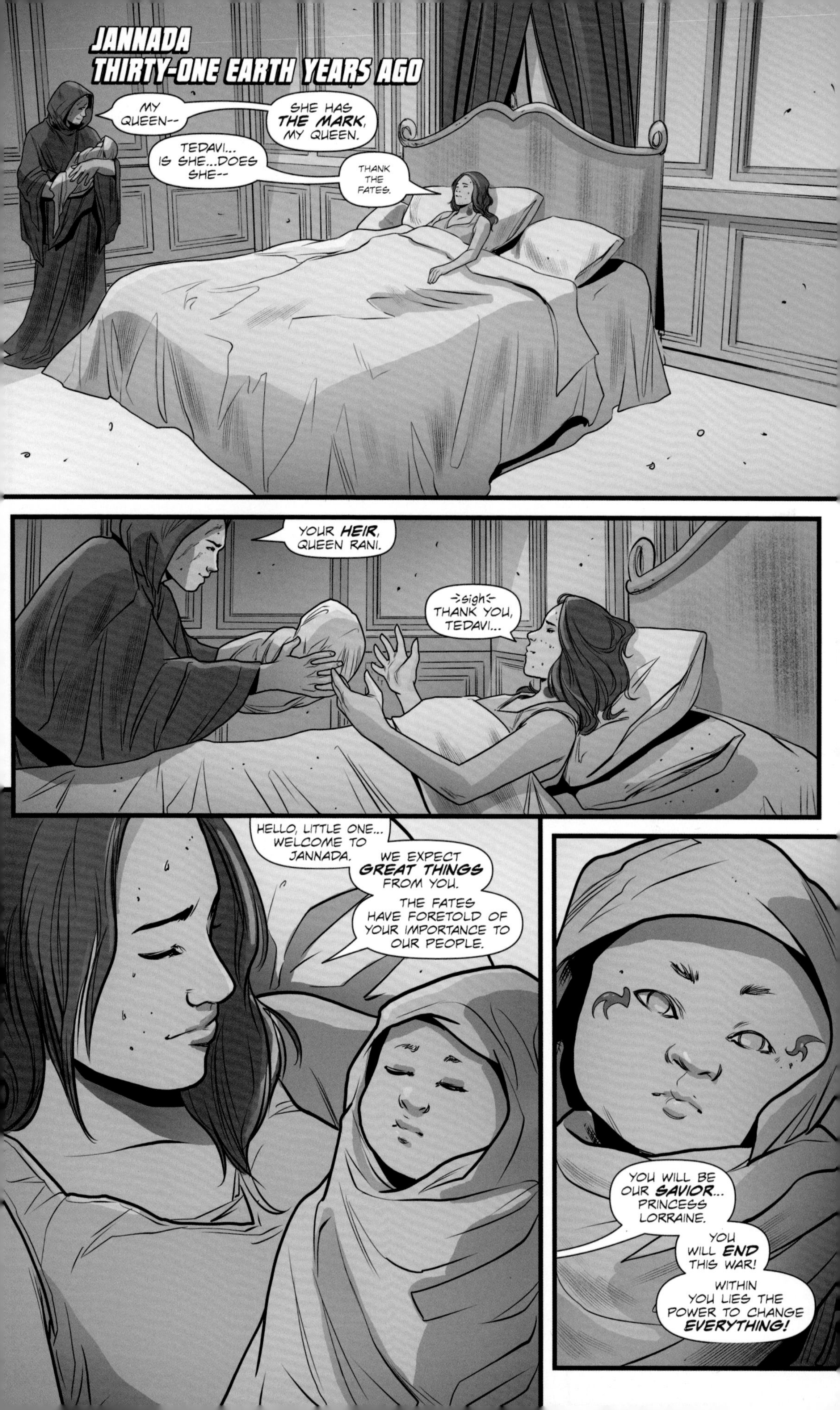

JANNADA
THIRTY-ONE EARTH YEARS AGO
MY QUEEN--
SHE HAS THE MARK, MY QUEEN.
TEDAVI... IS SHE...DOES SHE--
THANK THE FATES.
YOUR HEIR, QUEEN RANI.
sigh THANK YOU, TEDAVI...
HELLO, LITTLE ONE... WELCOME TO JANNADA.
WE EXPECT GREAT THINGS FROM YOU.
THE FATES HAVE FORETOLD OF YOUR IMPORTANCE TO OUR PEOPLE.
YOU WILL BE OUR SAVIOR... PRINCESS LORRAINE.
YOU WILL END THIS WAR!
WITHIN YOU LIES THE POWER TO CHANGE EVERYTHING!

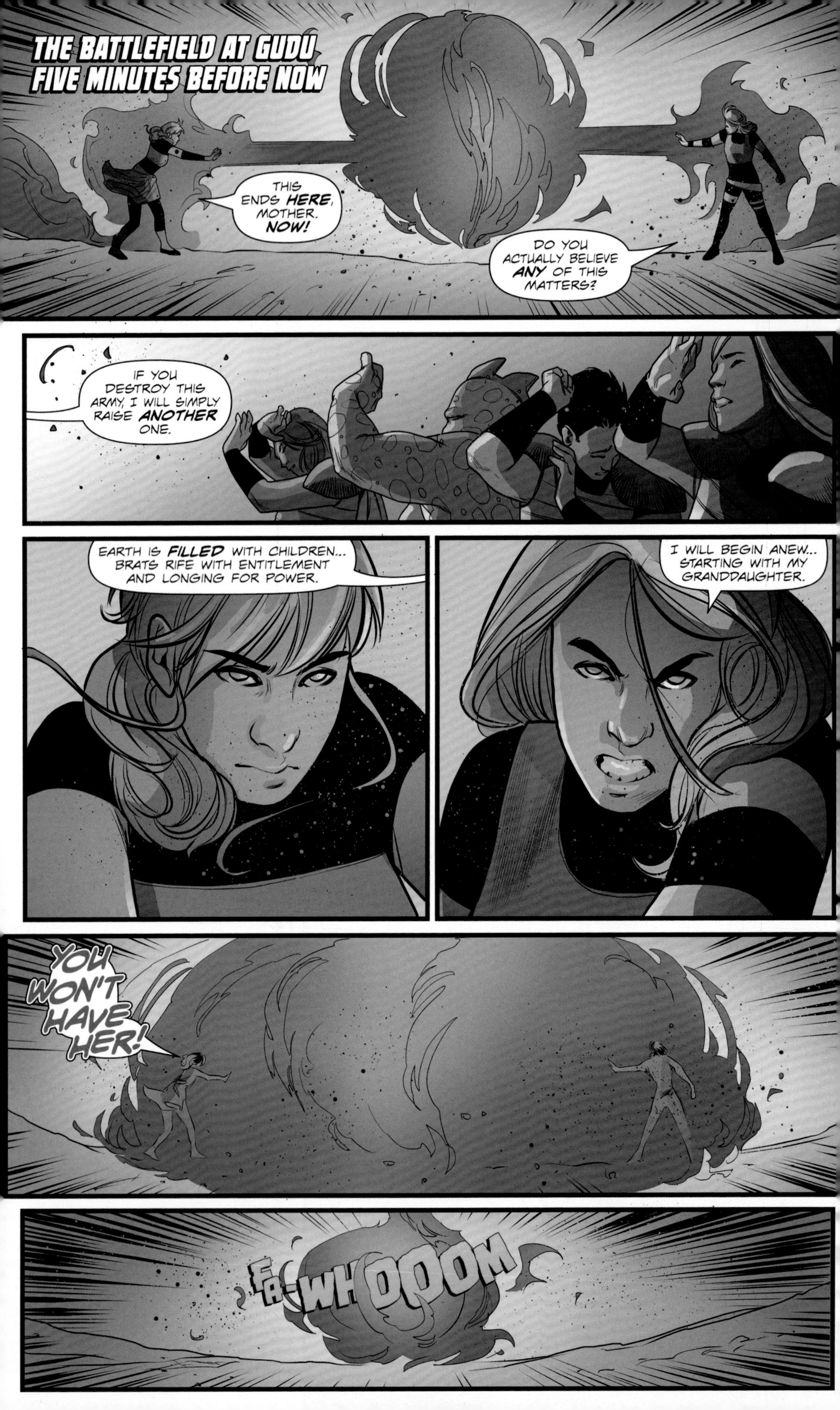
THE BATTLEFIELD AT GUDU
FIVE MINUTES BEFORE NOW
THIS ENDS HERE, MOTHER. NOW!
DO YOU ACTUALLY BELIEVE ANY OF THIS MATTERS?
IF YOU DESTROY THIS ARMY, I WILL SIMPLY RAISE ANOTHER ONE.
EARTH IS FILLED WITH CHILDREN... BRATS RIFE WITH ENTITLEMENT AND LONGING FOR POWER.
I WILL BEGIN ANEW... STARTING WITH MY GRANDDAUGHTER.
YOU WON'T HAVE HER!
FA-WHOOOOM

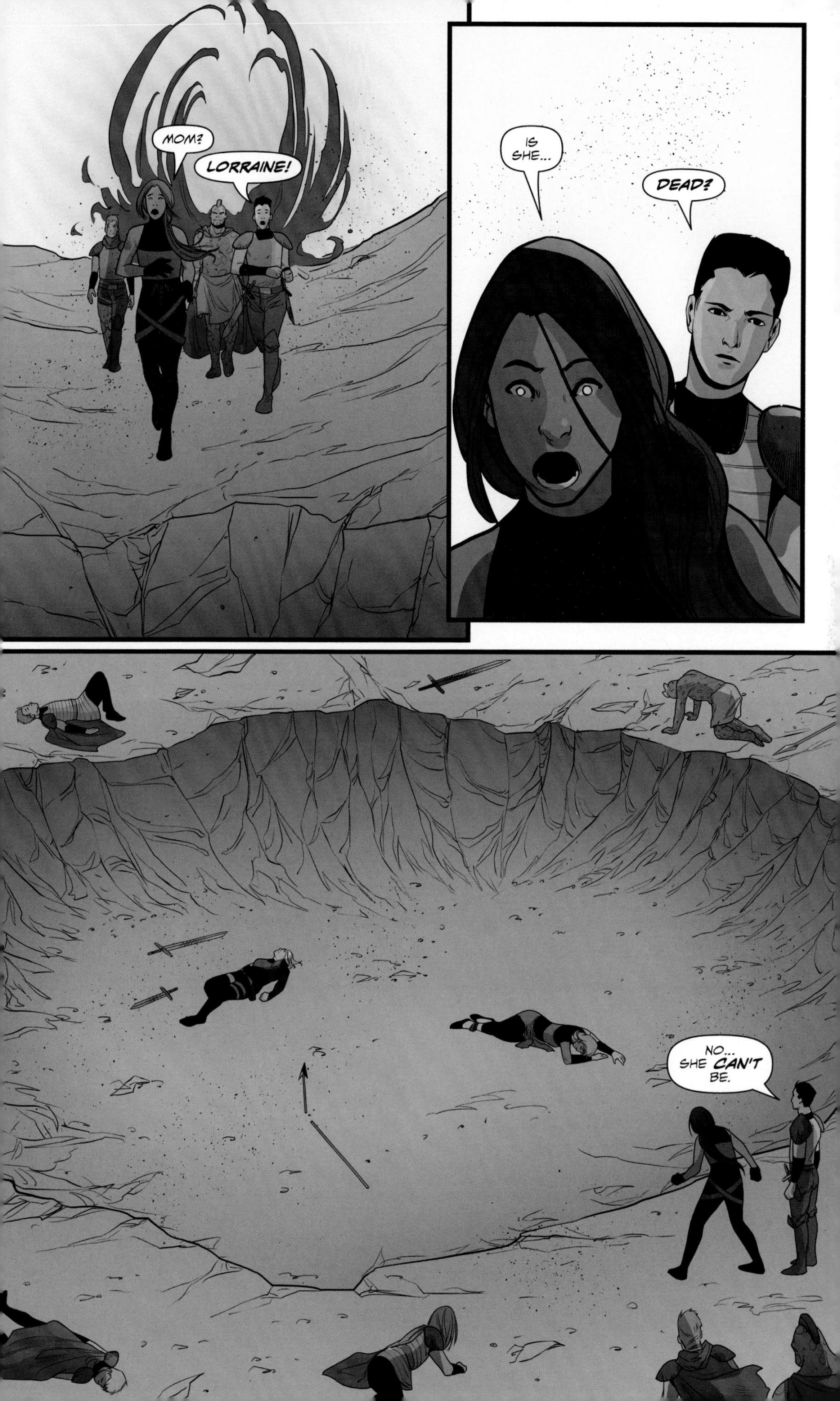
MOM?
LORRAINE!
IS SHE...
DEAD?
NO... SHE CAN'T BE.

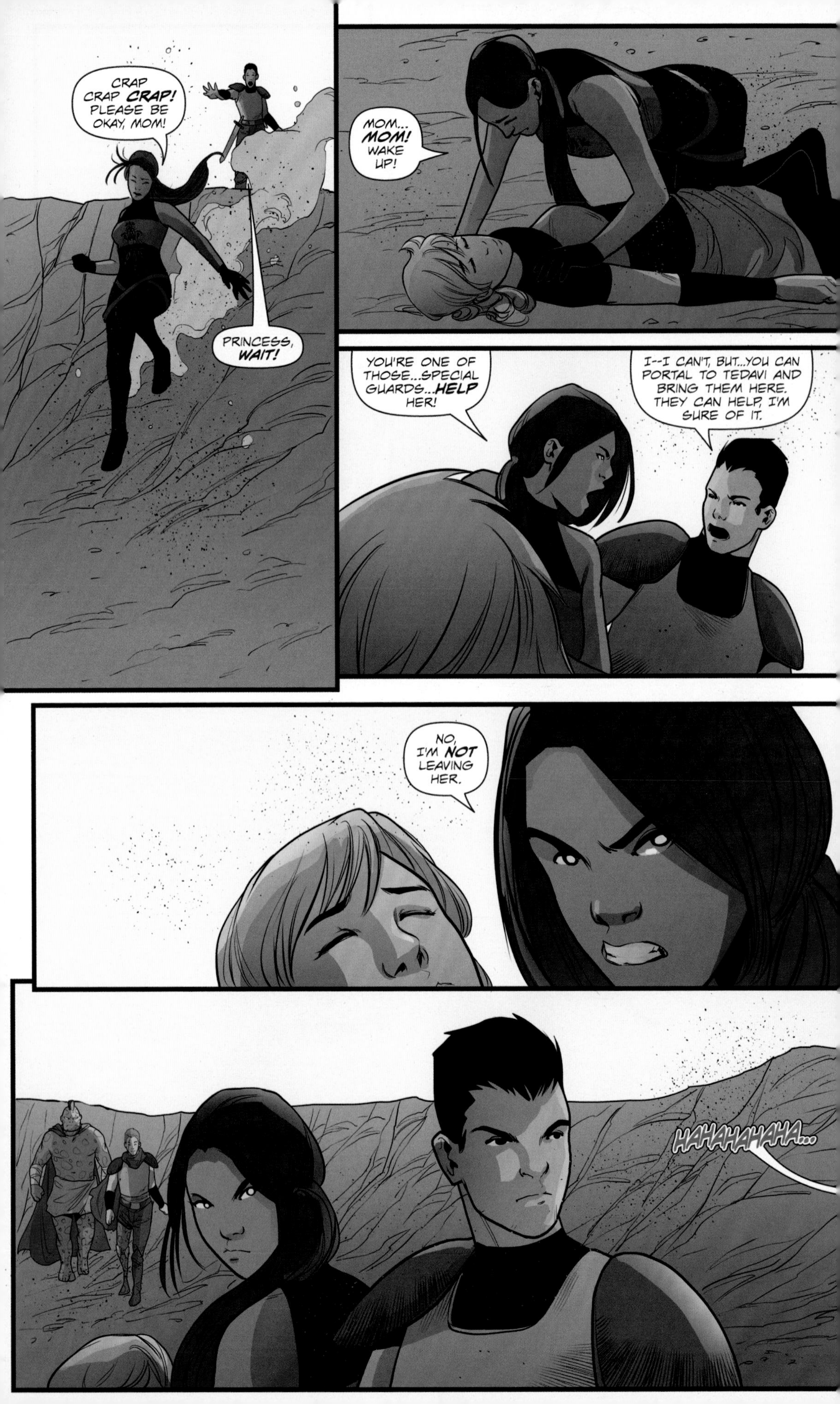
CRAP CRAP CRAP! PLEASE BE OKAY, MOM!
PRINCESS, WAIT!
MOM... MOM! WAKE UP!
YOU'RE ONE OF THOSE...SPECIAL GUARDS...HELP HER!
I--I CAN'T, BUT...YOU CAN PORTAL TO TEDAVI AND BRING THEM HERE. THEY CAN HELP, I'M SURE OF IT.
NO, I'M NOT LEAVING HER.
HAHAHAHAHA...

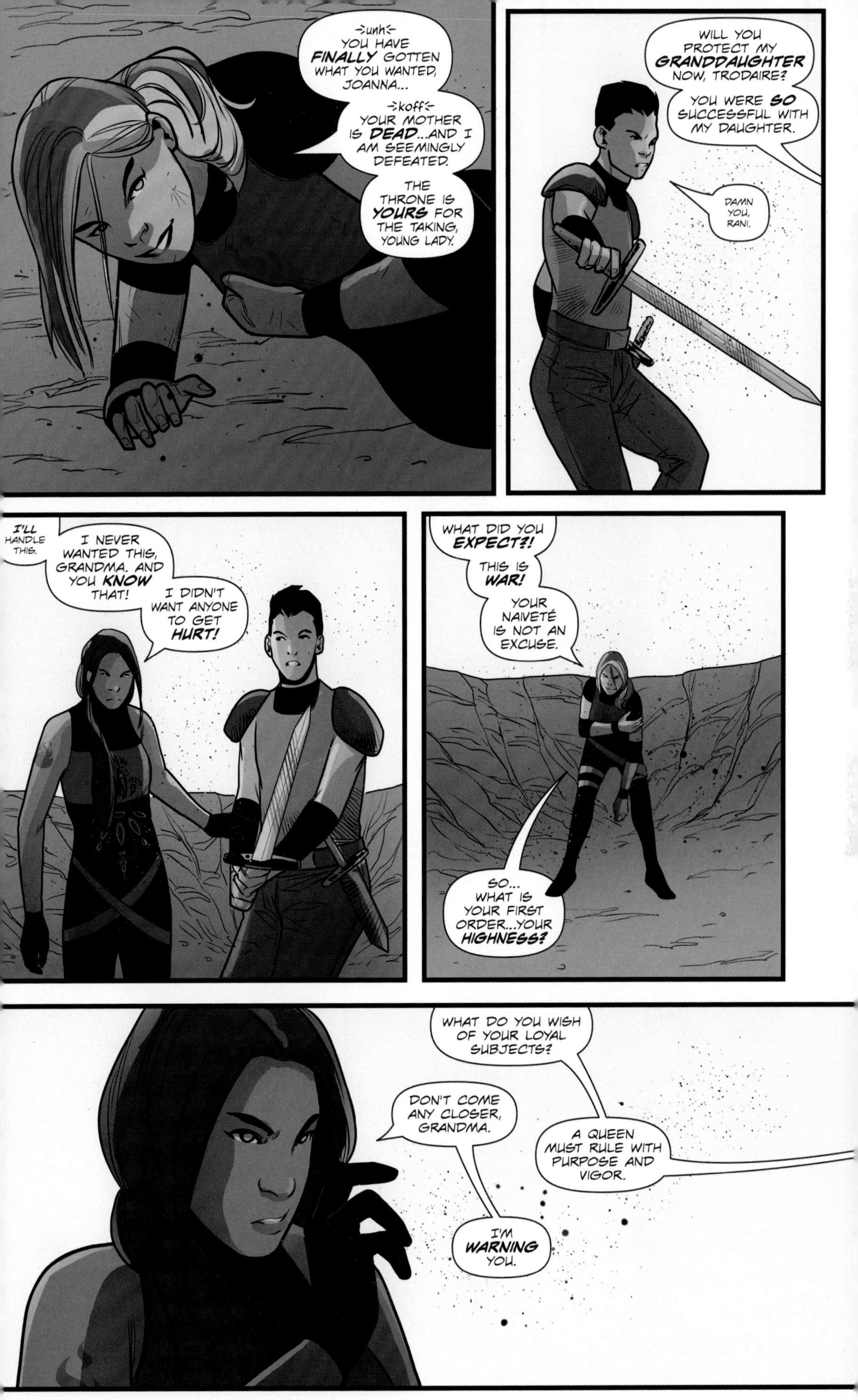

unh
YOU HAVE FINALLY GOTTEN WHAT YOU WANTED, JOANNA...
koff
YOUR MOTHER IS DEAD...AND I AM SEEMINGLY DEFEATED.
THE THRONE IS YOURS FOR THE TAKING, YOUNG LADY.
WILL YOU PROTECT MY GRANDDAUGHTER NOW, TRODAIRE?
YOU WERE SO SUCCESSFUL WITH MY DAUGHTER.
DAMN YOU, RANI.
I'LL HANDLE THIS.
I NEVER WANTED THIS, GRANDMA. AND YOU KNOW THAT!
I DIDN'T WANT ANYONE TO GET HURT!
WHAT DID YOU EXPECT?!
THIS IS WAR!
YOUR NAIVETÉ IS NOT AN EXCUSE.
SO... WHAT IS YOUR FIRST ORDER...YOUR HIGHNESS?
WHAT DO YOU WISH OF YOUR LOYAL SUBJECTS?
A QUEEN MUST RULE WITH PURPOSE AND VIGOR.
DON'T COME ANY CLOSER, GRANDMA.
I'M WARNING YOU.

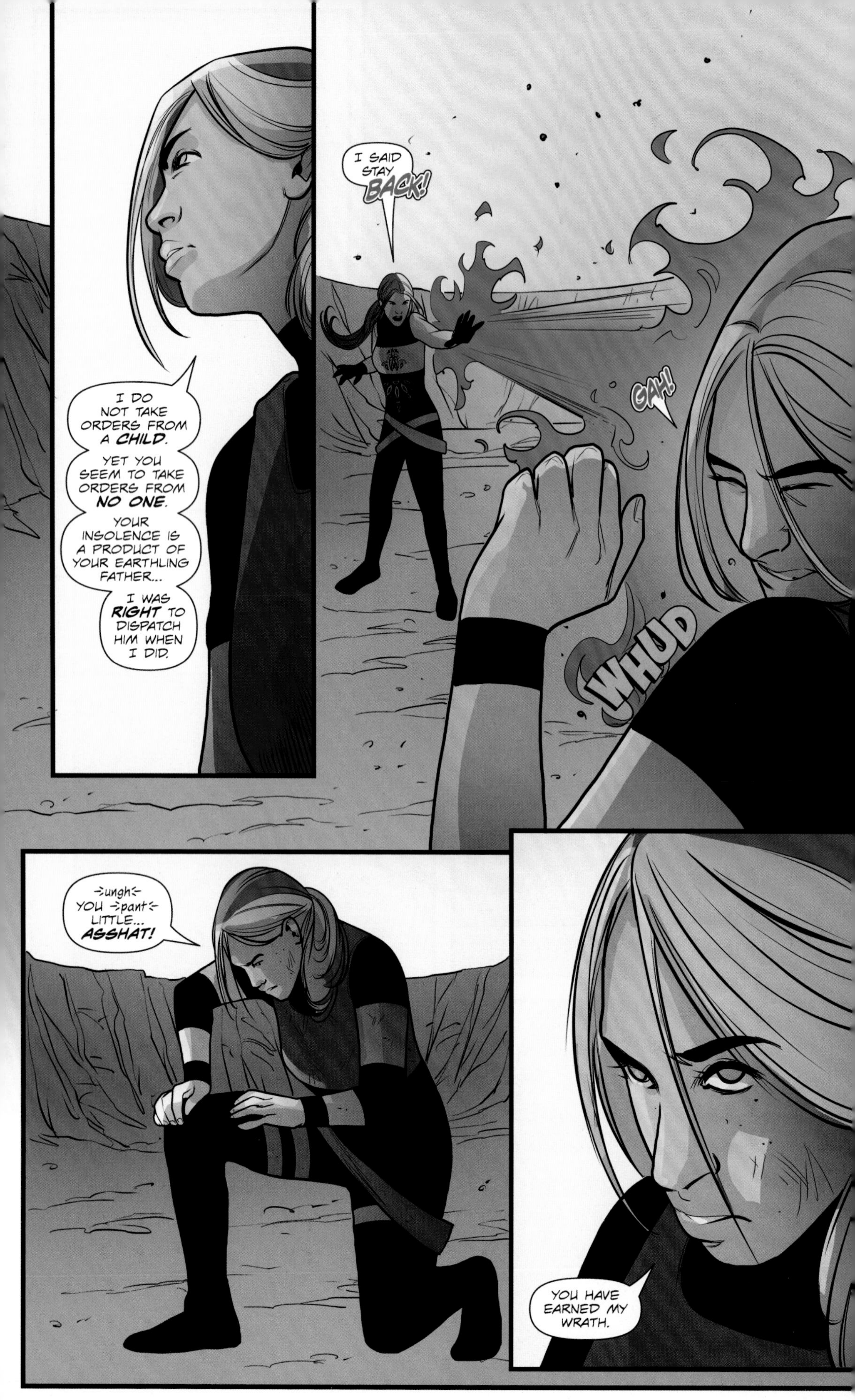
I DO NOT TAKE ORDERS FROM A CHILD.
YET YOU SEEM TO TAKE ORDERS FROM NO ONE.
YOUR INSOLENCE IS A PRODUCT OF YOUR EARTHLING FATHER...
I WAS RIGHT TO DISPATCH HIM WHEN I DID.
I SAID STAY BACK!
GAH!
WHUD
-ungh- YOU -pant- LITTLE... ASSHAT!
YOU HAVE EARNED MY WRATH.

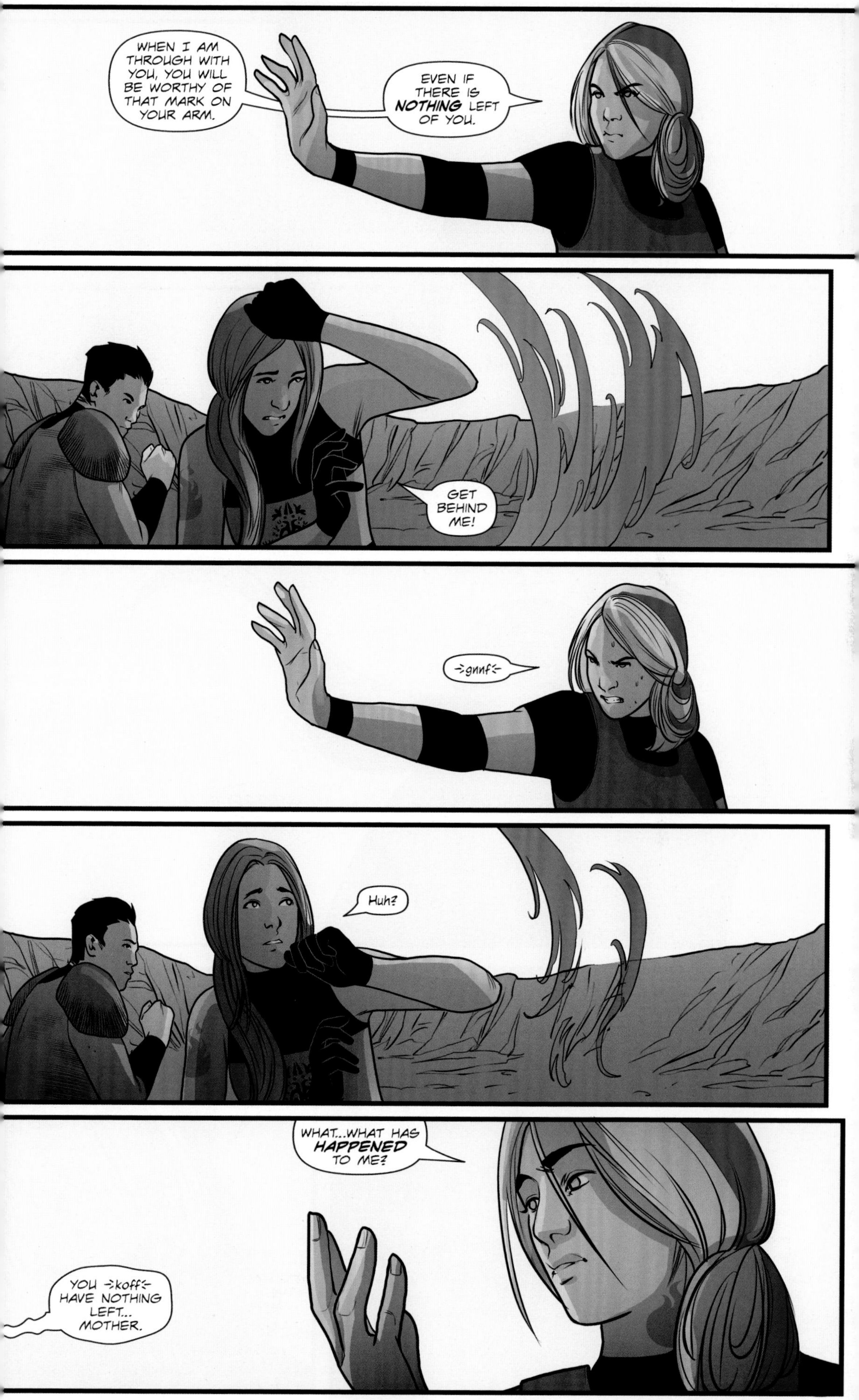
WHEN I AM THROUGH WITH YOU, YOU WILL BE WORTHY OF THAT MARK ON YOUR ARM.
EVEN IF THERE IS **NOTHING** LEFT OF YOU.
GET BEHIND ME!
-gnnf-
Huh?
WHAT...WHAT HAS **HAPPENED** TO ME?
YOU -koff- HAVE NOTHING LEFT... MOTHER.

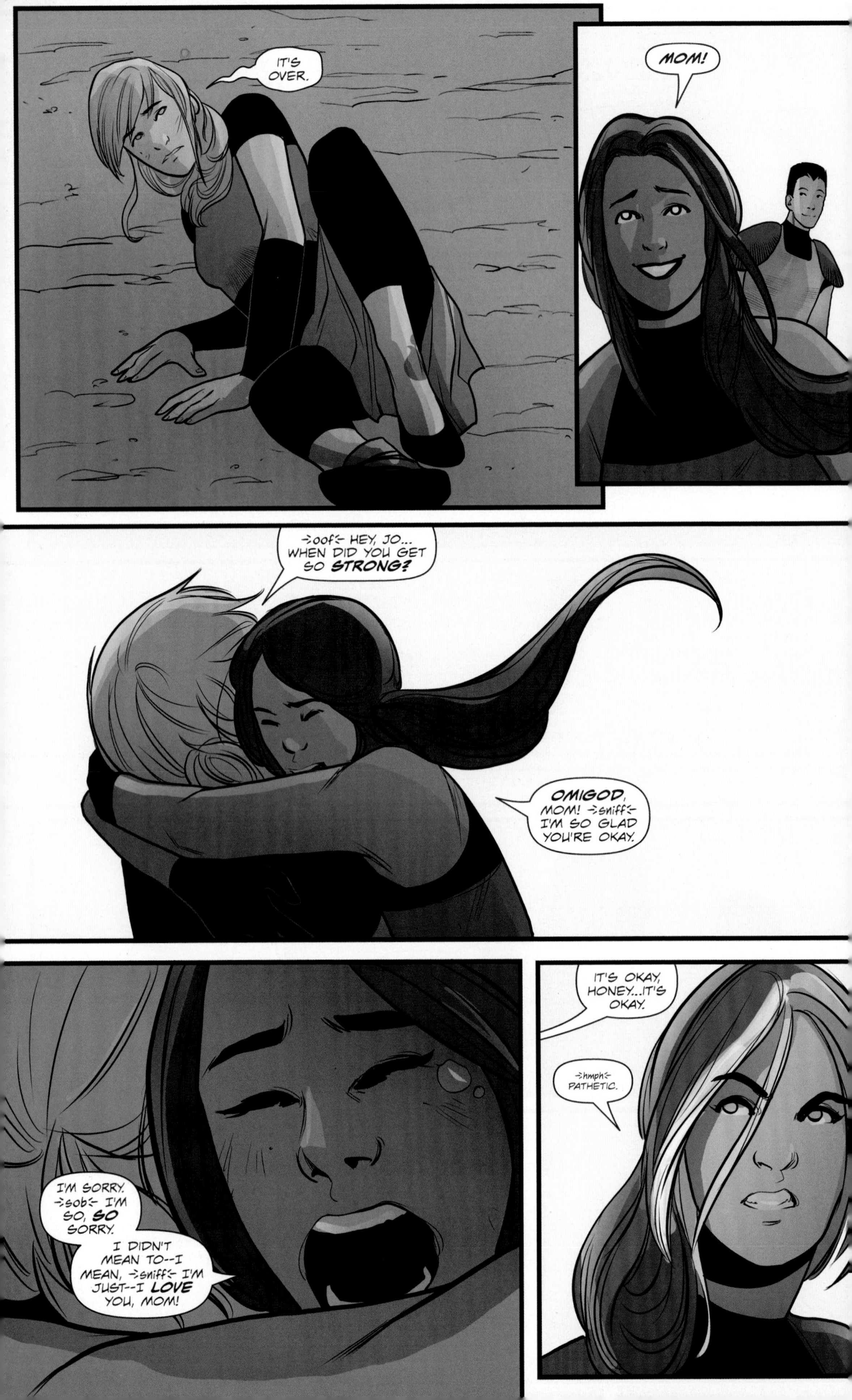
IT'S OVER.
MOM!
→oof← HEY, JO... WHEN DID YOU GET SO STRONG?
OMIGOD, MOM! →sniff← I'M SO GLAD YOU'RE OKAY.
I'M SORRY. →sob← I'M SO, SO SORRY.
I DIDN'T MEAN TO--I MEAN, →sniff← I'M JUST--I LOVE YOU, MOM!
IT'S OKAY, HONEY...IT'S OKAY.
→hmph← PATHETIC.

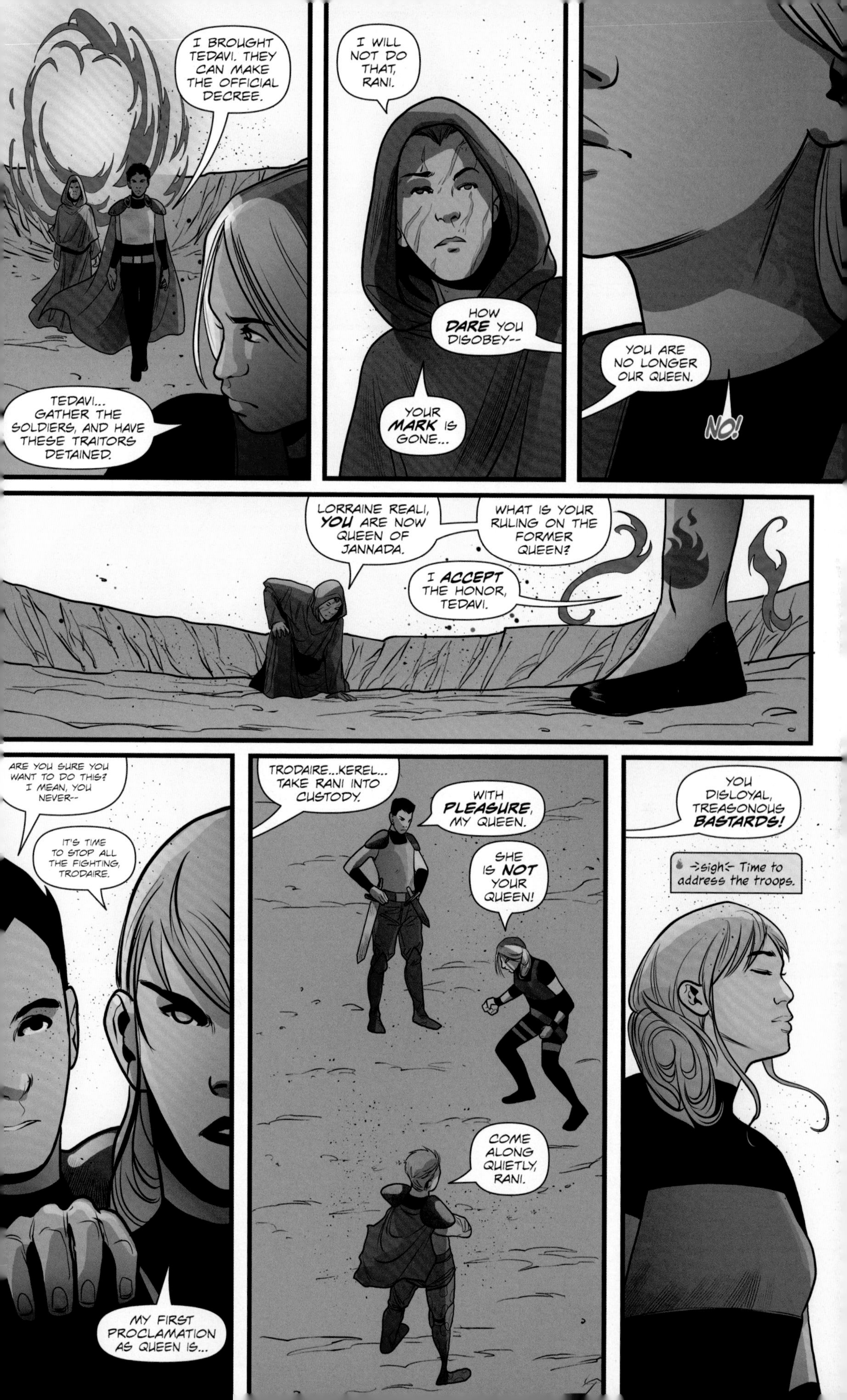
I BROUGHT TEDAVI. THEY CAN MAKE THE OFFICIAL DECREE.
TEDAVI... GATHER THE SOLDIERS, AND HAVE THESE TRAITORS DETAINED.
I WILL NOT DO THAT, RANI.
HOW DARE YOU DISOBEY--
YOUR MARK IS GONE...
YOU ARE NO LONGER OUR QUEEN.
NO!
LORRAINE REALI, YOU ARE NOW QUEEN OF JANNADA.
WHAT IS YOUR RULING ON THE FORMER QUEEN?
I ACCEPT THE HONOR, TEDAVI.
ARE YOU SURE YOU WANT TO DO THIS? I MEAN, YOU NEVER--
IT'S TIME TO STOP ALL THE FIGHTING, TRODAIRE.
MY FIRST PROCLAMATION AS QUEEN IS...
TRODAIRE...KEREL... TAKE RANI INTO CUSTODY.
WITH PLEASURE, MY QUEEN.
SHE IS NOT YOUR QUEEN!
COME ALONG QUIETLY, RANI.
YOU DISLOYAL, TREASONOUS BASTARDS!
->sigh<- Time to address the troops.

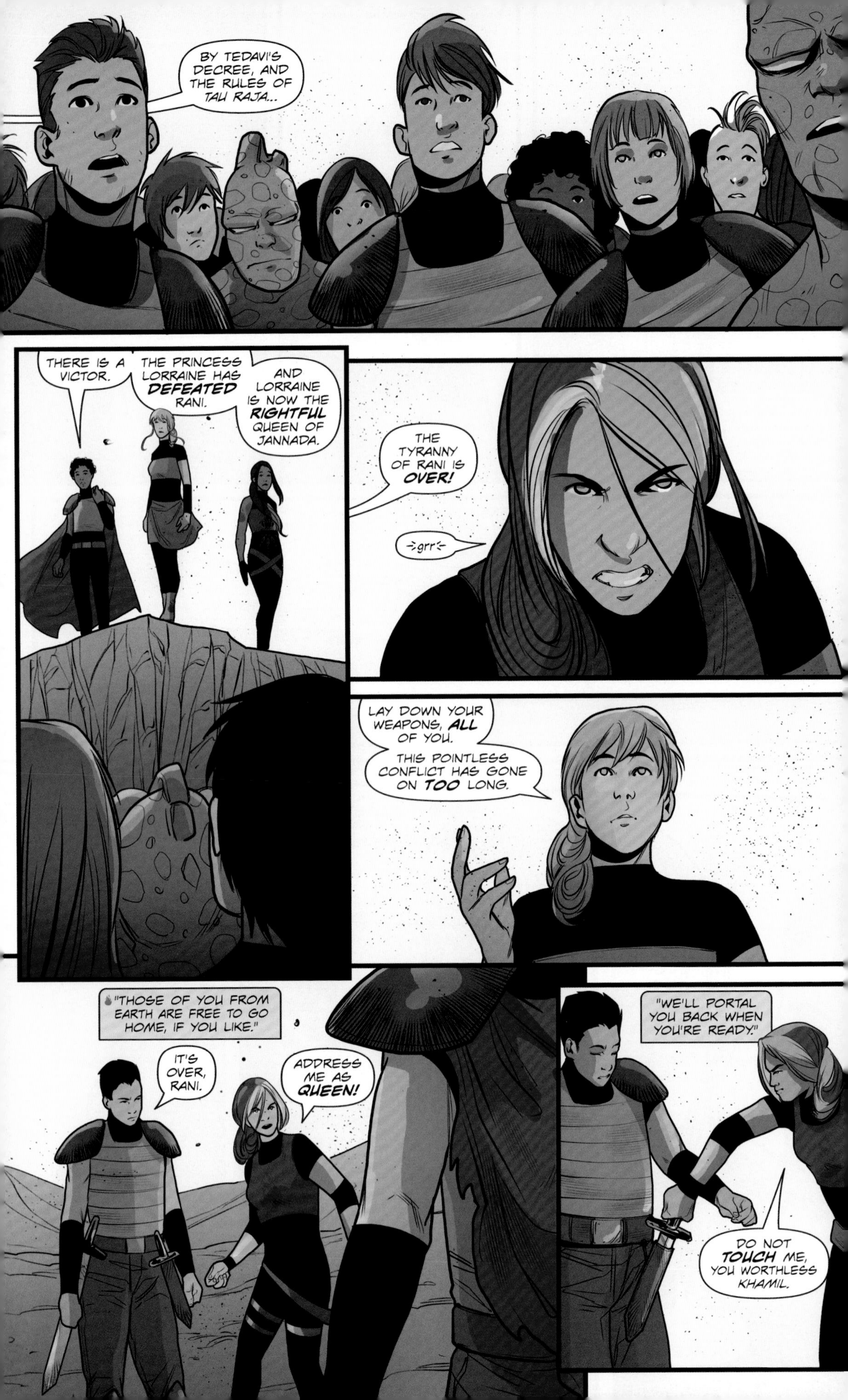
BY TEDAVI'S DECREE, AND THE RULES OF TAU RAJA...
THERE IS A VICTOR.
THE PRINCESS LORRAINE HAS DEFEATED RANI.
AND LORRAINE IS NOW THE RIGHTFUL QUEEN OF JANNADA.
THE TYRANNY OF RANI IS OVER!
grr
LAY DOWN YOUR WEAPONS, ALL OF YOU.
THIS POINTLESS CONFLICT HAS GONE ON TOO LONG.
"THOSE OF YOU FROM EARTH ARE FREE TO GO HOME, IF YOU LIKE."
IT'S OVER, RANI.
ADDRESS ME AS QUEEN!
"WE'LL PORTAL YOU BACK WHEN YOU'RE READY."
DO NOT TOUCH ME, YOU WORTHLESS KHAMIL.

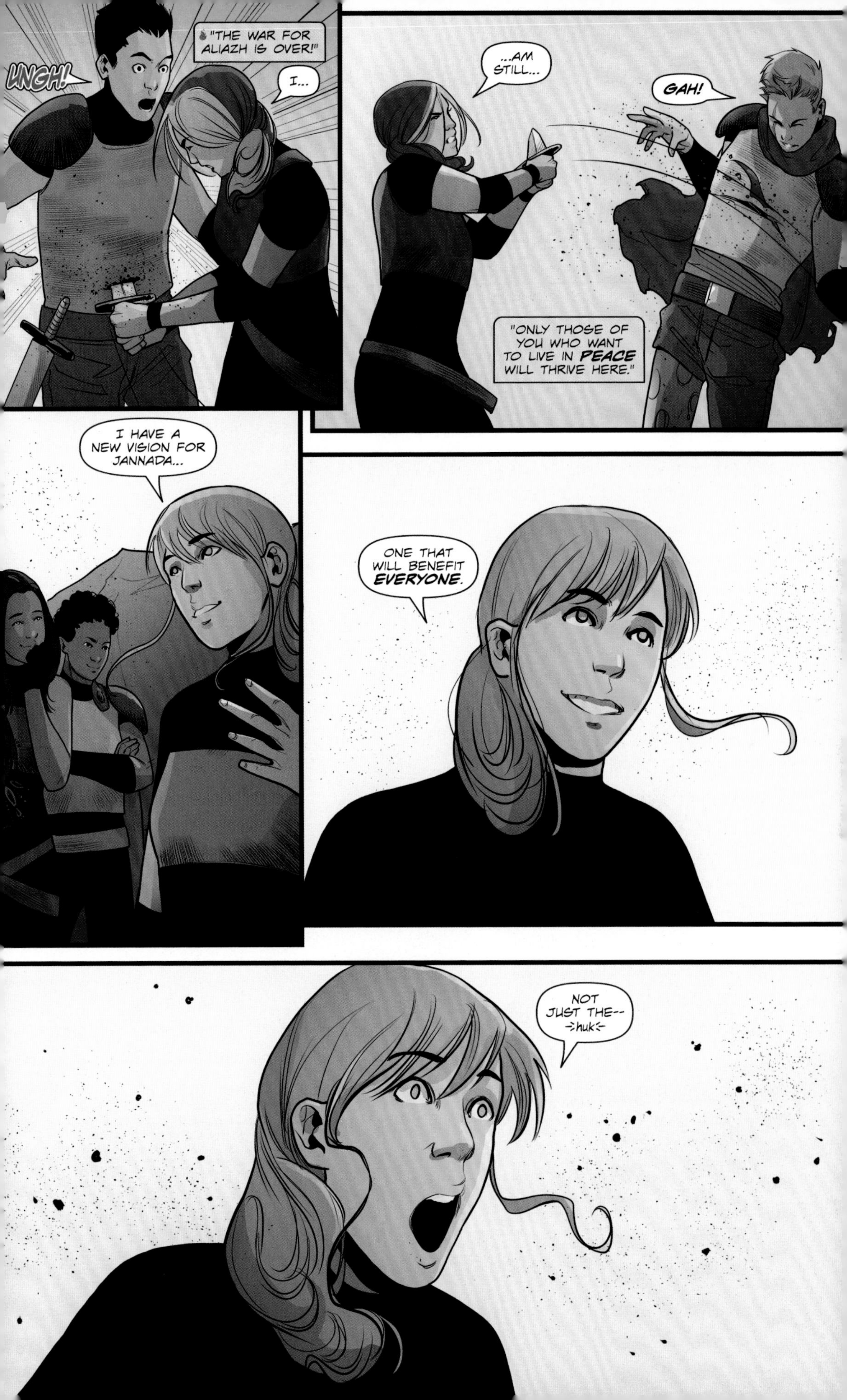
UNGH!
"THE WAR FOR ALIAZH IS OVER!"
I...
...AM STILL...
GAH!
"ONLY THOSE OF YOU WHO WANT TO LIVE IN PEACE WILL THRIVE HERE."
I HAVE A NEW VISION FOR JANNADA...
ONE THAT WILL BENEFIT EVERYONE.
NOT JUST THE-- huk

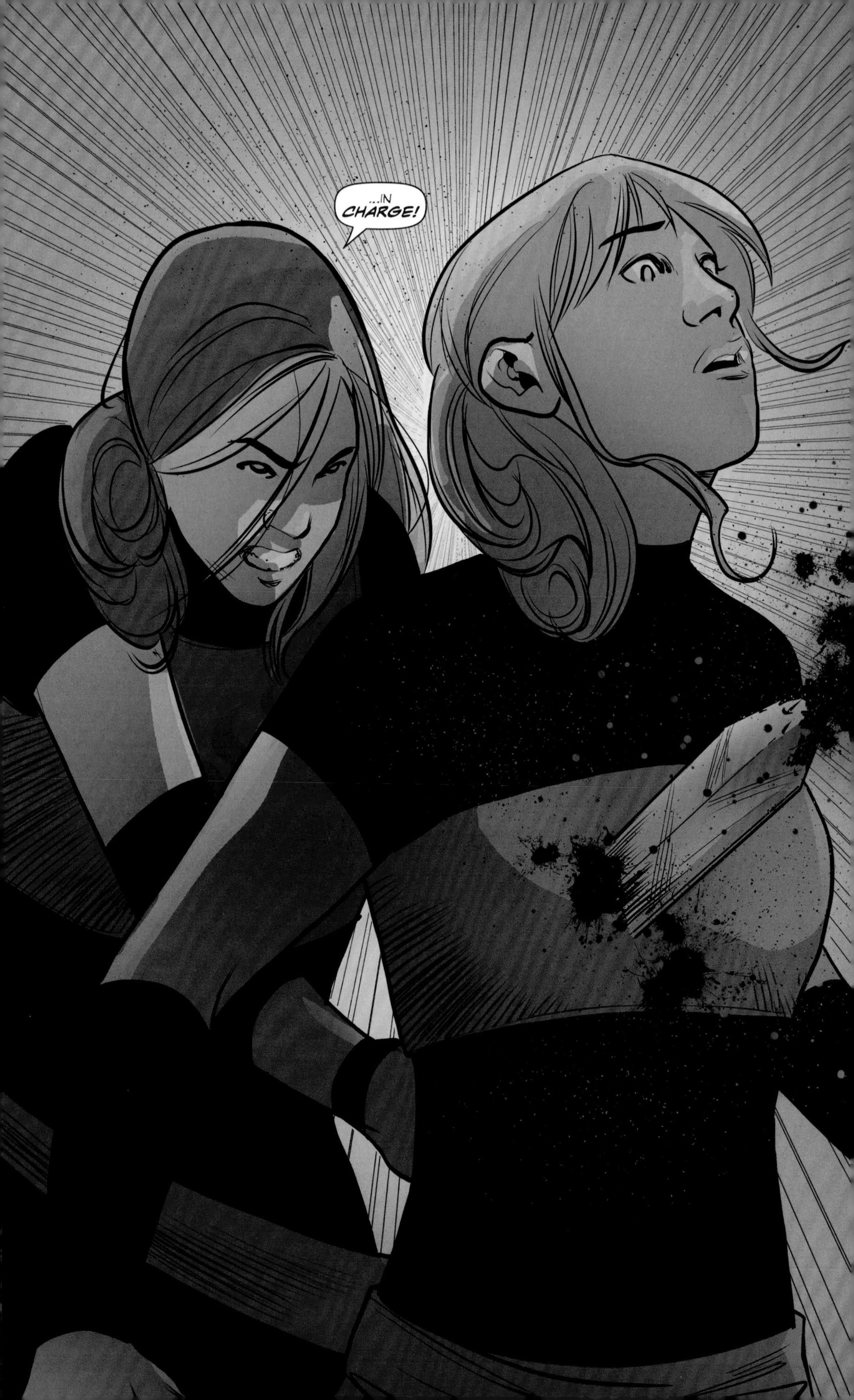
...IN
CHARGE!

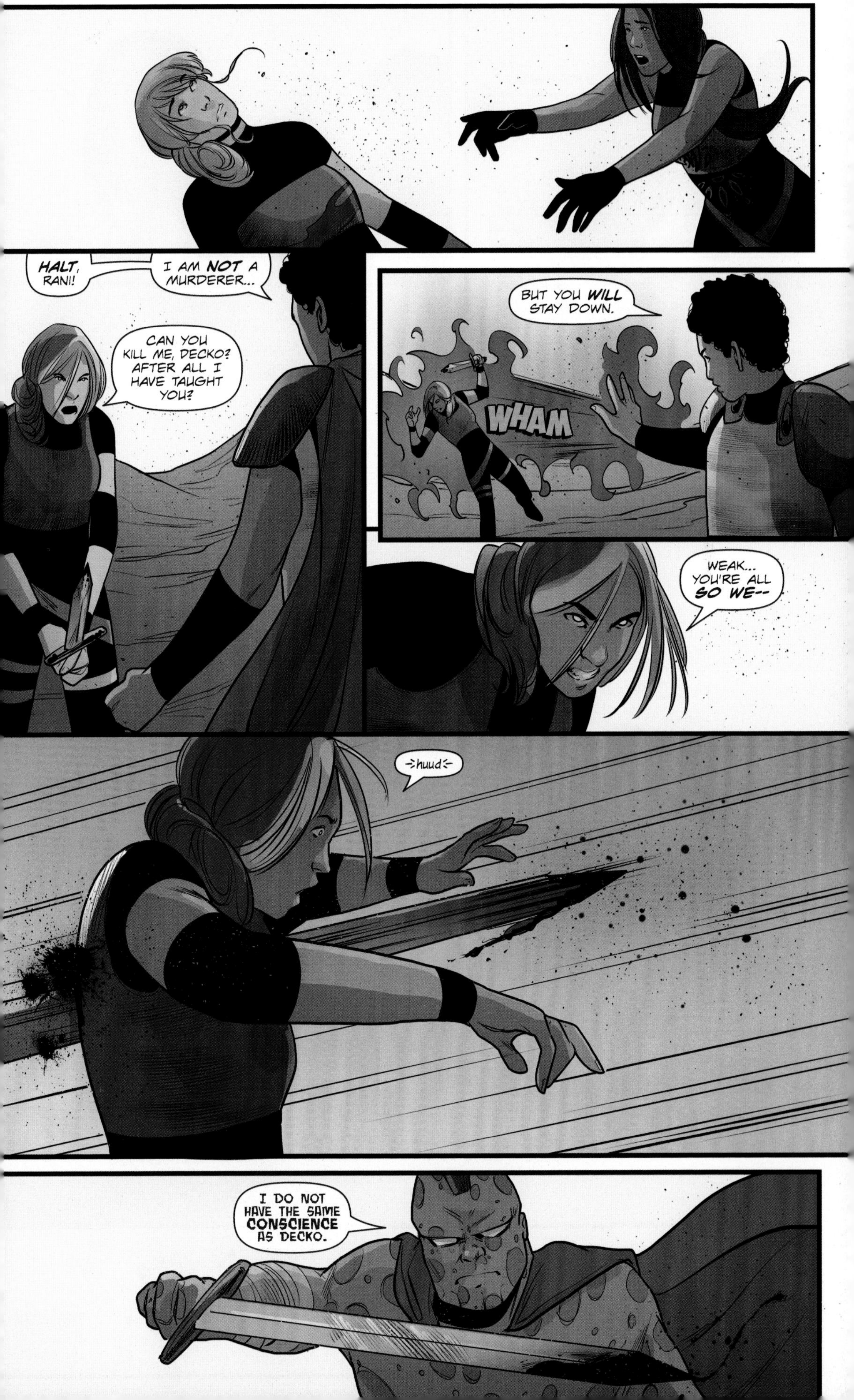
HALT, RANI!
I AM NOT A MURDERER...
CAN YOU KILL ME, DECKO? AFTER ALL I HAVE TAUGHT YOU?
BUT YOU WILL STAY DOWN.
WHAM
WEAK... YOU'RE ALL SO WE--
huud
I DO NOT HAVE THE SAME CONSCIENCE AS DECKO.

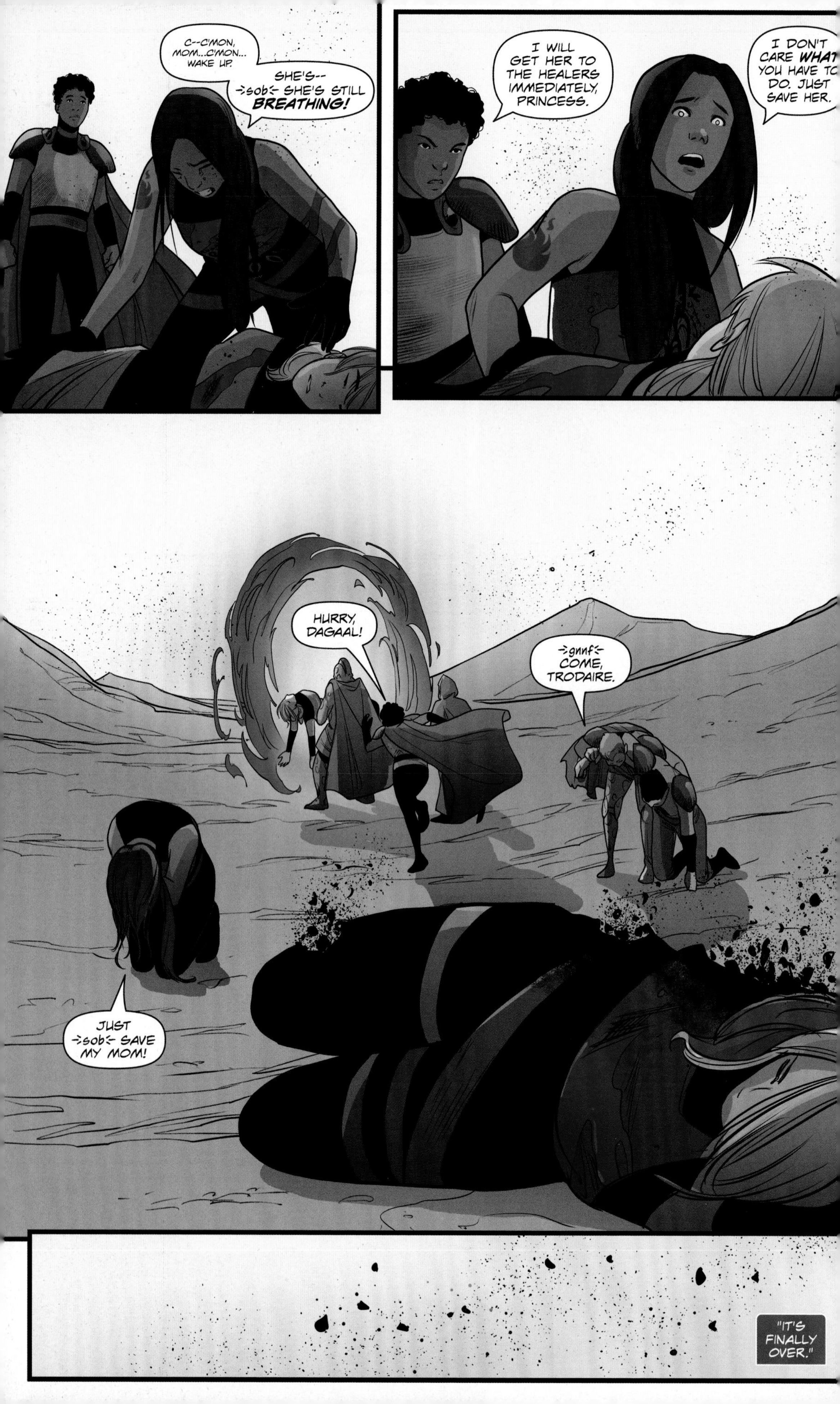

C--C'MON, MOM...C'MON... WAKE UP.
SHE'S-- ~sob~ SHE'S STILL **BREATHING!**
I WILL GET HER TO THE HEALERS IMMEDIATELY, PRINCESS.
I DON'T CARE **WHAT** YOU HAVE TO DO. JUST SAVE HER.
HURRY, DAGAAL!
~gnnf~ COME, TRODAIRE.
JUST ~sob~ SAVE MY MOM!
"IT'S FINALLY OVER."

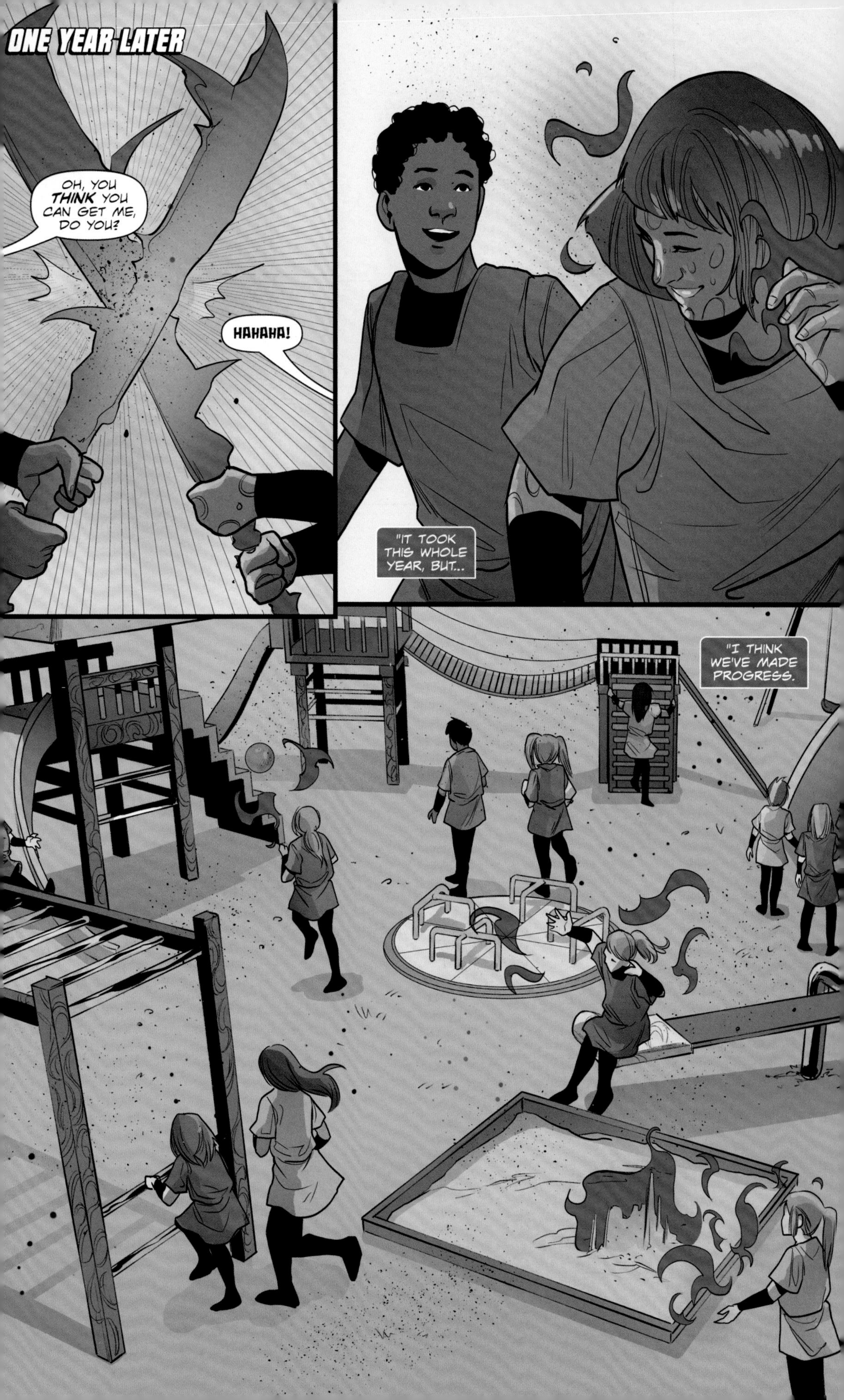
ONE YEAR LATER
OH, YOU THINK YOU CAN GET ME, DO YOU?
HAHAHA!
"IT TOOK THIS WHOLE YEAR, BUT...
"I THINK WE'VE MADE PROGRESS.

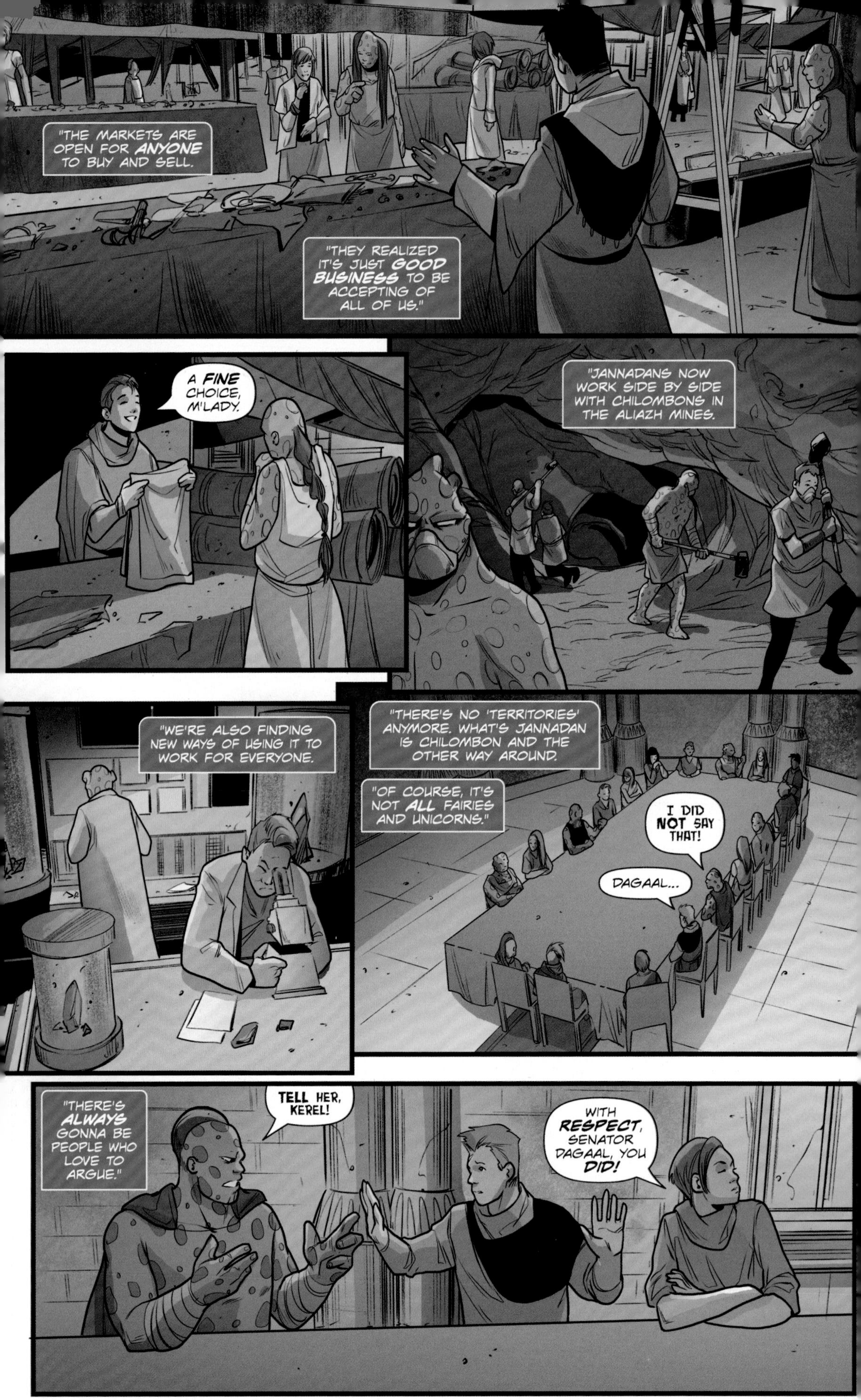
"THE MARKETS ARE OPEN FOR ANYONE TO BUY AND SELL.
"THEY REALIZED IT'S JUST GOOD BUSINESS TO BE ACCEPTING OF ALL OF US."
A FINE CHOICE, M'LADY.
"JANNADANS NOW WORK SIDE BY SIDE WITH CHILOMBONS IN THE ALIAZH MINES.
"WE'RE ALSO FINDING NEW WAYS OF USING IT TO WORK FOR EVERYONE.
"THERE'S NO 'TERRITORIES' ANYMORE. WHAT'S JANNADAN IS CHILOMBON AND THE OTHER WAY AROUND.
"OF COURSE, IT'S NOT ALL FAIRIES AND UNICORNS."
I DID NOT SAY THAT!
DAGAAL...
"THERE'S ALWAYS GONNA BE PEOPLE WHO LOVE TO ARGUE."
TELL HER, KEREL!
WITH RESPECT, SENATOR DAGAAL, YOU DID!

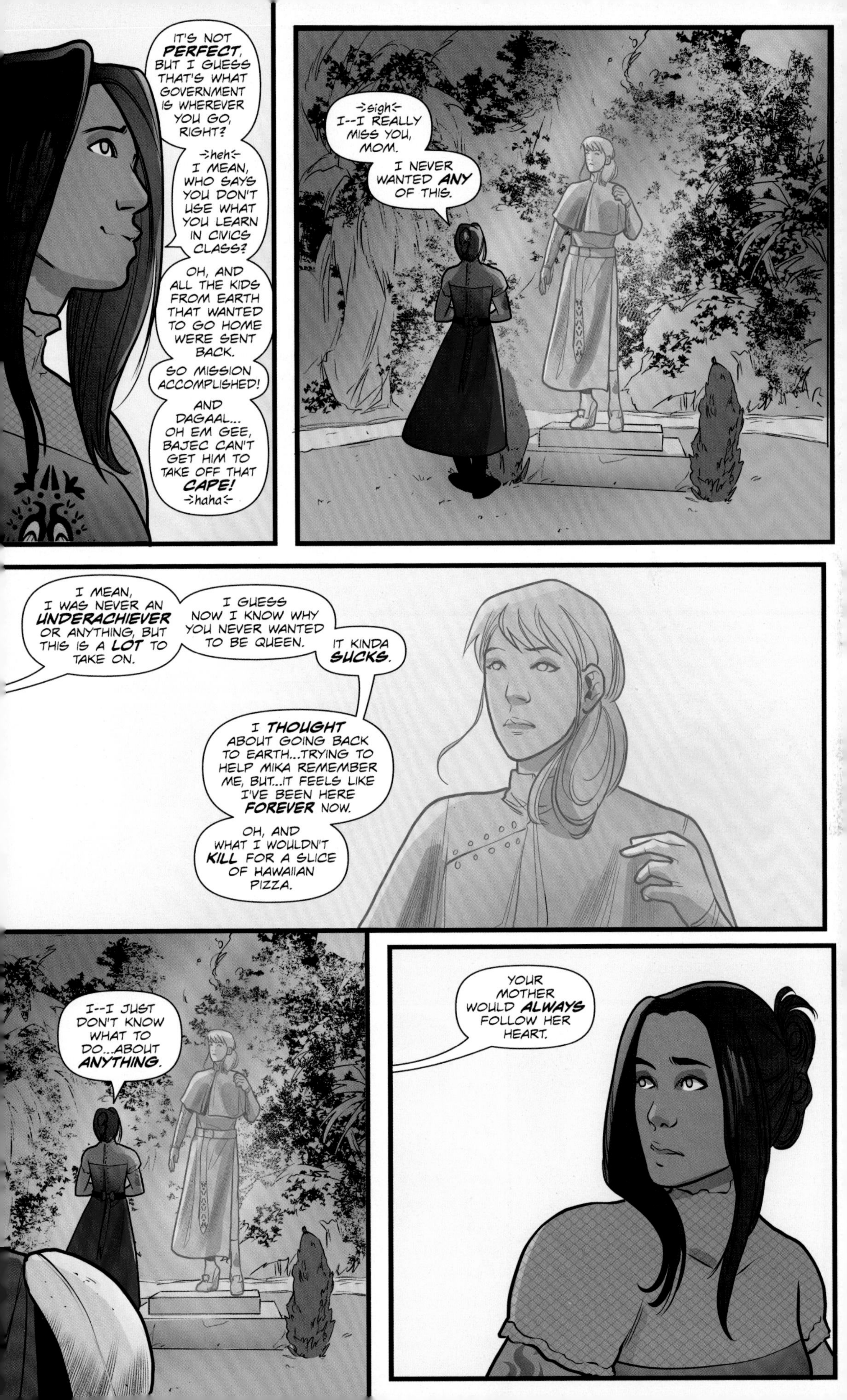
IT'S NOT PERFECT, BUT I GUESS THAT'S WHAT GOVERNMENT IS WHEREVER YOU GO, RIGHT?
-heh- I MEAN, WHO SAYS YOU DON'T USE WHAT YOU LEARN IN CIVICS CLASS?
OH, AND ALL THE KIDS FROM EARTH THAT WANTED TO GO HOME WERE SENT BACK.
SO MISSION ACCOMPLISHED!
AND DAGAAL... OH EM GEE, BAJEC CAN'T GET HIM TO TAKE OFF THAT CAPE! -haha-
-sigh- I--I REALLY MISS YOU, MOM.
I NEVER WANTED ANY OF THIS.
I MEAN, I WAS NEVER AN UNDERACHIEVER OR ANYTHING, BUT THIS IS A LOT TO TAKE ON.
I GUESS NOW I KNOW WHY YOU NEVER WANTED TO BE QUEEN.
IT KINDA SUCKS.
I THOUGHT ABOUT GOING BACK TO EARTH...TRYING TO HELP MIKA REMEMBER ME, BUT...IT FEELS LIKE I'VE BEEN HERE FOREVER NOW.
OH, AND WHAT I WOULDN'T KILL FOR A SLICE OF HAWAIIAN PIZZA.
I--I JUST DON'T KNOW WHAT TO DO...ABOUT ANYTHING.
YOUR MOTHER WOULD ALWAYS FOLLOW HER HEART.

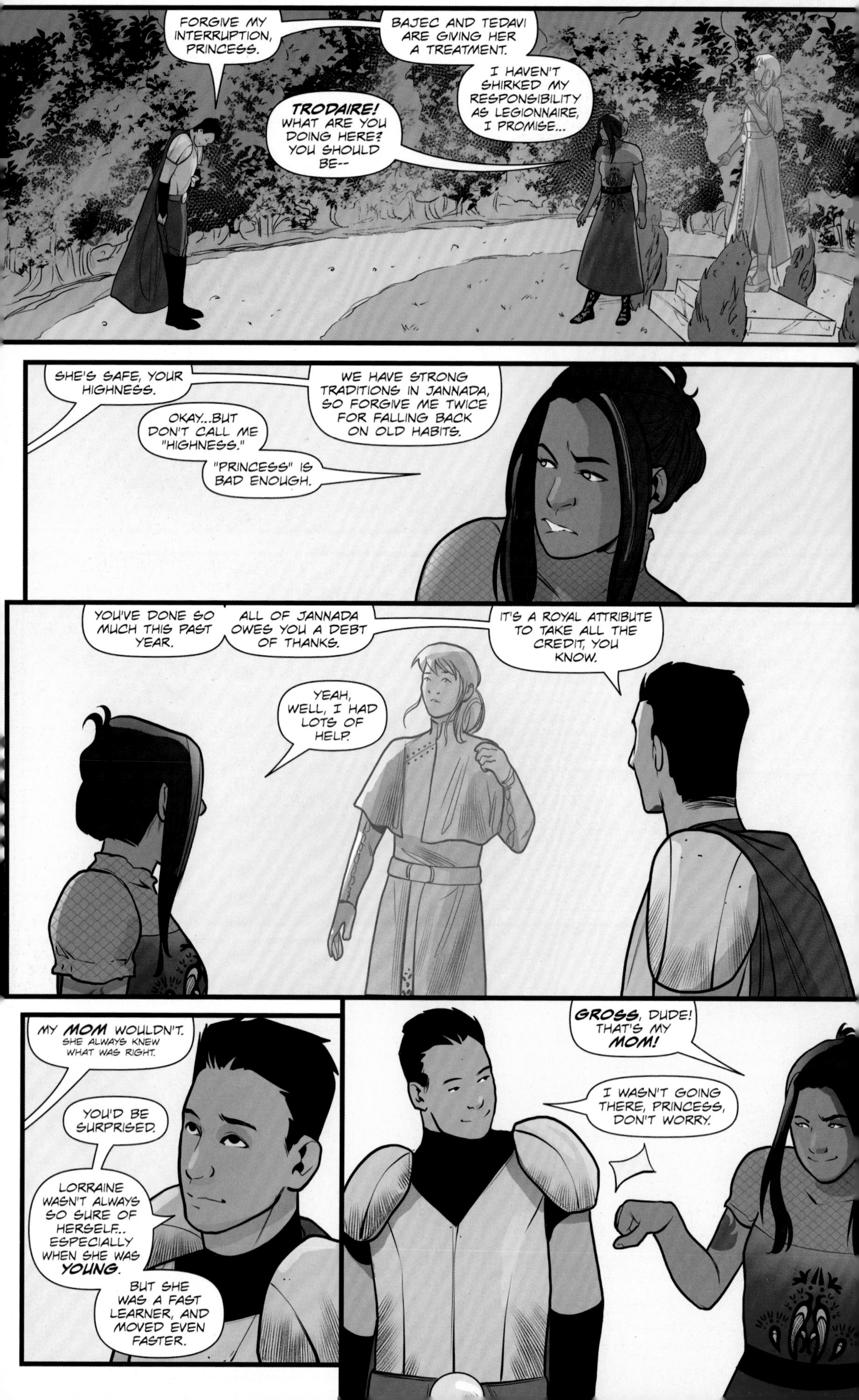
FORGIVE MY INTERRUPTION, PRINCESS.
BAJEC AND TEDAVI ARE GIVING HER A TREATMENT.
I HAVEN'T SHIRKED MY RESPONSIBILITY AS LEGIONNAIRE, I PROMISE...
TRODAIRE! WHAT ARE YOU DOING HERE? YOU SHOULD BE--
SHE'S SAFE, YOUR HIGHNESS.
OKAY...BUT DON'T CALL ME "HIGHNESS."
"PRINCESS" IS BAD ENOUGH.
WE HAVE STRONG TRADITIONS IN JANNADA, SO FORGIVE ME TWICE FOR FALLING BACK ON OLD HABITS.
YOU'VE DONE SO MUCH THIS PAST YEAR.
ALL OF JANNADA OWES YOU A DEBT OF THANKS.
YEAH, WELL, I HAD LOTS OF HELP.
IT'S A ROYAL ATTRIBUTE TO TAKE ALL THE CREDIT, YOU KNOW.
MY MOM WOULDN'T. SHE ALWAYS KNEW WHAT WAS RIGHT.
YOU'D BE SURPRISED.
LORRAINE WASN'T ALWAYS SO SURE OF HERSELF.. ESPECIALLY WHEN SHE WAS YOUNG.
BUT SHE WAS A FAST LEARNER, AND MOVED EVEN FASTER.
GROSS, DUDE! THAT'S MY MOM!
I WASN'T GOING THERE, PRINCESS, DON'T WORRY.

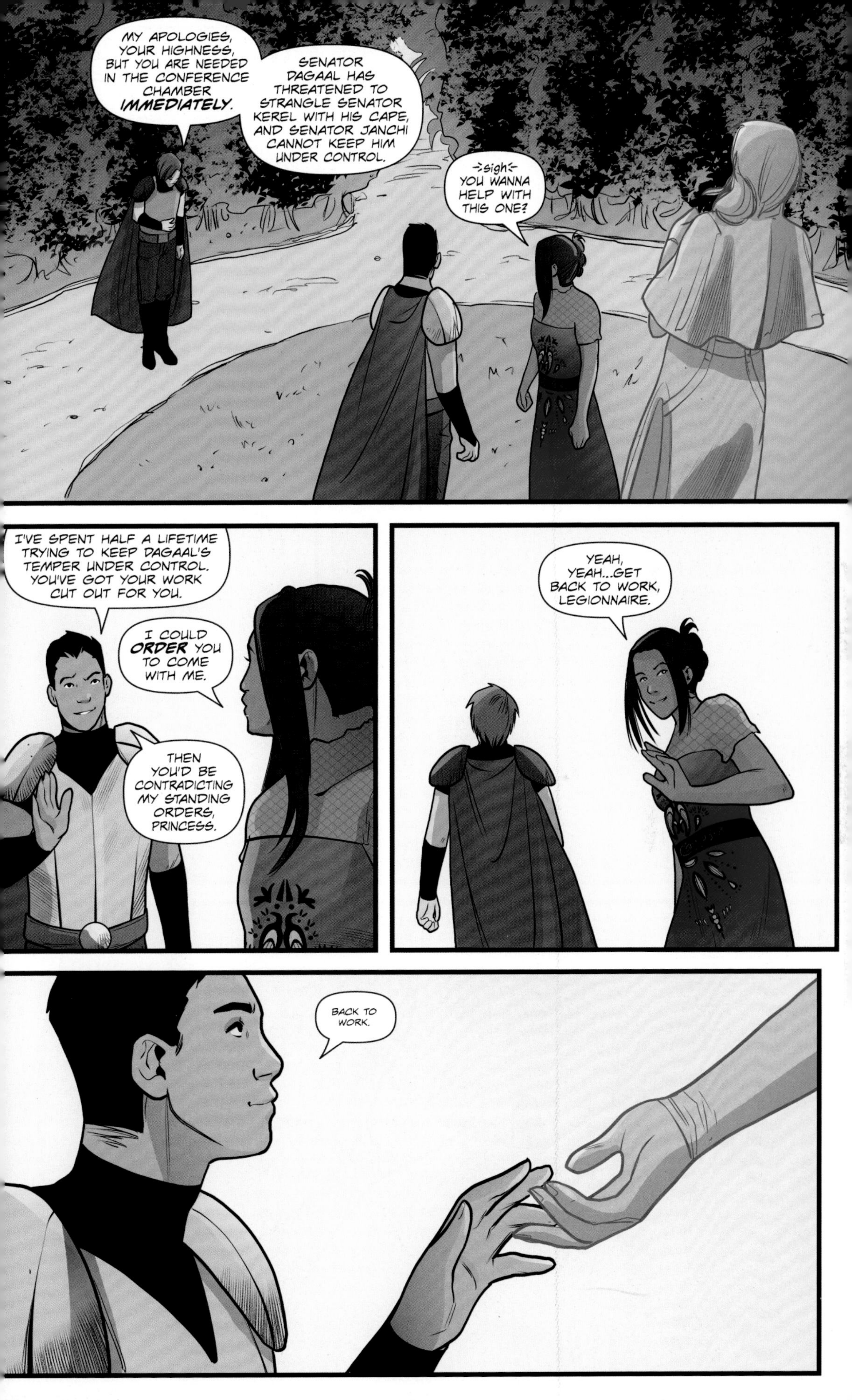
MY APOLOGIES, YOUR HIGHNESS, BUT YOU ARE NEEDED IN THE CONFERENCE CHAMBER *IMMEDIATELY*.
SENATOR DAGAAL HAS THREATENED TO STRANGLE SENATOR KEREL WITH HIS CAPE, AND SENATOR JANCHI CANNOT KEEP HIM UNDER CONTROL.
sigh YOU WANNA HELP WITH THIS ONE?
I'VE SPENT HALF A LIFETIME TRYING TO KEEP DAGAAL'S TEMPER UNDER CONTROL. YOU'VE GOT YOUR WORK CUT OUT FOR YOU.
I COULD **ORDER** YOU TO COME WITH ME.
THEN YOU'D BE CONTRADICTING MY STANDING ORDERS, PRINCESS.
YEAH, YEAH...GET BACK TO WORK, LEGIONNAIRE.
BACK TO WORK.

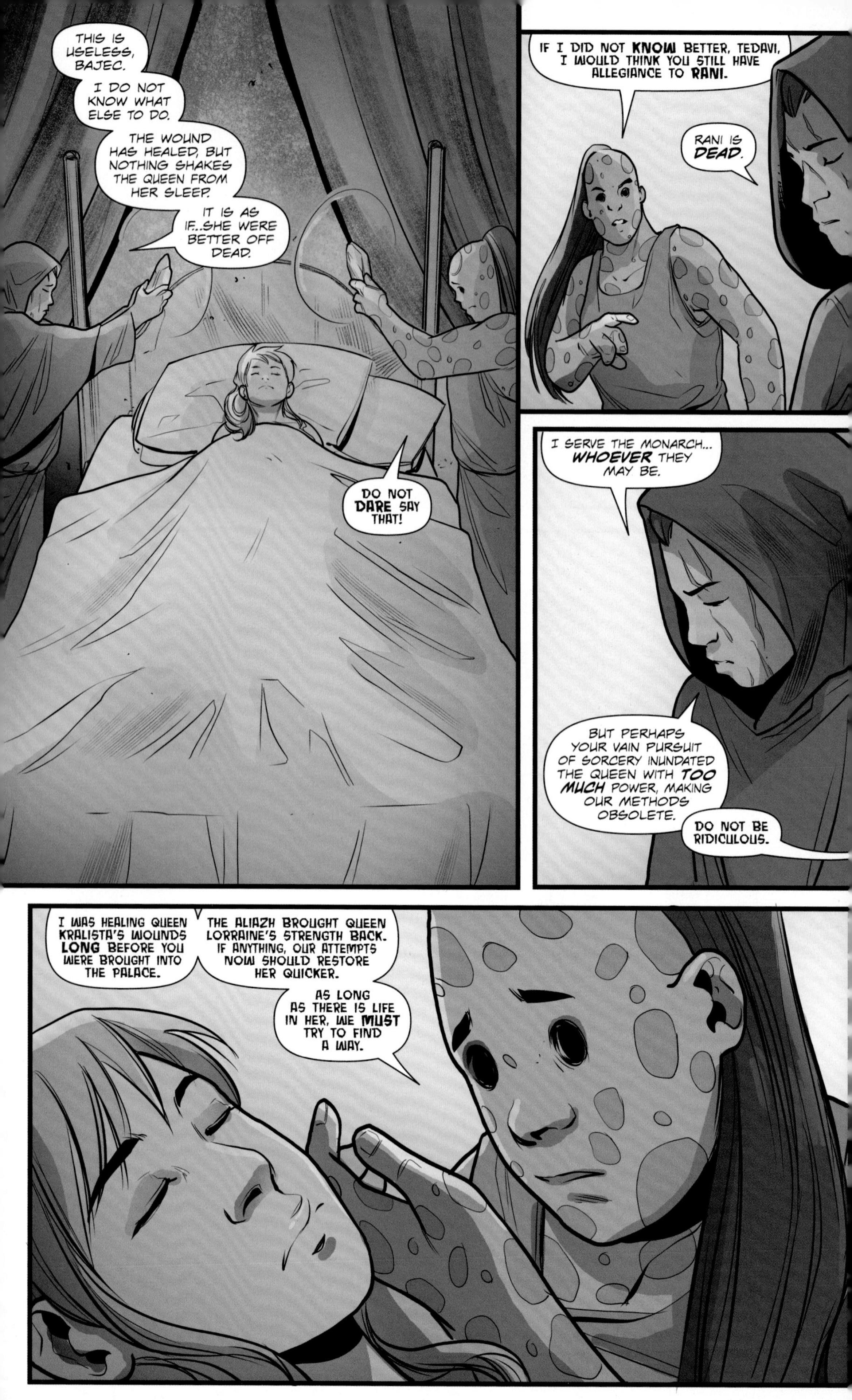
THIS IS USELESS, BAJEC.
I DO NOT KNOW WHAT ELSE TO DO.
THE WOUND HAS HEALED, BUT NOTHING SHAKES THE QUEEN FROM HER SLEEP.
IT IS AS IF...SHE WERE BETTER OFF DEAD.
DO NOT DARE SAY THAT!
IF I DID NOT KNOW BETTER, TEDAVI, I WOULD THINK YOU STILL HAVE ALLEGIANCE TO RANI.
RANI IS DEAD.
I SERVE THE MONARCH... WHOEVER THEY MAY BE.
BUT PERHAPS YOUR VAIN PURSUIT OF SORCERY INUNDATED THE QUEEN WITH TOO MUCH POWER, MAKING OUR METHODS OBSOLETE.
DO NOT BE RIDICULOUS.
I WAS HEALING QUEEN KRALISTA'S WOUNDS LONG BEFORE YOU WERE BROUGHT INTO THE PALACE.
THE ALIAZH BROUGHT QUEEN LORRAINE'S STRENGTH BACK. IF ANYTHING, OUR ATTEMPTS NOW SHOULD RESTORE HER QUICKER.
AS LONG AS THERE IS LIFE IN HER, WE MUST TRY TO FIND A WAY.

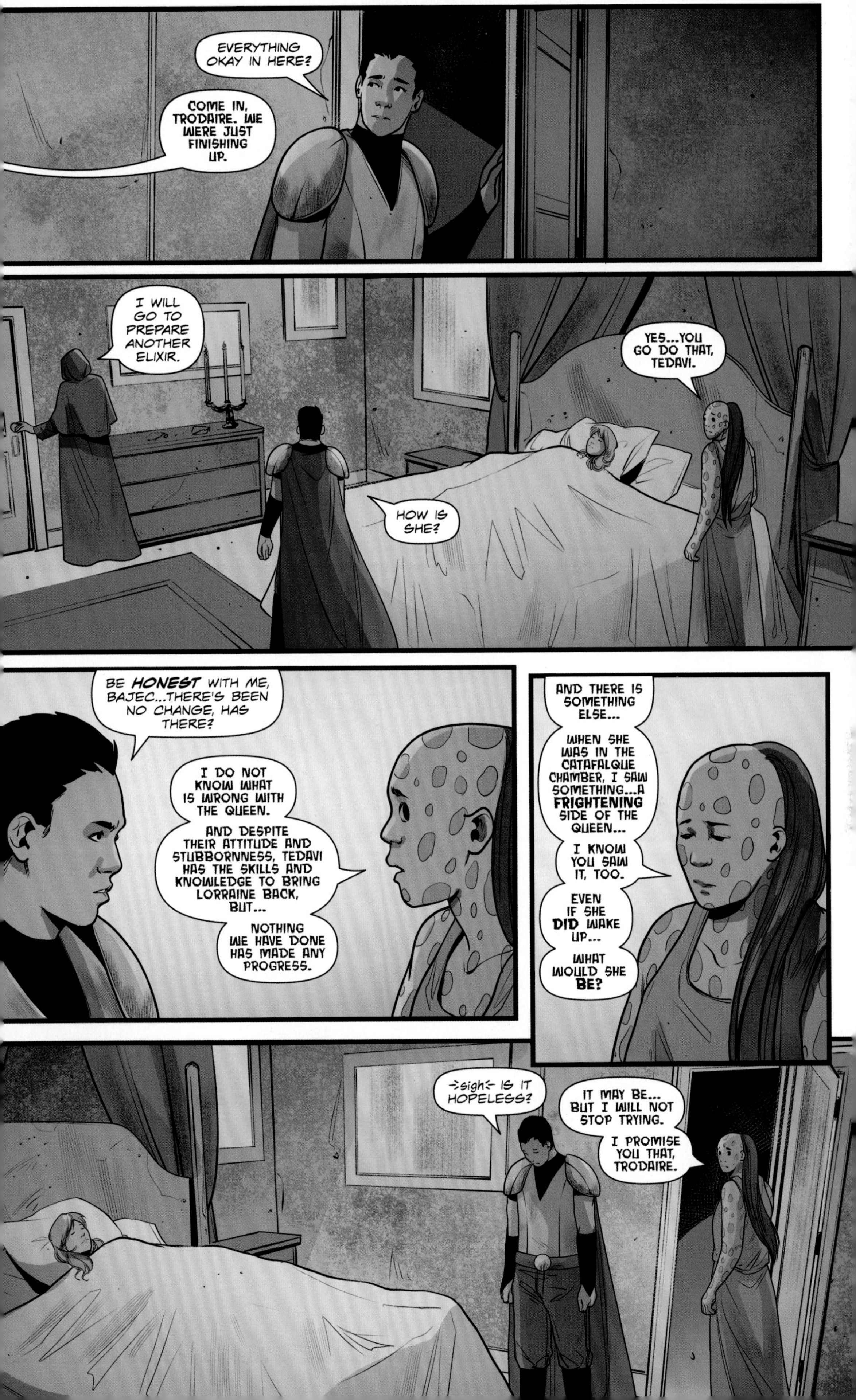
EVERYTHING OKAY IN HERE?
COME IN, TRODAIRE. WE WERE JUST FINISHING UP.
I WILL GO TO PREPARE ANOTHER ELIXIR.
YES...YOU GO DO THAT, TEDAVI.
HOW IS SHE?
BE HONEST WITH ME, BAJEC...THERE'S BEEN NO CHANGE, HAS THERE?
I DO NOT KNOW WHAT IS WRONG WITH THE QUEEN.
AND DESPITE THEIR ATTITUDE AND STUBBORNNESS, TEDAVI HAS THE SKILLS AND KNOWLEDGE TO BRING LORRAINE BACK, BUT...
NOTHING WE HAVE DONE HAS MADE ANY PROGRESS.
AND THERE IS SOMETHING ELSE...
WHEN SHE WAS IN THE CATAFALQUE CHAMBER, I SAW SOMETHING...A FRIGHTENING SIDE OF THE QUEEN...
I KNOW YOU SAW IT, TOO.
EVEN IF SHE DID WAKE UP...
WHAT WOULD SHE BE?
-sigh- IS IT HOPELESS?
IT MAY BE... BUT I WILL NOT STOP TRYING.
I PROMISE YOU THAT, TRODAIRE.

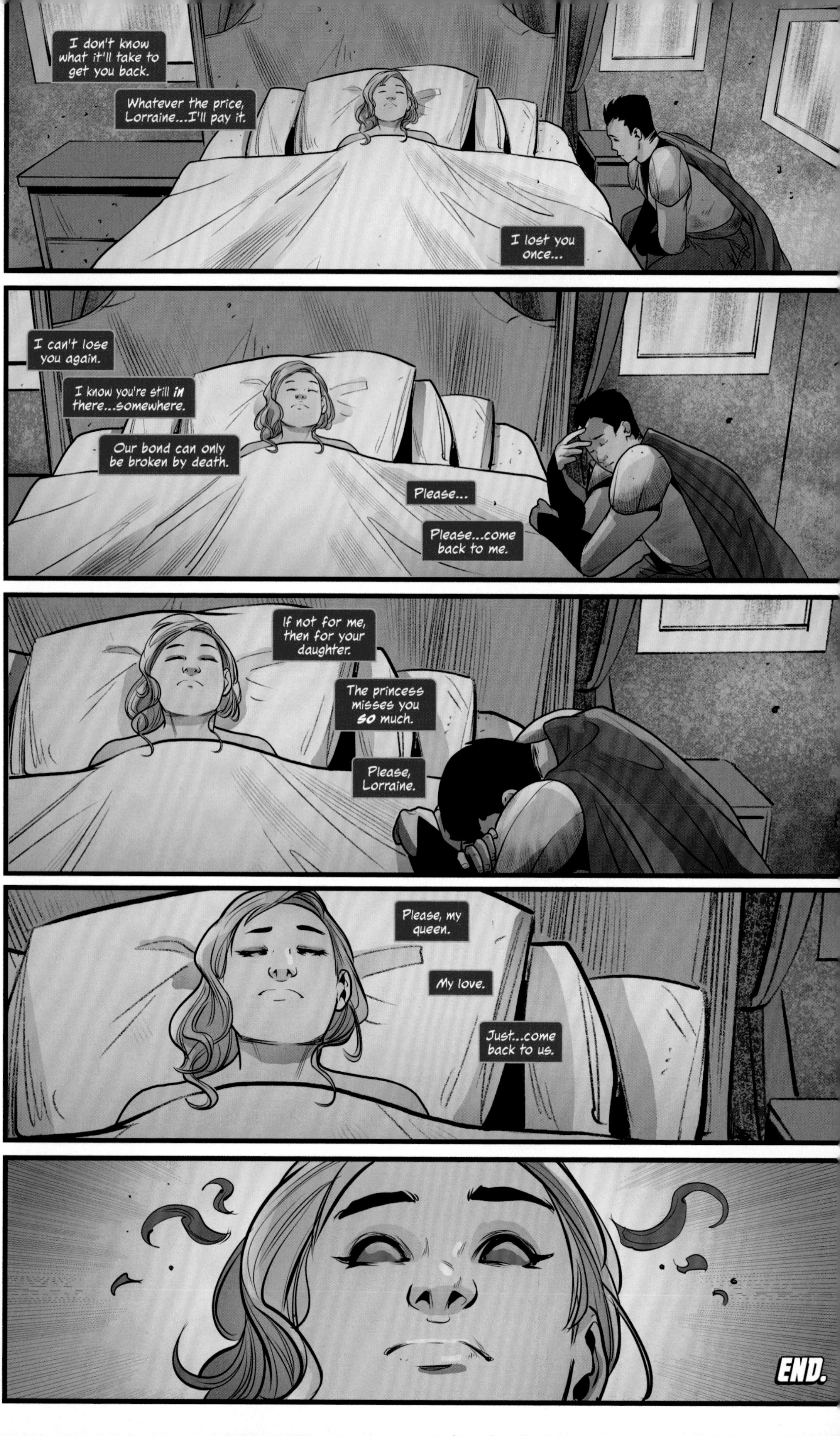
I don't know what it'll take to get you back.
Whatever the price, Lorraine...I'll pay it.
I lost you once...
I can't lose you again.
I know you're still in there...somewhere.
Our bond can only be broken by death.
Please...
Please...come back to me.
If not for me, then for your daughter.
The princess misses you SO much.
Please, Lorraine.
Please, my queen.
My love.
Just...come back to us.
END.

BEHIND THE MAGIC

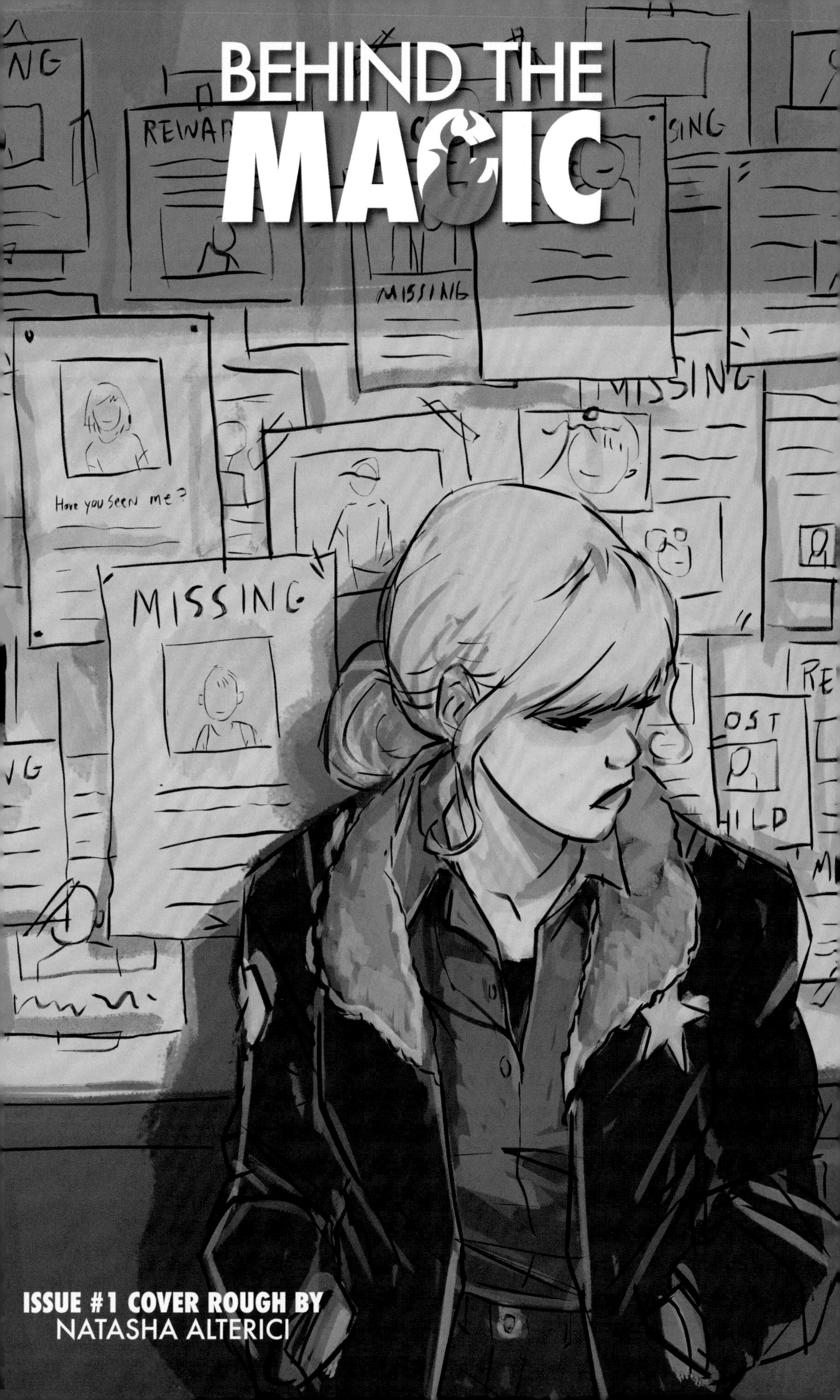
MISSING
Have you seen me?
MISSING
MISSING
MISSING

ISSUE #1 COVER ROUGH BY
NATASHA ALTERICI

DAREDEVIL #181 BY FRANK MILLER

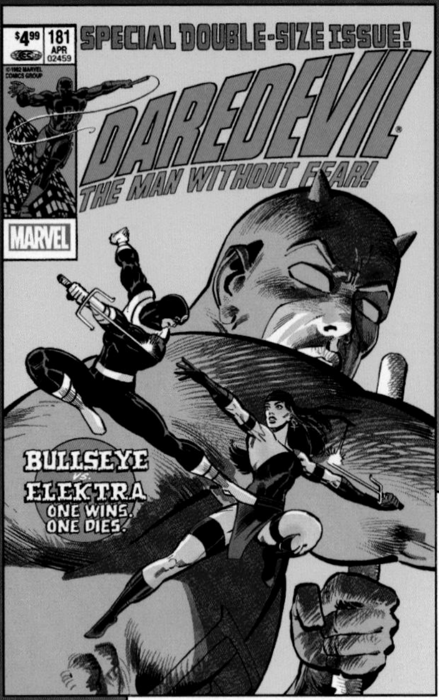
$4.99
181
APR
02459
SPECIAL DOUBLE-SIZE ISSUE!
DAREDEVIL
THE MAN WITHOUT FEAR!
MARVEL
BULLSEYE
vs.
ELEKTRA
ONE WINS.
ONE DIES.

For the last two covers of the series, we wanted to pay homage to some of the great comics creators who paved the way for complex storytelling.

Having had the honor of writing a *Daredevil* story and with Bill Sienkiewicz involved in *Forgotten Home*, we thought doing an homage to one of Frank Miller's famous covers would be apropos. —ES

FORGOTTEN HOME #7 COVER ROUGH BY NATASHA ALTERICI

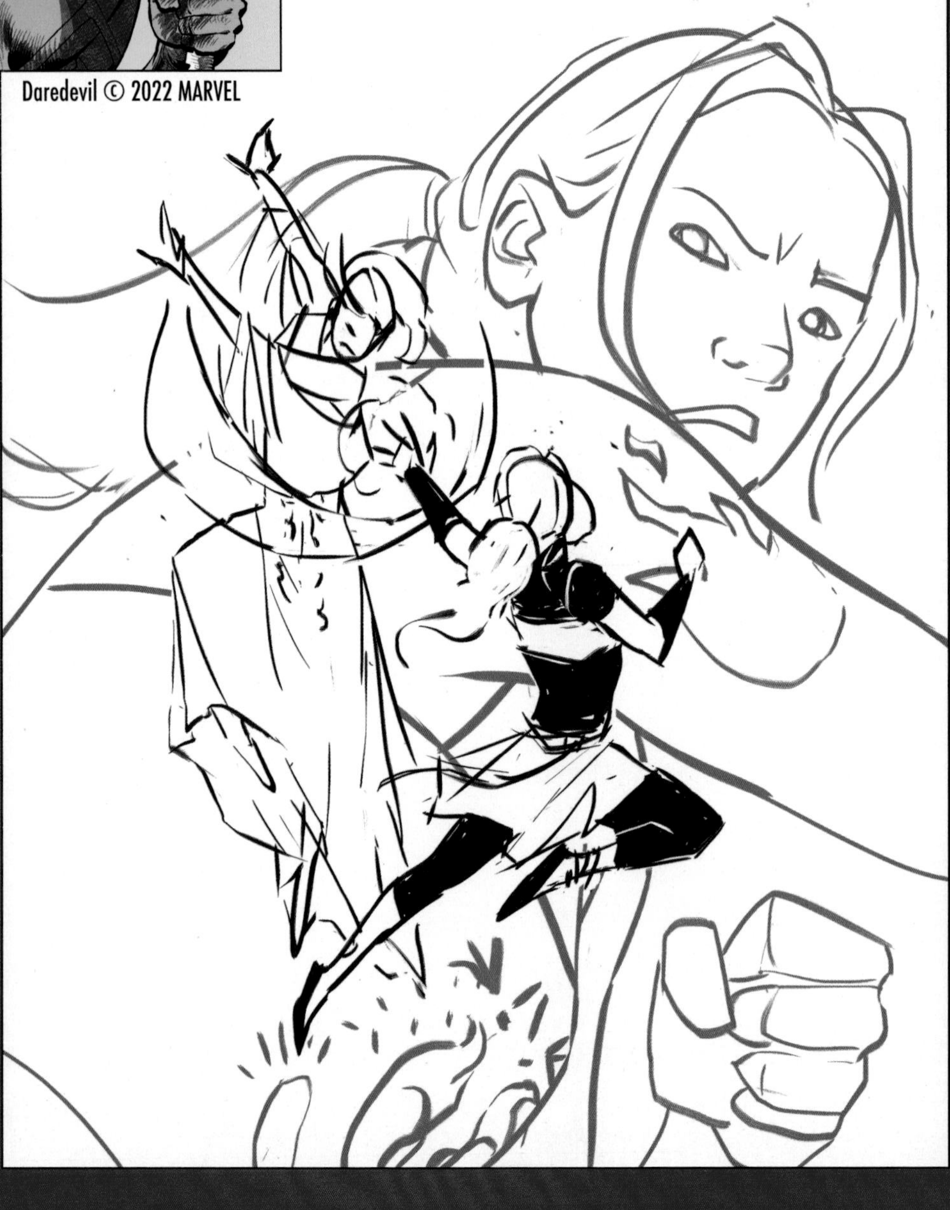

FORGOTTEN HOME #7 COVER FINAL BY
NATASHA ALTERICI

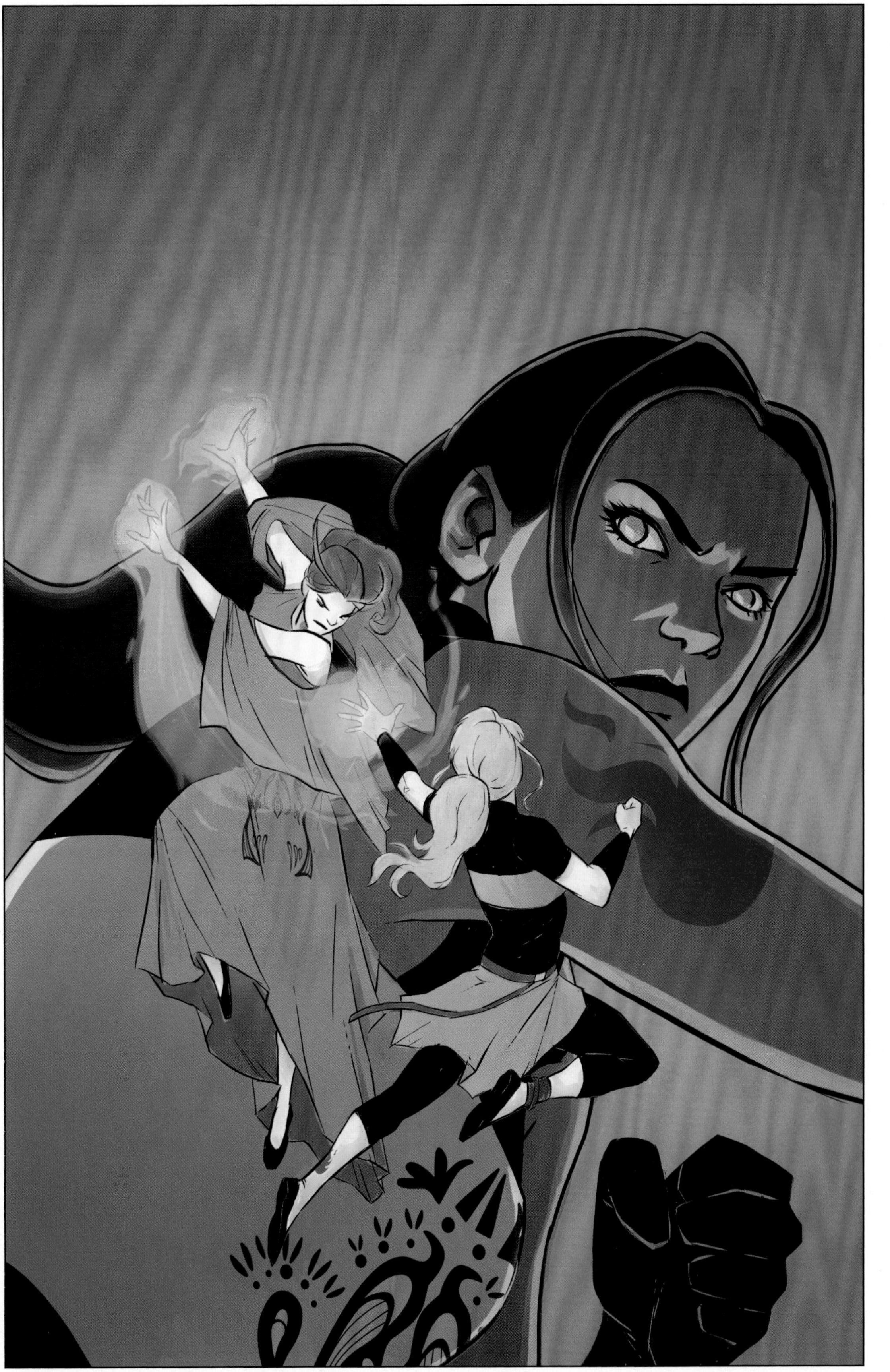

VARIANT COVER CONCEPTS BY KEVIN MAHER

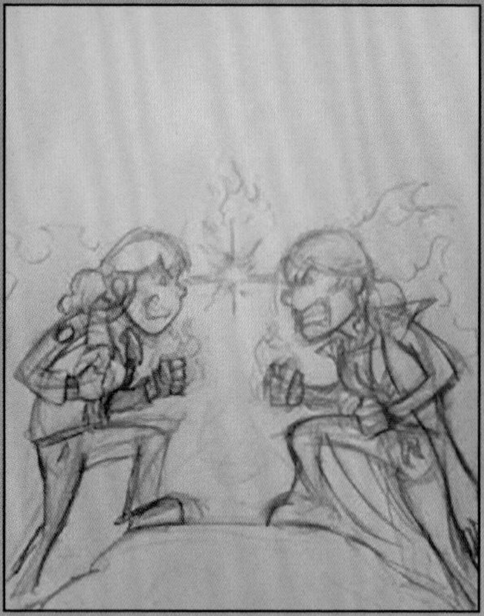

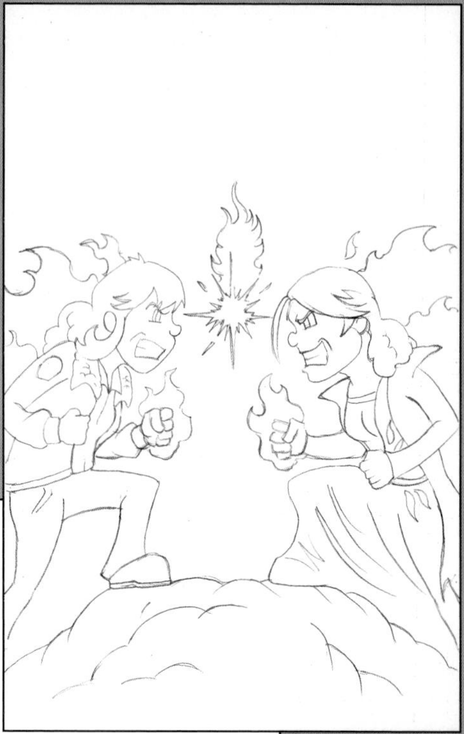

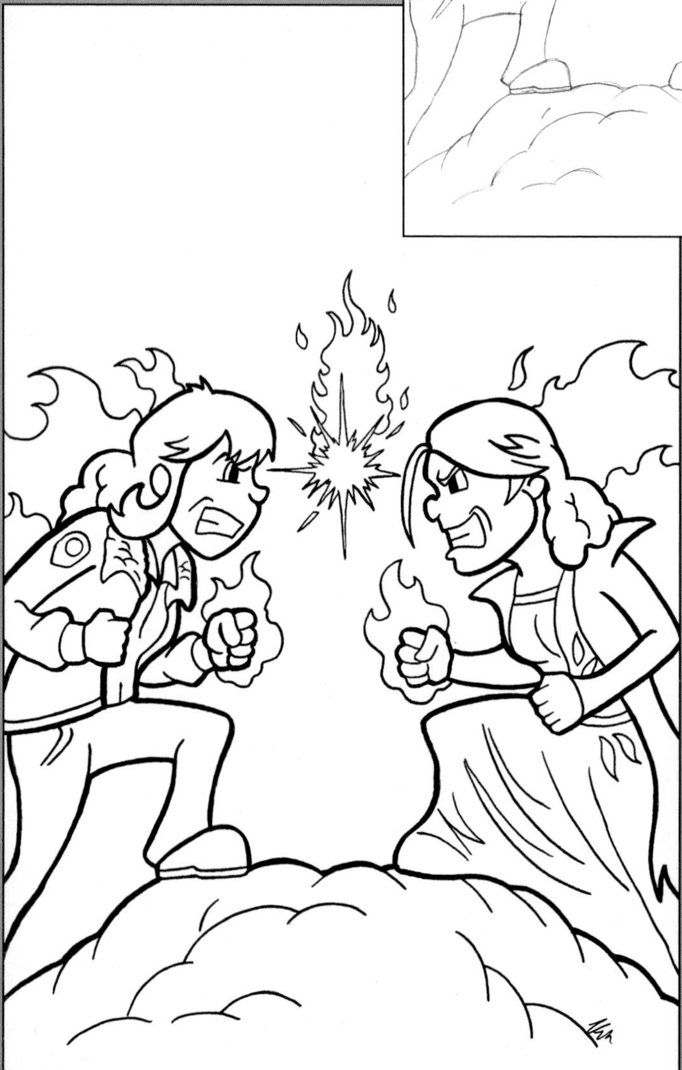

VARIANT COVER FINAL BY
KEVIN MAHER

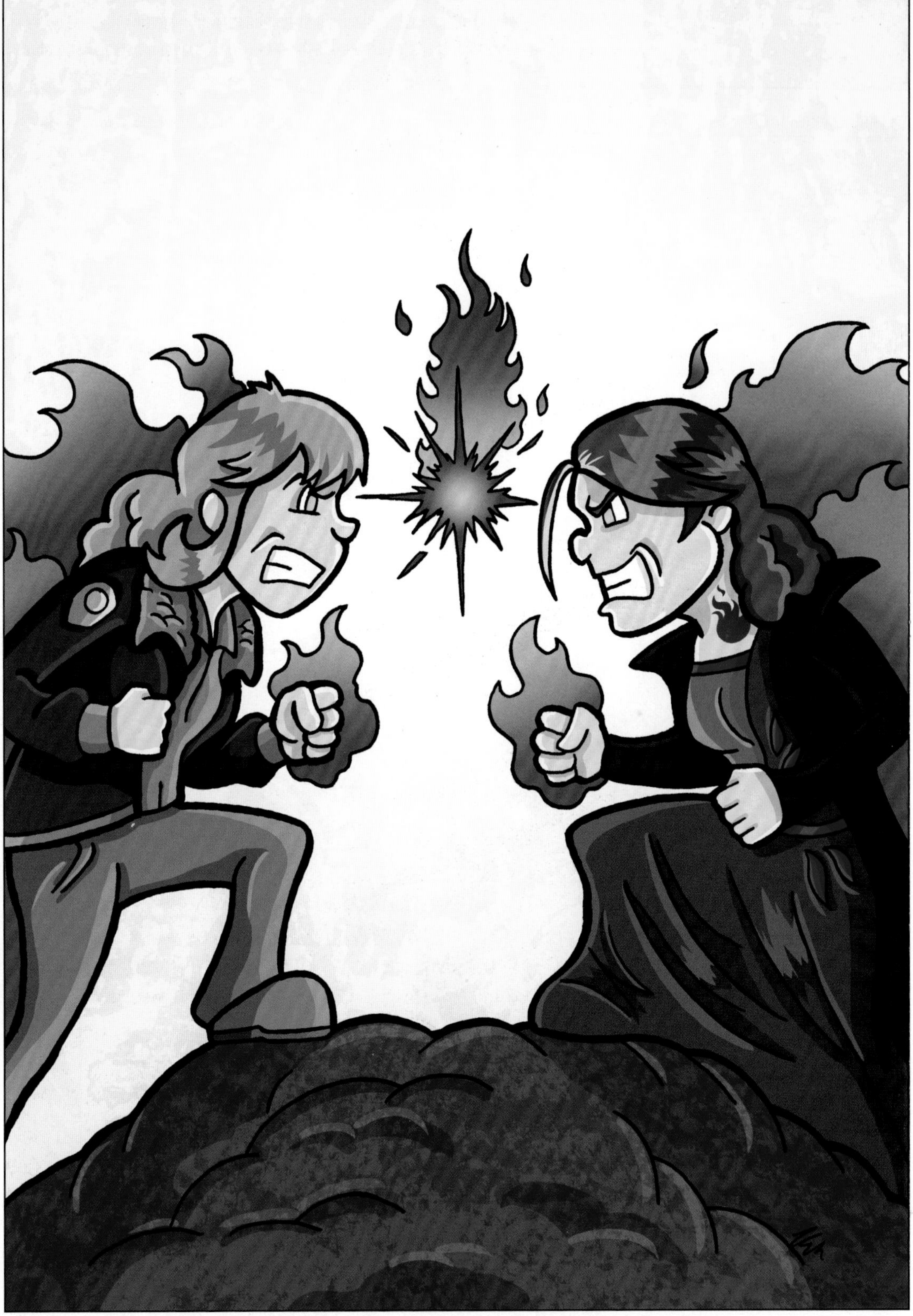

PROCESS

PAGE 19 PANEL 01
Cut to a large panel. It's an epic battle, think Helm's Deep from *Lord of the Rings: The Two Towers*. Child warriors from Jannada use magic to fight Chilombons who fight with spears, bows and arrows, and stone swords.

PAGE 19 PANEL 02
Kralista is the general, decked out in Jannadan armor, leading the troops. By her side is Rani, also in armor. Maybe they're each riding a horse-like creature. Rani has a sword drawn.

PAGE 19 PANEL 03
A Chilombon throws a spear toward the sisters.

PAGE 19 PANEL 04
Kralista is hit with the spear.

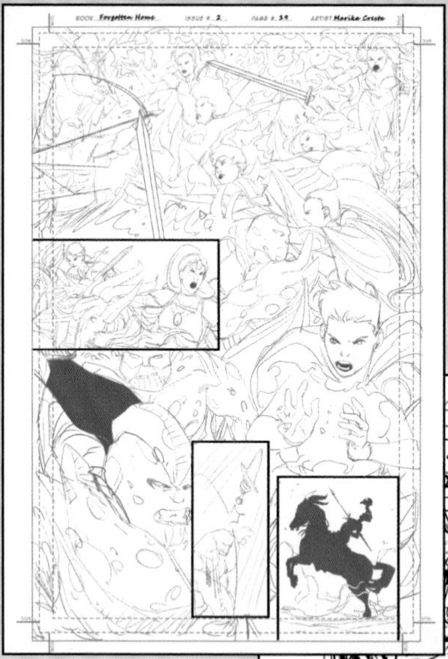

Forgotten Home
Marika Cresta

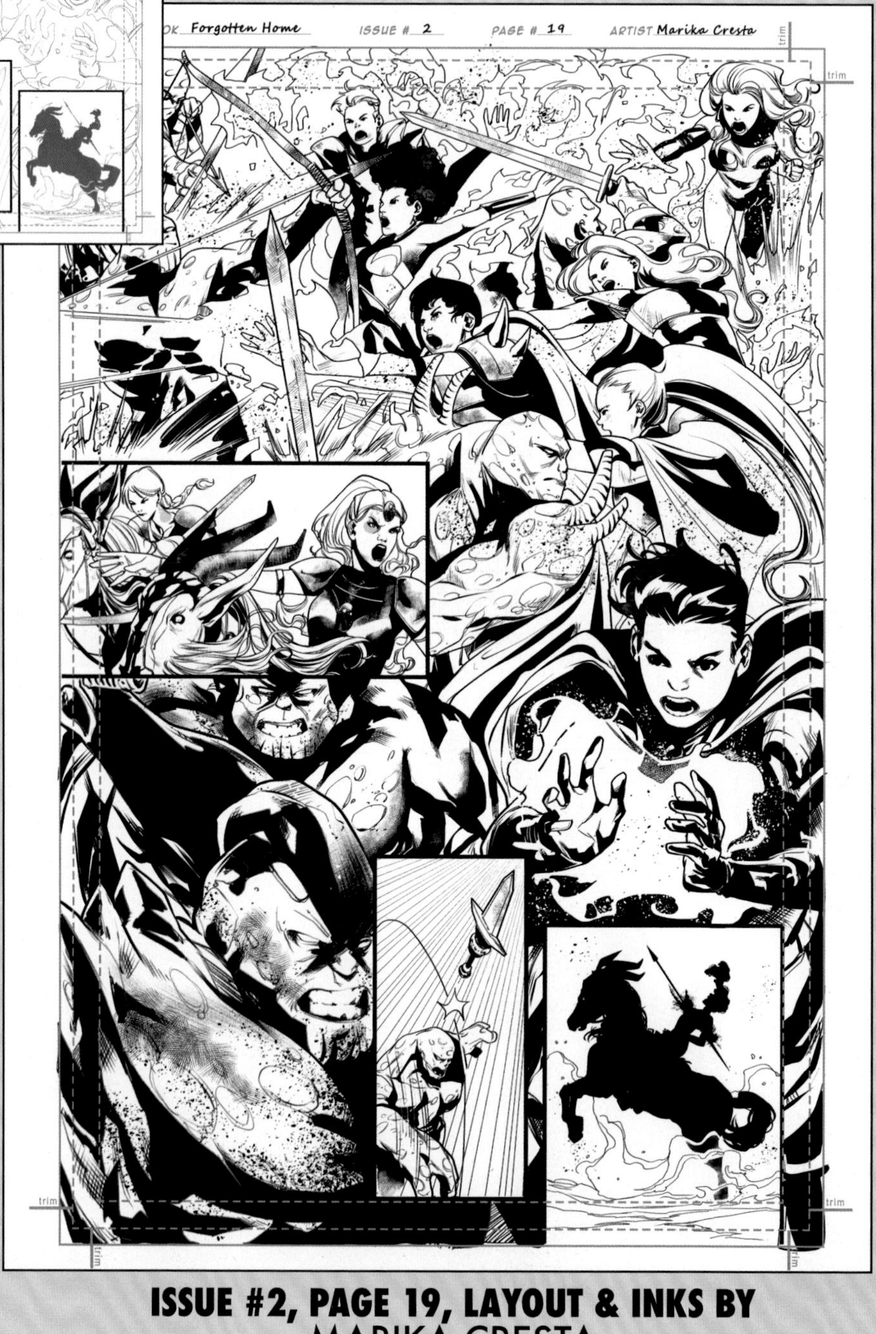

OK Forgotten Home
ISSUE # 2
PAGE # 19
ARTIST Marika Cresta
trim

ISSUE #2, PAGE 19, LAYOUT & INKS BY
MARIKA CRESTA

ISSUE #2, PAGE 19, FINAL ART BY
MARIKA CRESTA & MATT EMMONS

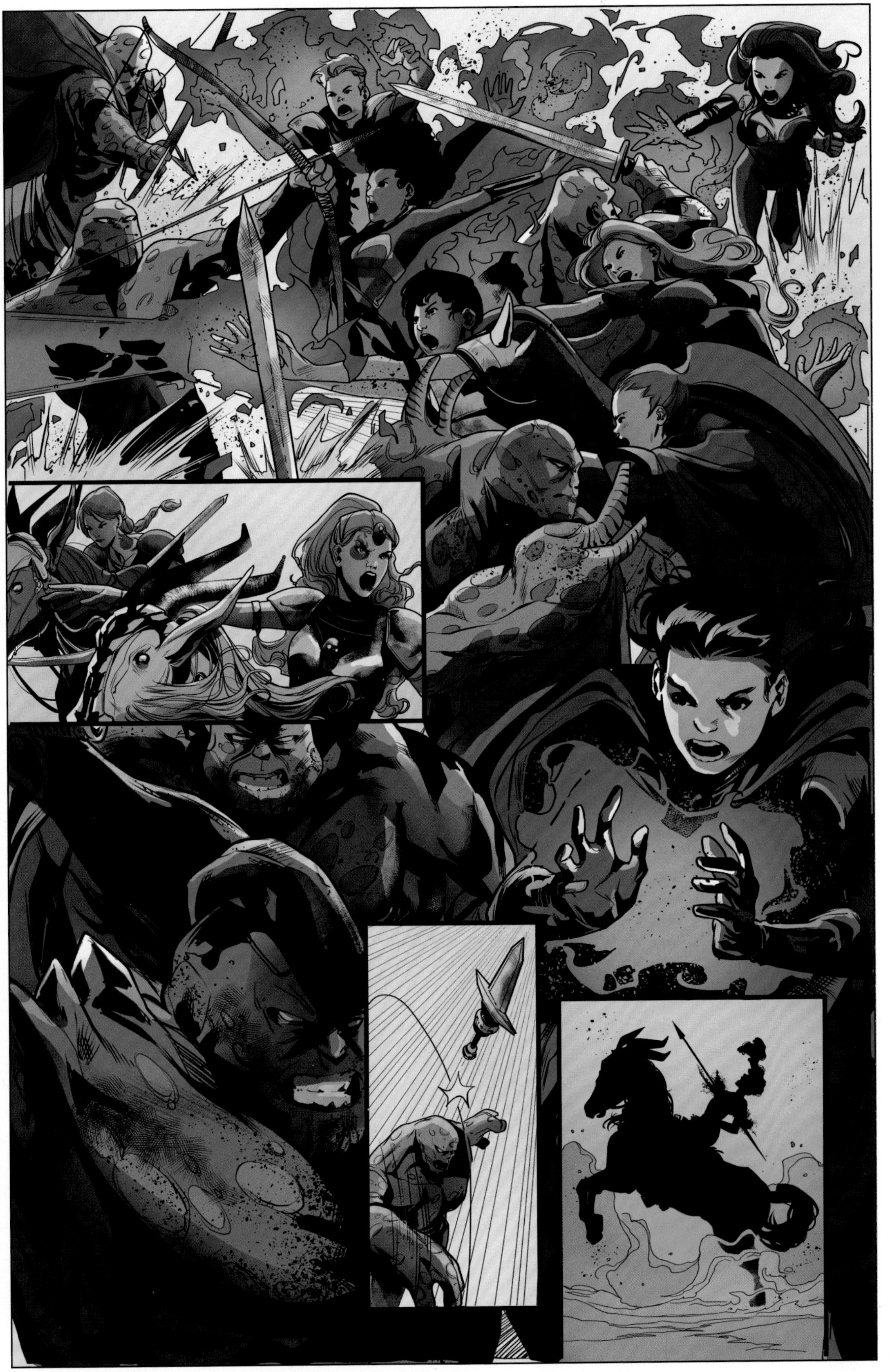

ORIGINAL DESIGN FOR RANI'S ROYAL JANNADAN GARMENTS BY
YISSEL AYALA

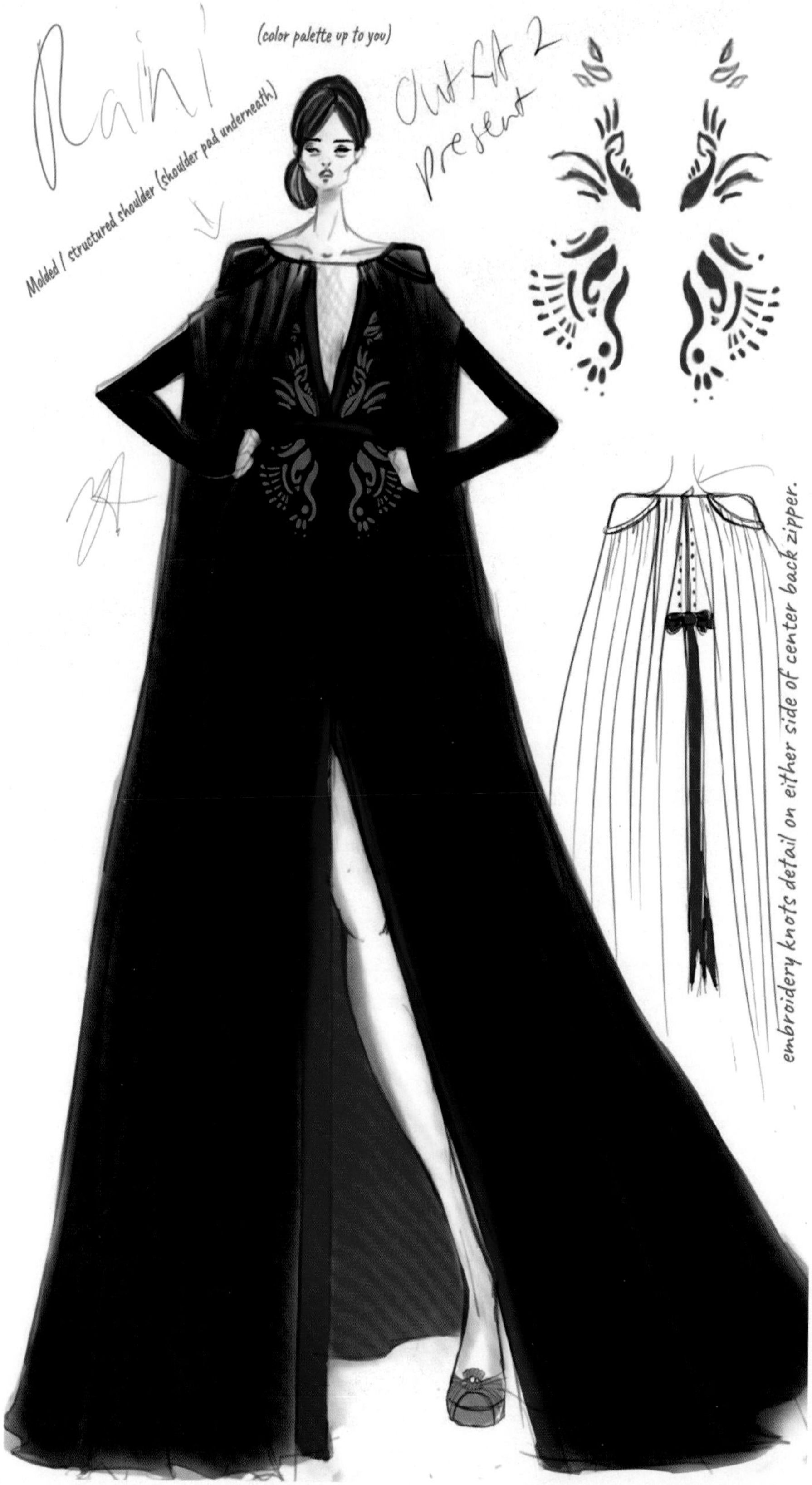
Rani
(color palette up to you)
Outfit 2
present
Molded / structured shoulder (shoulder pad underneath)
embroidery knots detail on either side of center back zipper.

FINAL ARTWORK BY
MARIKA CRESTA
& MATT EMMONS

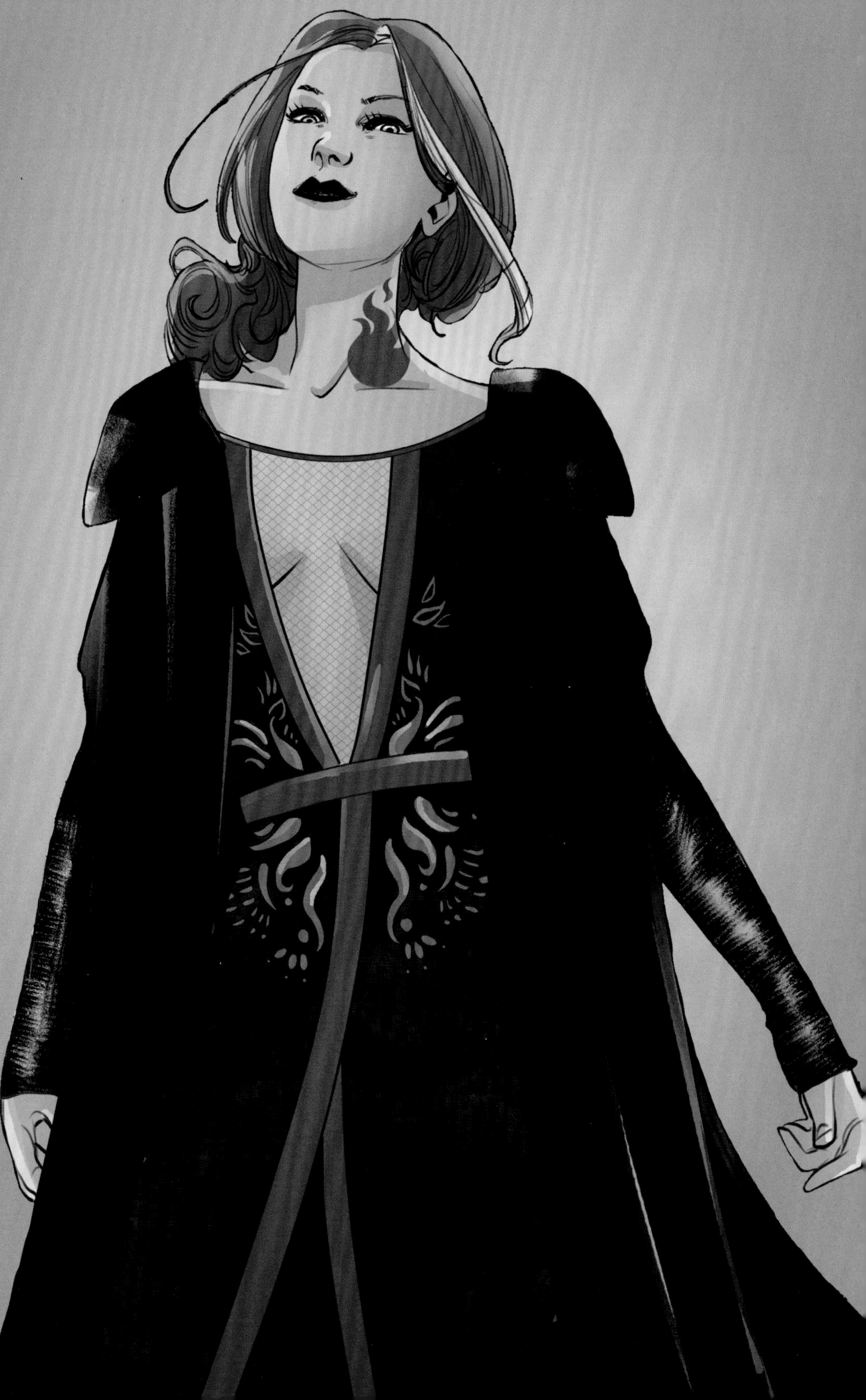

ORIGINAL DESIGN FOR JOANNA'S ROYAL JANNADAN GARMENTS BY
YISSEL AYALA

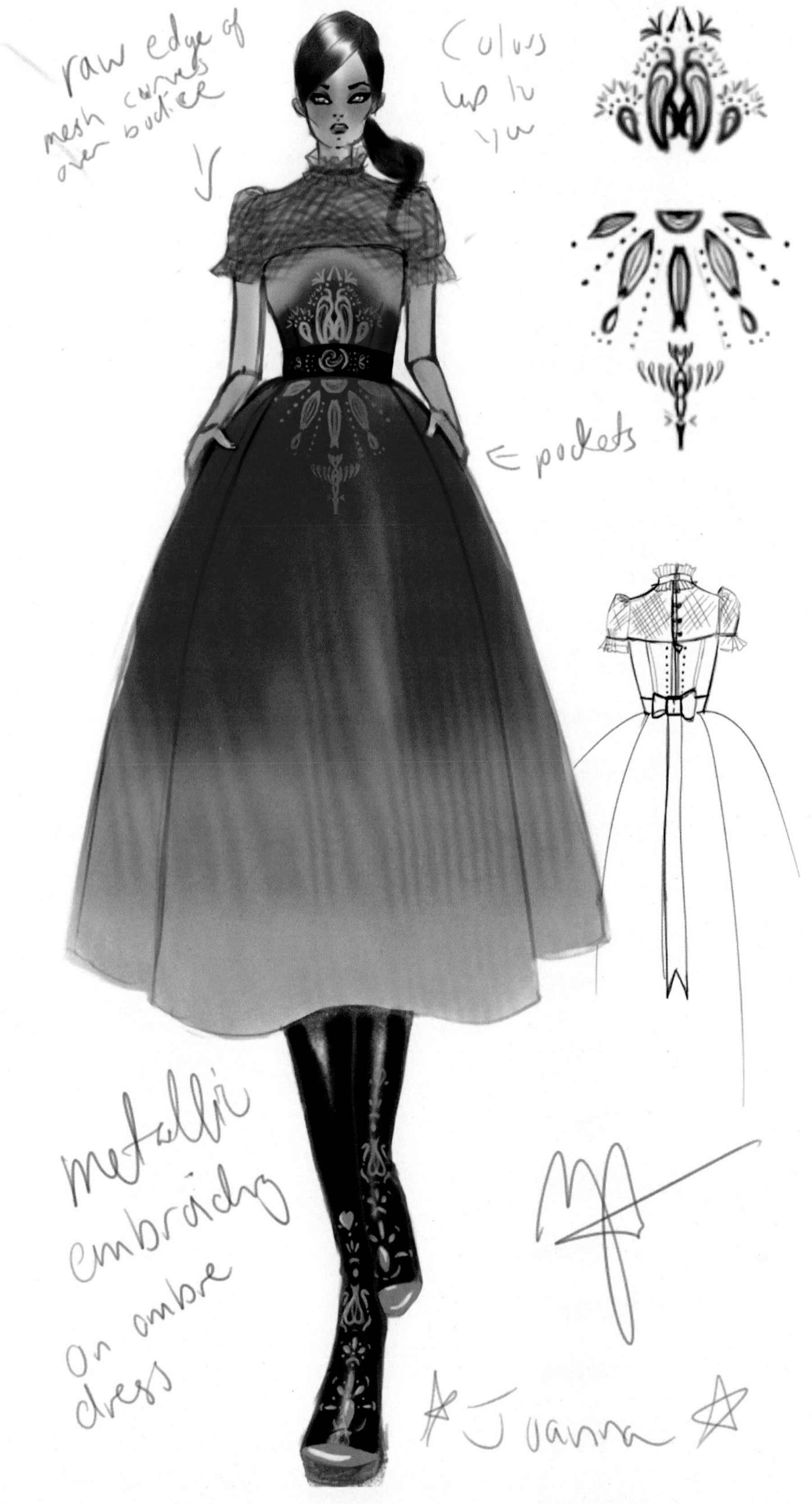

raw edge of mesh curves over bodice
pockets
on ombre dress
Joanna

FINAL ARTWORK BY
MARIKA CRESTA
& MATT EMMONS

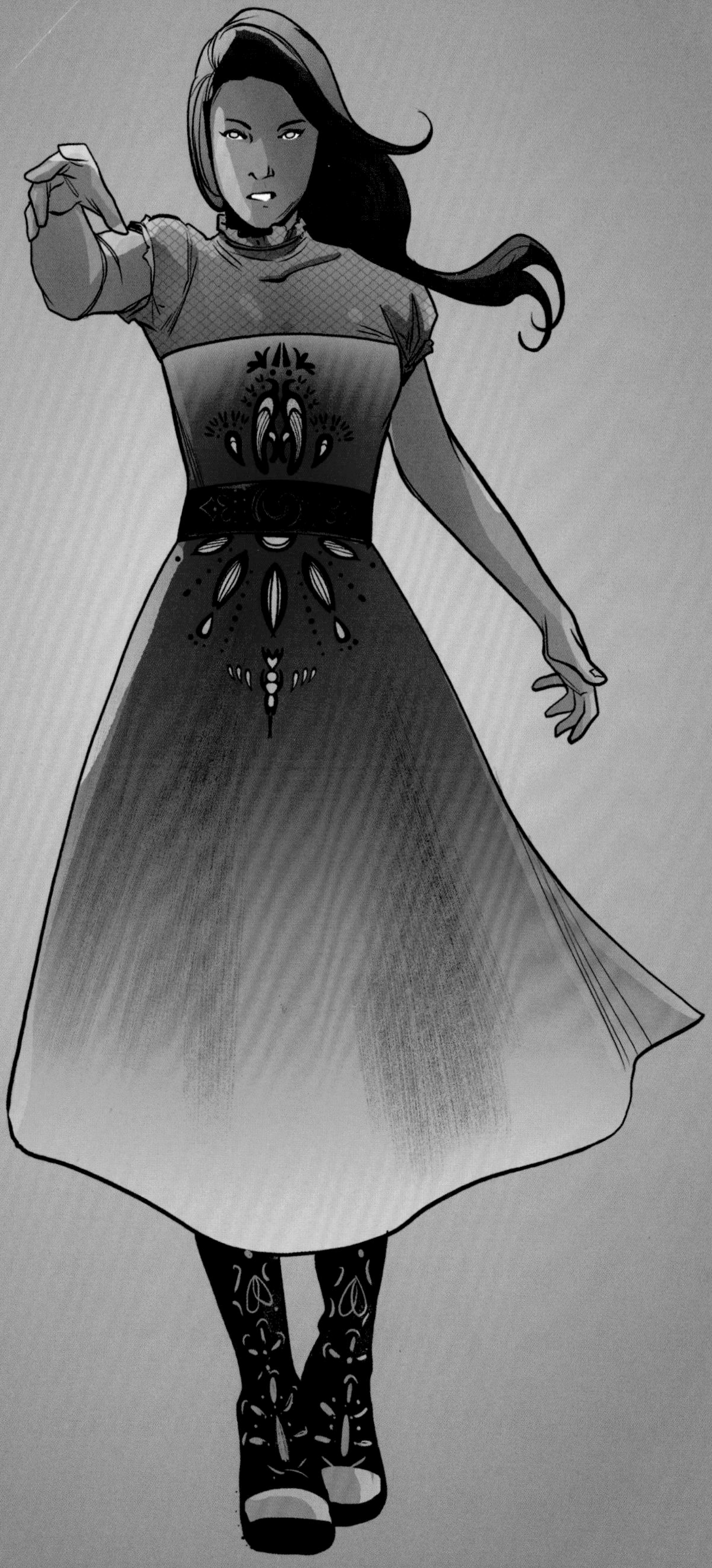

ORIGINAL DESIGN FOR LORRAINE'S ROYAL JANNADAN GARMENTS BY
YISSEL AYALA

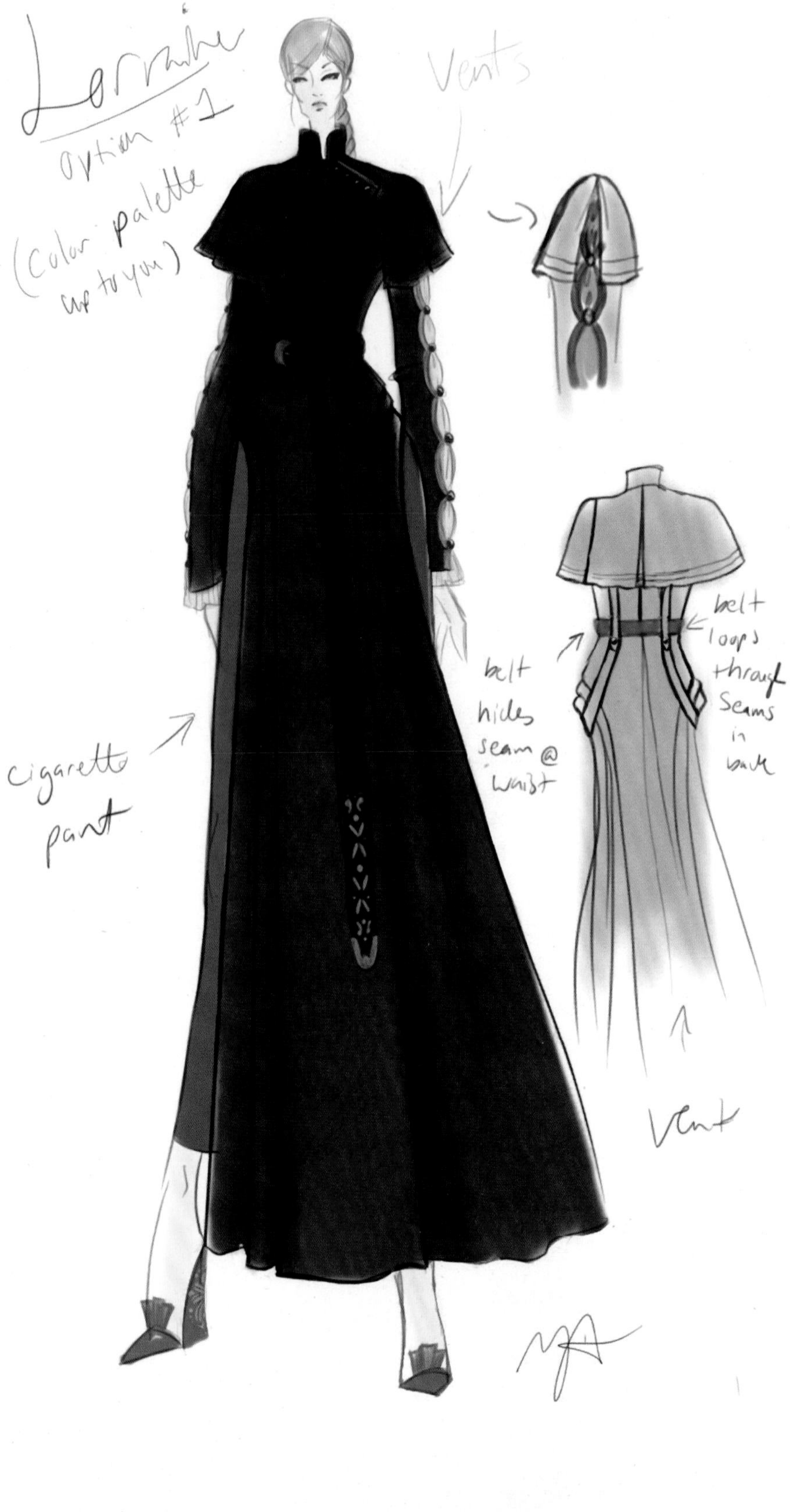

Lorraine
option #1
(Color palette up to you)
Vents
cigarette pant
belt hides seam @ waist
belt loops through seams in back
Vent

FINAL ARTWORK BY
MARIKA CRESTA
& MATT EMMONS

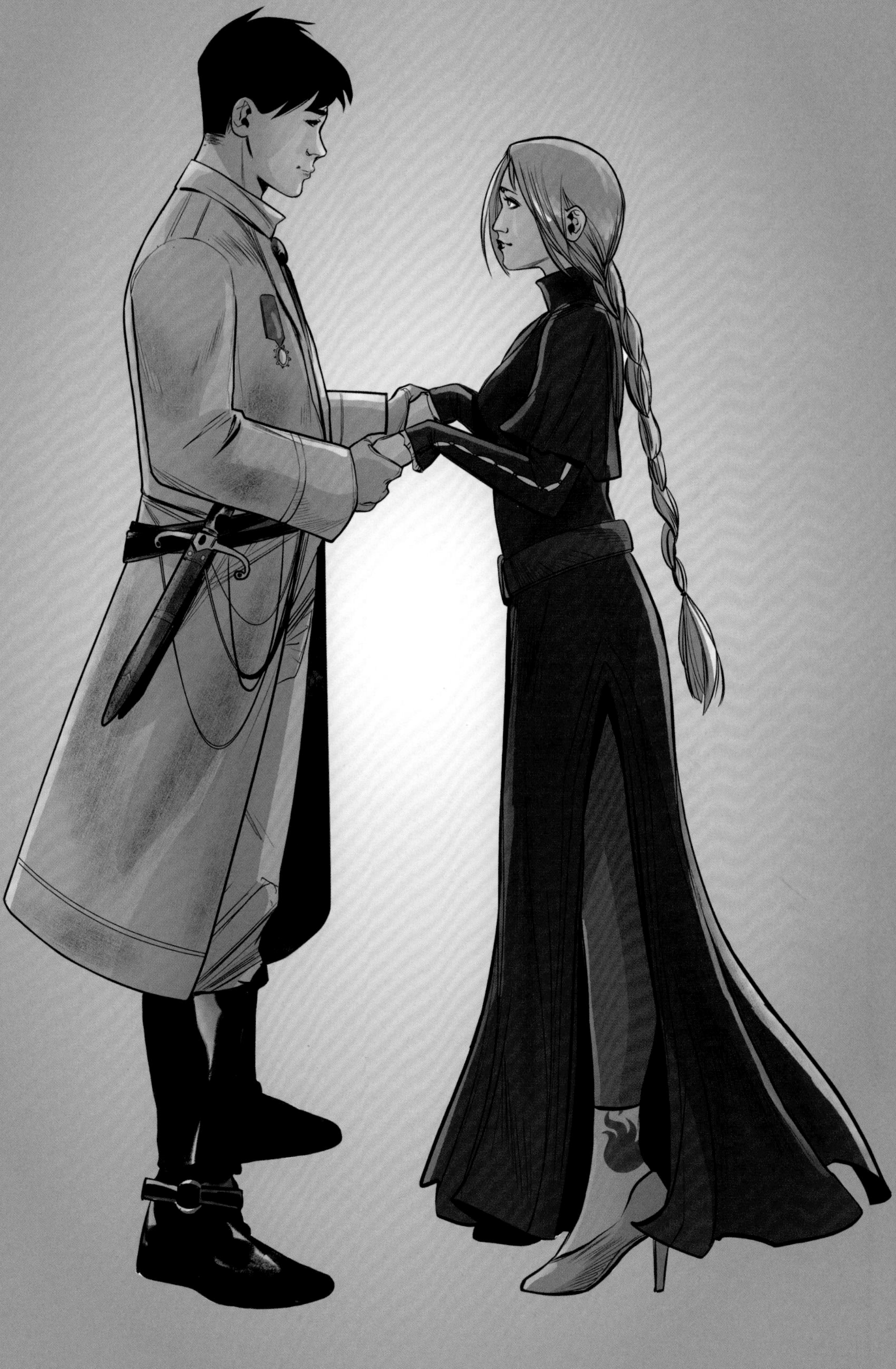

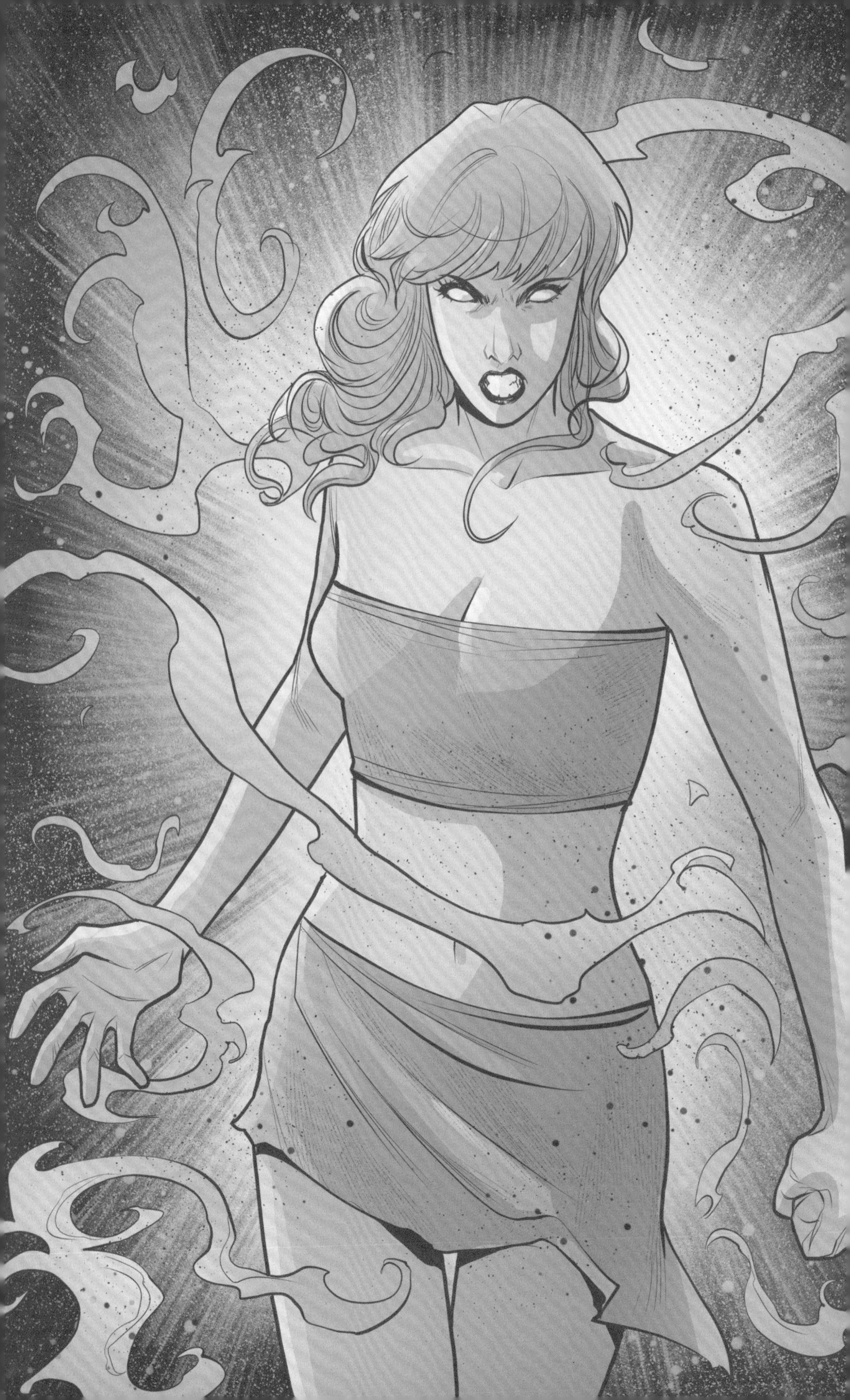

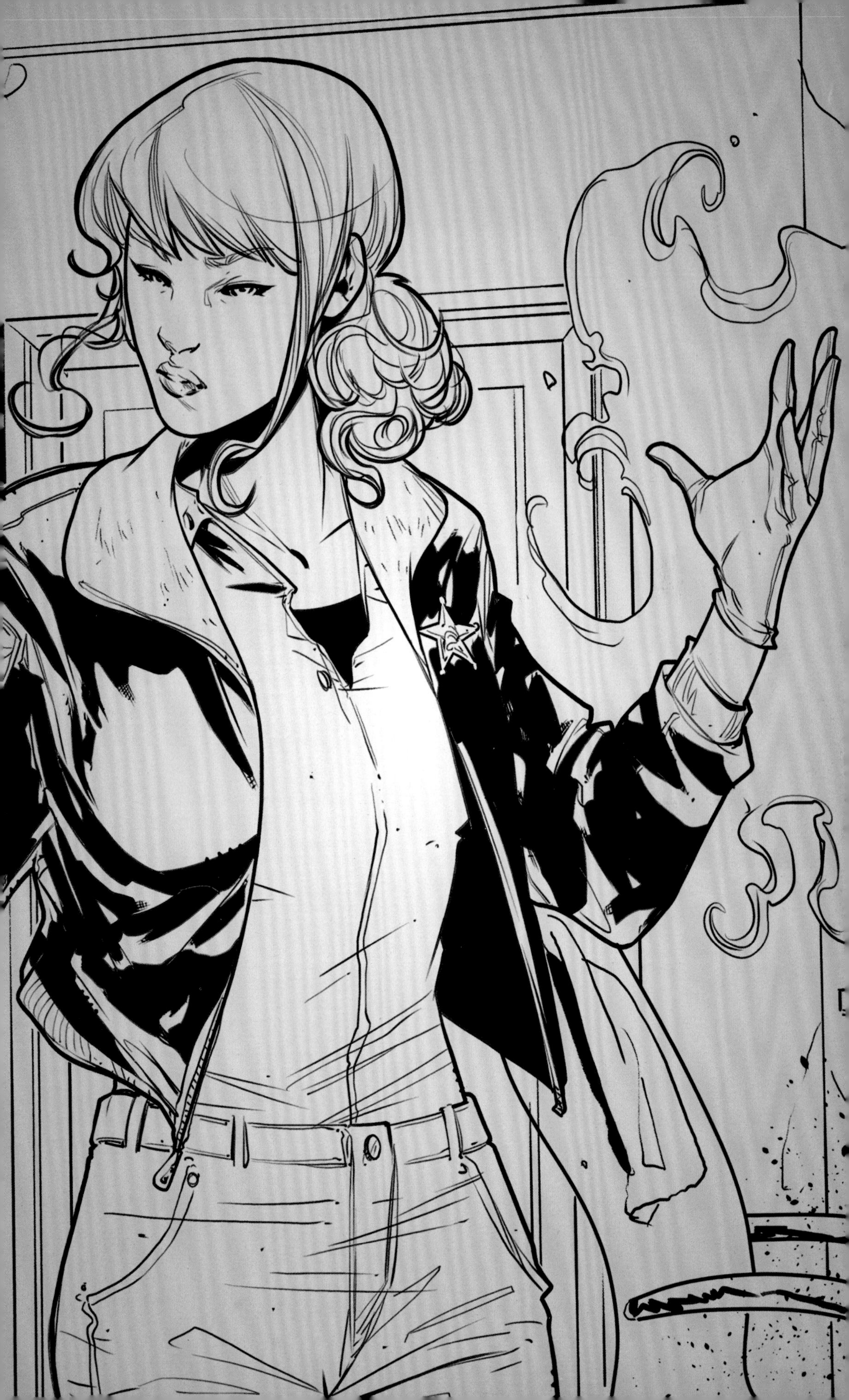

COMIXOLOGY COMES TO DARK HORSE BOOKS!

JASON LOO
CHIP ZDARSKY
AFTERLIFT
WILL EISNER

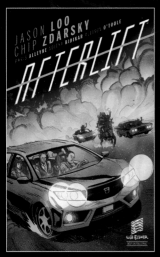

ISBN 978-1-50672-440-9 / $19.99

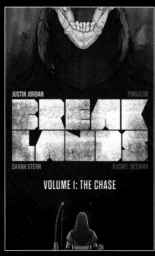

JUSTIN JORDAN
TYASSETA
BREAK LANDS
SARAH STERN
RACHEL DEERING
VOLUME I: THE CHASE

ISBN 978-1-50672-441-6 / $19.99

curt pires
alex diotto
dee cunniffe
micah myers
Youth
Named One of "10 Comics to Celebrate Pride" by the New York Times
"Bold, genre-defying and heartfelt. Youth hits a reader like the meteor in its own pages: an angry, wondrous and transformative book." —Scott Snyder (Batman, Justice League)

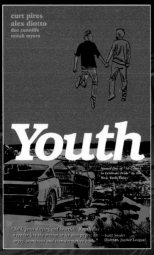

ISBN 978-1-50672-461-4 / $19.99

Named one of the "5 New Comic Book Series for the End of Summer" by the New York Times
THE BLACK GHOST
HARD REVOLUTION
ALEX SEGURA
MONICA GALLAGHER

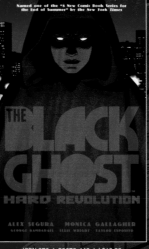

ISBN 978-1-50672-446-1 / $19.99

THE PRIDE
OMNIBUS

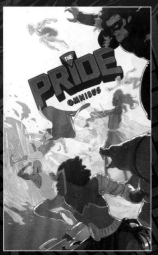

ISBN 978-1-50672-447-8 / $29.99

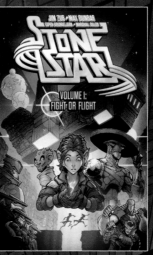

JIM ZUB
MAX DUNBAR
STONE STAR
VOLUME I: FIGHT OR FLIGHT

ISBN 978-1-50672-458-4 / $19.99

AFTERLIFT
Written by Chip Zdarsky, art by Jason Loo

This Eisner Award–winning series from Chip Zdarsky (*Sex Criminals*, Daredevil) and Jason Loo (*The Pitiful Human-Lizard*) features car chases, demon bounty hunters, and figuring out your place in this world and the next.

BREAKLANDS
Written by Justin Jordan, art by Tyasseta and Sarah Stern

Generations after the end of the civilization, everyone has powers; you need them just to survive in the new age. Everyone except Kasa Fain. Unfortunately, her little brother, who has the potential to reshape the world, is kidnapped by people who intend to do just that. *Mad Max* meets *Akira* in a genre-mashing, expectation-smashing new hit series from Justin Jordan, creator of *Luther Strode*, *Spread*, and *Reaver*!

YOUTH
Written by Curt Pires, art by Alex Diotto and Dee Cunniffe

A coming of age story of two queer teenagers who run away from their lives in a bigoted small town, and attempt to make their way to California. Along the way their car breaks down and they join a group of fellow misfits on the road. travelling the country together in a van, they party and attempt to find themselves. And then . . . something happens. The story combines the violence of coming of age with the violence of the superhero narrative—as well as the beauty.

THE BLACK GHOST SEASON ONE: HARD REVOLUTION
Written by Alex Segura and Monica Gallagher, art by George Kamabdais

Meet Lara Dominguez—a troubled Creighton cops reporter obsessed with the city's debonair vigilante the Black Ghost. With the help of a mysterious cyberinformant named LONE, Lara's inched closer to uncovering the Ghost's identity. But as she searches for the breakthrough story she desperately needs, Lara will have to navigate the corruption of her city, the uncertainties of virtues, and her own personal demons. Will she have the strength to be part of the solution—or will she become the problem?

THE PRIDE OMNIBUS
Joseph Glass, Gavin Mitchell and Cem Iroz

FabMan is sick of being seen as a joke. Tired of the LGBTQ+ community being seen as inferior to straight heroes, he thinks it's about damn time he did something about it. Bringing together some of the world's greatest LGBTQ+ superheroes, the Pride is born to protect the world and fight prejudice, misrepresentation and injustice—not to mention a pesky supervillain or two.

STONE STAR
Jim Zub and Max Zunbar

The brand-new space-fantasy saga that takes flight on comiXology Originals from fan-favorite creators Jim Zub (*Avengers*, *Samurai Jack*) and Max Dunbar (*Champions*, *Dungeons & Dragons*)! The nomadic space station called Stone Star brings gladiatorial entertainment to ports across the galaxy. Inside this gargantuan vessel of tournaments and temptations, foragers and fighters struggle to survive. A young thief named Dail discovers a dark secret in the depths of Stone Star and must decide his destiny—staying hidden in the shadows or standing tall in the searing spotlight of the arena. Either way, his life, and the cosmos itself, will never be the same!

AVAILABLE AT YOUR LOCAL COMICS SHOP OR BOOKSTORE / To find a comics shop near you, visit comicshoplocator.com / For more information or to order direct, visit darkhorse.com

DARK HORSE BOOKS

COMIXOLOGY ORIGINALS

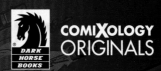